THE EVOLU
OF INTERNATIONAL

The Evolution
of International Arbitration

Judicialization, Governance, Legitimacy

ALEC STONE SWEET
and
FLORIAN GRISEL

OXFORD
UNIVERSITY PRESS

OXFORD

UNIVERSITY PRESS

Great Clarendon Street, Oxford, OX2 6DP,
United Kingdom

Oxford University Press is a department of the University of Oxford.
It furthers the University's objective of excellence in research, scholarship,
and education by publishing worldwide. Oxford is a registered trade mark of
Oxford University Press in the UK and in certain other countries

Published in the United States of America by Oxford University Press
198 Madison Avenue, New York, NY 10016, United States of America

British Library Cataloguing in Publication Data
Data available

Library of Congress Control Number: 2016960618

ISBN 978–0–19–873973–9 (pbk.)
ISBN 978–0–19–873972–2 (hbk.)

Acknowledgements

I am deeply indebted to Sheng Li, Meng-Jia Yang, Michael Chung, Moeun Cha, Tara Zivkovich, and Adam Saltzman, then students at the Yale Law School, for their dedication to the (often dreary) work of collecting and analyzing investment arbitration awards. I thank participants in seminars on arbitration and global law at Yale (2010-2015) for ideas and inspiration, in particular, Anthea Roberts, Jürgen Kurtz, Giorgio Sacerdoti, David Rivkin, Ralf Michaels, Emmanuel Gaillard, Rusty Park, Thomas Carbonneau, George Bermann, Stacie Strong, Giacinto della Cananea, and Gus Van Harten. The Camargo Foundation in Cassis, France, and its Director, Julie Chenot, provided peaceful settings in which to write, with gorgeous views. Martha Lewis, a painter of ideas and sophistication, has, once again, produced the cover art. I am grateful for her endless patience with book projects.

Alec Stone Sweet

I am grateful for the support and encouragement that numerous friends, family members and colleagues have provided, in many different ways, throughout this project. The research published in this book benefited from the institutional support of the *Centre national de la recherche scientifique* and King's College London. My work also benefited from the assistance of Helin Laufer Gencaga, who helped with great research and countless edits to the draft chapters. I also thank Alec Stone Sweet for his longtime friendship, mentoring and support, as well as Martha Lewis for the creative ways in which she captured the "evolution of international arbitration" in the cover art. Finally, I owe special thanks to Charlotte Collin, for her unfaltering support during the endless evenings, weekends and holidays spent on this book.

Florian Grisel

Contents

1

Judicialization and Arbitral Governance

This book focuses on the evolution of arbitral governance in the realms of transnational commerce and investment. The development of international arbitration as an autonomous legal order—connected to, but meaningfully autonomous from, state systems—comprises one of the most remarkable stories of institution building at the global level over the past century.[1] Efforts by representatives of transnational business to make arbitration a viable alternative to adjudication in national courts began in earnest in the 1920s, accelerated after the Second World War, and then came to full fruition with the explosive increase in global trade and investment since the 1980s. The result has been the steady development of a network of arbitral centres that compete with each other for docket, resources, and influence. The powerbrokers in the system are private actors. Large, multinational law firms are now heavily invested in arbitration practice, and their lawyers argue before tribunals staffed by a relatively small group of peers, specialists, and legal academics. Legal elites also manage the major international arbitration centres [IACs], in tandem with representatives of transnational business. Although the structure of authority in the field is non-hierarchical and pluralistic, the regime has gradually acquired the properties of a stable legal system.

In the world of transnational commerce, the community has sought and secured a 'global freedom of contract',[2] wherein private parties enjoy rights to choose their own law of contract, to contract out of national courts, and to select their own arbitrators and procedures. By the end of the twentieth century, as Juenger puts it, 'the tendency to keep transnational commercial disputes out of the courts, and thereby beyond the reach of local laws, is nearly universal'.[3] In 1999, Berger reported that more than 90 per cent of transnational commercial contracts of significance

---

[1] Yves Dezalay and Bryant G Garth, *Dealing in Virtue—International Commercial Arbitration and the Construction of a Transnational Legal Order* (University of Chicago Press, Chicago 1996) ['Dezalay and Garth']; Joshua Karton, *The Culture of International Arbitration and the Evolution of Contract Law* (Oxford University Press, Oxford 2013) ['Karton']; Walter Mattli and Thomas Dietz, *International Arbitration and Global Governance* (Oxford University Press, Oxford 2014); Jan Paulsson, *The Idea of Arbitration* (Oxford University Press, Oxford 2013) ['Paulsson'].

[2] See Chapter 2. Martin Shapiro and Alec Stone Sweet, 'Judges and Company' in Martin Shapiro and Stone Sweet (eds), *On Law, Politics, and Judicialization* (Oxford University Press, Oxford 2002) ['Shapiro and Stone Sweet'] Chapter 5.

[3] Friedrich Juenger, 'The Lex Mercatoria and the Conflict of Laws' in T E Carbonneau (ed), *Lex Mercatoria and Arbitration: A Discussion of the New Law Merchant* (Juris, Huntington 1998) 266.

The Evolution of International Arbitration: Judicialization, Governance, Legitimacy. First Edition. Alec Stone Sweet and Florian Grisel. © Alec Stone Sweet and Florian Grisel 2017. Published 2017 by Oxford University Press.

contained an arbitration clause;[4] in 2015, in the most authoritative survey of corporate counsel and the transnational bar, more than 90 per cent of respondents selected international arbitration as their preferred mode of dispute resolution, while only 2 per cent of respondents preferred litigation in national courts.[5] Traders value arbitration for its political neutrality, confidentiality, specialized expertise, and flexibility. In conjunction with arbitrators, the parties themselves help to determine the complexity, cost, and speed of the proceedings. They also have an abundant choice of fora. Over the past century, the number of established IACs has risen from 10 (in 1910) to more than 200 today (Chapter 2). The most important centre is the Paris-based International Chamber of Commerce [ICC]. Established in 1923, the ICC International Court of Arbitration[6] has registered more than 20,000 disputes, 17,000 of which since 1980.[7] A 2014 assessment of 'trends in arbitration' reports that twelve of the most important houses now process more than 3,000 new claims annually, worth more than $1.7 trillion.[8]

There would have been no boom in international commercial arbitration [ICA] had the community failed to resolve a crucial problem: how to enforce its awards. Because arbitrators are unable to compel compliance with judgments as national judges do—through commands backed by coercive state authority—the question of how to guarantee the 'finality', that is, the enforceability of awards has been a permanent preoccupation. The solution involved harnessing state power. Under its own initiative, the ICC drafted what became the 1958 New York Convention on the Recognition and Enforcement of Foreign Arbitral Awards,[9] and ICC associates closely supervised the process that led to its entry into force.[10] The New York Convention, now ratified by 155 states,[11] made national courts the public guarantors of private arbitral authority. Its provisions oblige national courts to 'recognize' the validity of arbitral agreements (the binding nature of arbitration clauses and agreements), and to enforce tribunal awards, subject to exceptions of 'inarbitrability' and 'public policy'. Beginning in the 1960s, judges and legislators in the

---

[4] Klaus Peter Berger, *The Creeping Codification of the Lex Mercatoria* (Kluwer, The Hague 1999) ['Berger'] 111.

[5] White & Case and Queen Mary, University of London, '2015 International Arbitration Survey: Improvements and Innovations in International Arbitration', <http://www.whitecase.com/publications/insight/2015-international-arbitration-survey-improvements-and-innovations> accessed 26 January 2016.

[6] The ICC International Court of Arbitration does not produce arbitral awards, but rather administers the resolution of disputes by ICC tribunals in accordance with the ICC Rules of Arbitration (see Chapters 2 and 3).

[7] We report data on the activities of major IACs in Chapter 2.

[8] Mark Bezant, James Nicholson, and Howard Rosen, 'Trends in International Arbitration: A New World Order' (*FTI Consulting*, February 2015) <http://www.fticonsulting.com/insights/fti-journal/trends-in-international-arbitration> accessed 26 January 2016.

[9] The United Nations Convention on the Recognition and Enforcement of Foreign Arbitral Awards (more commonly known as the New York Convention) was signed on 10 June 1958 (and entered into force on 7 June 1959).

[10] Chapter 2.

[11] United Nations Commission on International Trade Law, 'Status: Convention on the Recognition and Enforcement of Foreign Arbitral Awards' (New York, 1958) <http://www.uncitral.org/uncitral/en/uncitral_texts/arbitration/NYConvention_status.html> accessed 26 January 2016.

major states of the trading world have steadily narrowed these exceptions, in ways that have reduced the judicial review of awards to virtually nil. They had at least three good reasons to do so. First, traders strongly prefer arbitration, and states depend on transnational commerce for their economic well-being.[12] Second, in the context of overloaded court systems, arbitration has the advantage of draining off complex litigation for which many (generalist) national judges are ill prepared. Third, as arbitration has proved its worth, the 'competition for the "business" of … international arbitration' has intensified among states in the major trading zones.[13] Making national law more hospitable to arbitration is essential to attracting this business.[14]

The scope and importance of arbitration has also exploded in the world of foreign direct investment. The vast bulk of investor-state arbitration [ISA] takes place within a legal framework instantiated by a web of international investment agreements, the vast majority of which signed since 1990. As of the end of 2015, there were 3,304 such agreements: 2,946 bilateral investment treaties [BITs], ratified by some 150 different states; and 358 other arrangements, principally multilateral, economic agreements that contain investment provisions.[15] Through 2015, the number of known ISA cases reached 696, the majority brought since 2008.[16] Most cases fall under jurisdiction conferred on arbitrators by BITs; and most BITs provide for ISA under the auspices of the World Bank's International Centre for Settlement of Investment Disputes [ICSID]. BITs resemble one another in function and form (though important provisions may vary). Their purpose is twofold. First, they encourage investment by reducing its risk, typically precluding expropriation without adequate compensation, and requiring 'equitable' and non-discriminatory treatment, and other protections. Second, they remove disputes between the foreign investor and the host state from the diplomatic arena and domestic national courts, channelling them into arbitration. In the archetypal case, the investor initiates ISA in order to obtain compensation for an alleged breach of a BIT's protections by the host state. If the tribunal concludes that the state did violate the treaty, then it assesses and awards damages.

The stakes of arbitration are enormous and growing. In 2013, a survey of the leading law firms in the field reported information on 109 active ICA cases

---

[12] Between 1980 and 2010, the annual value of global trade has risen by more than 600 per cent, while the global GDP has risen only by about 300 per cent.

[13] Ulrich Drobnig, 'Assessing Arbitral Autonomy in European Statutory Law' in Thomas E Carbonneau (ed), *Lex Mercatoria and Arbitration: A Discussion of the New Law Merchant* (Juris, Huntington 1998) 196.

[14] Michael Mustill, 'The History of International Arbitration: A Sketch' in *The Leading Arbitrator's Guide to International Arbitration* (Juris, Huntington 2014) 30: 'International Arbitration has thus become, not just part of the risk management of international business, but really big business in itself. This fact has at last dawned on those who make economic policy at the national level … There is a fierce if genteel competition for this business …'.

[15] Chapter 2.

[16] United Nations Conference on Trade and Development, 'World Investment Report 2016' <http://unctad.org/en/PublicationsLibrary/wir2016_en.pdf> accessed 26 June 2016 ['World Investment Report 2016'], 118.

in which at least $500 million was 'in controversy', including fifty-eight cases
in which claims totalled more than $1 billion, and nine with claims over $10
billion.[17] In ISA, the survey found 165 active cases with claims totalling over
$100 million, forty-eight over $1 billion, and seven over $10 billion. In 2014, a
tribunal ordered Russia to pay investors more than $50 billion plus interests and
costs in the so-called 'Yukos' arbitration, the highest compensation awarded in
the history of litigation.[18] The monetary value of claims and awards is just one
measure of arbitration's increasing significance. Major disputes often involve
important issues of law and policy, and a mix of public and private interests that
arbitrators, like the judges they have displaced, must consider when they take
decisions.

This community—tribunals, the bar, and scholars in the field—once worked in
relative obscurity. Today, states, international bodies, non-governmental organizations, and the media monitor awards and actively debate reform proposals. While
few would deny that arbitrators help to govern international commerce and investment, there is a great deal of controversy about how they are, and should be, governing. In ICA, where the vast bulk of awards are covered by confidentiality rules,
these controversies are most visible when it comes to the recognition and enforcement of arbitral awards in national courts. 'Border skirmishes'[19] between judges
and arbitrators are as common as they are inevitable, given the growing complexity, significance, and adversarial nature of ICA. Although ISA is booming, some
observers claim that the regime is in the throes of a legitimacy crisis.[20] Some states,
claiming bias against capital-importing states, have refused to comply with decisions. Bolivia, Ecuador, and Venezuela have recently exited the regime altogether.
Others, including Canada, India, the United States, and the European Union, have
declared their interests in bolstering the status of public policy interests in new
treaties.[21]

---

[17] Michael Goldhaber, 'Arbitration Scorecard 2013: Contract Disputes' (*The American Lawyer*, 1 July 2013) <http://www.americanlawyer.com/id=1202607030865/Arbitration-Scorecard-2013-Contract-Disputes?slreturn=20160103181849> accessed 26 January 2016.
[18] Efforts to annul and enforce the *Yukos* award are now underway. See Jarrod Hepburn, 'Dutch Court Sets Aside US$50 Billion Yukos Award, Criticising Tribunal for Accepting Provisional Application of Energy Charter Treaty to Russia' (*Investment Arbitration Reporter*, 20 April 2016) <https://www.iareporter.com/articles/dutch-court-sets-aside-us50-billion-yukos-award-criticising-tribunal-for-accepting-provisional-application-of-energy-charter-treaty-to-russia/> accessed 24 June 2016.
[19] S I Strong, 'Border Skirmishes: The Intersection Between Litigation and International Commercial Arbitration' (2012) 1 Journal of Dispute Resolution 1.
[20] The flow of scholarship on the 'crisis' in ISA appears to be continuous. See Susan D Franck, 'The Legitimacy Crisis in Investment Treaty Arbitration: Privatizing Public International Law through Inconsistent Decisions' (2005) 73 Fordham Law Review 1521; Charles N Brower and Stephan W Schill, 'Is Arbitration a Threat or a Boon to the Legitimacy of International Investment Law?' (2008–2009) 9 Chicago Journal of International Law 471; Leon Trakman, 'The ICSID under Siege' (2012) 45 Cornell International Law Journal 604; Pia Eberhardt and Cecilia Olivet, *Profiting from Injustice: How Law Firms, Arbitrators and Financiers are Fuelling an Investment Arbitration Boom* (Corporate Europe Observatory and the Transnational Institute, Brussels 2012); Anthea Roberts, 'Clash of Paradigms: Actors and Analogies Shaping the Investment Treaty System' (2012) 106 American Journal of International Law 1.
[21] See Chapters 5 and 6 for analysis.

This rather breathless synopsis highlights important aspects of the current state of international arbitration, as well as outcomes that will help to determine the future. But it is not the end of the story. Indeed, international arbitration is now at a crucial point in its development, poised between conflicting conceptions of its nature, purpose, and legitimacy. Consider the types of questions that those who use, manage, and study the system are now intensively debating. Are arbitrators merely the 'agents' of the disputing parties? Or are they also meant to serve the interests of a wider, transnational community, even of the international economic order more broadly? To what extent do important, prior awards constitute a case law, having persuasive, precedential value when relevant to current disputes? Should the major centres, such as the ICC and ICSID, supervise proceedings, and review the content of awards? Would the creation of arbitral appellate bodies, proposed in the name of enhancing legal certainty and bolstering systemic coherence, undermine flexibility and efficiency? To what extent do arbitrators take authoritative decisions that impinge upon public policy and interests, and thereby constrain state officials? Has state 'sovereignty'—its regulatory prerogatives—been redefined, in the interest of promoting global commerce and investment?

Such questions concern the scope of arbitral *governance*. In this book, we conceive of governance in a generic sense, as the process through which the institutions that govern activity in any domain—for present purposes, (a) relevant state law as well as (b) arbitral rules, procedures, and jurisprudence that apply to transnational contracting, exchange, and investment—are adapted, on an ongoing basis, to changing circumstances. Our central thesis is that international arbitration has undergone a self-sustaining process of endogenous institutional evolution—which we call 'judicialization'—a process that has steadily enhanced governance capacities over the past century. In this chapter, we present the theory of judicialization[22] in an abstract and deductive form, elucidating specific mechanisms of institutional change, and then discussing how it applies to arbitration. These theoretical materials guided our empirical research, the results of which are reported in subsequent chapters.

The main features of the project deserve emphasis upfront. First, the book provides a macro-institutional account of the systemic evolution of international arbitration. We do not elaborate a distinctive normative theory of arbitration. One can read this book through normative lenses; readers may celebrate or deplore the judicialization of arbitration, for example. Instead, we survey and assess these controversies with reference to our findings, primarily in the final chapter. More generally, we explicitly adopt an 'external' perspective to our topic. Insiders—overlapping groups of arbitrators, counsel to the parties, and specialist law professors—have long dominated the literature in this field. In recent years, new styles of research have emerged, wherein legal scholars leverage theoretical materials and modes

[22] Alec Stone Sweet, 'Judicialization and the Construction of Governance' (1999) 31 Comparative Political Studies 147 ['Stone Sweet']; Alec Stone Sweet and Florian Grisel, 'L'arbitrage international: du contrat dyadique au système normatif' (2009) 52 Archives de philosophie du droit 75.

of analysis developed outside the study of arbitration to describe and assess how the system operates.[23] In this new wave, scholars routinely lament the paucity of explanatory empirical analyses of arbitral behaviour, which is, in fact, striking. The book, we hope, will contribute to filling this void.

Second, one standard account of the development of arbitration stresses the virtues of freedom of contract, including the contracting parties' rights to choose their own contract law, as well as arbitration. The political economy version of the argument lays emphasis on how these virtues reduce the costs of trade and investment, notably by resolving commitment problems, while enabling actors to escape the biases and inefficiencies that afflict many national court systems.[24] We embrace the basics of this account (Chapters 2 and 6). ICA's socio-political legitimacy is firmly rooted in party autonomy and freedom of contract, and ISA's legitimacy is anchored in inter-state contracting. Nonetheless, few if any arbitrators today are exclusively creatures of contract, if by that we mean their purpose is strictly limited to the resolution of discreet disputes between two parties. Rather, many are devoted to building the systemic coherence and authority of the arbitral order itself, which, in turn, enables them to govern in the name of a larger, transnational community (Chapters 4 and 5). As judicialization has proceeded, we will show, the regime has developed forms of hierarchy that enable it to impose its politico-legal choices on the parties (Chapter 3).

Third, we detect an emerging consensus on the view that ICA and ISA are developing quite differently, in effect, as separate regimes.[25] In contrast, we do not make a sharp analytical distinction between ICA and ISA; we see many of the differences between them as a matter of degree, not kind, which we exploit for comparative purposes. In certain respects, the judicialization of ISA has gone faster and further than in ICA. The reason is that some of the mechanisms of judicialization operate more robustly in ISA, not because they do not operate in ICA. In ISA, for example, virtually all final awards on liability are published, whereas in ICA the vast bulk of awards remain secret. This difference has consequences for the development of precedent-based argumentation and lawmaking (Chapter 4), public

[23] Following Dezalay and Garth (n 1) and including Karton (n 1), Susan D Franck, 'The ICSID Effect? Considering Potential Variations in Arbitration Awards' (2011) 51(4) Virginia Journal of International Law 825; Susan D Franck, 'Conflating Politics and Development? Examining Investment Treaty Arbitration Outcomes' (2014) 55(1) Virginia Journal of International Law 13; Stephan W Schill (ed), *International Investment Law and Comparative Public Law* (Oxford University Press, Oxford 2010) [Schill (ed)]; Gus Van Harten, 'Arbitrator Behaviour in Asymmetrical Adjudication: An Empirical Study of Investment Treaty Arbitration' (2012) 50 Osgoode Hall Law Journal 211.
[24] Alec Stone Sweet, 'Islands of Transnational Governance' in Martin Shapiro and Alec Stone Sweet (eds), *On Law, Politics, and Judicialization* (Oxford University Press, Oxford 2002) Chapter 2.
[25] See Anthea Roberts, 'Clash of Paradigms: Actors and Analogies Shaping the Investment Treaty System' (2012) 106 American Journal of International Law 1; Gus Van Harten and Martin Loughlin, 'Investment Treaty Arbitration as a Species of Global Administrative Law' (2006) 17 European Journal of International Law 121 ['Van Harten and Loughlin']; Nico Krisch and Benedict Kingsbury, 'Introduction: Global Governance and Global Administrative Law in the International Legal Order' (2006) 17 European Journal of International Law 1.

accountability (Chapter 5), and debates concerning the legitimacy of arbitral governance (Chapter 6).

The chapter proceeds as follows. Part I considers the book's themes in light of the scholarship that we engage. In part II, we present the theory of judicialization. To the extent that judicialization proceeds, the theory holds, dispute resolvers will act as agents of a larger community, not merely of two disputants, and will accrete capacity to govern. Part III considers judicialization in light of delegation (also known as Principal–Agent) theory, developing three distinct models of governance: (A) *the contractual*; (B) *the judicial*; and (C) *the pluralist-constitutional*. These models now compete for dominance, while resting on rather different foundations of legitimacy. As an empirical matter, with the movement from model A to B, or from model B to C, tribunals accumulate obligations to a wider community of stakeholders. We conclude with an overview of the book.

I. Orientations

The aim of the book is not to refute or debunk other approaches to international arbitration, or to champion our own. Instead, we seek to build constructively on existing scholarship, including traditional doctrinal commentary on specific awards,[26] the reflections of elite arbitrators and IAC officials,[27] and empirically based, critical reconstructions of the regime.[28] Here, we briefly discuss strains of scholarship that intersect with our basic orientations,[29] noting the handful of important monographs on the evolution of international arbitration that have been published to date.

Institutions and Change

This book builds on social science approaches to institution-building that coalesced in the 1990s as the 'new institutionalism'.[30] These approaches focus on the role of institutions, understood as norms (principles, standards, rules, procedures, and cultural dispositions) that constrain choices, fix roles and duties, enable the exercise of 'legitimate' authority, and organize the evolution of social systems in

---

[26] All of the major IACs edit specialized journals that publish such work.

[27] Lawrence Newman and Richard Hill (eds), *The Leading Arbitrators' Guide to International Arbitration* (3rd edn, Juris, Huntington 2014); William Park, *Arbitration of International Business Disputes: Studies in Law and Practice* (2nd edn, Oxford University Press, Oxford 2012); Paulsson (n 1).

[28] Klaus Peter Berger, *The Creeping Codification of the Lex Mercatoria* (2nd edn, Kluwer, Alphen aan den Rijn 2010) ['Berger 2010']; Gus Van Harten, *Investment Treaty Arbitration and Public Law* (Oxford University Press, Oxford 2007) ['Van Harten'].

[29] We reference more specialized literatures in subsequent chapters.

[30] For a synthetic overview, see Peter Hall and Rosemary Taylor, 'Political Science and the Three New Institutionalisms' (1996) 44 Political Studies 936. See also Walter W Powell and Paul DiMaggio (eds), *The New Institutionalism in Organizational Analysis* (University of Chicago Press, Chicago 1991) ['Powell and DiMaggio']; and Douglass North, *Institutions, Institutional Change, and Economic Performance* (Cambridge University Press, Cambridge 1990) ['North'].

path-dependent ways. The theoretical frameworks presented in parts II and III distil and integrate the main insights of this literature.

In sociological terms, the unit of analysis at the core of our project is a 'field'.[31] For our purposes, a field is an arena of activity that is created when actors operating in what had been previously separate and autonomous domains of action begin to orient their activities to one another. A new field is consolidated as these domains become embedded in one another, at which point domain autonomy becomes merely relative, in the sense that actors are no longer able to realize their goals successfully without reference to field-level 'institutions' (as just defined). The construction of new social fields, of course, needs actors—the builders of new institutions, and the agents of change. So-called 'skilled social actors'[32] are adept at building linkages between existing domains, and across pre-existing organizational ideologies and world views. Where they are successful, they fashion new templates for action that become normalized as best practice standards. In international law and politics, European integration is one of the best documented examples of the emergence and consolidation of new fields,[33] as are the effects of incorporating the European Convention on Human Rights into national legal orders.[34]

We do not claim that institutionalist and field-theoretic theory offers the best way to conceptualize the evolutionary dynamics of international arbitration, and we recognize that some legal scholars will see no need for theory developed outside of legal studies. We introduce these ideas because they provide a generic and coherent approach to institutional change. The ambition of this book is to describe, explain, and assess the development of arbitral order as a legal system, and arbitration as a system of transnational governance. To do so, we focused on the consolidation of institutions that have enabled arbitration to develop as a legal system and, hence, to defend its own claims of autonomy and legitimacy. Today, the arbitral regime remains decentralized—there is no sovereign legislator or dispute resolver in the regime—although the elites who run the system are tightly networked in a stable, competitive, market-based field. We then tracked the development of the interface—a transnational, legal field—between the arbitral system and domestic law and courts, under the 1958 New York Convention. This legal field regularly generates what sociologists call 'institutional isomorphism',[35] dynamics that produce doctrinal convergence across jurisdiction boundaries (Chapters 2, 4, and 5). Arbitrators incorporate general principles of law (most importantly, including due process norms), found in national systems, both to build their own effectiveness

---

[31] Neil Fligstein and Doug McAdam, *A Theory of Fields* (Oxford University Press, Oxford 2012).

[32] Neil Fligstein, 'Social Skill and the Theory of Fields' (2001) 19 Sociological Theory 105.

[33] Neil Fligstein and Alec Stone Sweet, 'Constructing Markets and Polities: An Institutionalist Account of European Integration' (2002) 107 American Journal of Sociology 1206 ['Fligstein and Stone Sweet'].

[34] Helen Keller and Alec Stone Sweet (eds), *A Europe of Rights: The Impact of the European Convention on Human Rights on National Legal Systems* (Oxford University Press, Oxford 2009).

[35] The classic account is Paul DiMaggio and Walter W Powell, 'The Iron Cage Revisited: Institutional Isomorphism and Collective Rationality in Organizational Fields' (1983) 48 American Sociological Review 147.

and to secure enforcement of their awards. And lawmakers and judges of the most powerful states in the major trading zones adapted to the rise of arbitration by adopting, gradually and at times only grudgingly, its core doctrines.

Agency and Ideology

The construction of new fields depends on agency, that is, on the activities of skilled actors who possess or accumulate the power to induce institutional transformation. The most important book on the evolution of international arbitration as a field remains Dezalay and Garth's *Dealing in Virtue* (1996), a field-theoretic study that highlights struggles for influence among elites within the regime itself.[36] The authors argued that the regime underwent a fundamental change in the 1980s, when litigation-savvy lawyers trained in the techniques of American adversarialism replaced the 'Grand Old Men', mostly of Europe, who relied on their status, charisma, and academic credentials to create the ICC and then to dominate the regime. *Dealing in Virtue* is the first social science study of the professional backgrounds and socialization of the actors that run the system. In a more recent book, Karton identifies and evaluates *The Culture of International Arbitration* (2013),[37] on the basis of extensive interviews with arbitrators, and analysis of their awards. Arbitrators, he finds, share powerful ideological commitments to an expansive notion of party autonomy, and to flexible modes of legal interpretation and dispute resolution that they create and curate, as transnational contract law. We address some of these authors' specific arguments in chapters to come. More generally, what we find important is their treatment of the evolution of arbitration as a macro-institutional phenomenon of broad socio-legal significance.

The Status and Autonomy of the Arbitral Order

The most venerable vein of scholarship on the evolution of arbitration is philosophical inquiry into the status of the regime as an autonomous legal system, as such.[38] In the 1960s, a first wave of scholars, the most important of whom were also leading arbitrators, began to formalize the dogmatic foundations of the arbitral order's autonomy claims. These theorists, including Goldman[39] and David,[40] emphasized

---

[36] Dezalay and Garth (n 1). The content and outcomes of these struggles, Dezalay and Garth emphasize, were partly determined by major shifts in geopolitics and the global economy.

[37] Karton (n 1).

[38] See, generally, Florian Grisel, *L'arbitrage international ou le droit contre l'ordre juridique* (LGDJ, Paris 2011).

[39] Berthold Goldman, 'Frontières du droit et "lex mercatoria"' (1964) 9 Archives de philosophie du droit 177; Berthold Goldman, 'Le droit applicable selon la Convention de la B.I.R.D. du 18 mars 1965 pour le règlement des différends relatifs aux investissements entre Etats et ressortissants d'autres Etats' in *Investissements étrangers et arbitrage entre Etats et personnes privées: la convention B.I.R.D. du 18 mars 1965* (Pédone, Paris 1969); Berthold Goldman, 'La lex mercatoria dans les contrats et l'arbitrage internationaux: réalité et perspectives' (1979) *Journal du Droit International* 475.

[40] René David, 'Arbitrage et droit comparé' (1959) 11 Revue internationale de droit comparé 5; René David, 'Arbitrage du XIXe et arbitrage du XXe siècle' in *Mélanges offerts à René Savatier* (Dalloz, Paris 1965).

two main factors of significance to systemic identity and legitimation: (a) party autonomy and freedom of contract; and (b) the customs, trade usages, and general principles of transnational commerce—called the *Lex Mercatoria*. Legal positivists immediately objected,[41] pointing to the importance of the national 'seat of arbitration' (held to be the source of arbitration's legitimacy) and of domestic courts as a mechanism of enforcement (held to be a necessary condition of arbitration's effectiveness). This debate continues to rage, producing increasingly esoteric versions of the argument, with no signs that it will be settled any time soon.

The autonomy of the arbitral regime and the status of arbitral lawmaking are major themes of this book. In designing our empirical research, we acknowledged that both sides of the debate can point to important empirical facts in support of their own positions.

Since the 1960s, the arbitral regime has evolved in ways that have rendered traditional doctrines of the seat all but obsolete (Chapters 2 and 3). Gaillard, in *Legal Theory of International Arbitration* (2010),[42] stresses this point as a crucial fact in support of the autonomy view. Gaillard recognizes, as Goldman did,[43] that the substantive law of arbitration is 'incomplete', even if the *Lex Mercatoria* is fully taken into account. Arbitrators should (and do) fill gaps with reference to general principles of law, which they find through comparative analysis of the jurisprudence of national courts. In this view, the autonomy of the arbitral order is both meaningful and relative. Berger's *The Creeping Codification of the Lex Mercatoria* (1996, 2010)[44] makes the case for a much fuller version of autonomy. Echoing the tenets of new institutional economics, Berger argues that domestic law and judicial doctrine, which he characterizes as deeply dysfunctional, impose intolerably high transaction costs on transnational commerce, a situation that has driven the construction of transnational law and dispute resolution over many decades.[45] Berger then documents the evolution of transnational institutions, which he conceptualizes as autonomous general principles that are constitutive of the system itself.

It is a matter of some importance that scholars can now sensibly claim that the arbitral order meets the classic criteria of legal positivism for the identification of a 'legal system'. In *Transnational Legality* (2014),[46] Thomas Schultz examines a host of structural properties that undergird the arbitral order and the *Lex Mercatoria*, including 'the complex union of primary and secondary rules' that Hart famously emphasized to differentiate 'legal' from other social systems.[47] Academic lawyers have long treated the investment regime, with ICSID at its core, as a legal system,

---

[41] Francis A Mann, 'Lex Facit Arbitrum' in Pieter Sanders (ed), *International Arbitration—Liber Amicorum for Martin Domke* (Martinus Nijhoff, The Hague 1967). See also Michael Mustill, 'Contemporary Problems in International Commercial Arbitration: A Response' (1989) 17 International Business Law 161.

[42] Emmanuel Gaillard, *Legal Theory of International Arbitration* (Martinus Nijhoff, Leiden 2010).

[43] Berthold Goldman, *Lex Mercatoria* (Kluwer Law and Taxation Publishers, Deventer 1983).

[44] Berger 2010 (n 28).   [45] Berger (n 4).

[46] Thomas Schultz, *Transnational Legality: Stateless Law and International Arbitration* (Oxford University Press, Oxford 2014).

[47] H L A Hart, *The Concept of Law* (3rd edn, Oxford University Press, Oxford 2012) ['Hart'] 114.

although there remain few political analyses of ISA in the legal literature. An important exception is Sornarajah, who emphasizes, in *Resistance and Change in the International Law on Foreign Investment*, that ISA owes its take-off in large part to the rise of neo-liberal ideology. The institutionalization of market-based dogmas within structures of global governance in the 1990s not only pushed states to buy into the ISA, it profoundly shaped the struggle for control of the regime's development, and constrained reform agendas.[48] Following a seminal paper by Van Harten and Loughlin,[49] scholars now routinely study the regime in the light of comparative public law materials, Van Harten's *Investment Treaty Arbitration and Public Law* (2007)[50] being a prominent example.

It remains a blunt fact that the arbitral regime needs courts to enforce its awards. For these and other reasons, a group of scholars continue to oppose the regime's autonomy claims, often in dismissive and bellicose terms.[51] As we stress throughout the book, states have freely chosen to recognize arbitral authority in treaties, some of which (the New York and ICSID Conventions) are of quasi-constitutional importance. If powerful trading and capital-rich states jointly chose to destroy the arbitral regime, they could do so. We approached these issues primarily from an empirical perspective, focusing on how state officials, including judges, interact with arbitrators, within an evolving pluralist, legal field (Chapter 2). That field would not exist, we argue throughout the book, without arbitration's steady judicialization.

II. Theory of Judicialization

We now present the theory of judicialization in its most basic, abstract, and deductive form. Judicialization refers to the process through which third-party dispute resolution [TDR] emerges in a community, and develops authority over its institutional evolution. The theory was elaborated without reference to arbitration,[52] and has been tested in various settings.[53] It predicts that TDR will develop as a mechanism of governance insofar as specific causal relationships are forged between three factors: (a) *dyadic exchange* (e.g. contracting); (b) *triadic dispute resolution* (including reason-based decision-making); and (c) *normative structure* (institutions, that is, the

[48] M Sornarajah, *Resistance and Change in the International Law on Foreign Investment* (Cambridge University Press, Cambridge 2015).
[49] Van Harten and Loughlin (n 24). See also Schill (ed) (n 23).
[50] Van Harten (n 28). See also Schill (ed) (n 23).
[51] Ralf Michaels, 'Dreaming Law without a State: Scholarship on Autonomous International Arbitration as Utopian Literature' (2013) 1 London Review of International Law 35.
[52] Stone Sweet (n 22).
[53] ibid. See also Alec Stone Sweet and Thomas Brunell, 'Constructing a Supranational Constitution: Dispute Resolution and Governance in the European Community' (1998) 92 American Political Science Review 63 ['Stone Sweet and Brunell 1998']; Alec Stone Sweet, *Governing with Judges: Constitutional Politics in Western Europe* (Oxford University Press, Oxford 2000); Alec Stone Sweet, *The Judicial Construction of Europe* (Oxford University Press, Oxford 2004).

procedural and substantive norms that govern exchange). Because actors can block the process at crucial stages, however, outcomes are contingent, not predetermined.

The first element, 'the simplest sociological formation',[54] is the *dyad*, defined as 'any pattern of [direct] exchange' between two individuals or groups.[55] The generic basis of social exchange is the norm of reciprocity: to keep one's promises, to repay one's debts, and to recognize and return kindnesses received. As Simmel puts it, reciprocity confers on the dyad 'a special consecration', by linking individuals to 'a common fate'.[56] At the same time, dyadic forms can be inherently unstable. The various dilemmas of the game theorist (assurance games and the prisoner's dilemma, for example) may infect virtually any dyadic relationship. Here, we focus on dyadic contracting. Contract law formalizes reciprocity norms, enshrining them in terms of expansive principles such as good faith, while producing demand for third-party enforcement.

The *triad*—comprised of two disputants and a dispute resolver—is a primordial mode of social organization, found in virtually every known human community. The underlying reason is straightforward: the triadic entity is the guarantor of reciprocity. Quite literally rooted in the dyadic form, the triad brings an external presence to the dyad, whose interest lies in 'a common fate'. The move from the dyad to the triad lays the foundations of a particular form of governance: the triadic. In dyads, conflict can be debilitating; but dyadic conflict is constitutive of the triad. Where effective, TDR will perform basic functions of governance: to sustain cooperation; to reinforce existing norms; to produce new guidelines for how one ought to behave; to stabilize one's expectations about the behaviour of others; to reduce the costs of contracting and disputing; and to alter the terms of exchange, thereby impinging prospectively on the distribution of values and resources.

Two ideal types of TDR are relevant to our concerns. The first is consensual TDR: two disputants, acting through a voluntary ad hoc act of delegation, recognize the authority of the triadic dispute resolver. Arbitration is a paradigmatic case of consensual TDR. The second is compulsory TDR: judicial office replaces delegation, and jurisdiction imposes the terms of dispute settlement on the disputants.[57] The paradigmatic form of compulsory jurisdiction is adjudication in a state court. Although the distinction can be crucial, we will show that even in situations in which the authority of the triadic figure is based on the free consent of the parties, judicialization can proceed.

The third factor is *normative structure*, what social scientists call 'institutions': those socially constituted constraints on behaviour that govern exchange in any

[54] Georg Simmel, *The Sociology of Georg Simmel* (Free Press, Glencoe 1950) ['Simmel'] 122.

[55] George Foster, 'The Dyadic Contract: A Model for the Social Structure of a Mexican Peasant Village' in S W Schmidt, J C Scott, C Landé, and L Guasti (eds), *Friends, Followers, and Factions* (University of California Press, Berkeley 1977) ['Foster'].

[56] Simmel (n 54), 123, 135.

[57] Martin Shapiro, *Courts: A Comparative and Political Analysis* (University of Chicago Press, Chicago 1981) ['Shapiro'] Chapter 1.

community. Broadly conceived, normative structure includes, in North's terms, 'law', 'rules of the game', 'conventions, codes of conduct, norms of behaviour', and 'customs and traditions'.[58] It conforms to March and Olsen's notion of *rules*, a term inclusive of legal norms, but also the panoply of 'paradigms, codes, cultures, and knowledge' that permit us to 'identif[y] the normatively appropriate behaviour',[59] as well as to ground the 'performance scripts'[60] through which actors perform their roles. Rule systems enable productive social exchange by simplifying the range of choices available, and investing those choices with value and meaning. Across the social sciences, change in normative structure has proved difficult to theorize. We understand better the logics of inertia. Rules facilitate exchange between individuals, creating opportunities for collective action; and behaviour that responds to these opportunities, once locked in (e.g. in dyadic forms), reinforces normative structure.

We now present a theory of the construction of triadic governance, focusing on dynamics of change that are endogenous to relationships between these three basic elements. The theory integrates, as tightly interdependent phenomena, (a) strategic behaviour, how individual actors conceive and pursue their interests, and (b) change in normative structure through TDR. It is important to stress two additional theoretical considerations upfront. First, we exclude, but only initially, hierarchy and coercion from consideration, doing some violence to reality.[61] Second, the causal system we theorize constitutes a mechanism for processing rising demand for change. Such demands are exogenous to the theory; they may be generated by an external shock or disruption, technological innovation, a shift in consumer taste, and so on. Research on the judicialization of any system of dispute resolution must identify the factors that stoke the demand for change, and assess how they are processed, with what rule-making effects.

Dyads, Triads, and Normative Structure

Figure 1.1 depicts the process through which a consent-based system of triadic governance evolves. The process is comprised of four chronological shifts, moving clockwise. Each shift conditions what will happen in subsequent stages. The discussion highlights tensions within dyads and triads that drive movement from one stage to another, generating the recursive effects (feedback) that produce(s)

---

[58] North (n 30), 3–5.

[59] James March and John Olsen, *Rediscovering Institutions* (Free Press, New York 1989) 22.

[60] Ronald Jepperson, 'Institutions, Institutional Effects, and Institutionalism' in Powell and DiMaggio (n 30), 145.

[61] All dyadic relationships reflect or organize ongoing power relationships that may contain elements of at least implied coercion. We begin with a consensual, rather than a coercive, model of governance in order to direct attention to outcomes that result exclusively from the internal logic of rules, dyads, and triads. Put differently, ours is a theory of ideational and normative—not physical or material—power and influence.

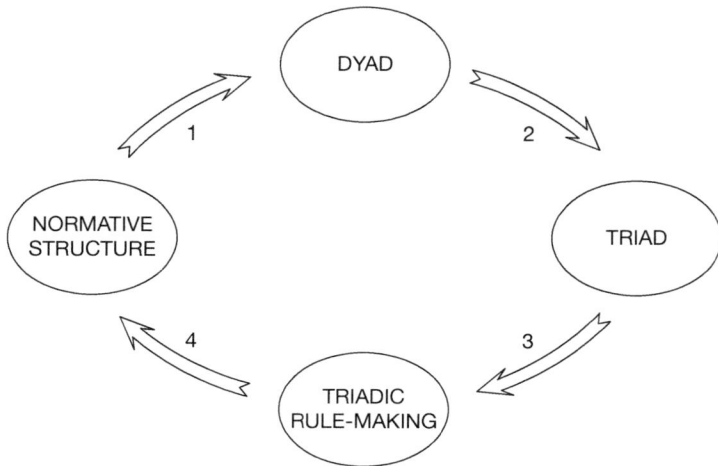

Figure 1.1 Judicialization and the Construction of Governance

normative change. Because judicial lawmaking[62] is the crucial catalyst of change, we give its microfoundations special attention.

Stage 1: From Norms to Contract

To get to a dyadic contract, we need two individuals and at least a rudimentary normative structure. By dyadic contract, we mean the rules of exchange (or, those promises) voluntarily entered into between two persons. Contracts can be implicit or explicit. The promises made in an 'implicit dyadic contract' are uncodified and 'lack ritual or legal basis'; explicit contracts codify promises meant to be legally binding.[63] Both forms establish reciprocal rights and duties among two contract-ants. In contracting, two individuals coordinate their self-interest in terms of some shared view of the future. Such coordination is difficult, if not impossible, without at least a primitive cultural framework: in the form of language (communication), and in the form of the norm of reciprocity, which is embedded in notions of individual commitment, reputation, and responsibility. In a strong sense, normative structure—a property of the social—is analytically prior to contracting.

Reciprocity, a crucial building block of society, enables the construction of the dyadic form; as Gouldner has it, the norm constitutes a 'starting mechanism' that 'helps to initiate social interaction'.[64] Contract law typically expresses the

---

[62] We are aware that 'judicial lawmaking' is a contested concept. We use the term in a generic sense to mean any decision that supplements the corpus of normative materials that can be used in any future episodes of TDR.

[63] Foster (n 55), 16.

[64] Alvin Gouldner, 'The Norm of Reciprocity' in S W Schmidt, J C Scott, C Landé, and L Guasti (eds), *Friends, Followers, and Factions* (University of California Press, Berkeley 1977) 39.

reciprocity norm through the *good faith* principle and its corollaries. Normative structure also helps sustain dyadic relationships over time, by facilitating dispute resolution. At the level of the single actor, norms derived from reciprocity—or a relevant rule, or an established manner of doing things—can prevent disputes, to the extent that the norm guides and constrains individuals in ways that lead them to honour their commitments. Once a dispute has erupted, norms provide the parties with materials for settling the dispute dyadically, insofar as they furnish standards for evaluating both the disputed behaviour and potential solutions to the conflict. The authority, or legitimacy, of these standards depends heavily on the fact that they existed prior to the dispute.

Stage 2: From Dyad to Triad

The legitimacy of dyadic exchange is rooted in the self-interest of the contracting parties. For each party, the contract must be functional in a specific sense: its existence depends on the parties' perception that the benefits of dyadic exchange outweigh the costs. The terms of a dyadic contract coordinate self-interest, in the form of reciprocal rights and obligations, for the duration of the dyad.

Contracting generates a massive functional demand for third-party interpretation and enforcement. Most contracts of any complexity are 'incomplete', in the sense that parties are unable to specify fully rights and obligations for all contingencies *ex ante*. Incomplete contracting is a basic source of the demand for TDR: the dispute resolver helps to complete the contract *ex post* in light of a dispute about the contract's terms. Further, as circumstances change, the meanings attached to the same terms may diverge; the value of the dyadic relationship may decline for one or both of the parties; or one party may succumb to incentives to renege on obligations (the prisoner's dilemma).

Parties often succeed in resolving disputes on their own. When they do so, the dyad comprises, in the parlance of legal anthropology, a specific 'legal level'. If disputants fail to resolve their dispute, they may choose to delegate the matter to a third party, thus constituting a new legal level: the triadic.[65] Such delegation is likely when, for each disputant, going to a third party is perceived as less costly than either breaking the contract, or attempting to impose a particular settlement against the wishes of the other. The risk of delegating to the triadic figure is the prospect that she will take an undesirable decision, or stigmatize one as a loser. In the longer run, the more intensively any pool of contractants interacts with one other, the less that risk matters. Parties may expect to win some disputes and to lose others, over time, against a backdrop of absolute benefit. The social logic of delegation, like that of the dyadic contract, is one of long-range utility: each party must believe that it is better off attempting to resolve a dispute than dissolving the relationship.

---

[65] Jane Fishburne Collier, *Law and Social Change in Zinacantan* (Stanford University Press, Stanford 1973) Chapter 1.

Yet the calculation of costs and benefits need not favour the move to TDR. One (or both) parties may choose to walk away from their relationship. Agreement on a dispute resolver, whose impartiality and wisdom is jointly recognized, may be elusive. One party may prefer sustaining conflict, rather than resolving it. The move to TDR may indeed help disputants restore their relationship—that is, after all, one of its functions—but the move itself is not automatic, since it requires a sufficient degree of trust and cooperation between the parties. Adversarialism heightens these problems in obvious ways. In response, contractants can lock in their commitment to TDR at the *ex ante* contractual moment, agreeing in advance to settle their disputes through TDR. It is precisely through such pre-agreements that most arbitral tribunals in the commercial world are constituted.

The delegation of dyadic conflict to a third party is the fuel that drives the system. If disputants choose not to delegate or are unable to agree on procedures, if disputants are able to settle their disputes dyadically, or if one of the disputants has the will and power to impose a solution on the other, there would be neither TDR nor evolution in forms of triadic governance.

Stage 3: The Crisis of Legitimacy, or, 2-Against-1

Once constituted, the triadic entity faces a potentially intractable dilemma. On the one hand, her reputation for neutrality is crucial to her legitimacy. Disputants would be loath to delegate disputes if it were otherwise. Yet, in resolving disputes, the third party may compromise her reputation for neutrality by declaring one party the loser, thereby creating a 2-against-1 situation.[66] In an adversarial situation, in particular, we can assume that each disputant hopes as much. In such a situation, the dispute resolver's interest, her existential priority, is to settle conflicts without destroying the perception of the neutrality of TDR, with respect to present and future disputants.

In pursuit of this objective—which we will call 'effectiveness'[67]—four basic tactics are available. First, the dispute resolver can develop procedures in order to persuade the parties of the fairness of the process; at a minimum, she must ensure that each is able to express its side of the dispute. Second, she can defend her decisions as constrained by existing norms. Norms provide ready-made, presumptively legitimate standards of appropriate behaviour that the dispute resolver can invoke as reasons. Social norms will, often enough to matter a great deal, express an interest beyond that of individuals or the dyad, in effect, reflecting the 'social interest'. Third, she can fashion compromise rulings, in effect, splitting the difference between the parties when it comes to finding fault and tailoring a remedy. Fourth, she can encourage the parties to settle their dispute, leading them to withdraw it, as a means of avoiding the 2-against-1 situation altogether.

---

[66] See especially Shapiro (n 57).

[67] We define effectiveness, more concretely for arbitration, in Chapter 2, and use that definition throughout the book.

No known, stable system of TDR fails to blend these elements, albeit in different ratios. Nonetheless, the values underlying these tactics may come into tension in specific cases. The friction between (concrete) facts and (abstract) norms is a generic source of such tensions. Thus, while laying down procedures may help the dispute resolver to 'get the facts right', these same facts may well expose the inadequacy of existing norms, pressuring the dispute resolver to innovate (shift 4). Invoking a rule might well complicate the crafting of a decision based on fairness considerations. In any event, restoring reciprocity through settlement is a radically different task from determining how much a loser owes to a winner. If the dispute resolver does designate one party the clear 'winner', and the other the 'loser', then her legitimacy is likely to rest all the more on the integrity of the procedures, the 'correct' determination of the facts, and the persuasiveness of normative reasoning and justification.

Stage 4: From Dispute Resolution to Lawmaking

Modes of TDR can be arrayed along a continuum constituted on one pole by mediation and on the other pole by adjudication. In mediation, the dispute resolver helps the disputants arrive at a mutually satisfactory settlement of the conflict. In adjudication, the dispute resolver authoritatively resolves the dispute, identifying the loser, and assessing the harm to the winner. In practice, dispute resolvers move back and forth along the continuum—or threaten to do so—continuously, to enhance their flexibility, limit their political exposure, and maximize their influence over the disputants.

In embracing adjudication, the dispute resolver is led, with increasing precision and formality, (a) to develop (or rely on pre-existing) procedural templates and (b) to provide a rule-based justification for her decisions. The more she does so, the more two forms of triadic lawmaking will become inseparable. The first type is *particular* and *retrospective*: the triadic figure settles a specific dispute about the terms of one dyadic contract, helping to 'complete' it. The decision—the law made—applies to the disputing parties. The stage for a second form of lawmaking is set once the dispute resolver seeks to justify procedural or substantive decisions normatively, with reasons. In telling us, for example, why a given act is or is not permitted, or how tensions between two norms or interests are to be resolved, she makes law of a *general* and *prospective* nature. This is so to the extent that her decision clarifies, alters, or creates elements of normative structure in ways that future dyads and triads will credit.

Triadic lawmaking constitutes a predictable response to the crisis faced by dispute resolvers (stage 3, tactic 2, above). Yet it raises a second-order legitimacy issue, in that the parties could not have ascertained the content of the governing norms at the time the dispute erupted. Put bluntly, the perception of the dispute resolver's neutrality erodes as her capacity to make law—imposed as a social interest congealed as a norm—becomes visible. Without dispensing entirely with reason-giving, which would leave her worse off, this problem cannot be resolved. She can seek to mitigate it, say, by portraying her lawmaking as a by-product of dispute resolution, rather than as an outcome that she desires. In effect, she tells the loser: 'You have lost not because I prefer your opponent to you, but because it is my responsibility to uphold what is right in our community, given our norms and the harm that has occurred in this instance.'[68] Her legitimacy (reputation for impartiality) will now rest, in part, on the perceived appropriateness of a third interest she has brought to bear on the parties: the 'social interest' as embodied in norms and reasons she gives.

Shift 1 (Again): Feedback—Reconstructing the Dyad

Moving through shifts 1 to 4 can knot together dyadic contracting, TDR, and normative structure. A dyadic dispute erupts; the disputants delegate the matter to a dispute resolver; the latter resolves the conflict in a process involving normative deliberation and reason-giving, revising (at least subtly) normative structure. In returning to shift 1, the impact of norms on exchange, we have come full circle, back to our initial starting point. But we find ourselves in a rather different world this time: the individuals comprising the dyad have learned something about the nature of their relationship and about the institutional environment that sustains it. The dispute resolver has re-enacted normative structure, asserting the social interest. She may have done so in a relatively conservative manner, devising a partial victory for each disputant and invoking rules whose prior existence is unquestioned. Or she may have done so more progressively, declaring one party to be the loser, while revising an existing norm or creating a new one. In the latter situation, she has made law that opens a path to future judicialization.

Given two conditions, triadic lawmaking becomes triadic governance. First, future contractants must perceive that they are better off in a world with triadic lawmaking than without it, and will evaluate potential actions in light of past decisions (undergirding the recursivity of shifts 1 and 2). Second, future contractants and dispute resolvers must understand that the procedures developed, and reasons given, to justify prior decisions have some prospective, pedagogical authority (grounding shifts 3 and 4). If these conditions are met, and if there is a steady stream of disputes and decisions, then TDR will inexorably become a mechanism of institutional change, and dyadic exchange will be placed in the shadow of triadic rule-making. A virtuous circle is completed. To the extent that TDR is effective, it will lower the costs of contracting; as dyadic exchanges increase in number, scope, and diversity, so will the demand for TDR; as TDR is exercised, the normative structure will expand and thicken; these rules will then feed back onto dyadic relationships, structuring future interactions, conflict, and dispute resolution. In sum, as the normative structure expands, so does the significance of community-level values, what we have called the social interest.

---

[68] Again, the insight is Shapiro's: see Shapiro (n 57).

Triadic Governance

The theory demonstrates how we can move, by virtue of a self-sustaining process, from disputes about the terms of dyadic contracts to a system of triadic governance, if shifts 1 to 4 are reiterated, and the conditions just stipulated are met. As decisions accumulate, the normative structure, registering the community's values, will become more elaborate and differentiated. The practices that lawyers associate with precedent—'persuasive authority'—will follow naturally, so long as triadic figures recognize that their legitimacy will depend in part on consistent reason-giving.[69] In encapsulating this sequence—dyadic contract → conflict → deliberation → triadic rule-making → precedent-based lawmaking—triadic governance will organize the future. But it will be sustained only so long as future dyads and triads are drawn into the process and help to perpetuate it.

To this point, we have considered the dynamics of judicialization within a consensual regime. Coercive sanctions and enforcement mechanisms are conspicuously absent. Movement from one stage to another depends on how actors identify their respective interests and behave accordingly. They are capable of blocking movement at crucial points. One or both disputants may choose to dissolve their contract rather than delegate to a third party, for example, or the dispute resolver may render capricious decisions, or refuse to give reasons at all. Where such behaviour is, or becomes, the normal state of affairs, triadic governance will not develop.

Sanctions buttress triadic governance. Yet even in the consensual world, sanctions—social provisions that stigmatize those who refuse to comply with existing norms or decisions issuing from TDR—can be effective. In a situation in which all actors possess good information about the reputations of one another, for example, no one will contract with those who persistently disregard their obligations under a dyadic contract, imposed by TDR. Banishment from the pool of contractants is the ultimate penalty associated with consensual governance (see Chapter 2). As classic legal anthropology[70] and contemporary economic approaches to norms[71] have shown, consensual TDR in close-knit societies usually operates to reassert pre-existing norms, or to evolve new ones only gradually, in light of changing external circumstances. By contrast, as the quantity and complexity of impersonal contracting and exchange grows and covers larger distances, the functional demand for TDR overlaps a growing need for general and prospective lawmaking (stage 4). Consensual TDR may not be sufficient to sustain increasing levels of social exchange. More robust commitment devices and enforcement—hierarchy—may be required (in particular, at stage 2). And the formalization of precedent, as binding law, is secured through hierarchical structures for appeal.

---

[69] For an explanation of the foundations of this view of precedent, see Alec Stone Sweet, 'Path Dependence, Precedent, and Judicial Power' in Shapiro and Stone Sweet (n 2), Chapter 2.

[70] Bronislaw Malinowski, *Crime and Custom in Savage Society* (Paul, Trench and Trubner, London 1932).

[71] Robert Ellickson, *Order without Law: How Neighbors Settle Disputes* (Harvard University Press, Cambridge MA 1991).

In compulsory triadic governance (ie the domain of state courts), explicit rules and coercive sanctions govern the following sequence: dyadic contract → TDR → decision → compliance → precedent. The move from dyad to triad occurs in the absence of the consent of one of the parties, obliges the triadic dispute resolver to consider the complaint, requires the parties to comply with the terms of the eventual decision, and specifies enforcement measures for non-compliance that enlist the coercive powers of other public officials. The transition from consensual to compulsory TDR is inherently the stuff of political evolution.[72]

More concretely, our account of triadic governance intersects with a range of social science approaches to contracting and the development of markets. Modern contract theory, for example, focuses on the linked problems of how to achieve optimal contracting, in which the parties maximize joint benefits while balancing *ex ante* commitment and *ex post* flexibility, in order to manage uncertainty. As we have stressed, those who contract need enforcement; those who write incomplete contracts need an interpreter; and those who interpret the law help to make it. Partly for these reasons, one predictable outcome of judicialization will be to lower the costs of exchange for the pool of potential contractants. Triadic governance, however, will undermine optimal contracting—from the standpoint of any specific contract—insofar as it brings to bear, on the dispute, social interests, against the will of the parties, and in tension with the terms of their agreement. Transaction cost approaches to market building also heavily emphasize the significance of effective TDR. Scholars have shown that triadic governance has played a crucial role in facilitating economic expansion, both within and across borders.[73] These results depend on the capacity of TDR to reduce transaction costs for long-range (non-local) trade, relative to pre-existing or presupposed alternative arrangements, not on the strict maximization of efficiency for any two parties.

Application to Arbitration

The theory of judicialization provides an abstract, deductive account of how a legal system evolves and reproduces itself. Although the theory was not developed with international arbitration in mind, its applicability to arbitration should be obvious: it is through consent that the authority of the tribunal in ICA is constituted, after all. One expects that rising contractually based trade and investment across

---

[72] With the development of the nation state, the authority to govern is shared among separate organs: legislatures and courts. These figures, however, are not easily detached from one another. Triadic lawmaking has a legislative aspect, evolving institutions on a case-by-case basis. For their part, legislators participate in dispute resolution: a function of statutes is to prevent conflict from arising in the first place, and to facilitate the settlement of disputes that do arise. Legislative authority, too, begets a crisis of legitimacy no less acute than the one that afflicts the dispute resolver. This crisis animates legislative and constitutional politics, and the endless quest to ground legislative authority in an external source of legitimacy (e.g. elections), while constraining its exercise (e.g. procedures and justiciable rights).

[73] See, for instance, Avner Greif, 'Contract Enforceability and Economic Institutions in Early Trade: The Maghribi Traders' Coalition' (1993) 83 American Economic Review 425; North (n 30); Stone Sweet and Brunell 1998 (n 53); Fligstein and Stone Sweet (n 33).

borders will generate the context for disputing, and a steady stream of adversarial disputes will activate and sustain the judicialization process.

The theory furnishes the basic empirical indicators of our inquiry, which can now be summarily stated. The first indicator concerns the nature of arbitration as a mechanism of TDR. As judicialization proceeds, the adjudicatory aspects of arbitration will be strengthened, weakening those associated with mediation. If so, a second set of indicators is implied. We can expect the process to generate institutions—procedures, substantive principles and rules, and precedent-based argumentation and justification—that will enable arbitrators to govern, in the face of rising adversarialism. The effectiveness of arbitral governance will depend on the development of elements of hierarchy, at the very least, in the form of commitment devices that keep disputants in the system. Third, governance entails the capacity of arbitrators to recognize the 'social' and the 'public' interest, and to impose it—in the form of applicable law—on present and future parties. This outcome, again, depends upon the construction of hierarchical authority.

Chapters 2 to 5 of this book chart the judicialization of arbitration with reference to these indicators. Earlier we noted the importance of exogenous factors that have driven the judicialization of the arbitral order over the past century, including the huge expansion in transnational trade and investment, and the attendant rise of adversarial legalism. From today's standpoint, we know that the process has generated three prominent, systemic outcomes (Chapter 2): (a) arbitral centres now operate as full-fledged substitutes for national courts; (b) transnational firms strongly prefer to arbitrate rather than to litigate their disputes; and (c) most states in the major trading zones have adopted strong, pro-arbitration policies. Taken together, these outcomes raise a fundamental issue, namely, the point at which a self-sustaining mode of triadic governance becomes a *bona fide* 'legal system'. Many social scientists conceptualize any stable mechanism of TDR, applying an identifiable normative structure, as a legal system; a court applying statutes is just one type of TDR.[74] This view has gradually influenced the thinking of academic lawyers,[75] including some who study international arbitration.[76] More traditional scholars, on the other hand, have been anxious to distinguish law from other social norms, and judges from other kinds of third-party dispute resolvers.[77] For present purposes, we conceptualize these latter distinctions as empirical indicators. One observes judicialization when one sees arbitration developing hierarchical features akin to those found in systems of adjudication, and when one sees arbitrators adopting the mantle of the adjudicator. In the next section, we contextualize these points further.

---

[74] See Sally Engle Merry, 'Legal Pluralism' (1988) 22 Law and Society Review 869 ['Merry']; Stone Sweet (n 22).

[75] Walter Otto Weyrauch and Maureen Anne Bell, 'Autonomous Lawmaking: The Case of the "Gypsies" ' (1993) 103 Yale Law Journal 323.

[76] See Stavros Brekoulakis, 'International Arbitration Scholarship and the Concept of Arbitration Law' (2013) 36 Fordham International Law Journal 745 ['Brekoulakis'].

[77] Following Hart (n 47).

III. Logics of Delegation

The Principal–Agent [P–A] framework is an adaptation of well-known concepts of contract law and practice to explain important aspects of economic and political governance.[78] Over the past three decades, social scientists have made P–A analysis a standard approach to research on the firm,[79] state organs,[80] and international regimes.[81] Although scholars use it for varied purposes, the framework is popular for three main reasons. First, it helps to explain the origin and persistence of specific modes of delegated governance in light of the functional demands of those who need them. Second, it offers ready-made, appropriate materials that the analyst can tailor to a wide range of situations. Third, it helps to organize empirical research on the dynamics of delegated governance, allowing the analyst to derive testable propositions about the consequences, *ex post*, of delegating in a particular form, *ex ante*. The approach neatly applies to arbitration, being a paradigmatic case of delegated authority; and it is easily adapted to the theory of judicialization. In this section, we introduce the basics of the P–A framework, and then develop three models of arbitral authority. We use these models as heuristic devices to chart the judicialization of arbitration throughout the book.

Principals and Agents

The P–A approach dramatizes the relationship between Principals and Agents, against the background of a specified set of governance problems. *Principals* are those actors who create *Agents*, whereupon the former confers upon the latter discretionary authority to take binding decisions. The Agent governs to the extent that her decisions influence the distribution of values and resources in the domain of her competences. By assumption, the Principals are initially in control, in that they possess the authority and resources to constitute (or not) an Agent. Since the Principals are willing to pay the costs of delegation, which include expenditures of resources to design a new institution, and to monitor the Agent's activities, one assumes that they expect the benefits of delegation to outweigh costs, over time. The analyst typically 'explains' the origin and persistence of an organization, or governance situation, in light of the specific needs of those who delegate. Delegation thus takes place insofar as it is 'functional' for principals, that is, in their interest.

---

[78] See generally, Mark Thatcher and Alec Stone Sweet (eds), *The Politics of Delegation* (Routledge, London 2003); Mark Thatcher and Alec Stone Sweet, 'Theory and Practice of Delegation to Non-Majoritarian Institutions' (2002) 25 West European Politics 1 ['Thatcher and Stone Sweet'].

[79] Jean-Jacques Laffont and David Martimort, *The Theory of Incentives: The Principal-Agent Model* (Princeton University Press, Princeton 2001); Paul Milgrom and John Roberts, *Economics, Organization and Management* (Prentice-Hall, Englewood Cliff 1992).

[80] Kaare Strøm, Wolfgang Müller, and Torbjörn Bergman, *Delegation and Accountability in Parliamentary Democracies* (Oxford University Press, Oxford 2006).

[81] Mark Pollack, *The Engines of Integration: Delegation, Agency, and Agency Setting in the European Union* (Oxford University Press, Oxford 2003).

Among other rationales, Principals create Agents to help them govern: to make rules and settle disputes; to guarantee the credibility of their commitments; to harness epistemic expertise; and to avoid taking blame for unpopular decisions.[82]

The Principals' capacity to control their Agent has been the central preoccupation of the approach. The potential for the Agent to develop and to act on her own interests poses an omnipresent problem. Because these and other 'agency costs' inhere in delegation, would-be Principals face a dilemma. In order for them to achieve their goals, they have to grant meaningful discretionary authority to the Agent; yet the Agent may use her powers to produce outcomes that the Principals would reject, or which are costly to eradicate, thereby undermining rationales for delegating in the first place. Sharing this anxiety, sophisticated Principals will seek to incentivize the Agent's work, by building procedures for oversight and override, for example.

In designing a new institution, Principals choose from a complex menu of options. They may give an Agent more or less authority to govern in a specific domain *ex ante*; they may create procedures enabling them to monitor the Agent's decisions; and they may choose to retain some or no power to undo an Agent's decisions, or to redirect her priorities *ex post*. The more Principals seek to pre-commit themselves to predetermined policy goals or outcomes, the analysis assumes, the more power and autonomy they are likely to delegate to their Agent. Indeed, some Agents' decisions are so highly insulated from override by those who create them that analysts label them 'Trustees', which are a type of 'super agent'.[83] Examples include supreme and constitutional courts (empowered to protect rights through constitutional judicial review), and central banks (tasked with controlling inflation). In contrast, if Principals seek a rich range of policy alternatives from which to select, on an ongoing basis, they will benefit from designing easy-to-use *ex post* mechanisms of supervision and control. Legislatures, for example, often retain the capacity to supervise policies produced by the 'independent' agencies they create, and to reconfigure their mandates if deemed necessary.[84]

The standard P–A approach generates what we will call an *agency control model*, focusing empirical attention on the goals of the Principals, and the extent to which Agents help to achieve them. A somewhat different, but not incompatible, approach to delegated governance highlights the role-oriented perspective of Agents, producing what we will call a *fiduciary model*. A fiduciary model stresses the formal obligations and social expectations that accrue to Agents by virtue of the roles they perform and the authority they exercise when they govern. An agency control model prioritizes the interactions between Principals and Agents, as conditioned by the

[82] Thatcher and Stone Sweet (n 78).

[83] Alec Stone Sweet, 'Constitutional Courts and Parliamentary Democracy' (2002) 25 West European Politics 77–100; Alec Stone Sweet and Thomas Brunell, 'Trustee Courts and the Judicialization of International Regimes: The Politics of Majoritarian Activism in the ECHR, the EU, and the WTO' (2013) 1(1) Journal of Law and Courts 61 ['Stone Sweet and Brunell 2012'].

[84] Martin Shapiro, 'Judicial Delegation Doctrines: The US, Britain, and France' (2002) 25 West European Politics 173.

decision rules that govern override. A fiduciary model emphasizes the duties Agents owe to those to whom their decisions apply, bringing third parties into the mix.[85]

An Agent is a 'fiduciary' if she possesses the formal, discretionary authority to determine the distribution of a specific bundle of goods (assets, values, legal entitlements, and interests) to which some set of beneficiaries hold claim. By definition, 'beneficiaries' are in a state of 'vulnerability' to the fiduciary, in the strict sense that their claims are subject to the latter's decision-making. Because of this vulnerability—which is itself a by-product of an act of delegation—the Agent is typically subject to a number of overlapping 'fiduciary obligations'. The most important of these duties are 'loyalty', 'accountability', and 'deliberative engagement', which we illustrate here with reference to a judge sitting on a court.[86]

At a minimum, 'loyalty' includes the judge's obligation to pursue and defend the values of the legal system, while maintaining impartiality with respect to the litigants that come before her. 'Accountability' requires the judge to give reasons for her decisions. Thicker versions of loyalty and accountability would include duties to seek doctrinal (jurisprudential) clarity and coherence, that is, to reduce both normative uncertainty and conflict between legal norms in order to strengthen the effectiveness of the legal system. 'Deliberative engagement', as Leib et al have it, comprises 'an affirmative duty to engage in dialogue' with beneficiaries, which entails 'an authentic effort to uncover preferences rather than a mere hypothetical projection of what beneficiaries might want'. On the 'input' side, judges depend heavily on dialogic materials and procedures, including written briefs, oral arguments, and expert testimony, to gauge preferences and the probable effects of potential rulings. On the 'output' side, they have a duty to report and justify their decisions in ways that 'facilitate understanding, engagement and monitoring'.[87]

Considered in light of judicialization theory, this list of basic fiduciary obligations appears as a response to the legitimacy crisis facing the triadic entity (shift 3 above); indeed, it is an elaborately formalized response. In Chapter 3, we chart the codification of the fiduciary duties of international arbitrators.

Three Models of Arbitral Governance

In this section, we develop three simple models of international arbitration: (a) the contractual; (b) the judicial; and (c) the pluralist-constitutional. The models are both descriptive and prescriptive, providing alternative notions of how legitimate arbitral power is, and ought to be, exercised. The contractual model rests upon the classic assumptions of party autonomy. In ICA, the sources of arbitral power are contracts, each of which constitutes its own autonomous legal 'system'. In ISA, each bilateral investment treaty (BIT) negotiated by contracting states does the same. The arbitrator is an Agent of the contracting parties: the Principals.

---

[85] We know of only two attempts to develop such models with reference to judging: Stone Sweet and Brunell 2012 (n 83); and David Leib, David Ponet, and Michael Serota, 'A Fiduciary Theory of Judging' (2013) 101 University of California Law Review 699 ['Leib, Ponet, and Serota'].
[86] Leib, Ponet, and Serota (n 85).   [87] ibid 742–3.

The judicial model presumes that the arbitrator acts, at least in part, as the Agent of a larger arbitral legal order, which is comprised of transnational firms and investors, arbitration houses, states, and other stakeholders. In moving from the first to the second model, we encounter nascent hierarchies, the development of more 'court-like' fiduciary obligations, and the routine imposition of the interests of the transnational business community, and of states. These are predictable outcomes of a sustained judicialization process. The principles of party autonomy and contract law that define the contractual model remain core features of the judicial model, but in the latter we expect IACs to (re)construct these principles in light of their own evolving purposes and policies (Chapter 3).

The pluralist-constitutional model embeds the arbitral order—conceived in terms of the judicial model—within a broader legal field. The law of this field flows from myriad sources: the New York and ICSID Conventions; general principles of law; the jurisprudence of international courts; property rights; and guarantees of due process. In this mode of governance, we expect to see the arbitral order, conceived as a legal system in its own right, defending its own autonomy and building its own effectiveness, through engagement with other legal regimes.

We developed these models as heuristic frames for organizing empirical research, to help us classify and analyse data relevant to arbitration's judicialization.[88] While judicialization can take place within each of the three models, we treat data that conforms to the dictates of the judicial model as evidence counting against the contractual model. Put differently, the consolidation of the judicial model entails the demise of the contractual model. In contrast, a necessary condition for the development of the pluralist-constitutional model is the existence of an arbitral order that functions along the lines of the judicial model. Expressed as a level of analysis distinction, the judicial model directs empirical attention to the development of hierarchical authority *within* an IAC or the arbitral order; the pluralist-constitutional model prioritizes the *external* effects of *internal* organization and hierarchy, focusing on interactions between (a) the arbitral order, as a relatively autonomous legal system, and (b) other legal regimes, both domestic and international.

---

[88] One might conceptualize these models as mutually exclusive accounts of the evolution of international arbitration. The contractual model would thus provide a 'bottom-up' account of the system, grounding each important level of analysis (the dispute, the tribunal, the arbitration centre, the New York Convention) in the basic norms of party autonomy and freedom of contract. On the other hand, a state-centric version of the pluralist-constitutional model—decidedly not our view—could provide a 'top-down' view of arbitration, framing party choice and arbitral authority as dependent on positive law, at the critical points where public international law and domestic law intersect. Much of the debate about the autonomy of the *Lex Mercatoria* and arbitral order is generated by incompatibilities between these two views. The judicial model, too, could be understood in insular terms. The ICC and other centres do not simply provide a neutral forum for resolving disputes; rather, the major IACs assert that their rules comprise an autonomous source of legitimacy, reflecting the transnational community's preference for arbitration, not simply the agreement of two parties to arbitrate a dispute arising out of contract. As we demonstrate in chapters to come, the arbitral order has developed its own general principles of contract, codes of procedures, and transnational public policy, many of which are not derived from party autonomy or state law.

The Contractual Model

When two contracting parties (the Principals) confer upon an arbitrator (the Agent) the authority to resolve disputes arising under the contract, they create a node of delegated governance. The contracting parties are free to select the law and procedures that will govern the proceedings, and these choices bind their Agent. Initially, at least, the legitimacy of arbitral power is unproblematic, issuing from an act of delegation to which the parties have freely consented. In the event of a dispute, the authority of the arbitrator is limited to the domain of activity governed by the contract. If need be, the arbitrator will 'complete' the agreement, interpreting disputed provisions in light of the facts and the law selected by the parties, and then applying these interpretations to resolve the dispute. Any law she makes is retrospective and particular, in that it applies only to a discrete dispute involving a pre-existing contract.

Arbitrators are a peculiar sort of Agents. In opposition to a situation in which a legislature creates an independent agency to help it govern the activities of actors in a particular regulatory domain, the tribunal possesses power over the parties (the Principals) themselves. Such a situation is more akin to trusteeship than to simple agency. The parties have agreed to include an arbitration clause in their contract. But, once a dispute has erupted, they may well have second thoughts, and they may disagree on how the arbitrator ought to perform her task. Most important, they will desire opposed outcomes: each prefers to side with the arbitrator against the other party. In response, tribunals have asserted, and steadily consolidated, their authority over the parties, once in dispute. As we discuss in Chapter 2, it is now settled doctrine that arbitration clauses are separable from the main contract,[89] and issues of *Kompetenz-Kompetenz* have been resolved in the arbitrator's favour.[90] These developments, while being important measures of judicialization, push in the same direction: to render more effective the arbitral process by strengthening the position of arbitrators. Both give arbitration the complexion of a compulsory system of TDR. A first-order hierarchy is the result: once the arbitration begins, the parties have little if any means of controlling their Agent.

As this example illustrates, the contractual model can accommodate a great deal of dynamic endogenous change. Most international arbitration today takes place in the wake of a destroyed commercial or investor-state relationship, wherein the goal of each party is to 'win', that is, to obtain the best monetary settlement possible. In such a situation—a paradigmatically *adversarial* one—the arbitrator will be under substantial pressure to show that she is neutral with respect to the parties, not least, by developing and ensuring fair procedures, and giving reasons for her decisions.

---

[89] That is, the validity of the arbitral clause is not affected by the legal nullity of the contract of which it is part. In essence, the doctrine forecloses moves by one of the parties to the contract to avoid arbitration by pleading the contract's nullity.

[90] *Kompetenz-Kompetenz* refers to the formal competence of a jurisdiction to determine its own jurisdiction or the jurisdiction of another organ. Modern arbitration statutes and case law largely accept that the arbitrator possesses the authority to fix the scope of its own jurisdiction subject, of course, to the will of the contracting parties.

Other variables push in the same direction. The greater the monetary stakes, the more likely the parties will be to tolerate, or to create themselves, complex and costly procedures (the terms of 'deliberative engagement' for the arbitrator-as-fiduciary). Further, the higher the stakes, the more likely it will be that a losing party will consider challenging an award, pushing enforcement into a national court. Thus, insofar as the parties treat arbitration as if it were a form of adversarial litigation, they will pressure the arbitrator to act as a judge. This is a rudimentary but not trivial form of judicialization, to the extent that it leads to the juris-generation, within the arbitral order, of the types of fiduciary duties that typically apply to judges.

The emergence of fiduciary duties, whose purpose is to ground and rationalize arbitral lawmaking in procedural rules, is a predictable response to heightened adversarialism. Consider the four 'principal obligations' of arbitrators that Rusty Park, a law professor and former President of the London Court of International Arbitration, has elaborated.[91] The first is to render 'an accurate award', a decision that maximizes fidelity to the 'context and relevant bargain' enshrined in a contract or investment treaty. The second duty is to ensure 'due process', both to fulfil the first duty and to strengthen the perception of arbitral impartiality and independence vis-à-vis the disputants. The third is to strive for 'efficiency', in the sense of reducing, as far as possible, 'undue costs and delays' of settling the dispute. Finally, the tribunal must produce 'an enforceable award', given that one of the parties may ask a national judge either to recognize or quash it. In practice, securing judicial recognition of an award entails providing reasons to justify the award, and a record of how deliberations proceeded. The arbitrator owes these obligations foremost to those who pay her: the parties. At the same time, fulfilling them helps tribunals to manage the 2-against-1 legitimacy problems that inhere in TDR, and which threaten its effectiveness. These 'four musketeers of arbitral duty', as Park call them, express the fiduciary duties of loyalty, accountability, and deliberative engagement in obvious ways.

As Park stresses, the good arbitrator seeks to strike a defensible balance between the multiple values that undergird these duties, when in tension. The predicate for producing an accurate award, for example, is getting the facts right, which can directly conflict with efficiency concerns. Striving for accuracy in complex cases may entail building burdensome procedures, which the arbitrator may have to impose upon a recalcitrant party under the rubric of due process. Reason-based justification has been subject to similar dynamics. Is it enough that arbitrators give an adequate reason? Or should they be anxious to give 'good reasons', or even 'the best reasons'?[92] Again, in higher stakes, adversarial proceedings, the tribunal will be concerned with the quality of its justifications, and their reception by the parties. In any event, insofar as 'good arbitrators', who are mutually regarding,

---

[91] William Park, 'The Four Musketeers of Arbitral Duty: Neither One-for-All Nor All-for-One' in *International Chamber of Commerce, ICC Dossiers* (ICC Publishing, Paris 2011) 8, 25.

[92] Martin Shapiro, 'The Institutionalization of European Administrative Space' in Alec Stone Sweet, Wayne Sandholtz, and Neil Fligstein (eds), *The Institutionalization of Europe* (Oxford University Press, Oxford 2001).

resolve a steady supply of disputes in ways that fulfil these duties, judicialization will proceed.

The Judicial Model

A second model rejects the view that arbitral authority is merely a creature of contract. Adding several layers of institutional complexity to the equation, it depicts arbitrators as Agents who owe the basic fiduciary duties discussed above not only to the parties in dispute, but to the arbitral system and the transnational community they serve. The 'skilled arbitrator' is a professional with an interest in ensuring her career. 'Success' will require performing the duties that define that role, in order to build a reputation for fairness and wisdom among the pool of *future* disputants, in competition with peers, and in light of the demands of the greater system. As noted in part I, scholars have shown that a 'distinct and cohesive legal culture' has grown up among prominent arbitrators,[93] which includes a strong orientation toward enhancing the effectiveness and autonomy of the arbitral order as a legal system in itself. At the same time, most of the major IACs have codified the basic fiduciary duties in their procedural codes (Chapter 3).

The judicial model explicitly acknowledges elements of hierarchy, both private and public. Institutionally, what distinguishes the judicial model from the contractual model is organization hierarchy. Today, far more than 90 per cent of all international arbitration takes place under the Rules and supervision of an arbitration house. IACs function as de facto legislators in the arbitral world, regularly revising their codes of procedures, often codifying best practices that had emerged through the arbitral process itself (Chapters 2, 3, and 4). Under the rules of every major house, arbitrators are required to justify their awards with reasons. The ICC announced, as early as 1924, that it would check the 'phraseology' of awards;[94] and the supervision of awards has become much more intrusive over the past two decades.[95] Today, the ICC's supervisory body—called the 'Court'—provides tribunals with a checklist of requirements when it comes to submitting awards; scrutiny of draft awards is mandatory; and the Court will refuse to certify an award that fails to give adequate reasons. It does so in order to maximize consistency across awards—what the ICC characterizes as promoting 'justice' for the parties—and to ensure that awards rendered will be enforceable in national courts under the New York Convention. Given that arbitration houses compete with one another for business, as well as with national courts, they have good reason to develop what is, in effect, a guarantee for the product they are selling.

The fact that national courts hold the power to vacate awards also leads IACs to invest in hierarchy, that is, the administrative capacity to control how tribunals

---

[93] Karton (n 1); Dezalay and Garth (n 1).

[94] International Chamber of Commerce, *The Arbitration of the International Chamber of Commerce* (ICC Publishing, Paris 1924) 7.

[95] Chapters 2 and 3.

perform their tasks, including their fiduciary obligations.[96] In P–A terms, what is crucial is that the arbitrator will normally be subject to the authority of multiple actors beyond the disputants, including officials of the IAC and national judges. IACs and domestic courts are able to exercise powers (of supervision and override) usually associated with Principals, but which the contracting parties themselves do not possess once the proceedings commence.

The judicial model portrays judges and arbitrators as performing similar functions. National judges (like arbitrators) regularly engage in mediation to cajole the parties to settle,[97] for example, and arbitral tribunals (like courts) regularly apply state law to resolve conflicts. Much depends on the fact pattern of the dispute, and the matrix of law that applies to it. In a commercial dispute that involves provisions of mandatory national regulations, the arbitrator will be compelled to consider, or to impose, state or other 'public policy' interests on the parties.[98] In *Mitsubishi*, a major ruling of the US Supreme Court, the majority expressly delegated[99] the task of interpreting and applying US anti-trust law to (non-American) arbitrators seated in Japan, while retaining authority to review how international arbitrators would apply mandatory law in future awards. Cases such as these eviscerate claims that the arbitrator, unlike the judge, owes duties only to the contracting parties (as Principals), or that they are not required to take into account wider social interests. Similarly, the model casts distinctions between 'private' and 'public' law as relative. No national contract law, whether legislated or judge-made, is strictly private, in that it has been constituted through the exercise of public authority, and is a direct form of business regulation more generally. Tribunals are routinely required to resolve disputes involving the interpretation and application of mandatory state law, in which case they expected to act, at least in part, as Agents of that legal order (Chapter 5).

To this point, we have portrayed the arbitrator's role in the judicialization process as essentially a defensive one: she develops procedures and reason-based justifications in order to secure and maintain her legitimacy with respect to present and future disputants, and with respect to IACs. Whereas the contractual model emphasizes the ad hoc character of arbitration, 'repeat players' striving to build their reputations as 'socially skilled' arbitrators dominate the field (Chapter 2). If, in fact, these arbitrators perform their fiduciary duties with an eye toward future professional prospects, then they may well be led to take into account the interests of a wider group of stakeholders, not just of two parties in a one-shot interaction.

---

[96] The mandatory scrutiny process produces, the ICC promotion materials emphasize, a 'stamp of approval' that will be recognized by national courts: International Chamber of Commerce, 'Ten good reasons to choose ICC arbitration' <http://www.iccwbo.org/Products-and-Services/Arbitration-and-ADR/Arbitration/Introduction-to-ICC-Arbitration/Ten-good-reasons-to-choose-ICC-arbitration/> accessed 26 January 2016.

[97] Section 278 of the German Civil Code, for example, requires German private law judges 'to seek an amicable resolution of the legal dispute' and details procedures for doing so. The analogue, in France, is Article L 611–4 to L 611–15 of the Commercial Code.

[98] Chapters 4 and 5.

[99] *Mitsubishi Motors Corp v Soler Chrysler Plymouth, Inc* (1985) 473 US 614.

If so, we can predict that the judicialization of the contractual model will favour the emergence of the judicial model.

In sum, the judicial model directs our attention to arbitration's autonomy as a 'legal system', the structural features of which can be observed and evaluated in their own right. While national courts and transnational arbitral tribunals remain different in significant ways, what is important is that the judicialization of arbitration has taken place despite these differences.

The Pluralist-Constitutional Model

While the judicial model attends to the internal development of international arbitration as a legal system in its own right, the pluralist-constitutional model focuses attention on how the arbitral order interacts with other legal regimes, externally as it were, in processes of transnational governance.

Pluralism is a structural property of certain legal systems.[100] Legal pluralism comes in two forms—'source' and 'jurisdictional' pluralism—and international arbitration mixes strong doses of both. Arbitrators routinely interpret and apply an eclectic mix of diverse, autonomous sources of law (contractual, national, international, transnational) in order to resolve the disputes that come before them. 'No law is "foreign" to the international arbitrator', the maxim has it. Jurisdictionally, the arbitral world is comprised of IACs who compete on the basis of their procedural and administrative offerings (Chapter 2), none of which can impose its policy choices on the others. Fragmentation is a fact of global law, and arbitration reflects as much. The 1958 New York and the 1965 ICSID Conventions, too, have been interpreted and applied in ways that have gradually institutionalized a pluralist legal order. Overlapping claims to authority emanate from domestic law and courts, international law, and arbitral centres (Chapter 2). But these systems lack an apex authority: there exists no organ possessing a final word when it comes to settling conflicts of jurisdiction or of norms.

Whether a pluralist legal order can be understood as 'constitutional' is more controversial.[101] The crucial issue, an empirical one, concerns the extent to which hierarchically organized rules structure these interactions in ways that constitute a system of otherwise autonomous legal regimes.[102] The 'constitutional' aspect of the model is rooted in two different claims that now, arguably, reinforce each other. First, treaty instruments of global scope have established a multi-level interface that serves to coordinate among jurisdictions found in three separate systems of law: the transnational-arbitral, the national, and the international. The New York

---

[100] See Merry (n 74); Paul Schiff Berman, 'The New Legal Pluralism' (2009) 5 Annual Review of Law and Social Science 225. For discussions of pluralism, as applied to international arbitration, see Chapter 2. See also Paulsson (n 1) and Brekoulakis (n 76).

[101] For a discussion of the concepts of pluralism and constitutionalism as properties of the same system, see Alec Stone Sweet, 'The Structure of Constitutional Pluralism' (2013) 11 International Journal of Constitutional Law 491 ['The Structure of Constitutional Pluralism'].

[102] Alec Stone Sweet, 'Constitutionalism, Legal Pluralism, and International Regimes' (2009) 16 Indiana Journal of Global Legal Studies 621.

and ICSID Conventions, which have been ratified by the vast majority of states, perform inherently constitutional functions. These treaties explicitly recognize arbitral authority, and require national judges to enforce awards, subject to exceptions such as 'public policy' and 'inarbitrability'.

The second claim, which is more embryonic, is that the New York and ICSID Conventions are foundational elements of an evolving international economic constitution that are grounded in general principles and fundamental rights. The central idea is that trade and investment combine with the activities of international organizations (including IACs) to drive the progressive construction of a system that has identifiable constitutional features. Conceptually, the claim is tied to the emergence of constitutional understandings of the international legal system, which presuppose a substantive body of 'higher law' norms that are binding on all international judges, including arbitrators.[103] The most commonly invoked elements are *jus cogens* norms, human rights, including property rights, and procedural guarantees associated with due process and access to justice. In the arbitral context, parties and tribunals typically invoke these norms in the guise of general principles of law, including principles of transnational public policy. Some scholars have pushed further, conceptualizing international human rights as itself a substantive constitution, which all judges are obliged to enforce.[104]

In ISA, the skilled arbitrator, mindful of the need to ensure and enhance the effectiveness of the arbitral order, will be adept at defending the regime's autonomy with respect to other established legal systems, which may well entail the identification and institutionalization of higher-order norms.[105] Building on the judicial model, one presupposes that the arbitral order possesses enough internal systemic coherence to assert its identity externally.[106] The 'good' arbitrator will also consider, when appropriate, the relevant jurisprudence of international courts. In any event, the obligation to engage with international law finds support in the 1969 Vienna Convention on the Law of Treaties, which directly applies to ISA under

---

[103] Erika de Wet, 'The International Constitutional Order' (2006) 55 International and Comparative Law Quarterly 51; Jan Klabbers, Anne Peters, and Geir Ulfstein, *The Constitutionalization of International Law* (Oxford University Press, Oxford 2009); Ernst-Ulrich Petersmann, 'Constitutional Theories of International Economic Adjudication and Investor-State Arbitration' in Pierre-Marie Dupuy, Francesco Francioni, and Ernst-Ulrich Petersmann (eds), *Human Rights in International Investment Law and Arbitration* (Oxford University Press, Oxford 2009).

[104] Ernst-Ulrich Petersmann, *International Economic Law in the 21st Century: Constitutional Pluralism and Multilevel Governance of Interdependent Public Goods* (Oxford, Hart 2012); 'The Structure of Constitutional Pluralism' (n 101).

[105] Arbitrators would be following down a path carved out by more established systems established by treaty. The Court of Justice of the European Union [CJEU] famously grounded its 'constitutional' doctrines (of direct effect, supremacy, and state liability for non-compliance) on the 'autonomy' of the legal system created by the Treaty of Rome and on the principle of 'effectiveness' of EU law which derives from it. The strategy has been followed, more or less successfully, by other international courts, including the European Court of Human Rights [ECtHR] and the Appellate Body of the World Trade Organization [AB-WTO].

[106] On the notion of constitutional identity, see Michel Rosenfeld, *The Identity of the Constitutional Subject: Selfhood, Citizenship, Culture, and Community* (Taylor and Francis, Abingdon and New York 2009).

investment treaties. Article 31(3) of that Convention requires the interpreter to take into account 'any relevant rules of international law applicable in the relations between the parties'. Further, international law explicitly recognizes, as an independent source of law, general principles of law, an uncodified, ever-expanding corpus of legal norms recognized in well-developed legal systems.[107] Today, tribunals routinely borrow principles from courts, and they develop general principles on their own (Chapters 4 and 5). In doing so, they create an arbitral common law, which enhances the autonomy of the arbitral regime and, arguably, contributes to the evolution of the economic constitution.

The model also applies to ICA. The claim is not that all transnational commercial disputes are inherently constitutional, but only that the arbitrator is under an obligation to issue awards that do not violate higher-law norms, as well as to take account of rights and normative hierarchies in other ways. As mentioned above, the 1958 New York Convention authorizes the national judge to refuse to enforce an award that offends 'public policy' or involves matters that are 'inarbitrable' altogether. In North America, most of Europe, and parts of Asia, states have reduced the scope of these exceptions to practical irrelevance. Significantly, this outcome has in large part depended on arbitrators demonstrating that they perform their fiduciary duties in ways that national judges will approve, including the construction of norms of 'transnational public policy' (Chapters 4 and 5). In most of the major trading states, the core exceptions that remain are linked to the same fundamental norms listed above, casting arbitrators and judges as partners in enforcing the 'constitution' in similar ways.

A glance at comparative contract law may help to clarify these claims. In an increasing number of national orders, judges are obligated to take into account constitutional norms when relevant to private law adjudication. The German Federal Constitutional Court, in its *Lüth* ruling of 1958, famously placed the civil courts under a duty to strike a proper balance between constitutional rights and the values that inhere in the private law, including freedom of contract.[108] Indeed, German judges must ensure the compatibility of 'every provision of the private law' with the constitution. The basics of *Lüth* have diffused beyond Germany, resulting in a process that has gradually 'constitutionalized' the private law. Proponents of the pluralist-constitutional model can therefore point to developments at both the international and domestic levels to support their claims.

Summary

As judicialization proceeds within any model, or provokes a move from model A to B, or facilitates arbitral decision-making congruent with expectations derived from model C, one finds arbitrators operating in an increasingly elaborate,

---

[107] Alec Stone Sweet and Giacinto della Cananea, 'Proportionality, General Principles of Law, and Investor-State Arbitration' (2014) 46 NYU Journal of International Law and Politics 911.
[108] *Lüth* (1958) BVerfGE 7, 198.

hierarchically defined legal system that they helped to construct. These transformations mean that arbitrators will conceptualize their roles, and perform their duties, differently. Consider the notion of 'justice'. In the contractual model, the arbitrator supplies justice by settling a dyadic dispute. For the parties, the prospect of an 'unjust' arbitral award is an inherent risk of any business deal that might sour; the award registers no impact beyond the dyad. In the judicial model, arbitrators render justice, at a minimum, by ensuring due process and maximizing legal certainty for present and future users of the system. In the pluralist-constitutional model, the arbitrator denies justice whenever she fails to uphold, or adequately take into consideration, applicable higher-law norms. And she may actively pursue just outcomes by developing general principles to fill gaps in the law when they appear. Thus, as we move from the judicial to the pluralist-constitutional model, the arbitrator accumulates duties to a wider community of stakeholders, and engages in lawmaking of a more prospective nature.

The theoretical materials presented here emphasize the functional logics that underlie delegation. But we do not mean to obscure the deeply political nature of the judicialization of arbitration. Those who seek to structure the arbitral order according to the terms of the judicial model are, in fact, waging an increasingly intense, real-world struggle against those wedded to representing arbitration in terms provided by the contractual model. The judicial model acknowledges that arbitrators and IACs are directly implicated in transnational governance, for example, whereas proponents of the contractual model are, in effect, denying the development of arbitral governance, or attempting to camouflage it. We chart the outcomes of this struggle in the chapters to come.

IV. The Institutional Evolution of International Arbitration

The theoretical materials presented in this chapter guided our empirical research. We used the propositions derived from these materials in two related ways: as hypotheses to be tested; and as heuristics for assessing the institutional evolution of judicialized governance. With respect to data collection, we endeavoured to be as systematic as possible. For ISA, we collected basic information on every publicly available final award on state liability, as well as for all decisions of ICSID ad hoc Annulment Committees. We coded for pleadings, outcomes, judicial decisions and arbitral awards cited, the counsel and arbitrators involved in the proceedings, and the types of state measures under review, among other information.[109] Each chapter reports our analyses of these data, which also helped to organize our qualitative research, in particular, on doctrinal development in ISA. For ICA, we examined published awards and judicial decisions issuing from annulment and enforcement

---

[109] *Yale Law School Data Sets on Investor-State Arbitration* (2016), compiled by Alec Stone Sweet as principal investigator, and Sheng Li, Meng-Jia Yang, Michael Chung, Moeun Cha, and Tara Zivkovich, as student research assistants.

proceedings in domestic courts. Because the vast majority of ICA awards remain confidential, we used a variety of less direct means to assess the field's evolution. We treated as data (for both ICA and ISA) information found in scholarly commentary and treatises, the published reflections of leading arbitrators, the annual and special reports of major IACs, and interviews with IAC officials and arbitrators. We examined all of the changes in the 'Rules of Arbitration' of the major IACs, focusing, in particular, on revisions of the ICC procedural code, the first edition of which dates from 1922. Further, each chapter reports our analysis of documents in the ICC's historical archives, many of which had not been examined before. Last, we tracked the emergence and revision of the hard and soft law instruments that ground the field: those treaties, model laws, and formalized texts, promulgated by transnational organs, purporting to express best-practice standards.

The book proceeds as follows. Chapter 2 provides a macro-institutional overview of the development of international arbitration as a pluralist legal system, defined by its own peculiar structures of authority. In Chapter 3, we analyse the evolution of arbitral procedures, paying particular attention to provisions that constitute organizational hierarchies, and formalize the fiduciary duties of arbitrators. Chapter 4 examines the dynamics of reason-giving and lawmaking, the emergence of stable conceptions of precedent, and the rising demand for mechanisms of appeal. In Chapter 5, we assess the extent to which arbitral tribunals take into account the public interest, and balance property rights against state regulatory prerogatives. Chapter 6 considers the legitimacy of arbitral governance in light of our empirical findings, and assesses a number of reforms designed to enhance arbitration's political legitimacy.

2

The Evolution of the Arbitral Order

In Chapter 1, we argued that the arbitral order will develop its own internal coherence and external autonomy as judicialization proceeds. We also elaborated three models of arbitral governance, each of which is subject to the dynamics of judicialization. This chapter gives empirical content to these claims, situating them in broad historical context. Part I examines how the generic problems of long-range trade have been resolved at different points in time, and how the present regime for international commercial arbitration [ICA] is organized. Part II considers the consolidation of arbitral power over the past century. We pay particular attention to the evolution of authority relationships between tribunals and disputants (at the contractual level of analysis), between international arbitration centres [IACs] and tribunals (within the judicial model), and between the arbitral order and national legal systems (in the context of the pluralist-constitutional model). Part III provides an overview of the evolution of treaty-based investor-state arbitration [ISA].

I. Islands of Transnational Governance

Over the past century, an expansive and increasingly cohesive community of actors has succeeded in constructing a transnational system of governance for transnational business. The space is comprised of a networked set of institutions and organizations—a patchwork of arrangements we call the new *Lex Mercatoria*—that makes no sovereignty claims over people or territory. These are 'islands of transnational governance'.[1] This part of the chapter takes a broad perspective on these developments. After discussing obstacles to the emergence of a stable trading system in a relatively abstract way, we examine how three different regimes have governed transnational commerce. We then map the contours of the present arbitral system.

Generic Problems of Trade

Assume the existence of a pool of actors who would trade with one another if it were profitable. The pool is comprised of *strangers* in that no pairing of them has had prior

---

[1] Alec Stone Sweet, 'Islands of Transnational Governance' in Martin Shapiro and Alec Stone Sweet (eds), *On Law, Politics, and Judicialization* (Oxford University Press, Oxford 2002) Chapter 2.

The Evolution of International Arbitration: Judicialization, Governance, Legitimacy. First Edition. Alec Stone Sweet and Florian Grisel. © Alec Stone Sweet and Florian Grisel 2017. Published 2017 by Oxford University Press.

dealings with one another. In such a context, traders will be able to sustain long-range, impersonal exchange only insofar as they are able to resolve three overlapping problems: of commitment, high transaction costs, and institutional choice. First, traders may fail to honour their commitments even if they are able to contract with one another. Second, transaction costs are usually higher for long distance than for local trade. Existing institutions, including state law and enforcement mechanisms, may impose costs, thereby discouraging the expansion of commerce outside of the local boundaries drawn by these rules. Third, our traders must organize a system of governance, and maintain it over time. The more they exchange with one another, the greater will be the demand for contractual interpretation and effective enforcement.

Problem 1: Cooperation and Commitment

The prisoner's dilemma (PD) game captures the core elements of the strategic context confronting our traders. Because the dominant move is to cheat, dyadic exchanges will tend to be one-shot deals. If so, iterative conditional strategies that may favour a move to cooperation, such as tit-for-tat,[2] are unavailable. Where contractants are not strangers, that is, where a pool of potential traders enjoys ongoing, face-to-face relations with each other within a shared normative framework, dilemmas of cooperation are more tractable.

In this latter situation, actors are far more likely to build and sustain a non-hierarchical trading regime.[3] All would-be traders in our pool know that they would be made better off through trade. At the same time, trader X recognizes that cheating trader Y will be advantageous if Y abides by contractual promises made (the PD). On the other hand, given adequate information about the past behaviour of potential contractants, incentives may reverse. X may learn that cheating Y today will make it more difficult to find new trading partners tomorrow, if cheating damages a trader's reputation for trustworthiness. Once the group establishes a means of curating reputations, they will exclude cheaters and exchange only with the trustworthy. This solution depends on the organization of information and monitoring capacities, collective goods that the group may or may not generate, given the costs involved. Grounding this type of regime, a 'reputational' system, is a rule: promises made must be kept—*pacta sunt servanda*.

Problem 2: Transaction Costs

If our traders have succeeded in stigmatizing cheating, then they are no longer quite 'strangers' to one another; at a minimum they recognize the legitimacy of

---

[2] Robert Axelrod, 'An Evolutionary Approach to Norms' (1986) 80 American Political Science Review 1095.
[3] Cooperation can be achieved by individuals and diffuses as the 'norm' within a group if each player possesses some knowledge about the preferences of other players or some means of assessing individual reputations for trustworthiness. See Michihiro Kandori, 'Social Norms and Community Enforcement' (1992) 59 Review of Economic Studies 63.

norms associated with reciprocity and good faith. The second problem they confront concerns relative transaction costs. We understand these costs to include all of the expenses incurred in commerce, including the costs of contracting and dispute resolution. Expenses related to the transport of goods, communications, insurance, letters of credit, and the costs of middlemen will almost always be less avoidable, and the outlays higher, for long distance, compared with local exchange. No long-range trading system can prosper without the development of some form of contract law, a stable pricing and payment system, and the availability of effective third-party dispute resolution [TDR]. If costs outweigh the potential gains of long-distance trade, or are smaller than the return to local exchange, trade will remain local.

For most of human history, most commercial activity has not been long distance and impersonal, but local. As North[4] has argued, sustaining arrangements that are capable of reducing these costs over time, as circumstances change, has been a necessary condition for the emergence of more cosmopolitan trading systems, whether across regions in a given national territory, or across state boundaries.[5] The details of how institutions are constructed will also be critical. Traders, one expects, will adapt their activities to arrangements that work well, reinforcing their resilience. And they will seek to replace dysfunctional institutions with more effective ones. Finally, there are usually actors and organizations, both public and private, who prefer autarky, support local hindrances to trade, and will seek to block changes desired by cosmopolitans.

Problem 3: Governance

The third problem is that of governance.[6] If our traders have overcome problems of commitment and high transaction costs, then they have also resolved some basic governance problems. What matters is how they have done so. A broad range of regime forms are potentially viable, the operational details of which may differ considerably. Both mediators and judges are dispute resolvers, for example, but the source and scope of their respective authority varies significantly. More generally, traders typically value both (a) freedom of contract and flexibility, and (b) security and legal certainty. Yet when it comes to the specifics of institutional design, these interests may clash. If trade-offs are inevitable, then the trick will be to find a way to balance them in sustainable ways. The trading community may also maintain

---

[4] Douglass C North, *Institutions, Institutional Change, and Economic Performance* (Cambridge University Press, Cambridge 1990).

[5] Alec Stone Sweet and Thomas Brunell, 'Constructing a Supranational Constitution: Dispute Resolution and Governance in the European Community' (1998) 92 American Political Science Review 63.

[6] For the purposes of this book (see Chapter 1), *governance* refers to the process through which institutions—rules, procedures, and organizational capacity to resolve disputes and make law—are adapted on an ongoing basis to the needs of those who exchange with one another.

multiple regimes that compete with one another, in order to maximize choice, responsiveness, and efficiency.[7]

In a world of sovereigns, where jurisdictions may overlap (medieval Europe), or where states are defined territorially (the Westphalian, state-centric world), traders may assign an existent set of law and court to their contract to enhance predictability and guarantee enforcement. The downside is that courts, far from being neutral dispute resolvers, engage in boundary maintenance, social control, and lawmaking. As Shapiro puts it, they routinely impose on the parties the interests of the state itself.[8] Our traders could also seek to construct and manage their own regime, to reduce costs and enhance their autonomy vis-à-vis pre-existing jurisdictions. If so, they will face problems inherent in all institutional design, including how best to keep the regime operating in light of their priorities. One should expect unintended consequences. Those who create new legal systems, for example, regularly find themselves in worlds that judges construct, to the extent that judges work to build the effectiveness of the system. Yet these worlds were hardly imagined, at the *ex ante* constitutional moment, by the designers.[9]

Regimes

For present purposes, a 'regime' refers to any durable set of institutional arrangements that enables traders to contract across borders and to resolve contractual disputes. Here we summarize how three different regimes have governed transnational commercial activity: the Medieval Law Merchant [MLM], the Westphalian state system, and the new *Lex Mercatoria*, with ICA at its core.

The Medieval Law Merchant

Prior to the emergence of the Westphalian nation state, the MLM—the 'old' *Lex Mercatoria*—governed large swathes of long-range, impersonal exchange. The MLM, which appeared between the eleventh and twelfth centuries, comprised a relatively comprehensive and efficient regime for trade beyond 'local' borders. Traders themselves managed the system. The regime's functional logic was straightforward. It enabled merchants to escape conflicts between various local customs and rules, to access third-party dispute resolution [TDR], and to avoid submitting

---

[7] While scholars recognize the topic's importance, the empirical literature on how actors make such decisions and with what consequences remains sparse.

[8] Martin Shapiro, *Courts: A Comparative and Political Analysis* (University of Chicago Press, Chicago 1981) Chapter 1.

[9] Hence the now extensive literature on the 'transformation' of international regimes through use, not design. See Joseph Weiler, 'The Transformation of Europe' (1991) 100 Yale Law Journal 2403; Alec Stone Sweet, 'The New GATT: Dispute Resolution and the Judicialization of the Trade Regime' in Mary Volcansek (ed), *Law Above Nations: Supranational Courts and the Legalization of Politics* (University of Florida Press, Gainesville 1997) 118–41; Joost Pauwelyn, 'At the Edge of Chaos? Foreign Investment Law as a Complex Adaptive System, How It Emerged and How It Can Be Reformed' (2014) 29(1) ICSID Review—Foreign Investment Law Journal 372 ['Pauwelyn'].

to the authority of judges attached to other jurisdictions, including the courts of feudal manors, city states, local gilds, and the Church.

By the close of the twelfth century, the MLM governed the vast bulk of long-distance trade in Europe and, through codes of conduct and middlemen, at critical points along the great Mediterranean and Eastern trading routes.[10] As Benson has it, the MLM was 'voluntarily produced, voluntarily adjudicated, and voluntarily enforced'.[11] The regime embodied certain constitutive principles, including: *pacta sunt servanda*; good faith; reciprocity and non-discrimination between 'foreigners' and 'locals' at the site of exchange; and the regularized provision of TDR. In practice, the MLM required traders to use contracts, which were gradually standardized, and to settle their disputes in courts staffed by other merchants—their peers. The community placed a premium on quick judgments, de-emphasized adversarial procedure, and favoured equity settlements.

A reputation-based system of enforcement comprises a core element of the regime. The primary purpose of TDR was not to declare a 'winner' or 'loser', but to resuscitate the contractual agreement, and to cajole the parties to get on with their business, using the norms of trade as a framework for settlement and decision-making. The effectiveness of the MLM depended critically on reputation effects, and the ostracization of those branded as untrustworthy.[12] The MLM served as a clearing house for such information, making of reputations a transferable good, or 'bond', within the community of traders. TDR reinforced the effectiveness of the system.[13] Because the merchant-judge recorded his decisions, traders could monitor one another's compliance with the community's codes. In sum, the institutional setting supplied by the MLM created the conditions necessary for constructing a trading regime in the absence of a coercive state apparatus, by making promises self-enforcing and by placing future contracting in the shadow of the law. Those who lost reputation lost trading partners, as well as access to the system.

The Westphalian State

Until well into the fifteenth century, the MLM provided the institutional underpinnings for most long-distance exchange in the trading world. Thereafter, European state rulers sought to emulate the main features of the MLM and to subordinate the merchant's regime to state control. New law, designed to 'move merchants into royal courts, and/or make merchants' courts less

---

[10] Avner Greif, 'Contract Enforceability and Economic Institutions in Early Trade: The Maghribi Traders' Coalition' (1993) 83 American Economic Review 425.

[11] Bruce L Benson, 'Customary Law as a Social Contract: International Commercial Law' (1992) 3 Constitutional Political Economy 1 ['Benson'], 15–19.

[12] The crucial problem facing medieval long-range trade was the 'costliness of generating and communicating information' about the histories of potential trading partners. See Paul Milgrom, Douglass North, and Barry Weingast, 'The Role of Institutions in the Revival of Trade: The Law Merchant, Private Judges, and the Champagne Fairs' (1992) 2 Economics and Politics 1.

[13] Avner Greif, Paul Milgrom, and Barry Weingast, 'Coordination, Commitment, and Enforcement: The Case of the Merchant Guild' (1994) 102 Journal of Political Economy 745.

desirable',[14] absorbed large parts of the old *Lex Mercatoria*, while gradually replacing more equity-based decision-making with enforceable judgments in law. At the same time, the European state gradually weaned itself off its more rapacious practices, such as repudiation of public debt and confiscations of property.[15] At the close of the sixteenth century, the private commercial law of the nation state and its law courts had reduced the significance and scope of the Law Merchant, while never quite extinguishing it. From the point of view of traders, state building had its advantages. The eighteenth and nineteenth centuries, for example, saw huge reductions in transaction costs, due to improvements in transportation and communication, in physical security and policing, and to the emergence of modern banking and insurance practices. By the end of the nineteenth century, national legal regimes, not the law of merchants, largely governed transnational commercial activity.

The state-centric system also introduced its own latent costs and inefficiencies, some of which we have already noted. In a world of sovereign states, each of which furnishes an authoritative law of contract and courts, it may be a point of contention as to which body of legal rules applies when contractual disputes of a transnational nature erupt. For one or more reasons, the dispute may involve the law of two or more state jurisdictions. If the dispute comes before a national judge sitting on a court of state X, she may assign the law of X to the case, and then proceed to resolve the dispute in the normal way. Frequently, however, the national law of the presiding judge is obviously not the appropriate law. The parties may have agreed, for example, that the law of state Y will govern their relationship. Or the dispute might involve the performance of obligations outside of X's territory, in state Z, the latter supplying authoritative rules relevant to performance. Or the deal concerned multiple contracts, entered into by a chain of parties operating in multiple locations under separate but mandatory national regulations. If our judge decides that a foreign legal system ought to provide the operative law, then she may well assign the law of that jurisdiction to the case. If so, the usual expectation is that she will act as if she were a judge trained in that latter system.

The practices meant to manage these problems go by two names, 'Private International Law' and 'Conflict of Laws'. We use the word 'practices' because conflict of laws has virtually no substantive content. Rather, it is a set of judge-made techniques that arose to respond to the challenges of increasing transnational activity.[16] In the past three decades, a substantial literature has appeared showing that

---

[14] Benson (n 11), 19.

[15] John M Veitch, 'Repudiations and Confiscations by the Medieval State' (1986) 46 Journal of Economic History 31.

[16] These techniques first developed in Italian city states (twelfth to fourteenth centuries), France (fourteenth to sixteenth centuries), and the Netherlands (seventeenth century), and, with the expansion of markets and trade, became widespread across Europe and North America in the nineteenth and twentieth centuries. See Kurt Lipstein, *Principles of the Conflict of Laws, National and International* (Martinus Nijhoff, The Hague 1981).

conflict-of-laws adjudication leads to wildly unpredictable decisions, even within the same jurisdiction. In Berger's survey,[17] scholars characterize conflict of laws variously but always contemptuously: 'an inveterate evil', 'a murky maze', 'creative chaos', 'alchemy', and a 'dismal swamp filled with quaking quagmires and inhabited by learned but eccentric professors who theorize about mysterious matters in a strange and incomprehensible jargon'. Juenger,[18] commenting on the American situation at the end of the twentieth century, states bluntly that, for proponents of the new *Lex Mercatoria*, 'it is a happy coincidence that, at this time in the United States' legal history, the conflict of laws lies in shambles'.

Concurrently, the view that national courts should generally be avoided has become orthodoxy within the transnational business and arbitral community. 'Litigation', as Newman puts it, 'means entanglement with a judicial process that is time-consuming, possibly biased in favor of locals, and perhaps even corrupt'.[19] Until recent decades, the most effective national legal systems in the world were deeply entrenched and slow to change to cosmopolitan inputs. Specialized courts were often unavailable to traders, and judges were often generalists with little experience in complex transnational disputes. Litigation meant 'waiting in line' for a court, and then suffering delays imposed by procedure, whereas the trading environment could change rapidly.

For these and other reasons, by the end of the twentieth century, national regimes had clearly lost their dominance, displaced by a new *Lex Mercatoria* with arbitration at its core.

ICA and the New Lex Mercatoria

In its heyday, the so-called Westphalian state constituted the centre of gravity for regulating trade across borders. *Governance* emanated from the hierarchical state, as authoritative state *government*. State-supplied institutions began to reach their functional limits for traders by the 1920s, at the latest, prompting the construction of a new *Lex Mercatoria*. Private actors—business leaders, lawyers, scholars—built the system. They founded new arbitral institutions, and initiated a major treaty project, which resulted in the 1958 New York Convention on the Recognition and Enforcement of Foreign Arbitral Awards.[20] Today, the New York Convention comprises the basic constitutional framework for ICA. As important, they developed a growing list of 'soft law' instruments, some of which states have adopted as 'hard law'. It is important to stress that the arbitral community does not sharply

---

[17] Klaus Peter Berger, *The Creeping Codification of the Lex Mercatoria* (Kluwer International, The Hague 1991) ['Berger'].

[18] Friedrich K Juenger, 'The Lex Mercatoria and the Conflict of Laws' in Thomas E Carbonneau (ed), *Lex Mercatoria and Arbitration: A Discussion of the New Law Merchant* (Juris, Huntington 1998).

[19] Lawrence Newman, 'A Practical Assessment of Arbitral Dispute Resolution' in Thomas E Carbonneau (ed), *Lex Mercatoria and Arbitration: A Discussion of the New Law Merchant* (Juris, Huntington 1998).

[20] United Nations Convention on the Recognition and Enforcement of Foreign Arbitral Awards (1958) 330 UNTS 38 (more commonly known as the New York Convention).

distinguish between hard and soft law. Instead, it often treats the norms, codes, and practices that traders use, and arbitrators apply, to be the 'real' law.

Efforts to codify transnational contract law have grown steadily since the 1950s. The most important of these have produced commercial codes of global and regional reach. In the 1970s, the International Institute for the Unification of Private Law [UNIDROIT] began work on what would become the UNIDROIT Principles of International Commercial Contracts, which purports to be a comprehensive, a-national code of contract for transnational commerce.[21] The UNIDROIT Principles (1994, 2004, 2010) state the fundamental notions of contract, including *pacta sunt servanda*, good faith and fair dealing, validity, interpretation, performance and non-performance, as well as *force majeure* and other defences. Significantly, the Institute decided not to submit the Principles to governments or to intergovernmental bodies, for fear that rounds of treaty negotiations would lead to changes and the reassertion of states' rather than traders' priorities. Today, the UNIDROIT Principles are constitutive elements of the *Lex Mercatoria*.

Proponents of the *Lex Mercatoria*, notably within the International Chamber of Commerce [ICC], have stressed the benefits of transnational contract law, while highlighting the failures of state law and courts.[22] Soft law like the UNIDROIT Principles can help parties reduce transaction costs and avoid bargaining stalemates. It can also facilitate the standardization of contractual instruments, and serve to ground arbitral interpretation and decision-making. In this undertaking, the ICC, and others engaged in developing a free-standing 'transnational' contract law, failed, at least at first glance. Parties based in states X and Y, after all, can just as well select the 'neutral' law of state Z to break stalemates. Although there is no systematic empirical research on the question, there is little doubt that, in the vast majority of important transnational contracts, the parties choose the national law of a small handful of states—notably of the United Kingdom, Switzerland, New York and California, France, and Singapore—as the applicable law.[23]

The ICC's bid to supplant national contract law is only a partial failure.[24] To understand why, we need to take into account the complex, symbiotic ways in which the *Lex Mercatoria* interacts with national law in the context of ICA. In a transformative process beginning in the 1960s, the states just mentioned (and many others) embraced broad conceptions of party autonomy, including the parties' freedom to choose arbitration. Today, the contract law of virtually every important trading

---

[21] International Institute for the Unification of Private Law, 'UNIDROIT Principles of International Commercial Contracts' <http://www.unidroit.org/publications/513-unidroit-principles-of-international-commercial-contracts> accessed 10 February 2016.

[22] Berger (n 17).

[23] International Chamber of Commerce, *The Secretariat's Guide to ICC Arbitration* (ICC Publishing, Paris 2012) ['The Secretariat's Guide'] 157.

[24] Even when parties include a choice of law provision designating state law as the applicable law, arbitrators and increasingly some national judges routinely treat the UNIDROIT Principles as a guide to interpretation, as well as to fill gaps in national contract law when it comes to transnational disputes. See Ralf Michaels, 'The UNIDROIT Principles as Global Background Law' (2014) 19 Uniform Law Review 643.

state either incorporates 'trade customs and usages' as implicit terms of commercial contracts, or treats them as background norms to 'fill gaps' in national contract law. Most major IACs require tribunals to apply trade usages along with any other law expressly chosen by the parties.[25] The upshot is that contractants have little need for transnational law, per se, as they can expect their choices to be honoured by both tribunals and courts, in light of transnational commercial custom. The ICC, for its part, has long laboured to codify usages. Since 1936, for example, the ICC has published the 'Incoterms', a compendium of basic commercial and trade terms of contract, which is now revised every ten years, the most recent dating from 2010. And, since the 1960s, the United Nations Commission on International Trade Law [UNCITRAL] has formally endorsed the Incoterms as the global standard for use in sale of goods contracts.[26] In the 1980s, UNCITRAL produced the United Nations Convention on Contracts for the International Sale of Goods,[27] which has been adopted by eighty-three state parties, including virtually every major trading state.[28] Once adopted, the Convention's provisions supplant national law,[29] while incorporating trade usages as directly enforceable, implied terms of contract.[30] The ICC integrates the UNCITRAL Convention into its Model International Sales of Goods Contract, which it offers online.[31]

The 'transnationalization of arbitration' story has a similar plot, with many of the same actors. In the late 1930s, UNIDROIT produced a Draft Uniform Law of Arbitration, now overtaken in importance by the UNCITRAL Model Law on International Commercial Arbitration (1985, amended in 2006). Prompted by what UNCITRAL officials decried as the 'inadequacy of domestic laws' and their 'disparity',[32] it embodies transnational business' preference for freedom to choose arbitration, enhanced arbitral autonomy, and routinized enforcement of awards. UNCITRAL openly declares its work to be in the service of transnational business. An intergovernmental organization,[33] policy is developed in highly specialized

---

[25] Chapters 3 and 4.

[26] International Chamber of Commerce, 'UN endorses Incoterms 2010, ICC Rules for international trade' (16 October 2012) <http://www.iccwbo.org/News/Articles/2012/UN-endorses-Incoterms-2010,-ICC-rules-for-international-trade/> accessed 10 February 2016.

[27] United Nations Convention on Contracts for the International Sale of Goods (1988) 1489 UNTS 3.

[28] Important exceptions include the United Kingdom and India.

[29] The Convention is, therefore, the law of Canada, the United States, and Mexico, each being parties to it.

[30] United Nations Convention on Contracts for the International Sale of Goods (1988), Article 9(2): 'The parties are considered, unless otherwise agreed, to have impliedly made applicable to their contract or its formation a usage of which the parties knew or ought to have known and which in international trade is widely known to, and regularly observed by, parties to contracts of the type involved in the particular trade concerned.'

[31] International Chamber of Commerce, 'Sale of Goods' <http://www.iccwbo.org/products-and-services/trade-facilitation/model-contracts-and-clauses/sale-of-goods/> accessed 10 February 2016.

[32] United Nations Commission on International Trade Law, 'UNCITRAL Model Law on International Commercial Arbitration (1985), with amendments as adopted in 2006' <http://www.uncitral.org/uncitral/en/uncitral_texts/arbitration/1985Model_arbitration_status.html> accessed 10 February 2016 ['UNCITRAL Model Law'], 24–5.

[33] UNCITRAL is a UN organ, composed of representatives of sixty Member States selected by the General Assembly.

committees that include representatives of the major arbitration centres.[34] The purpose of the 2006 revision of the Model Law was to strengthen its conformity with 'current practices in international trade and modern means of contracting'. To date, seventy-three states have enacted statutes based, at least in part, on the Model Law,[35] which has had the effect of harmonizing state law in support of arbitration. The organ has also produced a highly influential, and commonly used, set of procedures for the conduct of transnational arbitration: the UNCITRAL Arbitration Rules (1976, revised in 2010). Users are free to select, or adapt, these Rules as they see fit.

The codified rules of IACs, supplemented by soft law codes, comprise much of the procedural law of arbitration. As we detail in Chapter 3, one of the most important governance functions performed by the ICC is to revise its Rules, on an ongoing basis, in consultation with users. It does so against a background of a growing ratio of high stakes cases in which adversarial dispositions on the part of counsel can be presumed. All major IACs take their cues from the ICC, either by copying its innovations outright, or by branding themselves as distinct by declining to do so. Other private transnational organizations, notably the International Bar Association [IBA], have also been a source of normativity, including the generation of ethics codes for counsel and arbitrators, and guidelines on drafting arbitration clauses. The IBA Rules on the Taking of Evidence in International Arbitration (1999, 2010),[36] which draw from different national legal traditions, provide the standard for procedures governing document exchange, discovery, and the testimony of witnesses and experts. If parties incorporate such codes into their contract, or arbitral agreement, the rules become binding and will be enforced as, in effect, hard law. But the importance of these codes is even more far-reaching, indicative of the expansive nature of the *Lex Mercatoria* as a normative system that organizes day-to-day practice. 'Even if the parties do not refer to them', and 'even when the applicable rules are silent', Kaufmann-Kohler (a leading arbitrator) tells us, 'the arbitrators tend to refer consistently to the IBA Rules'.[37]

The Market for Arbitration

With the consolidation of the new *Lex Mercatoria* regime, ICA has become a highly structured, fiercely competitive market. Major law firms have invested heavily in transnational deal-making and arbitration practice; and they aggressively compete

---

[34] See Gabrielle Kaufmann-Kohler, 'Soft Law in International Arbitration: Codification and Normativity' (2010) 1 Journal of International Dispute Settlement 283 ['Kaufmann-Kohler'], 292: '... an increasing number of state delegates are recruited [from] within the arbitral community, and all major arbitral institutions and organizations not only participate as observers in the sessions of the working group on arbitration, but are also very active in the drafting [and reviewing] process'.

[35] UNCITRAL Model Law (n 32). Our count excludes federated entities such as the Canadian Provinces, counting such instances as one.

[36] International Bar Association, 'Practice Rules and Guidelines' <http://www.ibanet.org/Publications/publications_IBA_guides_and_free_materials.aspx> accessed 10 February 2016.

[37] Kaufmann-Kohler (n 34).

for corporate clients who need both. For their part, arbitral centres compete for market share, as well as for influence over the evolution of the domain. The major houses seek to structure the broader field in their own image; smaller ones work to develop regional, or niche, services that will enable them to survive and prosper. Courts are important underpinnings of this market. As crucial instruments of enforcement, they cast shadows on arbitration in myriad ways. Finally, arbitrators compete with one another both for lucrative appointments and for the top management positions in the major houses. A small cadre of elite arbitrators dominates the regime, networking it and reducing its fragmentation.

Here we provide an overview of the ICA regime, as currently constituted.

Arbitral Centres

No precise data on the number and activities of IACs exists. The most comprehensive compilation lists 207 established centres, operating in 102 countries, dispersed across all seven continents (Table 2.1). Every significant trading state in the world hosts at least one important IAC. These are all private entities, with the exception of a few inter-governmental organizations, the most important being the ICSID, the Permanent Court of Arbitration and the Iran–US Claims Tribunal.

Until the turn of the twentieth century, the Paris-based ICC (founded in 1919) was the only truly global arbitration house. Since 1922, the date of its first case, the ICC has processed more than 21,000 disputes involving parties hailing from virtually every state and independent territory in the world (about 200).[38] Figure 2.1 charts the average annual number of new arbitration cases filed at the ICC, by decade. In its first six decades (1921 to 1979), the ICC registered 3,790 new cases, a number surpassed by the 3,906 cases filed in just the last five years (2010 to 2014). In 2015, the ICC received 801 new requests for arbitration, brought by some 2,300 parties hailing from 133 countries, and its tribunals issued 498 awards, 343 of which were final. The vast majority of new cases filed involve parties based on different continents. That same year, ICC proceedings 'were seated in 97 different cities in 56 different countries', presided over by arbitrators of seventy-seven different nationalities. At the end of 2015, the aggregate value of pending claims at the ICC was more than 286 billion USD.[39]

Today, there are three global houses: the ICC, the AAA-ICDR (USA), and the LCIA (London). The SIAC (Singapore), the Stockholm Chamber of Commerce (SCC), and the Hong Kong International Arbitration Centre (HKIAC) are major centres with global aspirations. Table 2.2 presents information related to measures of the global scope of the operations of thirteen leading IACs. The AAA-ICDR receives the largest number of new filings per year (overtaking the ICC in 2001), but it is widely surpassed by the ICC and the LCIA when it comes to large sum disputes. With respect to national diversity of parties and arbitrators, the ICC is by

---

[38] International Chamber of Commerce, '2015 ICC Dispute Resolution Statistics' (2016) 26(1) ICC International Court of Arbitration Bulletin 9 ['2015 ICC Dispute Resolution Statistics'].
[39] ibid.

Table 2.1 Number of International Arbitration
Centres and Host States, Per Region, 2015

	IACs	States
Region		
Asia	34	17
Africa/Middle East	32	23
Latin America/Caribbean	47	17
North America	10	2
Eastern Europe	27	22
Western Europe	57	21

Source: 'Guide to Regional Arbitration 2015', *Global
Arbitration Review*, <http://globalarbitrationreview.com/
editorial/1037000/gar's-guide-to-regional-arbitration-2015>.

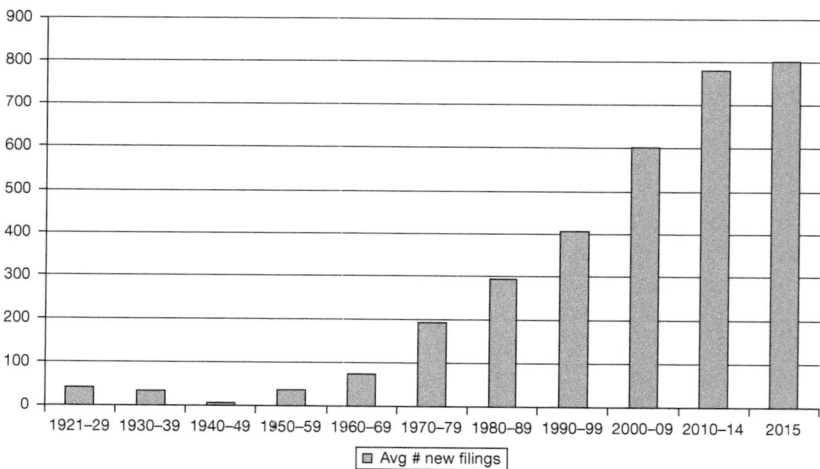

Figure 2.1 Average Annual Number of New Cases Filed at the ICC, 1921–2015
Source: The annual statistical reports of the International Chamber of Commerce (Paris).

far the most global centre: since 1996, a majority of the new cases filed annually are
brought by non-European parties hailing from two or more different continents.
Not shown in Table 2.2, American firms dominate the AAA-ICDR's caseload. In
2010, fully 90 per cent of cases registered included an American party,[40] which

---

[40] Sebastian Perry, 'Inside the ICDR: An Interview with Luis Martinez' (*Global Arbitration Review*,
19 October 2011) <http://www.globalarbitrationreview.com/news/article/29888/> accessed 24 June
2016 ['Perry'].

Table 2.2 New Filings for International Arbitration Registered Per Year: 2000–2014

	2000	2001	2002	2003	2004	2005	2006	2007	2008	2009	2010	2011	2012	2013	2014	Avg/Year
AAA-ICDR (USA)	510	649	672	614	646	580	586	622	703	800	888	994	996	1,165		745
ICC (Paris)	541	566	593	580	561	521	593	599	663	817	793	796	759	767	791	663
HKIAC (Hong Kong)	293	300	307	273	260	266	376	428	574	309	175	179	199	195		295
Domestic cases	5	7	13	14	20	15	18	20	28	120	116	96	94	65		45
SIAC (Singapore)														223	180	202
Domestic/international	58	64	64	64	78	74	90	86	99	160	198	188	235	259	222	241
LCIA (London)																
Domestic/international	147	158	159	192	191	205	251	270	243	272	246	224	265	290		222
SCC (Stockholm)	87	73	44	82	50	56	74	87	85	96	91	96	92	86	94	82
Domestic cases				67	83	91	120	106	103	85	117	89	89	87	73	44
KCAB (Seoul)	40	65	47	38	46	53	47	59	47	78	52	77	85	77	87	60
Domestic cases							168	261	215		264	246	275	261	295	248
CIETAC (Beijing)																
Domestic/international	633	731	684	709	850	979	981	1,118	1,230	1,482	1,352	1,435	1,060	1,256		1,036
BAC (Beijing)	8	10	18	33	31	53	53	37	56	72	32	38	26			36
Domestic cases	441	656	873	996	1,765	1,926	2,411	1,826	2,001	1,758	1,534	1,433	1,447			1,467
DIS (Cologne)						16	30	22	41	45	43	55	30			35
Domestic cases						56	45	78	81	127	112	119	91			89
SCCAM (Switzerland)																
Domestic/international								59	68	104	89	87	92	63	105	83
VIAC (Vienna)																
Domestic/international										60	68	75	70	56	56	64
DIAC (Dubai)																
Domestic/international								77	100	292	431	440	379	310		290

Note: Where entries are blank, either the IAC did not yet exist, or the data were not reported.

Source: The annual statistical reports of the International Arbitral Centres listed.

suggests that the AAA-ICDR is mostly 'global' because American firms operating globally prefer using its services. In contrast, French firms furnish the Paris-based ICC with barely 5 per cent of its arbitral filings,[41] and UK parties comprised only 18.6 per cent of the LCIA's users.[42] Of the more regionally based houses, the SIAC has exploded into prominence; Hong Kong has seen its business decline during this period; and Stockholm has consolidated a niche Nordic orientation to the Baltic republics, Russia, and other states of the ex-Soviet Union.

Marketing

The international arbitral order has been heavily structured by the activities of the ICC, which impact on every other important centre.[43] Today, the basic dimensions on which IACs compete have been fixed. Within these parameters, arbitration houses strive to build their brands, and to enhance their reputations and influence.

Every important centre, global or regional, trumpets its compliance with existing, best-practice standards. Every IAC claims:

(a) to respect the freedom of the contracting parties to determine how cases will proceed, while offering adaptable rules and in-house appointment of arbitrators when desired;

(b) to provide neutral, expert, flexible, efficient, and predictable administration of cases, including complex disputes involving three or more parties;

(c) to maintain a roster of highly competent, impartial arbitrators;

(d) to guarantee the confidentiality of awards, subject to waiver by the parties;

(e) to furnish modern facilities, equipped with state-of-the-art hearing rooms and technology, near comfortable hotels and world-class restaurants;

(f) to offer less-costly substitutes to arbitration, in the form of mediation and simplified, 'fast-track' procedures;[44] and

(g) to produce final, binding awards that will be enforceable in state courts, with little or no judicial review on the merits.

At the same time, each major IAC stresses its comparative advantage, seeking to differentiate itself by location, scope of operations, administrative capacities, procedural rules, and costs.

---

[41] The percentage of filings including a French firm was 4.8 per cent in 2013 and 5.13 per cent in 2014. See International Chamber of Commerce, '2013 Statistical Reports' (2014) 25(1) ICC International Court of Arbitration Bulletin 5; International Chamber of Commerce, '2014 Statistical Reports' (2015) 1 ICC International Court of Arbitration Bulletin.

[42] London Court of International Arbitration, 'Reports: Registrar's Report 2013' <http://www.lcia.org/LCIA/reports.aspx> accessed 10 February 2016.

[43] This outcome fits comfortably the core theoretical precepts of contemporary economic sociology. See Neil Fligstein and Doug McAdam, *A Theory of Fields* (Oxford University Press, Oxford 2012).

[44] An AAA-ICDR official reports that 'on average, between 8 and 12 per cent of parties will attempt mediation. The success rate for those that attempt it is approximately 90 per cent'. See Perry (n 40).

IACs based in important regional hubs, such as the Arab Gulf, Hong Kong, and Singapore, emphasize their close familiarity with the region's norms and customs. The Dubai International Arbitration Centre [DIAC] declares that it provides 'luxurious facilities' and a full range of services, designed to meet 'the needs of the global economy', while being situated in 'an Arabian oasis infused with modernity … connecting the East and West'.[45] The DIAC, and its regional rivals, also claim unique expertise in dealing with the complexities of enforcing awards in Gulf states, including the constraints of Sharia law (e.g. the effect of prohibitions on usury when it comes to awarding interest).[46] The HKIAC boasts that it possesses 'an excellent knowledge of China, including its commercial, regulatory and legal environments', while being supported by a 'common law court system overseen by an independent judiciary comprising local and international judges who are independent, professional and efficient'.[47] Singapore, exploiting the fact that the courts of neighbouring countries have dismal reputations, has rapidly secured its status as the major regional hub. The SIAC Secretariat, its publicity materials state, comprises 'experienced lawyers qualified in China, India, Indonesia, Malaysia, Singapore, the UK, and the USA', countries whose firms produce the vast bulk of the centre's caseload.[48]

The global IACs are the institutional entrepreneurs of the field, competing to shape it in line with their own models of governance.[49] The ICC possesses the resources and will to engage in continuous, highly structured consultations with users on procedures, administration, and policy and governance more broadly. Each new revision of the ICC Rules puts pressure on every other major house to follow suit, or to justify decisions not to do so. The centre of gravity for institutional innovation in the field is the ICC's Commission on Arbitration and Alternative Dispute Resolution, which functions as the house's legislative body (revising the Rules, promulgating codes, codifying best practices for transnational business, contracting, and arbitration), and a 'unique think tank' (generating white papers and policy recommendations).[50] The AAA-ICDR emulates the ICC. It has originated some innovations that have broadly diffused,[51] and produces white papers that also

---

[45] Dubai International Arbitration Centre, 'Why Arbitrate in Dubai?' <http://www.diac.ae/idias/services/dubai/> accessed 8 June 2016.

[46] Nayla Comair-Obeid, 'Salient Issues in Arbitration from an Arab Middle Eastern Perspective' (2014) 4(1) Arbitration Brief 52.

[47] Hong Kong International Arbitration Centre, 'Why Arbitrate in Hong Kong?' <http://www.hkiac.net/en/arbitration/why-hong-kong> accessed 10 February 2016.

[48] Singapore International Arbitration Centre, 'Why SIAC' <http://www.siac.org.sg/2014-11-03-13-33-43/why-siac> accessed 10 February 2016.

[49] The ICC notes that: 'Certain leading institutions have also assumed a role as industry regulators, setting standards and practices and offering training and conferences. Arbitral institutions, in particular ICC, have contributed significantly to the growth and success of international arbitration.' See International Chamber of Commerce, 'Arbitration' <http://www.iccwbo.org/products-and-services/arbitration-and-adr/arbitration/> accessed 10 February 2016.

[50] See International Chamber of Commerce, 'Commission on Arbitration and ADR' <http://www.iccwbo.org/about-icc/policy-commissions/arbitration/> accessed 10 February 2016; Chapter 3.

[51] In 2006, the AAA-ICDR introduced 'an emergency arbitrator procedure … whereby parties can obtain interim relief at the moment of filing', and the ICC adopted this innovation in its 2012 Rules. See Chapter 3.

purport to express best practices and other industry standards.[52] Most of the larger houses publish independent research in scholarly journals devoted to ICA.[53]

The globals have also invested heavily in widening the territorial scope of the arbitral order. Each has established regional 'satellites': the ICC in Hong Kong and New York; the AAA-ICDR in Bahrain, Seoul, Canada, and Mexico City; the LCIA in Dubai, India, and Mauritius. And each regularly organizes 'roadshow' events on every continent, in the form of conferences promoting arbitration, and training sessions for uninitiated lawyers and judges. As China, Brazil and other Latin American nations, Turkey, the United Arab Emirates, Ghana and Nigeria, Indonesia and India, and Russia have grown in importance as trading nations—while being reticent to embrace arbitration as an effective substitute for courts—so have the efforts of the global centres to convert them to the arbitral cause. The SIAC has recently opened a satellite in Mumbai, in order to stimulate demand for the SIAC's services, as well as to influence the direction of Indian legislation and the case law of the courts.[54] It has good reasons for doing so, given that Indian parties, on a par with those from China and the United States, are the most active users of the SIAC.

The global centres are capable of effectively administering an arbitration seated in any city likely to be chosen by the parties.[55] Each is able to provide an extensive menu of services to users. The ICC's offerings are particularly rich. Through its 'International Court of Arbitration' and Secretariat, ICC officials: certify arbitral agreements; supervise the preparation of procedural orders; 'confirm, appoint, and replace' arbitrators; fix costs (and readjust them when appropriate); support the tribunals' administrative work on a daily basis; monitor the compliance of tribunals with the ICC Rules; and review awards before they become final.[56] As early as 1976, the ICC established what is now called the International Centre for Expertise,[57] which helps parties find experts in such areas as accounting, construction, informational technology, and other relevant domains of science and

---

[52] International Centre for Dispute Resolution, 'Homepage' <https://www.icdr.org> accessed 10 February 2016.

[53] These journals include *Arbitration International* (LCIA), the *ICC International Court of Arbitration Bulletin* (ICC), and the *Stockholm International Arbitration Review* (SCC).

[54] Singapore International Arbitration Centre, 'SIAC Mumbai Office' <http://siac.org.sg/2014-11-03-13-33-43/about-us/siac-mumbai-office> accessed 10 February 2016: 'The primary objectives of the Indian liaison office are to … promote the use of institutional arbitration and SIAC as a leading international arbitration institution; to market the capabilities of SIAC in administering international commercial arbitrations to Indian parties … to create a line of communication for SIAC and the community in Singapore with key players for international arbitration in India; to provide practical information necessary to lawyers and corporate users for the effective use of SIAC arbitration as a dispute resolution option; [and] to work closely with the judiciary and the government in India on policy initiatives, regular exchange of ideas on live issues, and legislative change, amongst others.'

[55] For a detailed comparison of the administrative capacities of leading IACs, see Rémy Gerbay, 'The Functions of Arbitral Institutions: Theoretical Representations and Practical Realities' (PhD thesis, Queen Mary, University of London 2014) ['Gerbay'].

[56] Chapter 3.

[57] International Chamber of Commerce, 'Experts' <http://www.iccwbo.org/products-and-services/arbitration-and-adr/experts/> accessed 10 February 2016.

Table 2.3 Average Cost of Three-Member Tribunal Plus Administrative Fees

Amount in dispute	500K	5M	50M	500M	1B
Arbitral centre	ICC	ICC	SWISS	CIETAC	CIETAC
Costs	95K	307K	703K	2.37M	2.40M
	SWISS	SWISS	ICC	SWISS	SWISS
	93K	290K	613K	1.34M	1.78M
	SIAC	SIAC	SIAC	ICC	ICC
	78K	246K	541K	1.17M	1.55M
	HKIAC	DIAC	DIAC	SIAC	SIAC
	64K	211K	478K	1.04M	1.48M
	DIAC	SCC	HKIAC	HKIAC	HKIAC
	62K	175K	451K	901K	1.43M
	SCC	HKIAC	SCC	DIAC	DIAC
	57K	166K	339K	817K	1.19M
	CIETAC	CIETAC	CIETAC	SCC*	SCC*
	18K	72K	305K		

Note. * For disputes in which €100 million or more are at stake, the SCC Board determines fees through criteria that are 'undisclosed'. 'Arbitration Costs Compared', source citation below.

Source. Louis Flannery and Benjamin Garel, 'Arbitration Costs Compared: The Sequel', *Global Arbitration Reporter*, 15 January 2013.

knowledge, and to assign them to cases upon request.[58] The ICC maintains the most extensive bureaucracy of any IAC, and it is considered to be a relatively expensive venue though, in fact, its price competiveness rises dramatically with the sums at stake. As Table 2.3 on comparative costs shows, the ICC charges a 6.1 per cent fee for amounts in the $5 million range, but less than 0.23 per cent once sums reach $500 million.

Arbitrators

In ICA, the parties appoint their own arbitrators; only when they fail to agree do officials of the arbitral centre take charge. For three-member tribunals, by far the most common configuration for high stakes cases, each side typically nominates a co-arbitrator, and the co-arbitrators then name a president (discussed in detail in Chapter 3). The system gives strong advantages to repeat arbitrators. To be successful, competitors must build a reputation: for neutrality, fairness, and competence; for familiarity with the niceties of transnational business; and for capacity to

[58] Appointment of experts through the Centre has risen sharply. For a discussion and statistics, see James Nicholson and Matthias Cazier-Darmois, 'A Review of ICC Expert Services to Mark the Launch of New Rules in 2015' (2014) 25(2) ICC International Court of Arbitration Bulletin 5.

manage complex disputes that may involve diverse, at times contradictory, sources of law.

A relatively small number of individuals, each of whom occupies multiple positions of importance in the field, dominate arbitration. Consider the common attributes of a 'who's who' list of the twenty-five most highly regarded arbitrators in international commercial arbitration.[59] Every individual is a lawyer, and all have been partners in important law firms. Twelve of the twenty-five hold, or have held, a university professorship; all have published in scholarly journals, and eight have written prominent treatises and textbooks. This group has also dominated top management positions in the major IACs. Twenty-three of this 'elite twenty-five' have exercised executive functions in important IACs, including the ICC, LCIA, DIAC, SCC, SIAC, HKIAC, and the AAA-ICDR; seventeen have held management positions in two or more of these centres; and seven have held more than three such positions (the highest count is five). Among this group, we find: one Chairman of the LCIA's Board of Directors; two Presidents of the ICC Court; two Secretary-Generals of the ICC Court; two Presidents of the SIAC Court; and four Presidents of the LCIA Court. Thus, although the arbitral regime is organizationally fragmented, it is managed by a tightly networked elite.

II. Architectures of Authority

We now turn to the normative structure of arbitral authority—its institutional foundations—as these have evolved over time, at three levels of analysis. Our focus is on the system's *effectiveness*, defined simply as the capacity of the arbitral order to attract cases and to produce final awards that are binding on the parties. Effectiveness is a variable: it varies across time, tribunals, and IACs. Over the course of the past century, maximizing effectiveness has been the primary preoccupation of proponents of the new *Lex Mercatoria*, in particular, the ICC. The more the community demonstrates that is it able to resolve the dilemmas of exchange discussed above, the more likely traders will be to choose arbitration over national courts, and the more probable the arbitral order will develop as a legal system in its own right.

In Chapter 1, we generated three models of arbitral governance, blending the logics of (a) *agency control* (from the perspective of those who delegate authority in the first place—the 'Principals') and (b) *fiduciary duties* (from the perspective of their 'Agent'—the arbitrator). We will not repeat the discussion, other than to make the following summary points with regard to the field's evolution. First, within each model—which we treat as levels of analysis in this chapter—the course of judicialization tracks the growing effectiveness of the system. Second, as one moves from

---

[59] Who's Who Legal, 'Most Highly Regarded Firms: Arbitration 2014' (October 2013) <http://whoswholegal.com/news/analysis/article/30934/most-highly-regarded-firms-arbitration-2014> accessed 10 February 2016. On the basis of this list, we research backgrounds of each of these individuals.

one level of analysis to the next, arbitrators accrete duties, along with the authority that is necessary to perform them. Third, understanding the development of the arbitral order, as a meaningfully autonomous system, entails paying attention to how arbitral authority has evolved at each level of analysis: the contractual, the judicial, and the pluralist-constitutional. We focus here on the most important institutional components of arbitral authority. Although the discussion necessarily touches upon technical issues of law and doctrine, we give a relatively simplified treatment here.

Level 1: Parties and Arbitrators

Arbitral power is delegated power. Two disputing parties confer authority on a tribunal by virtue of an agreement to arbitrate, thereby creating a node of governance. A first-order determinant of effectiveness relates to the tribunal's authority to enforce that agreement, given strong incentives for one of the parties to renege on it. This is a basic problem of incomplete commitment within the 'contractual model', which is exacerbated by adversarialism. In the archetypal situation, a party asserts that the arbitration clause is without force because the contract containing it is invalid, or seeks access to a court despite the existence of an arbitration clause. In response, tribunals developed two doctrines of arbitral common law. The first— 'separability'—guarantees the autonomy of the arbitration agreement with respect to any other contractual instruments in play. The second—'*Kompetenz-Kompetenz*' [K-K]—makes the tribunal the sole judge of its own competence with regard to any aspect of a dispute covered by the agreement. Although these principles are today bulwark features of the *Lex Mercatoria*, both emerged only after the Second World War.

Separability

Under the doctrine of separability, the arbitration clause remains valid notwithstanding the termination or nullity of the contractual agreement in which it is contained. Questions concerning the tribunal's jurisdiction can thus be isolated from every other matter pertaining to the dispute. If the tribunal determines that the agreement to arbitrate is valid, then the arbitration will proceed despite the unwillingness of one of the parties, even one who refuses to participate at all. In its Rules of Arbitration of 1955, the ICC codified separability, while implying the principle of K-K:

Unless otherwise stipulated, the arbitrator shall not cease to have jurisdiction by reason of an allegation that the contract is null and void or non-existent. If [s/he] upholds the validity of the arbitration clause, [s/he] shall continue to have jurisdiction to determine the respective rights of the parties and to make declarations relative to their claims and pleas even though the contract should be null and void or non-existent.[60]

---

[60] ICC Rules of Conciliation and Arbitration (1955), Article 13(4).

Although enforcement problems may follow, separability enables the tribunal to produce a final award.

While these doctrines can be analysed narrowly, strictly from the perspective of the contractual model, it is also clear that their institutionalization depends heavily on their acceptance by national courts. To the extent that national judges recognize the separability of arbitral agreements and the K-K of tribunals, parties will be locked into arbitration. They are therefore potent mechanisms of effectiveness. Prior to the 1950s, in the vast majority of national legal systems that refused to recognize the arbitral order, awards were treated as an irrelevance in a law court. In 1929, Jean Robert published what we believe to be the first contemporary study of these issues. Tellingly, Robert, who would later become a prominent member of the ICC Court of Arbitration and one of the framers of the 1958 New York Convention, did not consider 'separability'. Instead, he analysed the legal remedies that were available if a party refused to respect an arbitration agreement, concluding that compelling the performance of the arbitration agreement was impossible. The 'situation', he declared, was 'quite harmful to arbitration as an institution', and 'full of dangers' for its future development.[61]

Kompetenz-Kompetenz

The so-called 'positive effect' of the doctrine of K-K holds that tribunals possess—with respect to any dispute falling within the scope of a valid agreement to arbitrate—complete authority to determine the nature and scope of their own competences. The 'negative effect' of the principle precludes a national judge from asserting jurisdiction over that same dispute. While tribunals initially developed K-K as a corollary of separability, they gradually asserted it as a fundamental tenet of the tribunal's authority per se. Today, separability and K-K comprise overlapping meta-principles of the *Lex Mercatoria*, finding their expression in the rules of virtually every major arbitration house.[62]

Where recognized, these doctrines establish a tribunal's power over the parties, while insulating the arbitral process from external interference. The 1958 New York Convention does not mention either doctrine. Nonetheless, beginning in the 1960s, the courts of the two most important states[63]—France and the United States—embraced both. In 1963, the French Supreme Court (the *Cour de Cassation*) recognized both principles, holding in particular that an arbitration agreement possessed 'complete legal autonomy' with respect to the contract

---

[61] Jean Robert, *La clause compromissoire et l'organisation de l'arbitrage* (Recueil Sirey, Paris 1929) 26.

[62] ICC Rules of Arbitration (2012), Article 6(5): 'In all matters decided by the Court under Article 6(4), any decision as to the jurisdiction of the arbitral tribunal, except as to parties or claims with respect to which the Court decides that the arbitration cannot proceed, shall then be taken by the arbitral tribunal itself.' This rule, according to the Secretariat of the ICC, derives from 'the well-known "competence-competence" principle, according to which an arbitral tribunal is empowered to rule on its own jurisdiction'—see The Secretariat's Guide (n 23), para 3–259.

[63] France is of enormous strategic importance because the ICC is located in Paris, and Paris is a common seat of arbitration. The United States is also an important seat of arbitration, and New York law is a popular choice when it comes to choosing the law in transnational contracts.

containing it, despite pleadings to the effect that the contract was invalid.[64] The US Supreme Court recognized both in 1967,[65] and then reinforced policy supporting international arbitral autonomy in a famous decision of 1985.[66] In the United Kingdom, the 1996 Arbitration Act[67] reflected the principles into English law, helping to spur the LCIA's bid to become a global ICA. The legislatures and courts of a long list of states have overtly copied these innovations, including most European states, Singapore, and Arab Gulf states. Meanwhile, the UNCITRAL Model Law on Arbitration (1985, 2006), which itself influenced the 1996 UK Act, also enshrines separability and K-K.[68] As states have adopted statutes based on the Model Law, the principles have widely diffused. Today, the national courts of the most important trading states enforce these principles, as hard law, upon verification of a valid arbitral agreement.

Logics of Hierarchy

The consolidation of the doctrines of separability and K-K transformed the contractual model of governance. Today, both are quasi-constitutional, *systemic* properties of the *Lex Mercatoria*, in that their existence: (a) is foundational of arbitral authority; (b) does not depend on the details of any particular contract or dispute, beyond an agreement to arbitrate; and (c) is recognized by the model law and statutes. Viewed functionally, the doctrines institutionalize solutions to the problems of incomplete contracting and commitment, while bolstering the effectiveness of arbitration in unstable, adversarial contexts. Viewed as judicialization, they constitute, within the arbitral order, features more akin to a system of compulsory TDR than to, say, mediation. Put in terms of delegation theory, once an agreement to arbitrate is activated, the contracting parties are denied any meaningful control of their Agent. Indeed, the arbitrator possesses and has a duty to exercise authority over the parties, subject to fiduciary duties owed to them (see Chapter 3). Through an expansive process of epistemically grounded juris-generativity and mimesis, the doctrines are today strongly supported by public law and courts.

Level 2: Arbitral Houses and Tribunals

The contractual model of arbitration conceives of any contract as a unique legal 'system', constituted by the two parties who delegate to an arbitrator the power to

---

[64] Cass Civ 1ère, 7 May 1963, *Gosset*, Bull No 246: '… en matière d'arbitrage international l'accord compromissoire, qu'il soit conclu séparément ou inclus dans l'acte juridique auquel il a trait, présente toujours, sauf circonstances exceptionnelles, une complète autonomie juridique, excluant qu'il puisse être affecté par une éventuelle invalidité de cet acte'.

[65] *Prima Paint Corp v Flood & Conklin* (1967) 388 US 395, 402, in which the US Supreme Court interprets the Federal Arbitration Act (1925) as containing the principles of separability and K-K, although the Act mentions neither.

[66] *Mitsubishi Motors Corp v Soler Chrysler Plymouth, Inc* (1985) 473 US 614.

[67] English Arbitration Act of 1996, Article 30(1) [*K-K*] and Article 7 (*separability*).

[68] UNCITRAL Model Law on International Commercial Arbitration (2006), Article 16(1).

resolve a dispute within the terms of that contract. With the judicialization of the contractual model, the systemic properties of the arbitral order (including separability and K-K) impinge directly on the authority relationship between the tribunal and the parties. Indeed, truly ad hoc arbitration is now virtually extinct, the vast bulk of arbitration taking place according to pre-existing procedural templates (Chapter 3). Required then is a second level of analysis—which the judicial model privileges—directing attention to the relationship between the IAC and its tribunals. The ICC, in particular, has steadily developed forms of hierarchy as a means of enhancing the autonomy and effectiveness of the arbitral order as a legal system in its own right.

The Judicialization of ICA and the Lex Mercatoria

When the ICC officials embarked on their project to relaunch the *Lex Mercatoria* in the early 1920s, they consciously sought to update the MLM. Arbitration, it was assumed, would enhance a 'reputation system' of contract enforcement. Officials disparaged adversarialism, and encouraged settlement and equity-based decisions by businessmen, not lawyers. Enhancing effectiveness—the capacity of the arbitrators to produce final, binding awards—was also a central goal. The ICC sought to do so by clearly distinguishing the respective functions of the arbitrator and the judge.

The 1922 Rules relied on reputational effects to enforce awards, through what the ICC labelled 'moral penalties'. A party that failed to comply with an award could be subject to two forms of 'punishment'. The first involved notification of the party's national chamber of commerce, along with a request for the latter to enact 'such disciplinary measures as it may think fit and proper under the circumstances, in respect of the defaulting member'.[69] Second, the Rules conferred on the ICC Court of Arbitration the authority to supervise compliance, and 'to publish the names of a defaulting party, together with the text of the award'.[70] Officials believed that the risk of 'dismissal from [the] group, loss of credit and of ... commercial reputation' would be enough to guarantee compliance in most cases.[71]

The ICC's attachment to (a) non-adversarialism, (b) equity-based TDR, and (c) a reputational system of enforcement, combined to foster an antagonism to reason-giving in the legal sense. Officials encouraged parties to use tribunals as *amiables compositeurs* (more of an umpire deciding the case in equity, rather than a judge deciding in law). At its London Congress of 1921, the ICC adopted a resolution according to which 'the diffusion of commercial arbitration is strictly connected to the possibility that arbitrators may be guided in their decision *by principles of*

---

[69] ICC Rules of Conciliation (Good Offices) and Arbitration (1922), Articles XX/XLI(b).
[70] ICC Rules of Conciliation (Good Offices) and Arbitration (1922), Articles XX/XLI(c).
[71] International Chamber of Commerce, *The Arbitration of the International Chamber of Commerce* (ICC Publishing, Paris 1924) 7: '[M]oral penalties are nearly always a sufficient guarantee for the execution of the award without having to refer to Civil Courts'.

equity rather than strict law.[72] In 1922, the Rules even distinguished between 'non-legal' and 'legal' arbitration, favouring the former, so as to place arbitrators under a duty to secure equity, not fidelity to law.[73] In an echo of the old MLM, Mr René Arnaud, the ICC's general counsel, portrayed the 'good arbitrator' as one who settles disputes 'as [would] a good businessman', in light of how transnational business is actually conducted, 'without being bound [by] written statutes or precedent'. The parties had a right, Arnaud declared, to expect 'technical competence, common sense and impartiality', rather than mastery of 'legal science'.[74]

Although this view of the arbitral function has left important traces,[75] the ICC abandoned these positions in the 1950s to meet the challenges of increased adversarialism. Success, it now believed, would depend upon strengthening the *systemic* authority of the *Lex Mercatoria*. As we will show, arbitral houses obligated tribunals to give legal reasons for their decisions, and developed their capacities to supervise the parties and tribunals. As important, ICC officials were instrumental in proposing, drafting, and overseeing the signing and ratification of the 1958 New York Convention, which created a quasi-constitutional framework for the recognition of arbitral authority by national courts. Judicialization then proceeded in earnest, so much so that, today, arbitration functions as a parallel form of adjudication in all but name.

Reason-Giving and Supervision

The dynamics of *reason-giving* constitute a basic mechanism of judicialization, insofar as they are capable of generating an expansive system of argumentation and justification (Chapter 1). We explore the effects of institutionalizing a reason-giving requirement in Chapters 4 and 5, including the extent to which a growing demand for law-making, precedent, and appeal has been met. Here we focus on the move to supervise the substantive merits of arbitral awards.

As noted, the ICC initially conceived of arbitration as a form of mediation, rather than a substitute for adjudication, to be conducted by businessmen, not lawyers. A 'non-judicial' approach made sense, given the centre's animosity toward adversarialism. From 1927 until 1955, the ICC Rules contained no general obligation to state reasons for awards. The supervision of awards by the so-called Court of

---

[72] Resolution No XIV adopted at the London Congress of 1921 (emphasis added).

[73] ICC Rules of Conciliation (Good Offices) and Arbitration (1922), Article VII.

[74] René Arnaud, 'Conseils pratiques pour l'arbitrage commercial international' (1930) 8 L'Economie Internationale 408, 413: 'Il est de votre intérêt que l'arbitre juge en équité, en bon homme d'affaires, sans être lié par des textes de loi écrite ou des précédents de jurisprudence. Vous attendez de lui moins la science juridique que la compétence technique, le bon sens et l'impartialité.'

[75] It was not until 1975, for example, that ICC Rules began to refer explicitly to the 'law' applicable to the merits of a dispute—see Chapter 3. Remnants of the system of the reputational system have also survived, notably, in the domain of commodities. Tribunals operating under the auspices of the Coffee Trade Federation and the Grain and Feed Trade Association, for example, publicize the name of a party that fails to comply with any award rendered under their respective rules. See Coffee Trade Federation Arbitration Rules (2008), Article 77; Grain and Feed Trade Association Arbitration Rules (2006), Article 22(1).

Arbitration was obligatory, but the Court concentrated on form, not substance.[76] The preference for equity decision-making, ICC officials believed, would help to insulate awards from judicial review on the merits. If tribunals did not give reasons in law to justify their decisions, then national judges would have nothing of substance to review. (The AAA would cling to this position until the 1990s.[77]) At the same time, the ICC recognized that, in some countries, including the Netherlands but not England, the failure to state reasons could lead to annulment at national bar. The ICC therefore gave its Court the competence to decide whether reasons should be provided, on a case-by-case basis. In its *Arbitration Report* of 1926, the ICC summarized its decision on the question:

It seemed impossible to place upon the arbitrator, who is often a businessman unfamiliar with foreign law, the onus of deciding whether he shall or shall not state the grounds of his award. But as the award must always be submitted to the Court of Arbitration, it was decided that the Court … itself should decide in each case whether the grounds … should be stated or not. Taking the case of a dispute between an Englishman and a Dutchman, if the arbitrator finds against the Englishman, the grounds of the award will not be stated; if he finds against the Dutchman, the grounds will have to be stated.[78]

In the 1930s, following the resolution of a wave of high profile cases involving currency fluctuations and other shocks related to the Great Depression, the ICC faced increasing demands for reason-giving, precedent, and appellate supervision of awards. Losing parties began formally to request that the Court of Arbitration sit as a 'Court of Cassation';[79] and proposals to create an internal appellate body, charged with merit review, were debated.[80] Moving cautiously, the ICC revised its Rules in 1934, referencing substantive review:

Before completing the award, the arbitrators … shall submit the same to the Court of Arbitration, which may lay down modifications as to its form. The Court of Arbitration is not precluded from calling the attention of the arbitrators … to points connected with the merits of the case, but with due regard to their liberty of decision.[81]

---

[76] The Court verified the validity of the arbitral agreement, the choice of arbitrators, and that the proper dates and signatures had been properly recorded.

[77] As late as 1993, Robert Coulson, a former president of the AAA, stated that: 'Arbitrators are not required to write opinions explaining the reasons for their decisions. As a general rule, AAA commercial awards consist of a brief decision on a single sheet of paper. Written opinions can be dangerous because they identify targets for the losing party to attack [before the courts]' (see Robert Coulson, *Business Arbitration: What You Need to Know* (5th edn, American Arbitration Association 1993) 30). The AAA's International Arbitration Rules of 1991 provided that: 'The tribunal shall state the reasons upon which the award is based, unless the parties have agreed that no reasons need be given.' The latest version of the AAA International Dispute Resolution Procedures (2014) contains a similar provision at its Article 30(1): 'The tribunal shall state the reasons upon which an award is based, unless the parties have agreed that no reasons need be given.'

[78] International Chamber of Commerce, *ICC Arbitration Report No 6* (ICC Publishing, Paris 1926) 5.

[79] Ordre du jour de la soixante-et-unième session du Comité Exécutif de la Cour d'Arbitrage du 26 mars 1930.

[80] Procès-verbal de la soixante-huitième session du Comité Exécutif de la Cour d'Arbitrage du 25 février 1931, 5–6.

[81] ICC Rules of Conciliation and Arbitration (1934), Article 22.

Although this part of the Rules changed little over the next four decades, the Court steadily consolidated its review authority. In 1975 and again in 1988, the ICC authorized the Court of Arbitration to review the 'reasons for awards' with respect to the 'mandatory rules' of the seat of the arbitration.[82] The location of the seat (a city) determines the site of annulment in a national court (see Chapter 3).

While guaranteeing the effectiveness of awards remains a central purpose of supervision, the procedure is now highly judicialized.[83] A tribunal may not communicate an award to the parties without prior approval of the Court of Arbitration. The Court is the high administrative authority of the ICC, overseeing all proceedings, and supervising respect for the Rules (Chapter 3). If the Court withholds approval, then it will provide comments on revision. In 2015, the Court certified only 4 of 498 awards (less than 1 per cent) at the draft stage, without asking for modification. Sixty-two drafts were rejected outright, requiring resubmission.[84]

The ICC today champions robust 'award scrutiny' as one of the 'ten good reasons to choose ICC arbitration'.[85] In 2014, it described the goal of supervision of awards in the following terms:

The mandatory award scrutiny process … is renowned for improving both the convincingness and enforceability of awards. It involves a thorough review of all awards by at least four or five expert arbitration lawyers, including Secretariat staff and Court members. Potential problems are regularly discovered. Improving an award's convincingness increases its chances of being complied with voluntarily. Most ICC awards are, in fact, respected without the need for legal enforcement procedures. Where enforcement becomes necessary, ICC's stamp of approval together with the Court's careful monitoring of the proceedings and scrutiny of awards is intended to maximize the award's chances of being enforceable.[86]

These two goals—compliance by the parties, and recognition and enforcement of awards by courts—are, of course, measures of effectiveness.

Today, the default rules of all major arbitration houses require tribunals to justify awards with reasons. While SIAC is the only IAC to adopt the ICC's compulsory approach (in its Rules of 2013), the other leading centres engage in some degree of pre-certification scrutiny of awards, although such practices are not mentioned in the rules.[87]

---

[82] ICC Rules of Conciliation and Arbitration (1988), Appendix II, Article 17: 'When it scrutinizes draft arbitral awards in accordance with Article 21 of the ICC Rules of Arbitration, the International Court of Arbitration pays particular attention to the respect of the formal requirements laid down by the law applicable to the proceedings and, where relevant, by the mandatory rules of the [seat] of arbitration, *notably with regard to the reasons for awards*, their signature and the admissibility of dissenting opinions' (emphasis added).

[83] See Chapter 3.   [84] 2015 ICC Dispute Resolution Statistics (n 38).

[85] International Chamber of Commerce, 'Ten Good Reasons to Choose ICC Arbitration' <http://www.iccwbo.org/Products-and-Services/Arbitration-and-ADR/Arbitration/Introduction-to-ICC-Arbitration/Ten-good-reasons-to-choose-ICC-arbitration/> accessed 26 August 2014 ['Ten Good Reasons to Choose ICC Arbitration'].

[86] ibid.

[87] For a detailed comparison of other major IACs, see Gerbay (n 55), 101–9.

Logics of Hierarchy

An arbitral system based on (a) equity decision-making by businessmen and (b) a reputation system of enforcement requires very little investment in hierarchy. The IAC helps users find and coordinate with one another, provides logistical assistance, and curates reputations. In its early days, the ICC embraced such a system which, coupled with an animosity to adversarial legalism, led it to underestimate the need for more rigorous institutions of enforcement. Although the demand for internal merit review of awards was registered almost immediately, supervision developed only gradually. The ICC now champions it as an indispensable element of its business model.[88] The construction of hierarchy within the house made what it calls a credible 'stamp of approval' possible. More generally, all major IACs seek to guarantee the quality of their awards in the name of effectiveness, both to satisfy the demands of its users, and to make it as routine as possible for national judges to enforce them.

Level 3: The Arbitral Order and National Systems

The autonomy of the arbitral order depends critically on a combination of acquiescence and active support on the part of national officials, in particular, judges. This apparent paradox largely disappears when one considers the interdependence of legal systems within transnational regimes more generally. The effectiveness of transnational law (and of the case law of many international courts) is heavily contingent on the capacity of judges to interact productively across jurisdictional boundaries. Indeed, in an increasingly globalized world, inter-judicial dialogue and cooperation is basic to how transnational activity is regulated, boundaries negotiated, and disputes resolved.[89] It is quite unclear, however, precisely how such cooperation is to be achieved. In the case of arbitration, it is today obvious that the 1958 New York Convention comprises the basic constitutional framework of the present system.

The New York Convention of 1958

A concise treaty, containing a bare handful of important provisions, the New York Convention has generated profound changes in statutory law and judicial doctrine at the national level. Article II of the Convention requires national judges to 'recognize' the validity of arbitral agreements and to impose them on recalcitrant parties:

1. Each Contracting State shall recognize an agreement in writing under which the parties undertake to submit to arbitration all or any differences which have arisen or which may

---

[88] 'Ten Good Reasons to Choose ICC Arbitration' (n 85).

[89] Gunther Teubner, *Constitutional Fragments: Societal Constitutionalism and Globalization* (Oxford University Press, Oxford 2012).

arise between them in respect of a defined legal relationship, whether contractual or not, concerning a subject matter capable of settlement by arbitration.
...
3. The court of a Contracting State, when seized of an action in a matter in respect of which the parties have made an agreement ... shall, at the request of one of the parties, refer the parties to arbitration, unless it finds that the said agreement is null and void, inoperative or incapable of being performed.

Article III requires a national judge to treat 'awards as binding and enforce them in accordance with the [relevant] rules of procedure' in place in that state. Under Article V(2), judicial 'recognition and enforcement of an award may be refused' on the basis of certain irregularities of procedure, when the court of the seat of arbitration has annulled it, and insofar as the judge 'finds that':

(a) The subject matter of the [dispute] is not capable of settlement by arbitration under the law of that country; or
(b) The recognition or enforcement of the award would be contrary to the public policy of that country.

The treaty does not otherwise speak to the exceptions of 'inarbitrability' and 'public policy', leaving judges with substantial discretion to determine their nature and scope.

The Convention, which has now been ratified by 155 states (see Figure 2.2), is the first treaty of global scope to make decisions issuing from private, transnational legal process directly effective within national legal orders. Those who would deny that the arbitral order is a meaningfully autonomous, private legal system, significantly detached from state law, typically emphasize the role of the Convention in creating and sustaining it. In our view, it is perfectly defensible to model the arbitral order as a product of state delegation, notably, through the Convention. After all, even a relatively small number of important states possess the power to destroy it, if

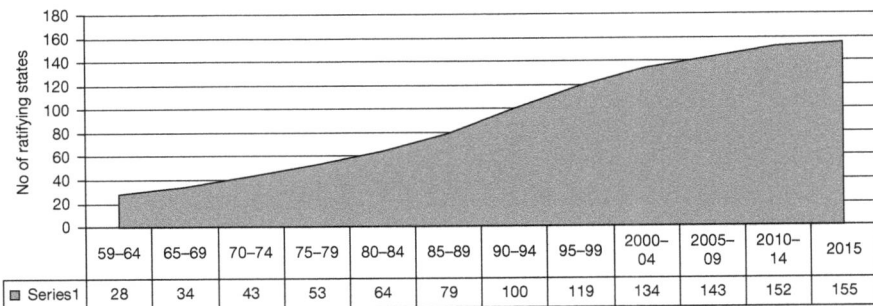

	59–64	65–69	70–74	75–79	80–84	85–89	90–94	95–99	2000–04	2005–09	2010–14	2015
■ Series1	28	34	43	53	64	79	100	119	134	143	152	155

Figure 2.2 Cumulative Number of State Ratifications of the New York Convention, 1959–2015

Source: Status: Convention of the Recognition and Enforcement of Foreign Arbitral Awards (New York, 1958), <http:// www.uncitral.org/uncitral/en/uncitral_texts/arbitration/NYConvention_status.html>.

they were, collectively, to withdraw support and recognition. But this view rests on a view that is both excessively formalist and a-historical.

The ICC, not states, drafted the initial version of the treaty, and expended enormous resources to ensure that the final text would reflect the priorities of transnational business and arbitrators. Immediately following the end of the Second World War, the ICC began working in earnest to reform the kaleidoscope of institutions that poorly served to coordinate state law and the arbitral order. At the national level, indifference and hostility to arbitration remained common. Internationally, the relevant treaty law—the Geneva Convention on the Execution of Foreign Arbitral Awards of 1927—did more to preserve existing dysfunctionalities than to dilute them.[90] The Geneva Convention required parties to obtain certification of the finality of an award by a judge in the seat of arbitration, before going to a second judge in the place of enforcement.[91] To make matters worse, in a conflict between (a) national procedural rules (of the seat) and (b) those chosen by the parties (or imposed by the house), it gave primacy to the former.[92]

ICC officials sought to produce a multilateral treaty that would abrogate the 1927 Geneva Convention, while requiring national judges to recognize the status of the arbitral order, and to enforce its awards. After nearly two years of work, it completed a draft in 1953. In the report appended to the proposed convention, the drafting committee summarized its approach in the following terms:

[T]he idea of an international award, i.e. an award completely independent of national laws, corresponds precisely to an economic requirement. [A] Commercial agreement between the parties, even for international transactions, will always be linked up with a given national system of law. Nevertheless, the fact that an award settling a dispute arising in connection with this agreement will produce its effects in different countries makes it essential that it should be enforced in all these countries in the same way.

In October 1953, the ICC submitted the draft to the United Nations Economic and Social Council [ECOSOC], which appointed a committee of eight to consider it. With one exception, none of them was an expert in the field of arbitration. Only in 1955 did the ECOSOC committee finally meet, and then only for two weeks. Expressing strong hostility to the ICC's approach, the ECOSOC produced its own text, which it modelled on the 1927 Geneva Convention, reproducing the same defects.

In response, ICC officials prepared a series of amendments to restore its priorities. They pressed to reverse the burden of proof, for example, when it came to enforcement, from the winning to the losing party. The losing party, in order to resist enforcement in *State Y*, would have to demonstrate that the award was not final at the seat of the arbitration, that is, under the law and in the courts of *State X*.

---

[90] For a detailed criticism of the 1927 Geneva Convention from the perspective of the ICC, see Edwin S Herbert, 'International Commercial Arbitration and Freedom of Contract' (ICC Publishing, Paris 1951).

[91] Geneva Convention on the Execution of Foreign Arbitral Awards of 1927, Article 1(d).

[92] Geneva Convention on the Execution of Foreign Arbitral Awards of 1927, Article 1(c).

The ICC also insisted on the primacy of the parties' choice of procedural rules, which would most likely be those of the house, rather than the rules of the seat. As the primary materials demonstrate, the ICC's preferences prevailed at the New York Conference. The critical moment occurred when Pieter Sanders—a drafter of the original proposal and the leader of the Dutch delegation—successfully proposed a series of amendments to reinstate the contested provisions of the ICC draft. As one of the Italian delegates, Eugenio Minoli, would later comment: 'the Conference decided in favor of a compromise undoubtedly nearer to the wishes of the ICC and of all those to whom arbitration appears to be an expression of legal regulation pertaining to the individual, rather than an institution coming under the legislation of the State'.[93]

National Legal Systems: Adaptation and Resistance

Three factors—(a) the global expansion in transnational commerce and arbitration, (b) the juris-generative activities of IACs and the professional organizations they serve, and (c) the demands of the 1958 New York Convention—combine to produce enormous pressure on national legal systems to recognize the autonomy and authority of the arbitral order. How they have done so is a complex topic on which there is virtually no systematic empirical research. Here we provide a response to the crucial questions: why, how, and to what extent, have national systems intensified their support for international arbitration?

The underlying strategic situation confronting states can be described simply. Assume a pool of trader-contractants, each of whom has a choice of partners located in different countries. Assume further that each trader prefers arbitration over litigation in the national courts, but only insofar as arbitration is effective, in that it produces final, binding, and enforceable awards. Other things equal, contractants will prefer partners from, or with assets within, those countries whose courts most intensively support arbitration and enforce awards with the lowest cost. And they will seek to avoid contact with states whose courts interfere with the arbitral process, engage in intensive merit review of awards, and hinder enforcement in other ways. In a situation in which trade explodes, these micro-level logics produce macro-level effects. The New York Convention and the UNCITRAL Model Law comprise the institutional framework for resolving systemic problems of enforcement, but success ultimately depends upon how they are deployed by national officials.

The explosion in trade, the development of arbitration as a substitute for courts, and enforcement of awards under the New York Convention combined to generate two dynamics serving to consolidate the domain of arbitration, as it has expanded. The first is enhanced regulatory competition among national legal orders. States compete with one another to show the world that they support transnational business, freedom of contract, and arbitral autonomy. It is of crucial importance

---

[93] Eugenio Minoli, 'The New York Convention on the Recognition and Enforcement of Foreign Arbitral Awards' (1958) Unification LYB 156, 161.

that the dominant competitor states are also the strategically most important: the United States, the United Kingdom, France, and—increasingly—Hong Kong and Singapore. Each is a major trading nation, with highly developed infrastructures, in law, banking and finance, insurance, and so on; and each hosts one of the global arbitral centres. Also crucial, the evolution of American, English, and French law heavily influences the development of most other important national systems, on every continent. When it comes to New York Convention obligations, all (through statutes and accompanying case law) preclude merit review of awards, while narrowing the inarbitrability and public policy exceptions to practical irrelevance. There are virtually no important instances of a court in the United States, the United Kingdom, or France refusing to enforce a major award on such grounds since the 1970s. Indeed, all three legal systems have gone beyond the requirements of the Convention in various ways. French law, for example, formally recognizes the transnational basis of awards, that is, their validity is not rooted into the law of any state; French courts have even enforced awards that have been annulled by a court at the seat of arbitration.

Arbitration is a lucrative business. Powerful private actors, including local and national bar associations, chambers of commerce, firms, and trade groups, now routinely build partnerships with public entities (such as federated states and cities) to promote the relative advantages of their law of contract, pro-arbitration policies, and courts as instruments of enforcement. In doing so, these actors help to institutionalize the market for arbitration, while generating a clear, best-practice template for what it means to be a 'pro-arbitration state'. The promotional materials of these entities highlight exactly those features that transnational business today expect: that the state's contract law will maximize party autonomy; that its courts will actively support arbitration as a matter of international, not simply national, public policy; and that host cities and states will furnish state-of-the-art, comfortable facilities. Germany, Hong Kong, Singapore, Sweden, and Switzerland among many others have fully embraced the pro-arbitration template, with dramatic results.

The second dynamic, closely related to that of regulatory competition, generates adaptation through network—'bandwagon'—effects rooted in logics of increasing returns to scale. To the extent that powerful states and private entities converge on emergent, best-practice standards, other states will be led to follow. Indeed, once the snowballing picks up speed, each state that buys into a nascent standard raises the probability that others will do so. The hypothesis is straightforward: the more any state is integrated into the global economy, the more it will be pressured to liberalize its policies toward arbitration by embracing elements of the template. States can do so by copying the approaches of major pro-arbitration states when it comes to recognition and enforcement, and by adopting a statute based on the UNCITRAL Model Law. In doing so, they deepen the constitutionalization—or institutional embeddedness, if one prefers—of the New York Convention regime.

The Model Law's basic purpose, after all, is to reconfigure national law as a structurally congruent interface with the New York Convention. The Model

Law: provides stand-alone procedures for international arbitration (displacing domestic codes); recognizes the defining features of arbitral autonomy, including separability and K-K; and harnesses the judiciary to ensure effectiveness. On recognition and enforcement, Article 35(1) states that: 'An arbitral award, irrespective of the country in which it was made, shall be recognized as binding' by the domestic courts, while 'the grounds on which recognition or enforcement may be refused' (Article 36) mirror those laid down in Article V of the New York Convention. In adopting an UNCITRAL-compliant statute, states 'internalize' or 'incorporate' the Convention into their national law, along with other values that find expression in the *Lex Mercatoria*. The seventy-three states that have passed legislation based on UNCITRAL comprise an expanding global patchwork of pro-arbitration zones. These zones are now found on all continents and major regions of the globe: Europe (Belgium, Germany, Ireland, Norway, and Spain); Russia and most states in post-Soviet Central and Eastern Europe; the Middle East (Egypt, Jordan, and Turkey); Asia and Oceania (Australia and New Zealand, Hong Kong, India, Japan, Korea, Malaysia, Thailand, and Taiwan); the Americas (Canada, Costa Rica, Honduras, Mexico, Nicaragua, Brazil, Chile, Paraguay, and Peru); and Africa (Kenya and Nigeria). Draft statutes based on the Model Law have appeared and await adoption in the Gulf (Saudi Arabia, the United Arab Emirates), while other important trading states have recently revised their laws to reduce gaps (Ghana and Italy).

While these developments have transformed the relationship between national law and the arbitral order, zones of resistance also exist. Resistance takes various forms. Some important trading states—the most important being China (with the exception of Macau and Hong Kong), Argentina, Indonesia, South Africa, and most Arab states in the Gulf—have not adopted, or expressly delayed consideration of, UNCITRAL-based statutes; and their judges are not loath to review a tribunal's decisions on the scope of its competence, and of its reasoning, to more searching judicial review. As important, the courts of a long list of countries, including others in Asia, Africa, and Latin America, have maintained parochial notions of public policy, weakening the enforcement system, notwithstanding ratification of the New York Convention.

Logics of Hierarchy

The New York Convention organizes a pluralist system of dispute resolution and enforcement. Lacking any supervisory or coordinative organ, the treaty establishes a decentralized enforcement regime, in which the courts of any signatory state are expected to enforce valid arbitral awards emanating from a long list of IACs. The dependence of arbitrators on national courts for enforcement does not deprive the arbitral order of its claims to autonomy. On the contrary, under the New York Convention, national courts owe positive duties to arbitrators, leaving judges to regulate the overall system only on the margins, as exceptions to core obligations. Powerful trading states could have blocked the expansion of the arbitral order. Instead, they have continuously adapted to the demands of transnational business, and the needs of the arbitral community, not least to facilitate trade and to enhance their own competitive positions in the market for arbitration.

III. Investor-State Arbitration

The generic issue facing transnational investment is, again, one of commitment. Assume a world in which private investors (X) in some states hold stocks of investment capital, while capital-poor states compete to attract investors. Assume that X is risk-averse, and will therefore prioritize investing in relatively stable environments. In this situation, to attract foreign direct investment [FDI], any state (Y) must persuade X that her investment will be safe, and that Y will not expropriate it (at least not without adequate compensation), or subject it to ruinous regulatory changes that would destroy its profitability (so-called 'indirect' expropriation). A standard solution—creating judicially enforceable property rights for investors against the state—is viable only if X trusts Y's courts. Because X may have good reason to wish to avoid Y's courts, harnessing 'a-national' arbitration to enforce X's rights is an obvious solution to these problems.

As in the case of trade, solving imperfect commitment dilemmas requires institution-building. As we have seen, the transnational community has succeeded in developing extensive private systems of governance for contract-based transactions. When it comes to FDI, however, regime-building requires the active participation of states. As Pauwelyn rightly stresses, the crucial question is 'why [would states] ever agree—and continue to agree—to limit their sovereign powers over foreign investors' through the delegation of judicialized authority to international arbitrators?[94] One part of the answer is that states possess joint interests in promoting and attracting FDI, for which they compete with one another. In expressing the matter so simply, we do not mean to understate the fierce complexity of the processes through which, in fact, these interests become manifest and are transformed into law and policy. But another part of the answer concerns state preferences to depoliticize dispute resolution. In line with broader trends in international economic law, states replaced dyadic systems—which were based on brute force, diplomacy, and unilateral assertions of jurisdiction—with rule-based TDR. States had long relied on diplomatic means of protecting 'aliens' and their investments, to which, after the Second World War, they added more articulated legal instruments, best exemplified by treaties of Friendship, Navigation, and Commerce. But these treaties did not provide for TDR. Beginning in the 1980s, a new generation of investment agreements combined with the 1965 Convention on the Settlement of Investment Disputes between States and Nationals of Other States [ICSID Convention] to constitute a new arbitral regime based on compulsory jurisdiction.

---

[94] Pauwelyn (n 9), 373.

Both capital-exporting and -importing states had reasons to buy in, which they have done on a steady basis ever since.[95] Here we provide a synoptic overview of how the ISA domain has evolved, comparing it to key features of ICA as we go along.

Institutions, Organizations, Actors

After the Second World War, the polarized ideological context of decolonization and the intensification of the Cold War made wide agreement on basic principles of FDI within the developing world, and international development policy more generally, all but impossible. Whether developing states had a right to expropriate foreign investors (as a means of furthering development goals), and how takings should be compensated (if at all) were core questions. As Oscar Schachter put it in 1984: 'Apart from the use of force, no subject of international law has aroused as much debate and strong feelings as standards for payment of compensation' following expropriation.[96] By the end of the 1980s, the situation had changed, as the strictures of neo-liberal economics diffused from advanced industrial to developing states,[97] and the developing world abandoned Marxist-inspired policies. Most important for our purposes, the demand for FDI in capital-poor states soared, in order to fund new infrastructure projects, modernize manufacturing and service industries, and privatize public utilities and other poorly performing, state-held assets. Capital-rich states welcomed this new openness, which the World Bank and International Monetary Fund also strongly supported. The initial bargain was relatively straightforward: in return for new FDI, host states would agree to arbitrate investment disputes.

Since the 1990s, the regime has developed at a spectacular rate, while generating controversy among state officials, and within the arbitral profession and scholarly community.

Treaties

The trading world is governed by two regimes of global scope. The first is a public law regime embodied by the World Trade Organization [WTO]. The second is ICA, a private law regime backed up by the public enforcement mechanisms of the New York Convention. For FDI, there is no equivalent of the WTO. Instead, investment disputes are resolved through different routes. Investors may sue public authorities in the courts of the host state. Or a state entity and a foreign investor—as parties to a contract—may agree to arbitrate; being contractual disputes, they are typically processed through the ICA regime, the ICC having long experience of

---

[95] ibid, 15–26.

[96] Oscar Schachter, 'Comment: Compensation for Expropriation' (1984) 8 American Journal of International Law 121.

[97] See M Sornarajah, *Resistance and Change in the International Law on Foreign Investment* (Cambridge University Press, Cambridge 2015) Chapter 1.

Annual
number of IIAs

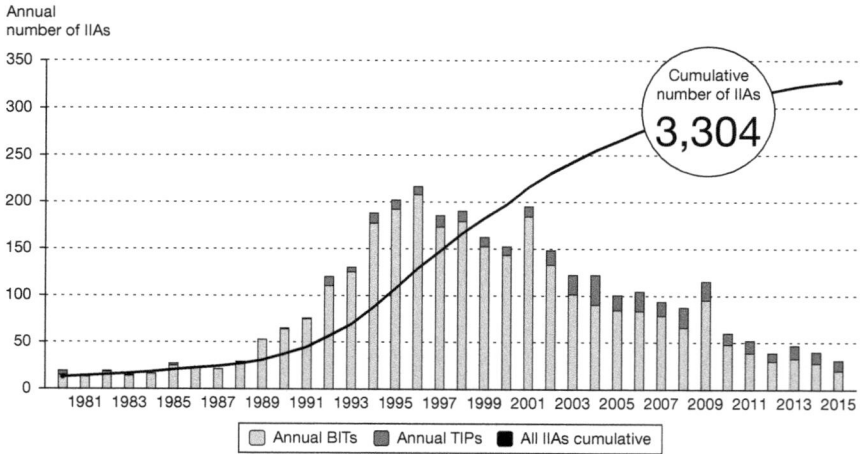

Figure 2.3 Trends in International Investment Agreements (IIAs) Signed, 1980–2015
Note: TIP—Treaty with Investment Provision.
Source: Annual UNCTAD World Investment Reports.

doing so. Since the late 1990s, the most common basis for ISA is a treaty, whether bilateral (a BIT), regional (e.g. chapter 11 of NAFTA), or sectoral (e.g. the Energy Charter, signed by European and Central Asian states).

Figure 2.3 tracks the annual and cumulative numbers of new international investment agreements concluded since 1980. By the end of 2015, the total stood at 3,304, consisting of 2,946 bilateral investment treaties [BITs] and 358 other agreements.[98] Despite these vertiginous numbers, most of these agreements share common features. First, they create substantive law for FDI. Provisions typically prohibit expropriation (direct and indirect) without a compelling public interest justification, followed by full and adequate compensation; they announce principles of non-discrimination (national and 'most favoured nation' [MFN] treatment); and, as tribunals have construed the ubiquitous 'fair and equitable treatment' standard [FET], they confer on investors a wide range of due process guarantees, as well as an obligation to honour investors' 'legitimate expectations' with regard to regulatory stability. Second, they establish state liability for the violation of an investor's rights. Third, they commit states to compulsory arbitration. Most BITs pre-commit the parties to arbitration at the International Centre for Settlement of Investment Disputes (ICSID), under the ICSID Convention and Rules. But agreements may also give parties a choice of arbitral venue, including at any major arbitration house under UNCITRAL Rules, or at ICSID.

---

[98] United Nations Conference on Trade and Development, 'World Investment Report 2016' <http://unctad.org/en/PublicationsLibrary/wir2016_en.pdf> accessed 26 June 2016 ['World Investment Report 2016'], 101.

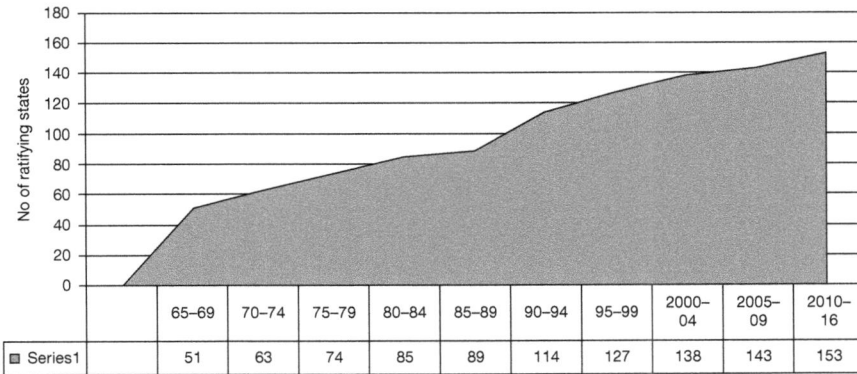

	65–69	70–74	75–79	80–84	85–89	90–94	95–99	2000–04	2005–09	2010–16
▣ Series1	51	63	74	85	89	114	127	138	143	153

Figure 2.4 Cumulative Number of State Ratifications of the ICSID Convention, 1965–2016

Source: 'List of Member States—ICSID', <https://icsid.worldbank.org/apps/ICSIDWEB/icsiddocs/Pages/List-of-Member-States.aspx>.

ICSID dominates the world of ISA. Figure 2.4 plots the cumulative number of ratifications by states of the Convention, which has reached 153.[99] The ICSID Convention established the Centre and its competences, laid down a mix of mandatory and default rules of procedure, and required the domestic courts of member states to enforce ICSID awards, just as they would a 'final judgment' of their own legal system.[100] Standing alone, the Convention exhibits glaring gaps, which gave it a stillborn quality for much of its first three decades of existence. The Convention's provisions do not state the substantive law governing the treatment of foreign investors; it was the explosion of BITs and other agreements in the 1990s (Figure 2.3) that would provide that law. As important, in providing pre-consent to ICSID jurisdiction, BITs gave a crucial, if completely 'unplanned' and 'unexpected',[101] boost to the Centre's mission.

Activity and Outcomes

Figure 2.5 charts the annual and cumulative number of known ISA cases covered by treaties.[102] In the 1965 to 1994 period, arbitral centres registered an average of

[99] International Centre for Settlement of Investment Disputes, List of Contracting States and Other Signatories of the Convention <https://icsid.worldbank.org/apps/ICSIDWEB/icsiddocs/Documents/List%20of%20Contracting%20States%20and%20Other%20Signatories%20of%20the%20Convention%20-%20Latest.pdf> accessed 10 February 2016.
[100] ICSID Convention, Article 54(1): 'Each Contracting State shall recognize an award rendered pursuant to this Convention as binding and enforce the pecuniary obligations imposed by that award within its territories as if it were a final judgment of a court in that State.'
[101] Andreas Lowenfeld, 'The ICSID Convention: Origin and Transformation' (2009) 38 Georgia Journal of International and Comparative Law 47, 57.
[102] The count excludes contractually based investment disputes processed through ICA.

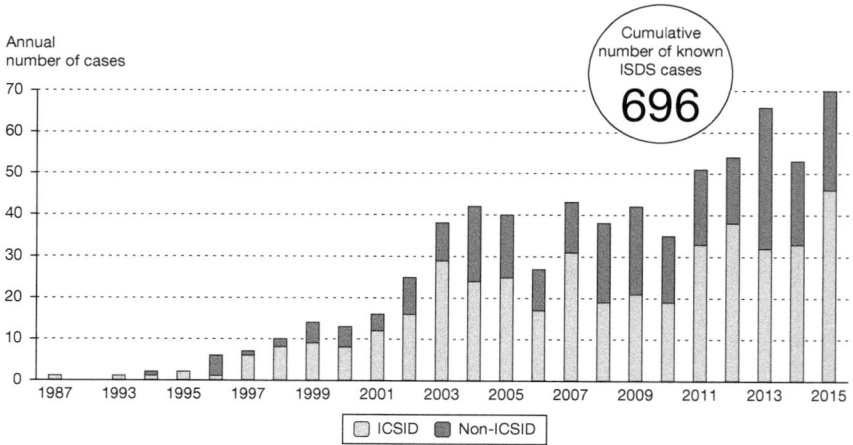

Figure 2.5 Known Treaty-Based Investor-State Arbitration Cases, 1987–2015

Note: ISDS—investor-state dispute settlement.

Source: Annual UNCTAD World Investment Reports.

less than one case per year. Filings increased dramatically in the 2000s, as the mass of investment agreements adopted in the 1990s started to bite. Through 2015, one counts 696 known cases of ISA involving 107 different respondent states, of which 60 per cent are classified by UNCTAD as 'developing'. With regard to basis of consent, BITs cover the vast bulk of cases, while the Energy Charter has generated eight-seven cases (12.5 per cent), followed by NAFTA with fifty-six (8 per cent of the total).[103]

ICSID has administered 82 per cent (497) of all known disputes through 2013, 90 per cent of which under ICSID Convention Rules, the remainder processed mostly under the Additional Facility. Figure 2.6 plots the number of new cases registered at ICSID by period. In its first two decades (1972 to 1991), ICSID processed only twenty-six cases. In 2015 alone, ICSID administered a record 243 cases, registered 52 new ones, and concluded 53 arbitrations.[104] The Permanent Court of International Arbitration, the ICC, the Stockholm Chamber of Commerce, and the Singapore centre also administer disputes, both treaty- and contractually based.

In contrast to the situation in ICA, where confidentiality of awards remains the norm, virtually all ICSID, NAFTA, and Energy Charter awards (or extracts thereof) are made public, as well as most of the awards rendered under UNCITRAL and IAC rules. It is therefore possible to compile and analyse

---

[103] World Investment Report 2016 (n 98), 105.

[104] International Centre for Settlement of Investment Disputes, 'ICSID Annual Report 2015' <https://icsid.worldbank.org/apps/ICSIDWEB/resources/Documents/ICSID_AR15_ENG_CRA-highres.pdf> accessed 6 July 2016.

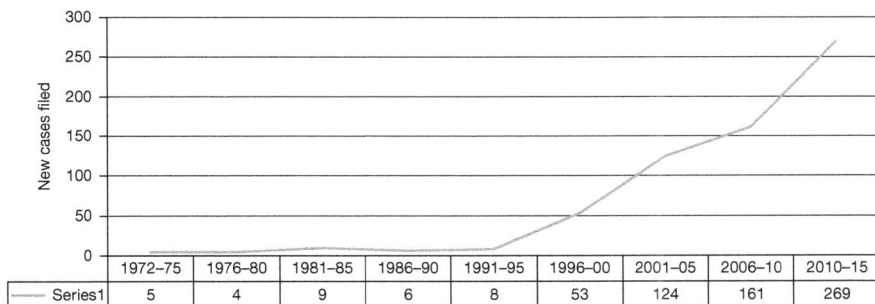

	1972–75	1976–80	1981–85	1986–90	1991–95	1996–00	2001–05	2006–10	2010–15
Series1	5	4	9	6	8	53	124	161	269

Figure 2.6 New Cases Registered at ICSID, 1972–2015
Source: 'ICSID Reports' (annual), <http://www.lcil.cam.ac.uk/publications/icsid-reports>.

relatively comprehensive data on outcomes. Through 2015, the known number of concluded cases is 444. States 'won' in 36 per cent of these cases: either jurisdiction was denied, or investors' claims for compensation were rejected in final awards. Investors 'won' in 27 per cent of the cases, that is, a tribunal issued a final award ordering the respondent state to compensate the investor. Of the remaining cases, 26 per cent were settled; 9 per cent were 'discontinued'; and in the remaining 2 per cent, 'liability [was] found but no damages [were] awarded'.[105]

Arbitrators

Virtually all ISA is conducted within three-member tribunals which are constituted when two party-appointed co-arbitrators nominate a president. At ICSID, the Secretary-General supervises the process and will appoint the president from the so-called 'panel of arbitrators', a list of arbitrators named by states and ICSID officials, if the co-arbitrators fail to do so.[106] The market for arbitrators in ISA is highly structured; the core repeat-arbitrators are easily identified; and many in this group are among the list of top arbitrators in ICA.

Publication also makes statistical analysis of appointments possible. In the most comprehensive study to date, Sergio Puig analysed 1,412 appointments involving 419 different arbitrators.[107] Puig found that 10 per cent of the appointment pool comprised 50 per cent of all appointments, and identified the twenty-five 'top arbitrators' that lead the field. Our data set contains appointment information on 166 final awards on liability (the merits). The top ten co-arbitrators[108]—those

---

[105] World Investment Report 2016 (n 98), 107.   [106] Chapter 3.

[107] Sergio Puig, 'Social Capital in the Arbitration Market' (2014) 25 European Journal of International Law 387 ['Puig']; Daphna Kapeliuk, 'The Repeat Appointment Factor—Exploring Decision Patterns of Elite Investment Arbitrators' (2010) 96 Cornell Law Review 47.

[108] The number is actually eleven, as there was a three-way tie for the tenth spot.

appointed by parties at least four times—were found on seventy-six (46 per cent) of the tribunals. With respect to the presiding arbitrator, individuals on our top-ten list (those presiding over at least four tribunals) comprise 38 per cent (n = 63) of all presidents. Twenty arbitrators have chaired at least three tribunals, meaning that experienced, repeat players drafted the majority of all final awards on the merits (54 per cent, n = 90). As in ICA, elite arbitrators compete on the basis of their reputations, which are built through serial appointments, work as counsel, and scholarly publications. As a result, a relatively small college of elite arbitrators play an outsized role in the system, giving the field more coherence than it might otherwise have.[109] The fact that fewer than twenty presiding arbitrators have produced most final awards—and thus are responsible for injecting reason-based justifications of awards into the system—favours the development of a more consistent arbitral case law, for example.

Although some arbitrators specialize in either ICA or ISA, we find significant overlap among elites. All of the 'elite twenty-five' in ICA (discussed above) have arbitrated investor-state disputes; a majority have served as counsel for states or investors in ISA proceedings; and seven of the 'top twenty-five' arbitrators identified by Puig are also members of the 'elite twenty-five' in ICA.

Arbitral Authority

ICA and ISA overlap in undeniable ways, and combine to constitute a broader legal field. Investors, for instance, can forum shop. When an investment dispute is registered in an arbitral house as a contractual dispute, the basic ICA regime applies.[110] Yet, when a contract is involved, investors may also file virtually the same case under a BIT at ICSID (or another arbitral centre), as a form of insurance or as leverage toward settlement. Further, many important treaty arrangements (including chapter 11 of NAFTA) permit investors to initiate ISA outside of ICSID, most commonly, under the UNCITRAL Rules of Arbitration. ISA and ICA are not sharply differentiated in terms either of procedures, or of the fiduciary obligations of arbitrators (Chapter 3). Indeed, the UNCITRAL Rules are routinely used to arbitrate both private commercial disputes and investor-state disputes; and the ICC, SCC, and SIAC Rules, too, apply to both ICA and ISA. All of these procedural codes expressly provide for separability and K-K; they require arbitrators to justify written awards with reasons; and the 1958 New York Convention governs the enforcement of awards. Thus, our analysis of the structure

---

[109] Puig (n 107), 407, Table 1: A lack of representativeness has received wide critical comment from scholars and some arbitrators. Puig found that only 19 of the 419 arbitrators appointed to date were female and that 46 per cent of all appointees hailed from just five states (the United States, France, the United Kingdom, Canada, and Switzerland—in that order), although eighty-seven nationalities are represented in his data set.

[110] See ICC Commission Report, *States, State Entities, and ICC Arbitration under the ICC Rules of Arbitration* (ICC, Paris 2012): 'Claims arising out of commercial contracts constitute the largest category of cases involving states or state entities.'

of arbitral authority within the ICA context (part II) also applies to a significant range of ISA activity.

Most disputes are settled at ICSID, which operates as a self-contained legal system, including mandatory Rules, annulment procedures, and robust administrative capacities. Because the ICSID system dominates ISA in distinctive ways, it merits separate analysis.

Level 1: Jurisdiction and Arbitral Authority

The Convention stipulates that ICSID's jurisdiction 'shall extend to any legal dispute arising directly out of an investment, between a Contracting State ... and a national of another Contracting State, which the parties to the dispute consent in writing to submit to the Centre.'[111] A BIT or other investment agreement that designates ICSID as forum constitutes consent, thereby conferring upon a foreign investor the right to bring suit at ICSID. Respondent states routinely raise jurisdictional challenges seeking the suit's dismissal. These challenges have produced an important jurisprudence (e.g. on the meaning of 'any legal dispute arising directly out of an investment') which has, in turn, generated a lively scholarly debate on the 'activism' of tribunals. Van Harten, for example, has demonstrated that tribunals have favoured an expansive notion of jurisdiction which, he rightly emphasizes, favours investors.[112] As a comparative matter, it is worth noting that new international legal regimes often adopt lenient rules on jurisdiction, not least, to jumpstart the system by building the docket.

The Convention firmly establishes the authority of tribunals over the disputing parties in ways that will by now be familiar. It stipulates that once 'the parties have given their consent, no party may withdraw its consent unilaterally',[113] for example, and lays down the principle of K-K.[114] Indeed, in light of its consolidation in ICA, the Convention's founders referred to K-K as a 'well-established' general principle of international arbitration.[115]

Level 2: Reason Giving and Annulment

Similar to the situation at the ICC, arbitrators owe a set of fiduciary duties to the parties and the house (see Chapter 3). Under the Convention, for example,

---

[111] Convention on the Settlement of Investment Disputes between States and Nationals of Other States (1967) 575 UNTS 159 ['ICSID Convention'], Article 25(1).

[112] Gus Van Harten, 'Arbitrator Behaviour in Asymmetrical Adjudication: An Empirical Study of Investment Treaty Arbitration' (2012) 50 Osgoode Hall Law Journal 211.

[113] ICSID Convention, Article 25(1). The ICSID Additional Facility Rules (which apply in the absence of consent to the ICSID Convention) expressly refer to the separability principle, Article 45(1) stating: 'For the purposes of this Article, an agreement providing for arbitration under the Additional Facility shall be separable from the other terms of the contract in which it may have been included.'

[114] ICSID Convention, Article 41(1): 'The Tribunal shall be the judge of its own competence.'

[115] International Centre for Settlement of Investment Disputes, 'Report of the Executive Directors on the ICSID Convention' <https://icsid.worldbank.org/ICSID/StaticFiles/basicdoc/partB.htm> accessed 10 February 2015, para 38.

arbitrators must 'state the reasons upon which [the award] is based'[116] and failure to do so can lead to the annulment of the award. Because virtually all ICSID awards are now made public, the system has generated a precedent-based jurisprudence that heavily conditions how parties argue cases, and how arbitrators justify awards. We examine the nature and impact of this case law at length in Chapters 4 and 5.

A unique feature of ICSID arbitration is the availability of annulment, through the decisions of 'Ad Hoc Annulment Committees' [ACs]. The procedure introduces a dose of hierarchical control. Parties activate the procedure, but otherwise have no control over how it operates. The Chairman of the Administrative Council of ICSID appoints the three-member ACs, who will then proceed under mandatory rules. ACs are empowered to annul awards on five grounds: 'failure to state the reasons'; 'manifest excess of powers'; 'that the Tribunal was not properly constituted'; 'that there was corruption on the part of a member of the Tribunal'; and 'that there has been a serious departure from a fundamental rule of procedure'.[117] While ACs are not authorized to annul an award for a tribunal's 'errors-in-law', they regularly identify and address such errors in *dicta*. Indeed, some Committees have positioned themselves as appellate courts in all but name, venturing to annul awards for faulty legal reasoning, under 'the failure to state the reasons' or the 'manifest excess of powers' headings. We examine the law and politics of annulment, in light of the development of precedent-based case law, and the demand for appeal, in Chapter 4.

Level 3: ICSID and Other Legal Orders

The 1958 New York Convention is the only instrument of international public law that directly furnishes foundational elements for ICA.[118] The New York Convention characterizes international arbitral awards as 'foreign', while recognizing prerogatives of courts at the 'seat of arbitration' with regard to annulment. The ICSID Convention establishes its own autonomous enforcement regime: there is no 'seat', and the courts of 'each contracting state' are to enforce the Centre's awards 'as if [they] were a final judgment in that State'.[119] Thus, with respect to transnational coordination and enforcement, the ICSID Convention exhibits even stronger, quasi-constitutional features than does the New York Convention.

The ICSID Convention combines with international investment agreements to position ISA at ICSID squarely in the broader realm of international law. Because these treaties provide sources of consent and substantive law, for example, arbitrators are bound by the Vienna Convention on the Law of Treaties when they apply them, which can add duties beyond those required by the contractual model (see Chapter 1). Further, in a provision of the Convention that has provoked a great deal of debate, Article 42(1) of the Convention states that:

---

[116] ICSID Convention, Article 48(3).   [117] ICSID Convention, Article 52.
[118] General principles of law and the mandatory law of national systems are applicable or come into play in a wide range of cases—see Chapters 4 and 5.
[119] ICSID Convention, Article 54(1).

The Tribunal shall decide a dispute in accordance with such rules of law as may be agreed by the parties. In the absence of such agreement, the Tribunal shall apply the law of the Contracting State party to the dispute (including its rules on the conflict of laws) *and such rules of international law as may be applicable* (emphasis added).

Some scholars, tribunals, and annulment committees have interpreted the phrase— '*and such rules of international law as may be applicable*'—as incorporating general norms of international law into investment agreements, including judge-made general principles of law.[120] In a seminal paper of 2003, Gaillard and Banifatemi argued that such law comprises a 'truly independent body of substantive rules which may be applied by itself, and not [merely] through the filter of the law of the host State',[121] a view that subsequent case law supports. The theory firmly denies the appropriateness of the contract model—that each investment treaty, in effect, establishes a closed legal system—and gestures toward the networking of treaties and tribunals, progressive arbitral lawmaking, and constitutionalization. Finally, in a related set of developments, scholars have begun to consider linkages between the investment, trade, environmental protection, and human rights regimes, while tribunals now routinely cite to other international courts, not least, to borrow doctrinal solutions to common problems.[122]

States

ICA and ISA resemble and are connected to one another in myriad ways. Of course, a fundamental difference is that states play a much more direct role in building and maintaining the latter. From the perspective of delegation theory, in treaty-based ISA, states are Principals, arbitrators are their Agents, and public international law mediates the relationship. At the same time, states are always the defendants in any suit. Over the past fifteen years, tribunals have developed an increasingly dense and articulated jurisprudence, generating agency control issues. Today, such questions dominate the politics of ISA, for reasons we briefly summarize here.

Network Effects

International investment treaties are networked in structural ways that have enabled arbitrators to develop ISA as a relatively unified legal domain. The vast majority of investment agreements contain similar provisions. States copied provisions from one set of BITs to another, relying heavily on relatively vague standards to protect foreign investment. Put in terms of delegation theory, states negotiated incomplete contracts, on the basis of a common template, thereby conferring on tribunals implied lawmaking powers. The contracting states, for example, gave no

---

[120] Statute of the International Court of Justice (1945), Article 38.
[121] Emmanuel Gaillard and Yas Banifatemi, 'The Meaning of "and" in Article 42(1), Second Sentence, of the Washington Convention: The Role of International Law in the ICSID Choice of Law Process' (2003) 18 ICSID Review—Foreign Investment Law Journal 375.
[122] See Chapters 4, 5, and 6.

interpretive guidance as to the meaning or scope of the FET standard that host states owe to investors. Yet one finds a FET provision in virtually every investment agreement; investors systematically raise FET claims; and ISA tribunals have found more violations of FET than they have of any other substantive provision of investment law. For their part, arbitrators have generated an expansive, self-sustaining jurisprudence on FET, treating it as an integrative norm of investment law, in the aggregate (detailed in Chapter 5). Other important streams of arbitral case network and 'complete' treaty provisions through similar processes.

As a result, every state-as-respondent (rather than Principal) finds itself being subjected to a system that tends to treat investment treaties in the aggregate. Moreover, most BITs contain a 'most favoured nation' clause. Under what is now settled jurisprudence,[123] the standard MFN rule means that claimants may request the tribunal to 'incorporate' from the host state's corpus of BITs any substantive provision that is not found in the BIT that directly applies to the dispute.[124] The highest standard of protection in a state's corpus of BITs thereby becomes the minimal standard, effectively obliterating differences between that state's BITs. MFN clauses network treaties in a formalized way, standardizing their terms, an outcome that is congruous with the judicial model.

Review of State Acts and Remedies

Under an investment agreement, every case involves an action brought by an investor (the claimant) against a state (the respondent). The tribunal's task is to review the lawfulness of state acts under the terms of a BIT or other agreement, which supplants the judicial review functions of national courts. For these reasons, some scholars conceptualize the networked treaty system as a type of 'global public law',[125] with ISA operating as a new form of administrative (or constitutional) judicial review. Proponents of this perspective tend to distinguish ICA from ISA on the basis of the latter's more 'public' nature. Nonetheless, ISA tribunals—unlike domestic administrative or constitutional courts—do not possess the authority to annul or quash state acts, or to compel the state to take a general or particular measure. If state liability under the treaty is found, the remedy on offer is compensation for losses. In this sense, ICA and ISA are more like than unlike one another, a point we explore further in Chapter 6.

---

[123] *EDF International SA, SAUR International SA and Leon Participaciones Argentinas SA v Argentina* (ICSID Case No ARB/03/23, award of 11 June 2012), para 932: 'To ignore the MFN clause in this case would permit more favorable treatment to investors protected under third countries, which is exactly what the MFN Clause is intended to prevent.' The question of whether the MFN applies to dispute resolution procedures remains a controversial one; Stephanie L Parker, 'A BIT at a Time: The Proper Extension of the MFN Clause to Dispute Settlement Provisions in Bilateral Investment Treaties' (2012) 2(1) Arbitration Brief 30.
[124] That is, an investor from *State X* hosted by *State Y* may plead any provision found in a BIT entered into by Y, even if that provision is absent in the BIT concluded by X and Y.
[125] Gus Van Harten and Martin Loughlin, 'Investment Treaty Arbitration as a Species of Global Administrative Law' (2006) 17 European Journal of International Law 121; see also the literature discussed in Chapters 1 and 6.

Legitimacy Debates

As ISA has taken off, the regime has steadily revealed its capacity for creative law-making, intensifying debate on its political legitimacy. The fact that state treasuries are exposed to the rulings of foreign arbitrators, upon review of the lawfulness of domestic regulations presumptively enacted in the public interest, gives legitimacy questions salience. In Chapter 6, we assess this debate in light of the book's findings. At this point, it is enough to highlight three main points.

First, no one knows the extent to which international investment agreements have actually increased FDI in capital-poor states. Some major recipients of FDI—Brazil being the most prominent—have not ratified BITs and are not signatories of the ICSID Convention. Of course, we cannot know if such countries would have received even more FDI had they joined the system. A review of the scholarly literature in this regard suggests, at most, that BITs do increase investment for some (but not all) countries, in certain sectors of the economy, probably in tandem with other propitious domestic factors.[126] Even accepting such findings, the debate now includes the issue of whether the costs imposed on states—including the payment of large awards and a reduction in regulatory flexibility—can ever be worth the benefits. In contrast, the positive effect of ICA on trade goes largely unchallenged; indeed, the world's most powerful trading states have adopted pro-arbitration positions that serve to legitimize ICA.

Second, unlike the situation for ICA, the politicization of ISA is in full swing. Until a decade ago, ISA could be characterized as relatively insulated from the greater political environment in which it is embedded. Only specialists in certain national ministries, elite law firms, and business associations, together with a handful of legal academics, paid much attention to the work, opaque and technical, of tribunals. Today, politicians, trade unions, NGOs, international organizations, and scholars have joined tendentious debates on the question of whether the ISA regime should be preserved, radically reformed, or scrapped altogether. The fact that the regime continues to expand, with new investment agreements being initiated and signed each year, sustains controversy.

Third, States-as-Principals have re-materialized, placing reform at the top of the agenda. For most of the past two decades, arbitrators have been the architects of the system, with little push-back from states. Since 2010, the situation has dramatically changed. Bolivia, Ecuador, and Venezuela have denounced the ICSID Convention, and terminated some BITs, in protest of what they consider to be systemic, pro-investor bias.[127] Others have threatened exit for the same reason,

[126] See Chapter 1.

[127] Ecuador terminated nine BITs in 2008; Venezuela terminated one BIT in 2009; and, since 2014, Indonesia has terminated fourteen BITs. Bolivia (2007), Ecuador (2009), and Venezuela (2012) denounced the ICSID Convention. See Gabrielle Kaufmann-Kohler and Michele Potestà, 'Can the Mauritius Convention Serve as a Model for the Reform of Investor-State Arbitration in Connection with the Introduction of a Permanent Investment Tribunal or an Appeal Mechanism? Analysis and Roadmap', Geneva Center for International Dispute Settlement (paper commissioned by UNCITRAL), 3 June 2016, 10.

and some have refused to pay awards. Indonesia and South Africa have begun to withdraw from BITs.[128] In 2014, UNCTAD—which has called for a recalibration of the relationship between states, investors, and arbitrators—counted more than fifty states actively revising their 'model' investment agreements. These efforts are important, in that such model treaties serve as codified expressions of state interests, as well as the basis for negotiating new treaties. This group includes both capital-rich and -poor states, on every continent. As Kurtz convincingly argues, the political 'landscape' of ISA is changing in the face of 'an overdue and hugely important reassessment by a broad range of states of their optimal level of investment treaty exposure'.[129] It is of critical importance for future development that major capital-exporting states, including the United States, Canada, and members of the European Union, are increasingly recipients of new FDI, and are thus more exposed to the system—as respondents. In Chapters 5 and 6, we examine in detail what states have actually done in response to arbitral lawmaking and the alleged 'crisis' in ISA.

IV. Conclusion

In the 1920s, a transnational business community based in Paris sought to revive elements of the old *Lex Mercatoria* in order to promote, and to meet the demands of, international commerce. The ICC took pains to stress the *non-judicial* features of the new regime. Arbitral proceedings would be relatively non-adversarial; tribunals would favour settlement, and produce equity-based judgments; and the regime would eschew procedural rigidity and precedent-based doctrines, thereby attracting users. The project failed. Successive waves of highly adversarial cases, and explosive increases in trade, led the ICC to explore another path of development: to emulate courts. Since the 1950s, the ICC has steadily developed its capacity to manage highly adversarial, high-stakes disputes, with the express goal of supplanting domestic systems. Today, a fiercely competitive market for ICA is managed by an elite corps of arbitrators dedicated to the development of ICA as an autonomous legal system. The domination of ICA, the community can defensibly claim, results from the fact that tribunals are positioned to perform the functions for which transnational business needs courts, but better.

The effectiveness of arbitration depended upon its judicialization. The regime has built hierarchy-based structures of authority at precisely those pressure points in the arbitral process where effectiveness is threatened. At a first level of analysis—that

---

[128] See 'South Africa Begins Withdrawing from EU-Member BITs' (*Investment Treaty News*, 30 October 2012) <https://www.iisd.org/itn/2012/10/30/news-in-brief-9/> accessed 10 February 2016; Ben Bland and Shawn Donnan, 'Indonesia to Terminate More than 60 Bilateral Investment Treaties' (*Financial Times*, 26 March 2014).

[129] Jürgen Kurtz, 'The Shifting Landscape of International Investment Law and Its Commentary' (2012) 106 American Journal of International Law 694.

of any specific proceeding—the doctrines of separability and K-K confer authority on tribunals to manage situations in which a party may threaten to defect. At the organizational level, IACs have generated an increasingly dense corpus of mandatory procedures, as a means of controlling tribunals, and of securing the finality and enforceability of awards. We chart the evolution of such procedures in Chapter 3. A third level of analysis focuses attention on interactions between the arbitral order and domestic courts. Under the 1958 New York Convention, an ICC initiative, pro-arbitration states in the major trading zones have explicitly recognized the autonomy and authority of the arbitral order as a legal system.

Since the late 1980s, in wide swathes of the world, states have also locked themselves into the arbitration of foreign investment disputes. ISA differs from ICA in that consent to the jurisdiction of arbitral tribunals prospectively covers an unknown number of foreign investments disputes, rather than being conferred on a case-by-case basis. ISA is further distinguished by the fact that, in all cases, the lawfulness of state acts (that is, their conformity with the provisions of an investment treaty) is under review. These features combine to intensify the salience of Principal–Agent dynamics (Chapter 1). As a formal matter, state courts exercise the functions of the Principal under the New York Convention. In ICA, judges do not do so either robustly, or in ways that scholars or the public can adequately assess. In treaty-based ISA, by contrast, the analyst can assess state responses to arbitral lawmaking relatively systematically, from an agency control perspective (Chapters 5 and 6).

3

Procedures and Hierarchy

When parties contemplate arbitration, the choice of procedures is primordial. All major international arbitral centres [IACs] promulgate, and regularly revise, a procedural code—called the Rules. The Rules comprise the basic institutional infrastructure of the house. They codify the fiduciary duties of the arbitrators, confer discretion to tailor procedures to the case, and enable them to proceed at crucial stages of the proceedings, despite the resistance of a party. The Rules determine the extent to which a centre will administer cases and supervise tribunals. Thus, the progressive elaboration of arbitral procedure tracks closely how structures of arbitral authority have evolved within the judicial model.

We begin by considering the evolution of arbitral procedure in light of themes developed in previous chapters. The autonomy of the arbitral order is partly measured by its gradual emancipation from constraints emanating from the domestic law of the seat of arbitration. It is also a function of the capacity of IACs to legislate codes of procedure, some provisions of which will be non-derogable and authoritative in other ways. Our primary focus is on how the dominant centre in the field, the International Chamber of Commerce [ICC], has revised its code over time, to serve its own policy choices and to manage increasing adversarialism. The ICC Rules have grown in sophistication, while remaining incomplete. Indeed, they are under continuous construction. Finally, we consider the code in light of three overlapping, but at times contradictory, systemic goals: to build the effectiveness of the arbitral order; to maintain efficiency; and to secure the autonomy of the arbitral order with respect to other legal systems. Along the way, we compare this development with the situation in other IACs, and at ICSID.

I. Procedural Codes and Arbitral Authority

Arbitral procedures constitute a complex and highly technical topic of professional and academic discourse, generating literally hundreds of books and articles each year, for a growing audience of users and specialists. The underlying reason for this complexity lies in the pluralist nature of arbitration and its symbiotic relationship to other legal orders, both national and international. Because organizational authority in the domain is fragmented, there is no unified code. Instead, various, often cumulative, bodies of rules govern proceedings. The domestic law covering the

The Evolution of International Arbitration: Judicialization, Governance, Legitimacy. First Edition. Alec Stone Sweet and Florian Grisel. © Alec Stone Sweet and Florian Grisel 2017. Published 2017 by Oxford University Press.

territory of the 'seat' once provided an important part of the procedural framework, since the courts of the seat were the privileged forum for annulment of awards. As a source of mandatory procedures, however, the importance of state law has steadily declined since the 1960s. Today, virtually all arbitration takes place under preestablished procedural templates—laid down by the house or in the UNCITRAL rules—which tribunals may then supplement with specific measures, in consultation with the parties. In elaborating the codes, the major arbitral centres function as legislatures, competing with each other in light of users' demands. One crucial measure of their success is external to the arbitral order: the extent to which state officials adapt to best-practice standards and institutional innovation, not least, in order to demonstrate the state's 'pro-arbitration' *bona fides* (discussed at length in Chapter 2).

The Decline of the Seat and the Rise of Transnational Freedom of Contract

Adopting the perspective of the national judge and state law provides a relatively simple way to understand the nature and scope of arbitral authority. Long-standing doctrine holds that every arbitral tribunal must be seated in a specific city, called 'the seat of arbitration', which subjects it to national law, under the territorial principle. A domestic court of the seat possesses the authority to supervise an arbitral tribunal, in effect, as a subsidiary organ within the legal system of that state.[1] States can and do impose their own mandatory rules on tribunals, which the courts may enforce at the behest of a disgruntled party. Because judges of the seat possess the power to annul awards, the mandatory requirements of national law weigh heavily on the work of any tribunal seated within it. The perspective of the arbitral community on these same issues, of course, stresses the intrinsic autonomy of the arbitral order, not the arbitration's subservience to the law of the state.[2] But such views do not make the constraints of the seat disappear.

The domestic law pertaining to international arbitration varies widely, including with respect to enforcement under the 1958 New York Convention. Arbitral houses and scholars devote enormous resources to the comparative analysis of relevant state law, and they continuously monitor the annulment and enforcement decisions

---

[1] Francis A Mann, 'Lex Facit Arbitrum' in Martin Domke and Pieter Sanders (eds), *Liber Amicorum for Martin Domke* (Martinus Nijhoff, The Hague 1967) 160.

[2] Gary Born summarizes the view succinctly: 'Historically, it was frequently said or assumed that arbitrators were required to apply the domestic procedural rules applicable in national courts in the arbitral seat. For the most part, it is now widely accepted that the domestic procedural rules of local courts are not applicable—mandatorily or otherwise—in international arbitrations seated on local territory. Rather, one of the most fundamental characteristics of contemporary international arbitration is the parties' broad freedom to agree upon the procedures to be followed in their arbitration.' See Gary Born, *International Commercial Arbitration* (1st edn, Kluwer Law International, Alphen aan de Rijn 2011) 715. The decline in the importance of the rules of the seat is a core component of Emmanuel Gaillard's theory: see Emmanuel Gaillard, *Legal Theory of International Arbitration* (Martinus Nijhoff, The Hague 2010).

of domestic courts.[3] Crucial for present purposes is the fact that, within the major trading zones, the most important courts have converged on robust pro-arbitration policies anchored in the recognition of a transnational freedom of contract, itself rooted in an extensive notion of party autonomy (see Chapter 2). For courts, this freedom entails (a) deference to the parties' choice of arbitration and procedures, and (b) a commitment to impose arbitral authority upon recalcitrant parties at crucial stages of the process.

Disputing parties and IACs choose the cities in which to seat the arbitration; and the major arbitral centres are capable of administering cases in virtually any city chosen by the parties. Users prefer to locate the arbitration in a pro-arbitration seat, in order to maximize the tribunal's autonomy and effectiveness. The most commonly selected seats at the ICC are Paris, London, Geneva, Singapore, New York, and Zurich,[4] cities located in states that have also invested significantly in the arbitral industry. These countries host a major arbitration centre. Their domestic statutes and case law reflect a broad conception of freedom of contract, while explicitly recognizing arbitral autonomy. And, significantly, the mandatory rules imposed in such jurisdictions, the most important of which are related to procedural due process and respect for transnational 'public policy', are virtually identical to the mandatory rules of the major arbitral centres (as far as procedural rules are concerned).

As we stressed in Chapter 2, islands of effective transnational governance emerge only to the extent that national legal orders adapt to the arbitral order, over time, as the latter evolves. The process, isomorphic in character, has generated important symmetries between state law and the arbitral order, at least in the major trading zones.

The Decline of Ad Hoc Arbitration

In so-called ad hoc arbitration, the ideal type of which is associated with the contractual model, the parties and the arbitrator negotiate their own binding procedural rules. In practice, institutional rules govern about 90 per cent of all proceedings, with most of the remaining 10 per cent taking place under the UNCITRAL Rules.[5]

---

[3] Since 1976, more than 1,700 national court decisions on annulment, recognition, and enforcement have been published in the ICCA Yearbook Commercial Arbitration: see International Council for Commercial Arbitration, 'ICCA Yearbook Commercial Arbitration' <http://www.arbitration-icca.org/publications/yearbook_table_of_contents.html> accessed 3 January 2016. See also New York Arbitration Convention, 'Court Decisions' <http://www.newyorkconvention.org/court+decisions> accessed 3 January 2016. The ICC Commission (discussed below) regularly updates the compendium. See International Chamber of Commerce, *Guide to National Procedures for Recognition and Enforcement of Awards under the New York Convention* (ICC, Paris 2012).

[4] International Chamber of Commerce, '2015 ICC Dispute Resolution Statistics' (2016) 26(1) ICC International Court of Arbitration Bulletin 9 ['2015 Statistical Report']. See also the findings and commentary in Queen Mary University of London and White & Case, 'The 2015 International Arbitration Survey: Improvements and Innovations in International Arbitration' (2015) <http://www.arbitration.qmul.ac.uk/research/2015/> accessed 3 January 2015.

[5] Queen Mary University of London and PricewaterhouseCoopers, 'International Arbitration: Corporate Attitudes and Practices 2008' (2008) <http://www.pwc.co.uk/services/forensic-services/insights/international-arbitration-2008.html> accessed 3 January 2016, 4.

All Rules contain gaps, many of which are intentional; IACs presume that tribunals and parties will seek to customize some rules for themselves. The situation is functional for users insofar as it blends efficiencies associated with pre-made institutions (saving the costs of negotiating rules for each case) and choice (enabling the tailoring of procedures to specific circumstances). Over time, however, the major arbitral centres have reduced this zone of choice, through legislating mandatory procedures from which counsel and tribunals may not derogate. Put in terms of judicialization theory, the contractual model has steadily given way to the judicial model, wherein each arbitral house operates as a quasi-autonomous legal system through Rules that establish some meaningful degree of hierarchy. The rest of this chapter provides, in more fine-grained detail, overwhelming evidence in support of this claim.

The House as Legislator

IACs compete with one another on the basis of procedural offerings.[6] The codes constrain users and determine the scope of in-house administrative capacity. Every major centre is continuously engaged in an assessment of their Rules with an eye to improving them. Highly structured consultations with users serve to identify recurrent problems and emergent needs. Over the past two decades, the arbitral domain has also seen the consolidation of a market-based 'field' in the sociological sense:[7] each major house closely monitors the legislative activities of every other house, as they seek to increase caseload and influence; and the leading arbitrators ply their trade in all of the major centres (Chapters 1 and 2). As we will show, once a major IAC has shown that a procedural innovation has successfully resolved a particular problem, in a form that users approve, other IACs will typically incorporate a version of the rule as their own. IACs may also seek to differentiate themselves by maintaining distinctive procedures. Lawyers and arbitrators, for their part, track changes and evaluate differences in making their own choices of forum.

The ICC is the heavyweight in ICA, and has been a major player in contract-based ISA. It has generated the basic institutional models that have structured the field, to which every other important house reacts one way or another. The ICC's legislative organ—a standing body called the Commission on Arbitration and ADR—has a wide mandate, which the ICC currently describes as follows:

The Commission on Arbitration and ADR is the ICC's rule-making body and unique think tank in the field of international dispute resolution. [It] drafts and revises the various ICC rules ... including the Rules of Arbitration, the Mediation Rules ... and the Rules for Expertise. In its research capacity, it proposes new policies in the interest of efficient and cost-effective dispute resolution and provides useful tools for [users].[8]

The Commission, composed of ICC officials, arbitrators, representatives of the bar, corporate counsel, and law professors, drawn from more than ninety countries,

---

[6] Chapter 2.   [7] Chapter 1.
[8] International Chamber of Commerce, 'Commission on Arbitration and ADR' <http://www.iccwbo.org/about-icc/policy-commissions/arbitration/> accessed 9 June 2016.

aggregates interests and epistemic expertise. Specialized committees draft amendments of the codes, which are then debated and adopted in the Commission's plenary sessions (of around 700 members), which meet twice per year. The Commission also produces white papers that float prospects for future reform, and reports meant to express best practices for the field.[9]

ICC officials not only legislate, they administer and judge, through powers centralized in the International Court of Arbitration [the Court], as supported by its Secretariat. Created in 1923, the Court is currently made up of around 125 members, who are 'experts and specialists' in arbitration, and the law of international commerce and investment.[10] It administers all arbitrations under ICC Rules, of which it is the authoritative interpreter. Specific functions include: (a) aiding the parties in constituting tribunals; (b) fixing the fees of arbitrators and administrative expenses; (c) supervising the compliance of tribunals with the various mandatory timetables and deadlines for the different phases of the proceedings; and (d) scrutinizing draft awards before certification as final. The Court's adjudication of disputes on the Rules has accreted into a dense, de facto jurisprudence that it communicates to users through the Secretariat. The Secretariat, which possesses broad powers of supervision, is involved in managing every proceeding, providing the interface between the tribunal and the Court.

II. Evolution

As arbitral centres displaced national judiciaries as preferred sites of dispute resolution for transnational business, their codes of procedure have grown in length and sophistication. Viewed functionally, the outcome is hardly surprising. The arbitral order processes the vast bulk of all complex transnational disputes with high monetary values at stake, and the number of such cases has risen sharply over the past two decades. With high-stakes disputing comes the potential for intensive party conflict, and a predisposition on the part of counsel to approach arbitration as a species of litigation. These factors have combined to generate a continuous demand for procedural innovation, to which IACs have responded. They have done so in order to secure the centrality, effectiveness, and autonomy of the arbitral order in the face of heightened adversarialism. Today, international arbitration can no longer be described in terms of its 'striking lack of formality',[11] once considered to be a defining feature.

---

[9] International Chamber of Commerce, 'ICC Arbitration Commission Report on Techniques for Controlling Time and Costs in Arbitration' (2015) <http://www.iccwbo.org/Advocacy-Codes-and-Rules/Document-centre/2012/ICC-Arbitration-Commission-Report-on-Techniques-for-Controlling-Time-and-Costs-in-Arbitration/> accessed 3 January 2016.

[10] Jason Fry, Simon Greenberg, and Francesca Mazza, *The Secretariat's Guide to ICC Arbitration* (ICC, Paris 2012) ['the *Guide*'], para 3-14.

[11] Alan Redfern, J Martin Hunter, Nigel Blackaby, and Constantine Partasides, *Redfern and Hunter on International Arbitration* (Oxford University Press, Oxford 2009) para 1.04.

In this section, we examine the evolution of arbitral procedures at the ICC. It is important to note in advance that the scholarship in this area is primarily descriptive, aimed at guiding users through the arbitral process. There is also a normative strain, the thrust of which is to critique and improve the codes. To our knowledge, no theory-based, explanatory account of this evolution exists. Although this chapter lays out a proto-explanation, our more modest ambition is to assess procedural change in terms of the theory of judicialization elaborated in Chapter 1. Several points of departure deserve emphasis up-front, because they are basic to our overall approach.

In Chapter 2, we dwelled at length on the ICC's evolution as an arbitral organization, tracing the fate of its self-appointed mission to relaunch a system of private dispute resolution for transnational business. Viewed from a procedural standpoint, the ICC (founded in 1919) has gone through four main phases of development. We do not claim that all that matters fits into neat temporal containers, of course. We recognize the messiness of procedural change; indeed, each successive period layered new institutions onto pre-existing foundations. Some legacies of the past have survived relatively intact (e.g. important functions of the Court), while others (e.g. mediation services) have been transformed, as actors adapted them to new conditions. Box 3.1 summarizes the main features of our periodization.

As previous chapters emphasized, the central factor driving procedural evolution—and the construction of arbitral authority more generally—is the growing intensity of party conflict, which has led IACs to institutionalize 'legal adversarialism' in various ways. We adapt Robert Kagan's widely accepted definition of such adversarialism, which has two components.[12] The first he calls 'legal contestation', wherein the 'disputants readily invoke legal rights, duties, and procedural requirements, backed by recourse to formal law enforcement'. The second component is 'litigant activism', which Kagan defines as 'a style of legal contestation in which the assertion of claims, the search for controlling legal arguments, and the gathering and submission of evidence are dominated not by judges or government officials but by disputing parties or interests, acting primarily through lawyers'. Taken together: 'Adversarial legalism combines formal decisionmaking style with participatory decisionmaking.' We would add one addendum, a caveat, to the application of the concept to ICC arbitration. As we will show, there is a great deal of participatory, 'litigant activism' in high stakes arbitration. But there is also a significant place for tribunals to activate themselves in fact-finding processes, and 'the search for controlling arguments'. These elements of hierarchy are necessary, if arbitration is to be effective in adversarial proceedings.

In counsel-driven, high stakes contests—wherein claimants will seek to maximize an award of damages, and the respondent's goal is to limit liability and damages—we can expect tactical negotiation and exploitation of procedures to be the norm. The tribunal, for its part, will seek to manage the situation

---

[12] Robert A Kagan, *Adversarial Legalism: The American Way of Law* (Harvard University Press, Cambridge 2003) 9.

Box 3.1 The Evolution of the ICC: Procedures

Period 1: Reviving Transnational Dispute Resolution

In a first period, 1920 to the outbreak of the Second World War, ICC officials sought to resuscitate certain core elements of the old *Lex Mercatoria*. They gave mediation and settlement a prominent place; they preferred the appointment of influential businessmen, rather than lawyers, to tribunals; and they encouraged awards in equity, rather than in law. While this effort largely failed, the house proved itself capable of responding to users' demands for a more judicialized system.

Period 2: Constructing an Enforcement Regime

In a second period, the decade of the 1950s, ICC officials concentrated their efforts on strengthening the arbitral order's capacity to produce final awards that would be enforced routinely in national courts. Most important, they initiated, and then actively participated in, the final drafting and ratification of the 1958 New York Convention. In this period, arbitral awards began to take the form of judicial rulings.

Period 3: Consolidating the New York Convention System

The third period—roughly the 1960s, 1970s, and 1980s—was dominated by the construction and consolidation of the New York Convention system. This process involved sustaining dialogues, both cooperative and conflictual, with other arbitration houses, the bar, national officials, and scholars concerning the nature and scope of arbitral authority. Although not all of its goals were attained, the ICC's success at assuring the relative autonomy of the arbitral order, and its own internal coherence as a legal system, cannot be overstated. By the end of the 1980s, legislatures and courts of the leading states in the major trading zones had firmly adopted pro-arbitration positions; and a highly structured market for arbitral business had emerged, one in which a growing number of important cities and states would aggressively compete for shares.*

Period 4: Institutionalizing the Legal System

Since 1990, a fourth period, the ICC has invested heavily in its capacity to meet the challenges of a diverse and ever-expanding docket. In particular, the house has developed new services, including: fast-track arbitration; a program to provide tribunals with 'neutral' technical experts; and a system for processing requests from parties for interim measures; and enhanced supervision in adversarial cases. These new services required new procedures and the building of new administrative competences. The present period is, in effect, one of full-fledged judicialization.

---

* See Chapter 2.

---

through the competences given to it by the Rules, which enable arbitrators, backed by the house, to control the parties. In state law, codes of judicial procedure have also evolved to manage increasing legal adversarialism, sometimes serving to intensify it,[13] and the same applies to arbitration. In the United

---

[13] Carl Tobias, 'Public Law Litigation and the Federal Rules of Civil Procedure' (1989) 74 Cornell Law Review 270.

States,[14] a series of amendments to the Federal Rules of Civil Procedure beginning in 1983 have 'cast the judge, not the litigants or their lawyers, as making the executive decisions in litigation'.[15] As Donald Elliot puts it: 'The notion that judges are to decide certain issues as "managers" implies that they must take into account the hard economic reality that procedural resources are limited and that decisions must be made on a sound, "business-like" basis as to which opportunities to pursue and which to pass by.'[16] As we will see, the presiding arbitrator in complex, adversarial cases at the ICC is also a manager, exercising 'executive' functions when it comes to controlling timetables, and disciplining the parties in other ways.

In the parlance of social science, our dependent variable—the legal phenomenon we are tracking and seeking to explain—is change in the Rules. In this chapter, we discuss every important change of the ICC's code, taking place across twelve versions.[17] The current 2012 Rules are contained in fifty-eight pages, forty-one articles, and five appendices, whereas the 1922 Rules comprised just eleven pages and twenty-four articles. In addition, the Secretariat provides detailed, official commentary on the code, and the jurisprudence of the Court. Currently, *The Secretariat's Guide to ICC Arbitration* ['the *Guide*'] comprises 506 pages, whereas the first *Explanatory Commentary* (1925) totalled all of five pages. As discussed below, the *Guide* is much more than a compendium of expert practical advice. It also lays down quasi-official interpretations of the Rules and the Appendices, which officials can force upon tribunals and the parties as mandatory. As we will show, the more adversarial the proceedings, the more counsel, arbitrators, and ICC staff will be governed by the commentary in the *Guide*.

In comparison, ICSID procedures have remained relatively stable.[18] The ICSID's founders designed a highly judicialized system from the outset, expecting adversarialism to be the normal state of affairs.[19] In the ICC, procedures, and their attendant administrative functions, have steadily evolved in light of users' demands and the house's own policy choices, which themselves have changed significantly over time. ICSID institutions, however, are strongly entrenched. Fundamental changes require treaty revision, and the decision-rule governing amendment is the unanimous consent of the contracting states (now totalling 153).[20] The ICSID Convention exhibits rigidity in another way: the Arbitration Rules, including

---

[14] For an overview of these changes, see Steven S Gensler, 'Judicial Case Management: Caught in the Crossfire' (2010) 60 Duke Law Journal 669. For their wider constitutional implications, see Judith Resnik, 'Trial as Error, Jurisdiction as Injury: Transforming the Meaning of Article III' (2000) 113 Harvard Law Review 924.

[15] E Donald Elliott, 'Managerial Judging and the Evolution of Procedure' (1986) 53 University of Chicago Law Review 306, 310.

[16] ibid 311.

[17] The ICC issued its first arbitration rules in 1922, subsequently amended in 1927, 1928, 1932, 1934, 1939, 1947, 1955, 1975, 1988, 1998, and 2012.

[18] The ICSID issued its first Arbitration Rules in 1966, subsequently amended in 1968, 1985, 2003, and 2006.

[19] It is worth recalling that the ICSID Convention lays down a detailed code of procedure, but not the substantive law of foreign investment (which was supplied only later by BITs and other treaties).

[20] Convention on the Settlement of Investment Disputes between States and Nationals of Other States (1967) 575 UNTS 159 ['ICSID Convention'], Article 66(2): 'Each amendment shall enter into

any procedures developed by tribunals for a specific case, cannot conflict with the Convention. The Arbitration Rules are slightly less entrenched, in that amendment requires a two-thirds majority of state representatives.[21] States have agreed to only three important revisions, all in 2006. The amendments conferred authority on tribunals to (a) admit third-party *amicus* briefs (which they had already begun doing on their own), (b) open and broadcast hearings to the public, and (c) hear preliminary motions to dismiss meritless claims.[22]

We now turn to how ICC procedures have developed to govern selected stages of the arbitral process, which we compare to ICSID Rules summarily. The ICC code reflects the fact that it operates a self-contained judicial system featuring a significant measure of hierarchy. Mechanisms of control, enshrined in the procedures, ensure the authority of (a) tribunals over the parties, and (b) the house over tribunals. In particular, the Rules serve three main (overlapping) functions. First, they establish the competences of the house's administrative apparatus, including the supervision of tribunals. Second, they codify the 'fiduciary duties' of the arbitrators, which is a relatively direct indicator of the consolidation of the judicial model (Chapter 1). The Rules impose at least five binding duties: (a) to arbitrate in accordance with the Rules; (b) to maximize the efficiency of the proceedings; (c) to remain impartial with respect to the parties and to guarantee procedural due process; (d) to enforce the applicable law; and (e) to justify awards with reasons. Third, the Rules confer specific powers on tribunals with respect to the parties, not least, in order to enable tribunals to perform these duties in the face of conflict. Table 3.1 summarizes the fiduciary obligations of ICC and ICSID arbitrators, as codified in the Rules (see 'Conclusion' below).

Initiation

Arbitral proceedings can be long and costly. The parties will therefore consider the range of available alternatives before filing a dispute, and arbitral houses provide a menu of such options. The major houses offer mediation services, as well as fast-track arbitration (wherein time limits and costs are agreed upon in advance). While both the ICC and ICSID encourage parties to settle, house-organized mediation (also called 'conciliation') is only a very small part of their activity.

Yet, in the beginning, the ICC took a strong position in support of mediation.[23] Disputes were best resolved, it insisted in 1922, 'without recourse either to [national] courts or to arbitration properly so called'.[24] The 1922 Rules required parties to use

---

force 30 days after dispatch by the depositary of this Convention of a notification to Contracting States that all Contracting States have ratified, accepted or approved the amendment.'

[21] ICSID Convention, Article 6: 'The ICSID Administrative Council amends the Rules. The Administrative Council is composed of representatives of each Contracting State, and is chaired by the President of the International Bank for Reconstruction and Development (who has no vote).'

[22] For a detailed treatment, see Aurélia Antonietti, 'The 2006 Amendments to the ICSID Rules and Regulations and the Additional Facility Rules' (2006) 21 ICSID Review—Foreign Investment Law Journal 427.

[23] International Chamber of Commerce, *International Commercial Arbitration—Practical Hints* (ICC, Paris 1935) [*Practical Hints*], 3: 'Conciliation should be tried before arbitration.'

[24] ICC Rules of Conciliation (Good Offices) and Arbitration (1922), Introduction (as cited in Stuart Hamilton, 'ICC Conciliation: A Glimpse into History' in *Special supplement 2001—ADR: International Applications* (ICC Publishing, 2001) 23–4).

the ICC's 'good offices' for mediation before proceeding to arbitration. Parties were to submit their disputes to a standing body, called the 'Administrative Commission', which would then make 'friendly suggestions' toward settlement.[25] Initially, the procedure appeared to be quite successful: between 1923 and 1925, only five of the ninety-one cases (95 per cent) submitted to the ICC went to arbitration; in the 1934 to 1938 period, even after the 1934 Rules made the mediation phase voluntary, the parties settled 81 per cent of the cases without the help of arbitrators.[26] As discussed in Chapter 2, mediation fitted the ICC's early mission, to revive the old *Lex Mercatoria* ideal of dispute resolution. The central purpose of third-party dispute resolution was to restore good relations between traders, through mediated settlements or equity decisions of peers versed in trade usages and customs, rather than to declare a winner or loser through a judgment in law.[27]

By the mid 1950s,[28] the ICC had committed to making arbitration a full substitute for litigation in domestic courts. The success of this project had the effect of marginalizing its mediation services, which now operate as a subsidiary settlement regime. Arbitration dominates the house's activities.[29] In 1997, it registered 462 arbitration cases, but only seven requests for mediation.[30] The next year, the ICC christened the new version of the code, the 'Rules of Arbitration' replacing the 'Rules of Conciliation [Mediation] and Arbitration' (a title dating from the 1920s).[31] In 2015, parties filed sixteen requests for mediation, of which twelve were required by prior contractual agreement. In three of the remaining four requests (each a unilateral filing), the other disputing party rejected mediation.[32]

In ISA, the story ends on a similar note. ICSID offers mediation services under its Rules[33] and the founders of ICSID apparently expected 'conciliation' to be a central activity of the Centre.[34] Although ICSID still encourages recourse to

---

[25] ICC Rules of Conciliation (Good Offices) and Arbitration (1922), Section A, Article I.

[26] International Chamber of Commerce, *Brochure from the International Chamber of Commerce* (ICC Publishing, Paris 1938) 14.

[27] *Practical Hints* (n 23), 4: 'The more conciliatory the parties show themselves, the more likelihood there is that they will remain on good terms and continue to do profitable business together in the future.'

[28] As late as 1954, the ICC still counselled that '[c]onciliation is always to be preferred to Arbitration …'. See *Practical Hints* (n 23), 4.

[29] In 1969, the ICC reported that users filed only a 'relatively modest number' of mediation cases. See '50 ans d'arbitrage de la CCI' *Nouvelles de la CCI* (Paris, June–July 1969) 35, No 5–6: '… le nombre relativement modeste des recours à la conciliation'.

[30] International Chamber of Commerce, '1997 Statistical Report' (1998) 10(1) ICC International Court of Arbitration Bulletin 4 ['1997 Statistical Report'].

[31] The ICC then elaborated a separate code to govern the various modes of mediation on offer: the 2001 Alternative Dispute Resolution Rules ['ADR Rules']. In 2012, only 21 new cases were filed under the ADR Rules compared to 759 arbitration cases. See International Chamber of Commerce, '2012 Statistical Report' (2013) 24(1) International Court of Arbitration Bulletin. In 2014, a new code, the Mediation Rules, superseded the ADR Rules.

[32] International Chamber of Commerce, '2015 ICC Dispute Resolution Statistics' (2016) 26(1) ICC International Court of Arbitration Bulletin 9 ['2015 ICC Dispute Resolution Statistics'].

[33] Chapter 3.

[34] The founders began developing what would become the ICSID system in the wake of mediation efforts on the part of the World Bank in the early 1950s: see the World Bank, 'Oral History Program:

mediation, 'as a relatively low-cost alternative to arbitration that may better preserve business relationships between the parties',[35] the core of the Centre's business is ISA. In its history, ICSID has administered 497 arbitrations, but only nine mediations.[36]

In ICA, parties choose arbitration, rules of procedure, and an arbitral centre at the *ex ante* contracting moment, or they may do so after the eruption of a dispute, by agreement. All of the major houses strongly encourage pre-consent. The ICC asks parties to incorporate the following standard clause into their contract, the current version stipulating that:

All disputes arising out of or in connection with the present contract shall be finally settled under the Rules of Arbitration of the ICC by one or more arbitrators appointed in accordance with the said Rules.[37]

In 2012, the ICC modified its Rules to make it clear that it could arbitrate investor-state disputes arising under a treaty, and not only those involving state entities that are parties to a contract with an investor.[38] The move has apparently paid off: the ICC registered eighteen filings for ISA under bilateral investment treaties in the 2013 to 2015 period.[39] For virtually all ICSID Convention cases, a treaty provides the basis of pre-consent (see Chapter 2).

The most important preliminary procedures concern (a) the filing, (b) payment of fees, (c) the selection of arbitrators, and (d) the determination of the seat. Developments in each of these areas reflect the evolution of the ICC, from a less formal regime modelled on an older conception of the *Lex Mercatoria*, into a more autonomous, judicialized legal system.

Transcript of Interview with Aron Broches' (1984) <http://documents.worldbank.org/curated/en/269421468179649792/pdf/789460v20TRN0B0ion010April018001984.pdf> accessed 3 January 2016, 29.

[35] ICSID Secretariat, 'Possible Improvements of the Framework for ICSID Arbitration' (Discussion Paper of 22 October 2004) <https://icsid.worldbank.org/apps/ICSIDWEB/resources/Documents/Possible%20Improvements%20of%20the%20Framework%20of%20ICSID%20Arbitration.pdf> accessed 3 January 2016, [18]. See also the follow-up white paper: ICSID Secretariat, 'Suggested Changes to the ICSID Rules and Regulations' (Working Paper of the ICSID Secretariat of 12 May 2005) <https://icsid.worldbank.org/apps/ICSIDWEB/resources/Documents/Suggested%20to%20the%20ICSID%20Rules%20and%20Regulations.pdf> accessed 3 January 2016, para 5.
[36] ICSID, 'Cases' <https://icsid.worldbank.org/apps/ICSIDWEB/cases/Pages/AdvancedSearch.aspx?cte=CD18> accessed 3 January 2016.
[37] International Chamber of Commerce, 'Standard ICC Arbitration Clauses' <http://www.iccwbo.org/products-and-services/arbitration-and-adr/arbitration/standard-icc-arbitration-clauses/> accessed 3 January 2016.
[38] The *Guide* (n 10), para 3-2: 'The term "disputes" in Article 1(2) has replaced "business disputes of an international character" found in Article 1(1) of the 1998 Rules. This change removes any doubt that all disputes, including ... investor-state disputes concerning claims made under a treaty ... may be resolved by arbitration under the Rules.' For related changes and a commentary, see International Chamber of Commerce, 'ICC Arbitration Commission Report on Arbitration Involving States and State Entities under the ICC Rules of Arbitration' (2015) <http://www.iccwbo.org/Advocacy-Codes-and-Rules/Document-centre/2012/ICC-Arbitration-Commission-Report-on-Arbitration-Involving-States-and-State-Entities-under-the-ICC-Rules-of-Arbitration/> accessed 3 January 2015.
[39] International Chamber of Commerce, '2013 Statistical Report' (2014) 25(1) ICC International Court of Arbitration Bulletin 5; 2015 ICC Dispute Resolution Statistics (n 32).

The filing of a request for arbitration binds the parties to the Rules and subjects them to the house's administrative authority. Claimants file by way of a summary brief of the case. The 1922 Rules required three items to be furnished: the names and address of the parties; a copy of the contractual instruments relevant to the transaction and the dispute; and a brief description of the claim.[40] The current Rules demand much more, inter alia: a full explication of the dispute and the '[legal] basis upon which the claims are made'; 'a statement of the relief sought, together with the amounts of any quantified claims and … an estimate of the monetary value of any other claims'; and 'all relevant particulars' concerning 'the number of arbitrators and their choice', as well as 'any observations or proposals as to the place of the arbitration, the applicable rules of law, and the language of the arbitration'.[41] The ICC Secretariat transmits this information to the respondent(s), who is expected to answer within thirty days.

Initiating arbitration entails charges, in the form of a flat-fee payment at filing, and advances on the tribunal's fees, the amounts of which the Court sets.[42] Arbitration is today an expensive venture. It was not always so. Under the ICC Rules of 1922, arbitration was a freely provided service: '[t]he arbitrators … shall render their services gratuitously'.[43] Appointments were taken to be 'honorary'[44] and prestige conferring. In 1934, the Court acquired the authority to fix fees, along with a mandate to keep costs 'as low as possible'.[45] In 1950, the ICC announced that the fees amounted to approximately 1 per cent of the disputed amounts,[46] a formula replaced by a fee schedule in 1955. Under the schedule, the ICC calculates costs primarily with respect to the amount in dispute.[47] Before certifying an award as final, the Court of Arbitration will fix the precise amount of the fees of the arbitrators. The parties also pay an administrative charge directly to the ICC for support services. Upon registration of an arbitration, the ICC Secretariat assigns a group—called the 'team' (*l'équipe*) in ICC parlance—to assist the parties through each stage of the proceedings, on a day-to-day basis if needed. According to an in-house audit of 2007, of the total cost of the arbitration, the parties can expect to pay, on average, 82 per cent to counsel, 16 per cent to arbitrators (in fees and expenses), and 2 per cent to cover administrative support.[48]

ICC officials have always been involved in 'the constitution of the tribunal'. In the 1920s and 1930s, the Executive Committee of the Court of Arbitration appointed the arbitrators,[49] with little or no direct involvement of the parties. In its view, the

[40] ICC Rules of Conciliation (Good Offices) and Arbitration (1922), Article X/XXX.
[41] ICC Rules of Arbitration (2012), Article 14(3).
[42] The filing fee is now set at US$3,000: see ICC Rules of Arbitration (2012), Article 4(4)(b).
[43] ICC Rules of Conciliation (Good Offices) and Arbitration (1922), Articles XIX(e)/XL(e).
[44] *Practical Hints* (n 23), 7. It was not unusual for arbitrators to refuse the payment of fees in exchange for their services. In ICC Award No 301, for example, the arbitrator refused their fees.
[45] ICC Rules of Conciliation and Arbitration (1934), Annex on 'Costs and Expenses of Procedure'.
[46] See 'Un arbitrage vaut mieux qu'un procès' (1950) 16(10) L'Economie Internationale 5.
[47] Chapter 2 on costs. See also 1997 Statistical Report (n 30).
[48] International Chamber of Commerce, *ICC Arbitration Commission Report on Techniques for Controlling Time and Costs in Arbitration* (ICC, Paris 2007) 11.
[49] ICC Rules of Conciliation (Good Offices) and Arbitration (1922), Articles VI/XXVI: the Court of Arbitration 'shall request the National Committees to furnish it with the names of technically

'presence of an arbitrator nominated by the parties adds nothing to the fairness of the trial, the single arbitrator being quite as capable as an umpire of arriving at an impartial and just decision.'[50] The Court, in fact, strongly preferred one-person tribunals, although parties could request a three-member body.[51] Arbitrators selected were typically influential businessmen, and only rarely lawyers.[52] These dispositions fit the house's wider goal of building a resilient web of 'trust' relationships of global scope. The ICC boasted that it could select representatives of 'all the great industrial and trading industries of nearly every country in the world'.[53]

The regime did not last long, undermined by a burst of fiercely conflictual disputes. The wave of filings flooding the system in the 1930s, in the wake of currency devaluations and global depression, starkly revealed the system's incapacity to deal with heightened adversarialism. These cases also led to calls from users for awards-in-law, rather than equity, and for appellate review.[54] In response, the ICC increased the number of lawyers and judges in its pool of recommended arbitrators. In 1938, the house's list of fifty-six arbitrators included fifteen lawyers.[55] In the 1950s, the ICC abandoned the notion that the system's effectiveness depended primarily on 'trust',[56] prioritizing instead its capacity to produce final awards, enforceable in the courts. Five years after the signing of the 1958 New York Convention, the house reported that 'the [intrinsically] legal nature of international arbitration leads to a predominance of personalities drawn from the legal professions'.[57]

Parties also demanded direct input into the appointment of arbitrators. In its revision of the Rules of 1947, the ICC relented,[58] and for high stakes cases, party-dominated appointments of three-member tribunals quickly became the norm. In the most commonly selected procedure, Party X (claimant) and Party Y (respondent) each appoint a 'co-arbitrator'; the two co-arbitrators then select a presiding arbitrator. The president of the tribunal will take the lead in organizing the proceedings, interfacing with the ICC team and other officials, and drafting the final award.[59]

We can specify a simple model of appointment procedures under adversarial conditions,[60] in which each party seeks to control the appointment of the tribunal. For

---

qualified arbitrators, as and when required, for appointment as arbitrators in the cases submitted to it, and from amongst them the Committee shall proceed to appoint'.

[50] *Practical Hints* (n 23), 5.

[51] ICC Rules of Conciliation (Good Offices) and Arbitration (1922), Articles XII/XXXII. This rule was amended in 1928 in order to allow the Court of Arbitration to appoint three-member tribunals 'if the importance of the case warrants the appointment of three arbitrators'.

[52] International Chamber of Commerce, 'Explanatory Commentary of the Rules of Conciliation (Good Offices) and Arbitration' (1925) Appendix to Brochure No 21, 4. See also *Practical Hints* (n 23), 6–7.

[53] *Practical Hints* (n 23), 7.   [54] Chapters 2 and 4.

[55] Here, the term 'lawyer' encompasses attorneys, judges, law professors, and in-house lawyers.

[56] In 1963, the Chairman of the ICC Court stated that 'arbitration has progressively lost its old characteristic of being founded on personal trust; this has given way to an increasingly marked institutionalisation.' See International Chamber of Commerce, *Guide to ICC Arbitration* (ICC Publishing, Paris 1962) 6.

[57] ibid 10.   [58] ICC Rules of Conciliation and Arbitration (1947), Article 12(1).

[59] ICC Rules of Arbitration (2012), Article 12.

[60] We offer a simple model of the strategic situation, not a perfect representation of reality. Put differently, the model generates a hypothesis; the hypothesis is supported to the extent that it applies, in general or on average.

Party X, the optimal procedure would be to appoint a sole arbitrator unilaterally, at its own discretion. Since the same is true for Party Y, stalemate is the likely result. A second best procedure, which appeals to rationales of both choice and fairness, would be to permit each party to name a co-arbitrator. The formation of a two-member tribunal is not a viable option: to the extent that the co-arbitrators reflect the respective legal positions of each party, deadlock will be the result. The present system solves the dilemma: X and Y each name a co-arbitrator, and the co-arbitrators select a third member, the president or chairman. If the co-arbitrators fail to agree, the ICC steps in. In such a system, both parties are equally vulnerable to the tribunal and, in particular, to the presiding figure, but they expect a co-arbitrator to ensure that the tribunal takes their interests into account. These logics have been institutionalized. In the 2007 to 2011 period,[61] parties selected co-arbitrators in 95 per cent of all three-member tribunals constituted. So long as each party believes it will be better off by reciprocally agreeing not to challenge the other's arbitrators, it would seem, the present system will remain stable. When it comes to a single-person tribunal, the unacceptable option for each party is to allow the other to name the arbitrator. The likely result, deadlock again, means that the ICC will act as appointing authority. During the 2007 to 2011 period, the ICC appointed 77 per cent of all single-arbitrator tribunals.[62]

Appointment procedures are one important area in which adversarialism has hindered, rather than driven, the move from the contractual to the judicial model. As leading arbitrators report, counsel now routinely engage in the vetting of candidates, through background checks and interviews, which may now 'be becoming part of the unwritten code of . . . selection';[63] counsel even instruct their co-arbitrator on the choice of chairman.[64] From the standpoint of the contractual model, participants and observers may not be bothered much by such practices. With judicialization, however, anxiety has mounted, and become public. To guarantee the system's integrity and long-term legitimacy, some important figures advocate the creation of an elite college of arbitrators, from whom the house, or some 'neutral body', would select.[65] We discuss these issues in Chapter 6.

The last important preliminary choice concerns the seat. Since 1927, the Rules have conferred upon the Court the authority to specify the seat, unless the parties agree otherwise.[66] In its early days, the members of the Court were clearly disposed to selecting the defendant's residence as the place of arbitration. This reflected the view, now obsolete, that the arbitral award comprised an act (akin

---

[61] The *Guide* (n 10), para 3-431 (Table 13), para 3-457 (Table 17).

[62] Overall, 60 per cent of all cases were handled by three-member tribunals and 40 per cent by a sole arbitrator.

[63] Gerald Aksen, 'The Tribunal's Appointment' in Lawrence W Newman and Richard D Hill (eds), *The Leading Arbitrators' Guide to International Arbitration* (Juris Publishing, New York 2014) 337–8.

[64] ibid 341.

[65] Jan Paulsson, *The Idea of Arbitration* (Oxford University Press, Oxford 2014) Chapters 5 and 9. See also Jan Paulsson, 'Moral Hazard in International Arbitration' (2010) 25 ICSID Review—Foreign Investment Law Journal 339.

[66] ICC Rules of Conciliation and Arbitration (1927), Rule 18(1): 'The place of the arbitration shall be fixed by the Court, unless agreed upon by the parties.'

to a judgment of dispute resolver of first instance) that was fully controllable at appeal.[67] Even before the development of the New York Convention system, the Court (or the parties, or the tribunal) took great pains to select arbitration-friendly seats.[68] As the Convention system took root, national courts in the main trading zones renounced routine merit review of awards, judicial annulments became exceedingly rare events, and the number of viable seats expanded. Today, given that the courts of the seat remain privileged sites of annulment actions, the house and its tribunals pay close attention to the seat's law, in particular, to applicable mandatory law (state law that cannot be modified by agreement between the parties).[69]

Today, the ICC encourages parties to select seats on their own, as part of the arbitral agreement. In the 2007 to 2011 period, the Court fixed the seat in only 12 per cent of all cases,[70] falling to just 7 per cent in 2014.[71] Transactional lawyers and the arbitral bar possess good information on the relative advantages of potential seats. Arbitration-friendliness remains a key consideration, but other factors may determine choice from among the options, including the quality of the arbitration facilities, transport, and the availability of comfortable hotels and restaurants. Dominating this part of the market are Paris, London, Geneva, Singapore, New York, Zurich, Hong Kong, and Vienna. Each of these cities is located in states that devote enormous resources to maintain their competitiveness in the market for arbitration.[72]

At ICSID, the investor-claimant initiates the process by providing the basic information on the parties, the instruments of consent, and observations as to why the dispute constitutes 'a legal dispute arising directly out of an investment',[73] the latter demonstration being a basic requirement for jurisdiction. The Secretariat will then review the content of the request for the purposes of registration, which the Secretary-General will reject if 'the dispute is manifestly outside the jurisdiction of the Centre'.[74] Claimants pay a filing fee,[75] and both

---

[67] In 1924, the ICC put it this way: 'The Court decides where the arbitration shall take place. It tries if possible to choose the country of the defendant; in other words, that of the debtor. When an award is made in the country of the party who will have eventually to pay, the award has the character of a *national award* and it is easier, in case of dispute, to have the award enforced than if it were made in another country' (emphasis added). See International Chamber of Commerce, *The Arbitration of the International Chamber of Commerce* (ICC Publishing, Paris 1924) 6.

[68] In 1949, the ICC chose Amsterdam, Basel, The Hague, Lausanne, Paris, and Stockholm—all places known to be arbitration-friendly—as seats even where the defendants resided in other countries. See *World Trade* (May 1949) 31.

[69] Under Rule 6 of Appendix II of the ICC Arbitration Rules (2012), the Court has a duty to do so in its scrutiny of draft awards.

[70] The *Guide* (n 10), para 3-686: When it does, '[t]he quality of the arbitration law and the courts is crucial'.

[71] International Chamber of Commerce, '2014 ICC Dispute Resolution Statistics' (2014) 25(1) ICC International Court of Arbitration Bulletin.

[72] ibid.   [73] ICSID Institution Rules (2006), Rule 2.

[74] ICSID Institution Rules (2006), Rule 6.

[75] The fee is now set at US$25,000: see ICSID Administrative and Financial Regulations (2006), Regulation 16; ICSID Schedule of Fees (2013), para 1.

parties are required to give periodic advances on administrative charges and expenses,[76] as well as those of the arbitrators,[77] as determined by the Secretary-General. Unlike ICC arbitration, the total amount of the arbitrators' fees will depend on the time spent by the arbitrators on the case,[78] not on the values at stake.[79] Tribunals at ICSID are composed of three members: each party names 'an arbitrator appointed by it', and suggests or agrees on a second name, proposed as president. If the parties fail to agree on the president, the Chairman of the Administrative Council will appoint one, typically on a recommendation by ICSID's Secretary-General.[80] Finally, ICSID Convention proceedings dispense entirely with the notion of a seat, annulment functions taking place in house under the 'annulment procedure'.

The Arbitration

Once an ICC tribunal is established, it will seek the parties' agreement on the basics of the case: a relatively comprehensive overview of the dispute and a clear statement of claims; a statement specifying the scope of the tribunal's authority; and the details of procedure, including a timetable for the proceedings. Three Articles of the 2012 Rules now govern these consultations. Rule 22(1) demands that the tribunal and the parties 'make every effort to conduct the arbitration in an expeditious and cost-effective manner, having regard to the complexity and value of the dispute'. Rule 22(2) grants discretion to the tribunal to 'adopt such procedural measures as it considers appropriate, provided that they are not contrary to any agreement of the parties'. It then places arbitrators under a general obligation to ensure due process, under Rule 22(4): 'In all cases, the arbitral tribunal shall act fairly and impartially and ensure that each party has a reasonable opportunity to present its case.' Rules 23 and 24 establish the procedures for developing the procedural framework that will govern the case.

A distinctive feature of ICC arbitration,[81] dating from the 1920s,[82] is the tribunal's duty, now specified as Rule 23 (2012), to produce a legally binding

---

[76] The charge is now US$32,000: see ICSID Schedule of Fees (2013), para 5.

[77] ICSID Schedule of Fees (2013), para 6; ICSID Administrative and Financial Regulations (2006), Regulation 14.

[78] The arbitrators' fees, not including expenses, amount to US$3,000 per day: see ICSID Schedule of Fees (2013), para 3.

[79] We are not aware of any substantial research on costs in ISA. To take one example, in the case of *Vigotop Ltd v Hungary*, the arbitral fees and expenses amounted to a total of US$664,855.07 (for a disputed amount of approximately €300 million): see *Vigotop Ltd v Hungary* (ICSID Case No ARB/11/22), Award of 1 October 2014, [635–6].

[80] ICSID Administrative and Financial Regulations (2006), Rules 3 and 4, implementing ICSID Convention, Article 37(2)(b).

[81] Although '[a]ll the arbitration rules made in the last two decades or so make it a duty on the tribunal to draw up a procedural timetable', only the ICC requires parties to sign the Terms of Reference: see Paulo Patocchi and Robert Briner, 'The Role of the President of the Arbitral Tribunal' in Lawrence W Newman and Richard D Hill (eds), *The Leading Arbitrators' Guide to International Arbitration* (Juris, New York 2014) 289–93.

[82] The Terms of Reference appeared in the ICC Arbitration Rules of 1922 (under the name of 'form of submission to arbitration'): see ICC Rules of Conciliation (Good Offices) and Arbitration (1922), Article XXXIV.

document called the 'Terms of Reference'.[83] This text, which tribunals may only revise with the agreement of the parties, 'anchors the arbitration and serves as a guide to which the parties and the arbitral tribunal may refer throughout the proceedings'. The *Guide* casts the process of fixing Terms in a positive light:

> It forces arbitrators to engage with the file at an early stage of the proceedings and develop an understanding of the case. Further, it encourages the parties to determine the parameters of their dispute and identify those issues on which the arbitration hinges. If done properly, this exercise allows the parties to construct their cases clearly and comprehensively, making subsequent written and oral submissions more focused. The collaborative and cooperative atmosphere created by the process of preparing the Terms of Reference can even lead to settlement on some or all issues or at least a more cooperative approach to the subsequent arbitration proceedings.[84]

The *Guide* contains eighty-five paragraphs of detailed commentary on Rule 23. It provides: quasi-official interpretations of each of the four clauses of that Article; practical advice to arbitrators, illustrated by examples of what the house considers to be best practices; blunt assessments of the relative costs and benefits of the various approaches to the negotiations available to parties and arbitrators; and discussion of how the Secretariat and the Court supervises this process, including with respect to submission of the Terms, and the Court's authority to approve or reject them.

According to Rule 23(2), the tribunal must submit the Terms to the Court, signed by the parties, within two months of receiving the file. The *Guide* makes it clear that, in managing this process, the tribunal owes duties both to the parties, and to the house (mandatory Rules being non-derogable). While the general due process clause contained in Rule 22(4) also applies, the *Guide* stipulates that: 'the tribunal must provide all parties with a reasonable opportunity to participate in the preparation of the Terms of Reference and to sign them'.[85] Rule 23(3) anticipates the possibility that one of the parties will refuse to participate in the negotiations,[86] or may refuse to sign the Terms. In such cases, the ICC Court may extend the time limit, or approve the Terms on its own.[87]

---

[83] The *Guide* (n 10), para 3-862: 'The arbitral tribunal and the parties should remember that the Terms of Reference are a mandatory initial step in the arbitral process and that delaying their completion will diminish their utility.'

[84] ibid para 3-827.

[85] ibid para 3-873. See also para 3-831: 'Given the binding force the document has with respect to a number of procedural matters, and the fact that all parties' signatures are required, the parties necessarily have a role to play in drafting the document.'

[86] ibid para 3-873: '[The tribunal] must also exert discipline by promptly submitting the Terms of Reference to the Court for approval where it appears that a party's refusal to sign is dilatory or otherwise unreasonable.'

[87] ibid para 3-880: 'Article 23(3) empowers the Court to approve the Terms of Reference where one or more parties are unwilling to sign the document or are not participating in the proceedings. It offers an alternative means of giving formal recognition to the Terms of Reference to allow them to come into effect and enable the arbitration to proceed.'

The *Guide* frankly acknowledges that the adversarial postures of 'uncooperative'[88] counsel could paralyze the proceedings:

Regrettably, parties sometimes misunderstand the purpose of the Terms of Reference and adopt a litigious attitude when discussing their content. Such behaviour is generally unwarranted as the parties' positions can usually be protected by appropriate reservations or caveats. That said, the arbitral tribunal should avoid simply insisting on and pushing through its own ideas where a party expresses genuine concern or justified objections. Rather, it should seek to build consensus amongst all involved through persuasion and/or adapting the draft in a way that removes contentious elements or clarifies that they will be decided in the arbitration.[89]

The ICC Secretariat—through the conduit of the team—closely supervises these consultations. Even when they appear to be going smoothly, officials remain vigilant, not least, to strengthen the tribunal's position in later stages of supervision. 'The Secretariat knows the standards applied by the Court when approving Terms of Reference', the *Guide* warns, if the tribunal 'submits Terms … that are unlikely to be approved, the Secretariat will usually … request a modified version'.[90] Staff and repeat arbitrators know that the Court will refer back to the Terms when it engages in its review of the final draft of the award, not least, 'as a starting point for determining whether all claims have been dealt with in the final award'.[91] Although the Court's approval of the Terms is normally presumed 'if all parties have signed them',[92] the team and the Secretariat work to ensure that tribunals meet the house's standards.

In 2012, the ICC introduced Rule 24, which requires tribunals to organize a 'Case Management Conference' [CMC] for the tailoring of specific procedural orders,[93] and for establishing an overall timetable. This move was dictated by efficiency concerns in the context of increasing adversarialism. The *Guide* itself points to those 'regrettable situations' in which the parties 'adopt unnecessarily litigious tactics (sometimes called "guerrilla tactics")' as a major problem.[94] The practice developed under the tutelage of 'experienced' arbitrators, working under the 1998 Rules, before the ICC moved to codify it as a means of reducing the intensity of party conflict during the Terms of Reference stage.[95] In the CMC, the tribunal, in

---

[88] ibid para 3-873. [89] ibid para 3-831.
[90] ibid para 3-884. [91] ibid para 3-829. [92] ibid para 3-880.
[93] ibid para 3-912: 'The mandatory case management conference is a tool designed to ensure a tailor-made procedure. The new Appendix IV, to which Article 24(1) explicitly refers, provides some guidance on the topics that may be addressed during the case management conference.'
[94] ibid para 3-914.
[95] ibid para 3-856: 'Some arbitral tribunals … try to regulate as much of the procedure as possible in the Terms of Reference … The perceived advantage of this approach is that it elevates these orders to agreements between the parties from which they cannot deviate without a subsequent agreement. However, it also results in time and effort being spent on regulating matters that can prove controversial and delay preparation of the Terms of Reference. Many details may even prove redundant … Most importantly, rules agreed in the Terms of Reference may restrict the arbitral tribunal's procedural flexibility in responding to unforeseen situations at a later stage of the proceedings.'

consultation with the parties, works to 'devise procedures allowing the dispute to be dealt with as efficiently as possible'.[96]

Appendix 4 of the Rules (2012) and the *Guide* provide detailed commentary on best practices for organizing the CMC.[97] Tribunals, for example, should split a complex arbitration into its constituent parts (e.g. jurisdiction, requests for interim measures, liability, damages), anticipating that each may require separate proceedings and the rendering of a 'partial award', which will prepare the way for a 'final award'. Tribunals should focus counsel's attention on the most important issues, if need be using threats to punish parties (in its award on costs) that pursue an 'unwarranted complication of the proceedings'. The CMC sets the rules for the testimony of witnesses and experts, and for discovery and exchanges between the parties. Rule 24(2) obliges tribunals to fix timelines for each stage in the form of a 'procedural timetable'.[98] Due process obligations fully apply; and the timetable, and any subsequent modifications to it, must be submitted to the parties and the Court.[99] As with the Terms, the timetable focuses the house's supervisory functions. It 'has become', the *Guide* indicates, 'a means by which the Court can monitor the progress of a case'.

The next stage, the so-called 'instruction phase', is typically the longest of an ICC arbitration, and can take months, or even years. It usually consists of one or more exchanges of written submissions, the production of documents (discovery), and oral hearings for pleadings and the examination of witnesses. The evolution of rules governing this phase is an important measure of the judicialization of ICC arbitration. Here we will focus only on the production of documents and due process requirements.

The ICC has succeeded in blending procedural elements found in different national orders to create an autonomous, transnational evidentiary system.[100] At its founding, the practices of the French civil law system dominated ICC practice. In this tradition, the judge manages the case, including the active gathering of the evidence on which it will base its judgment. In 1928, the ICC announced that its arbitrators possessed 'full authority to take all steps necessary to ascertain the facts …';[101] and the 1947 Rules provided that the tribunal 'shall take such steps as [it] may think fit for the purpose of ascertaining the facts relating to the case …'.[102] But the consensual nature of arbitration constrained tribunals, which did not possess authority to compel disclosure, for example. Growing adversarialism intensified the demands for discovery, including on the part of the tribunals themselves.[103] Arbitrators will not be able to render an 'accurate

---

[96] ibid para 3-918.   [97] ibid para 3-913.   [98] ibid para 3-918.

[99] ICC Rules of Arbitration (2012), Article 24(2).

[100] Document production is 'one of the most remarkable examples of a merger between different civil procedure approaches': see Gabrielle Kaufmann-Kohler, 'Globalization of Arbitral Procedure' (2003) 36 Vanderbilt Journal of Transnational Law 1313, 1325.

[101] International Chamber of Commerce, *Arbitration by the International Chamber of Commerce* (ICC Publishing, Paris 1928) 12.

[102] ICC Rules of Conciliation and Arbitration (1947), Article 17(1).

[103] Sigvard Jarvin, 'Aspects of the Arbitral Proceedings' in *Special Supplement 1997—The New 1998 ICC Rules of Arbitration: Proceedings of the ICC Conference Presenting the Rules* (ICC Publishing, Paris 1997) 38, 40.

award',[104] after all, if material facts go unreported or unverified. In the 1980s and 1990s, the system, in effect, oscillated between (a) the civil law tradition, which takes a restrictive stance toward discovery, and (b) the adversarial tradition of common law countries, where judges commonly do possess the power to compel disclosure.

The Rules of 1998 struck a balance between these traditions, codifying the tribunal's authority to order a party to produce specific evidence, upon the request of another party, or upon its own initiative.[105] At ICSID, the Convention provides that arbitrators may, unless the parties otherwise agree, 'call upon the parties to produce documents or other evidence', and the tribunal can initiate its own investigations as well.[106] In practice, ICC and ICSID tribunals proceed in the same way. Party X files a request listing the documents sought from Party Y; insofar as Party Y does not comply with the demand, X may ask the tribunal to compel Y to produce the documents. In handling such requests, arbitrators routinely refer to a set of soft law rules, now taken for granted as authoritative by counsel and tribunals, the International Bar Association Rules on the Taking of Evidence in International Arbitration. In particular, Article 9 of the IBA Rules establishes grounds to reject X's demand, such as lack of relevance or materiality, presumptions of confidentiality, or consideration of efficiency.[107]

When it comes to discovery, there is an obvious tension between values associated with rendering an accurate award and economy. The present Rules require tribunals: 'to avoid requests for document production when appropriate in order to control time and cost'; 'to limit such requests to documents or categories of documents that are relevant and material to the outcome of the case'; and 'to establish reasonable time limits for the production of documents'.[108] The system relies on mechanisms of self-enforcement backed by sanctions. The IBA Rules, which virtually all arbitrators consult and apply in both ICA and ISA, provide that if a party fails to comply with an order to produce a document, 'the Arbitral Tribunal may infer that such document would be adverse to the interests of that Party'.[109]

The instruction phase deals with discovery in the context of due process. In this area, too, the ICC initially distinguished arbitration and adjudication, associating what it called 'the fairness of the trial' with the personal integrity of the arbitrators themselves. The process would be fair because the ICC would appoint impartial

[104] Chapter 1.
[105] ICC Rules of Arbitration (2012), Article 25(5): 'At any time during the proceedings, the Arbitral Tribunal may summon any party to provide additional evidence.'
[106] ICSID Convention, Article 43(1).
[107] IBA Rules on the Taking of Evidence in International Arbitration (2010), Article 9(2).
[108] ICC Rules of Arbitration (2012), Appendix IV, Article 3(d).
[109] IBA Rules on the Taking of Evidence in International Arbitration (2010), Article 9(5). Still, the ICC Secretariat advises arbitrators to 'exercise caution in drawing an adverse inference': see The *Guide* (n 10), 277.

arbitrators who would apply the best practice standards of transnational business. The 1935 guide for users announced that the ICC:

can always find the right man, no matter what qualifications the parties are entitled to expect. [Even] if arbitrations have to take place in a country far distant from the domicile of either or both of the parties—in Shanghai or Buenos Aires, Quebec or Calcutta, Mexico or Helsingfors—the International Chamber is always able to find a competent arbitrator of neutral nationality and prove[n] impartiality.[110]

In the 1930s, parties pressed not only for more say in appointments, but also for the right to challenge their impartiality. In 1932, the ICC added a new provision permitting such demands.[111] In practice, challenges of ICC arbitrators have remained low, largely because of the logics of the appointment process described above.[112] The 1988 Rules require 'every arbitrator' to 'remain independent of the parties involved in the arbitration'.[113]

Principles of due process have evolved far beyond the presumption of impartiality; indeed, the regime has derived standards from judicial practice. In 1998, the ICC added an explicit due process clause to its Rules,[114] which now appears as Rule 22(4), discussed above. Many leading arbitrators consider this clause to have formally incorporated an expandable corpus of unwritten general principles of due process that they had been developing on their own in the absence of express authority. In the *Guide*, the Secretariat describes the provision as an 'overriding and fundamental principle of arbitration'.[115]

At ICSID, too, administrative officials closely assist and monitor proceedings. Each tribunal is assigned a 'secretary', who formally represents the Secretary-General within the tribunal, and who will function as the 'channel through which

---

[110] *Practical Hints* (n 23), 7.

[111] ICC Rules of Conciliation and Arbitration (1932), Article 12(3). An ICC official explained this change in these terms: 'The confidence of both parties to the dispute in the impartiality of the arbitrator is one of the elements most essential to successful arbitration, and it is this very factor of confidence on which the argument is based in favour of the settlement of disputes between nationals of different countries by international arbitration instead of in a law court in which the foreign party frequently, though possibly without justification, has not complete confidence ... In view of this position, it was not considered sufficient to leave the right to challenge the arbitrator to be inferred from [the old rules].' See Robert Marx, 'The Court of Arbitration of the International Chamber of Commerce—Revision of the Rules' (1931) 11 World Trade 301.

[112] The *Guide* (n 10), 175 (Table 20, showing that challenges have been brought in approximately 4 per cent of the ICC cases between 2001 and 2011). For a contrary view, see Rémy Gerbay, 'Is the End Nigh Again? An Empirical Assessment of the "Judicialization" of International Arbitration' (2014) 25(2) The American Review of International Arbitration 223, 231.

[113] ICC Rules of Conciliation and Arbitration (1988), Article 2(7). It is obvious that the parties do not expect the same level of impartiality from the party-appointed arbitrators as from the presiding arbitrator or from those nominated by the ICC Court. Indeed, counsel, arbitrators, and ICC officials acknowledge that party-appointed arbitrators will often back the position of the party that appointed them (discussed in Chapter 2). See Serge Lazareff, 'L'arbitre singe ou comment assassiner l'arbitrage' in Gerald Aksen et al (eds), *Liber Amicorum in honour of Robert Briner—Global Reflections on International Law, Commerce and Dispute Resolution* (ICC Publishing, Paris 2005) 483.

[114] ICC Rules of Conciliation and Arbitration (1988), Article 15(2): 'In all cases, the Arbitral Tribunal shall act fairly and impartially and ensure that each party has a reasonable opportunity to present its case.' See also the *Guide* (n 10), para 3-814.

[115] The *Guide* (n 10), para 3-814.

the parties may request particular services'.[116] The first important task of a tribunal is to produce the procedural orders that are 'required for the conduct of the proceeding',[117] initially through a 'preliminary procedural consultation with the parties'.[118] Either the Secretary-General or the tribunal may initiate consultations, although some elements of the process are de facto mandatory.[119] A 'conference' then follows, to establish non-contested facts and to discuss settlement,[120] after which the tribunal will issue first procedural orders and the timetable. In each of these phases, tribunals are required to 'consult' with the Secretary-General.[121] While Rule 44 of the ICSID Convention expressly gives tribunals the authority to decide 'any question' concerning procedures,[122] orders may not conflict with the Convention, or those Arbitration Rules that derive from the Convention's mandatory rules.[123] The Secretary-General is responsible for ensuring compliance. The Convention further establishes the tribunal's duty to guarantee due process to the parties at every stage of the proceedings, and to avoid any 'serious departure from a fundamental rule of procedure' as grounds for annulment of the award.[124] Through the interpretation of tribunals and annulment committees, a long list of otherwise unwritten due process requirements have emerged in ISA (see Chapter 4).

The Award

After pleadings, the tribunal drafts the award. The Rule requiring tribunals to submit drafts to the ICC Court dates from 1925, while the reason-giving requirement appeared only much later (Chapter 2). During the 1927 to 1947 period, the Court determined, on a case-by-case basis, whether grounds should be stated in awards,[125] based on whether the law of the seat required reasons (the Dutch approach) or discouraged them (the English approach).[126] By the end of the 1960s, at the latest,

---

[116] ICSID Administrative and Financial Regulations (2003), Regulation 25.
[117] ICSID Arbitration Rules (2006), Rule 19.
[118] ICSID Arbitration Rules (2006), Rule 20.
[119] The ICSID Secretariat provides tribunals with a checklist: see Christoph H Schreuer et al, *The ICSID Convention—A Commentary* (2nd edn, Cambridge University Press, Cambridge 2009) ['*Commentary*'], para 29 on Article 44 and Rule 20.
[120] ICSID Arbitration Rules (2006), Rule 21.
[121] ICSID Arbitration Rules (2006), Rule 13.
[122] ICSID Convention, Article 44: 'Any arbitration proceeding shall be conducted in accordance with the provisions of this Section and, except as the parties otherwise agree, in accordance with the Arbitration Rules in effect on the date on which the parties consented to arbitration. If any question of procedure arises which is not covered by this Section or the Arbitration Rules or any rules agreed upon by the parties, the Tribunal shall decide the question.'
[123] ICSID Arbitration Rules (2006), Rule 20(2): 'In the conduct of the proceeding, the Tribunal shall apply any agreement between the parties on procedural matters, except as otherwise provided in the Convention or the Administrative and Financial Regulations.'
[124] ICSID Convention, Article 52(1)(d), which is interpreted to have incorporated such fundamental rules. See *Commentary* (n 119), 983–91.
[125] See, for instance, ICC Rules of Conciliation and Arbitration (1927), Article 16(2).
[126] International Chamber of Commerce, 'Revision of the Rules of Conciliation and Arbitration' (1927) Brochure No 50, 4–5.

virtually all ICC tribunals produced awards resembling written judicial decisions. Since 1998, the Rules have stipulated that: 'The Award shall state the reasons upon which it is based.'[127]

The duty to give reasons intersects with another fiduciary obligation: to resolve the dispute according to the 'applicable rules of law'. This obligation, first codified in the 1975 Rules,[128] is today expressed as Rule 21 (2012):

1. The parties shall be free to agree upon the rules of law to be applied by the arbitral tribunal to the merits of the dispute. In the absence of any such agreement, the arbitral tribunal shall apply the rules of law which it determines to be appropriate.
2. The arbitral tribunal shall take account of the provisions of the contract, if any, between the parties and of any relevant trade usages.
3. The arbitral tribunal shall assume the powers of an *amiable compositeur* [an umpire deciding the case in accordance with equity] or decide *ex aequo et bono* [on the basis of fairness, or equity] only if the parties have agreed[129] to give it such powers.

The *Guide* stresses that the parties' choice of substantive law binds tribunals,[130] whereas ICC Rules bind them procedurally. In the 2007 to 2011 period, the average annual percentage of cases filed in which parties had specified the controlling law was 85 per cent.[131] In the remaining cases, the tribunal decides what body of law will apply to the merits, with wide discretion to choose from 'an almost limitless range of options'.[132] While Rule 21 is silent on the question, the *Guide* commands tribunals to make such determinations in the form of an order or award, 'in writing and properly reasoned'. The Court strongly 'prefers' such decisions to take the form

---

[127] ICC Rules of Arbitration (2012), Article 31(2).

[128] ICC Rules of Conciliation and Arbitration (1975), Article 13(3): 'The parties shall be free to determine the law to be applied by the arbitrator to the merits of the dispute. In the absence of any indication of the parties as to the applicable law, the arbitrator shall apply the law designated as the proper law by the rule of conflict which he deems appropriate.' The rule was slightly reformulated in the next version of the Rules, ICC Rules of Conciliation and Arbitration (1998), as Article 17(1), removing the reference to the 'rule of conflict': 'The parties shall be free to agree upon the rules of law to be applied by the Arbitral Tribunal to the merits of the dispute. In the absence of any such agreement, the Arbitral Tribunal shall apply the rules of law which it determines to be appropriate.'

[129] The *Guide* (n 10), para 3-730: '[G]iven that the exercise of the power can be vague and uncertain, it is very rare for parties to give an arbitral tribunal the power to decide in this manner.'

[130] ibid para 3-752: 'Where parties have agreed on a substantive law, the arbitral tribunal must respect that choice. If it fails to do so, this might be considered as a failure to conduct the procedure in accordance with the parties' agreement, which would undermine the enforceability of a subsequent award.'

[131] ibid para 3-750 (Table 31).

[132] ibid para 3-761: 'The term "rules of law" encompasses an almost limitless range of options. These include, for example, transnational commercial law (also known as general principles of international commercial law or *lex mercatoria*) and non-national sets of rules or principles, such as the UNIDROIT Principles of International Commercial Contracts, the Principles of European Contract Law, INCOTERMS, model laws prepared by UNCITRAL and any principles of public international law that may be applicable (e.g. in investment treaty arbitration). Parties or the arbitral tribunal could even develop a legal framework that borrows and combines individual rules and principles or entire sets of rules and principles from a number of sources (e.g. combining provisions from one or several domestic legal systems with principles of international treaty law and transnational commercial law).'

of an award, the drafts of which are subject to mandatory scrutiny, 'at no extra cost to the parties or tribunal'.[133]

Parties that have chosen the law typically specify the contract law of a single domestic system.[134] Yet even in such cases, arbitrators are unlikely to apply that law as a national judge would do in a similar dispute. One key reason is Rule 21(2), which expresses, if somewhat obliquely, the meta-principal that arbitrators should give effect to the intent and expectations of the contracting parties. Tribunals typically give effect to these expectations in light of the customs and usages of transnational commerce, as they evolve.

In its early effort to revive the *Lex Mercatoria*, the ICC gave 'trade usages' a prominent place, as a necessary element of its strategy to encourage awards-in-equity, rather than in law.[135] Arbitrators operating in equity mode would, in effect, be applying usages. By the 1950s, the ICC held that the parties' decision to resort to ICA, rather than courts, entailed a choice to incorporate usages as an implicit term of contract. The subsequent formalization of the presumption into a rule allowed ICA to evolve toward a judicial model, while preserving the façade of arbitration's contractual foundations. In 1968, Pieter Sanders introduced a report on the topic to the ICC's legislative organ, the Commission on International Arbitration and ADR, in these terms:

> In practice, parties to an international contract do not think in terms of national law, but on international lines. What counts for them are the terms of the contract and the customs of international trade. It is to these that they look for the answer in the event of their contract giving rise to disputes. Firstly, the contract itself should be looked at to find the answer, and in case it does not yield one, international trade usages should fill the gap. Why do the parties insert an arbitration clause in their international contract? There may be many reasons for doing so but one of them certainly is that they want to avoid going to a national court in some remote country and running the risk of having the dispute decided on the basis of some national law, even more of mystery to them than their own national law. They have more confidence in arbitrators who know the trade and who will decide the case according to the customs of the trade.[136]

The provision codifying the obligation to incorporate usages appeared in the next revision of the ICC Rules, in 1975, Article 13(5) mandating that: 'In all cases the arbitrator shall take account of the provisions of the contract and the relevant trade usages.'[137] Today, in ICC arbitration, tribunals may always apply trade usages, irrespective of whether disputing parties have included a choice-of-law clause in their contract (Chapter 4).

---

[133] ibid para 3-755.   [134] ibid para 3-761.

[135] As a guide published by the ICC in 1935 put it: 'It is to the interest of the parties that the arbitrator should decide the case in equity, as a business man, without being bound by statutes or legal procedure.' See *Practical Hints* (n 23), 5.

[136] ICC Commission on International Arbitration, 'The Role of Arbitration in Developing International Trade Law—Note Submitted by Professor P. Sanders' (1968) Doc No 420/162.

[137] ICC Rules of Arbitration (2012), Article 21(2): 'The arbitral tribunal shall take account of the provisions of the contract, if any, between the parties and of any relevant usages.'

How tribunals justify their awards in law is subject to close administrative supervision. Rule 33 (2012) states:

Before signing any award, the arbitral tribunal shall submit it in draft form to the Court. The Court may lay down modifications as to the form of the award and, without affecting the arbitral tribunal's liberty of decision, may also draw its attention to points of substance. No award shall be rendered by the arbitral tribunal until it has been approved by the Court as to its form.

The parsimony of Rule 33 disguises what is in reality a complex system of interactions—or 'dialogues'—between the house and its tribunals.

At early stages of the drafting, the Secretariat encourages '[e]ven the most experienced international arbitrators' to use it as a 'sounding board', a reliable 'source of knowledge and practice'.[138] Upon submission, the draft will be reviewed by the house lawyer assigned to the team (the 'Counsel') and other Secretariat officials. Both authorities may return the draft to the tribunal with recommendations for revision.[139] Most important will be the position taken by the Court. Today, the 'vast majority' of the Court's decisions are adopted in weekly 'committee sessions', while monthly plenary meetings are reserved for adopting awards that either 'involve a state or state entity as a party', include a dissenting opinion, or 'raise a significant concern'.[140] In its decision, the Court will: (a) approve the award as submitted; (b) approve it 'subject to' the tribunal 'making certain modifications of form and/or considering the Court's comments on substance'; or (c) reject it. In the 2007 to 2011 period, 86 per cent of all awards are 'approved subject to', and only 7 per cent are either approved or rejected outright.[141] A tribunal that has had its award rejected by the Court will have to repeat the submission and scrutiny procedure. An award revised following an 'approved subject to' decision is resubmitted to the Secretariat, which may forward it again to the Court if problems persist.[142]

Decisions to 'reject' outright, and many that 'approve subject to', initiate dialogues on implementation. The dialogues are delicate interactions, given the terms of Rule 33. On the one hand, as the *Guide* puts it:

---

[138] The *Guide* (n 10), para 3-1198.   [139] ibid paras 3-1199, 3-1201, 3-1202.
[140] ibid para 3-1202.   [141] ibid para 3-1192 (Table 37).
[142] For 'approved subject to' decisions, the following procedure applies: the arbitral tribunal 'must send the revised draft to the Secretariat for review. A revised version of the award will not normally be resubmitted to the Court. Rather, the Counsel in charge of the file will verify whether the arbitral tribunal has duly considered all of the Court's comments. If in doubt about whether a comment has been adequately addressed, the Counsel will refer to the Secretariat's management. If an arbitral tribunal refuses to change a point of form or adequately to consider a point of substance, the Secretariat may put the issue to the Court for it to decide how to proceed. In so doing, the Court and its Secretariat will be mindful of Article 33's clear indication that the arbitral tribunal maintains the right to make the final decision on any point of substance' (the *Guide* (n 10), para 3-1214).

The language of Article 33 makes clear that the scrutiny process cannot require the arbitral tribunal to change the substance of its award. The Court can do no more than draw the arbitral tribunal's attention to matters of substance and the Court is careful to respect this limit, no matter how frustrating it may be for Court members when confronted with draft awards they simply do not agree with. While the scrutiny process may lead an arbitral tribunal to modify a substantive aspect of its decision, this will result from the Court's identifying a problem such as missing elements in the decision, weaknesses in the reasoning, inconsistencies, the failure to deal with certain issues or claims, or dealing with claims or issues not raised by the parties.[143]

On the other hand, the Secretariat insists on the importance of the Court's decision when it comes to 'apparent contradictions or inadequacies in [the tribunal's reasoning], potential flaws in its analysis, inconsistencies between the dispositive section and the body of the award, and mandatory requirements of the arbitration law at the place of the arbitration'.[144]

The Court's decisions in this realm are confidential. The *Guide*, however, comments on three 'possible outcomes' of these dialogues.[145] First, the tribunal may 'admit its own error' and modify the award accordingly. Second, it may assert that the Court has erred or misunderstood its award. If persuaded by the tribunal, the Court may be 'perfectly willing to withdraw a comment'. But, if the Court rejects the tribunal's defence of the award, 'there may be further dialogue between the Secretariat and the arbitral tribunal'. Last, a tribunal may reject outright the Court's views. The *Guide* contains an explicit threat to those who would ignore the Court on matters on which the latter has taken a strong position:

Ultimately, if the arbitral tribunal remains fixed on its initial decision, the Court is likely to withdraw a substantive comment. However, it has happened that the Court initiated replacement proceedings against an arbitrator who refused even to consider the Court's comments in relation to points of substance that concerned serious jurisdictional issues. The Court may consider the points to be so fundamental as to call into question the competence of the arbitrator concerned.[146]

This warning applies to all decisions, even those falling within the 'approved subject to' category.

An arbitral institution that requires tribunals to produce fully reasoned awards, based on law, and subject to the mandatory review and control of a centralized organ, is already a significantly judicialized, hierarchically constituted legal system. Given these trappings, it is hardly surprising to find other features of judicial decision-making influencing arbitral procedures. Dissenting opinions, for example, are typically written by co-arbitrators appointed by the parties that have lost the arbitration.[147] Arbitrators write them, in part, to show that they have defended

---

[143] ibid para 3-1207.   [144] ibid para 3-1210.   [145] ibid para 3-1212.
[146] ibid para 3-1212.
[147] An exhaustive review of ISA awards rendered throughout 2009 shows that 'dissenting opinions are almost universally issued in favour of the party that appointed the dissenter': see Albert Jan van den Berg, 'Dissenting Opinions by Party-Appointed Arbitrators in Investment Arbitration' in Mahnoush Arsanjani et al (eds), *Looking to the Future: Essays on International Law in Honor of W. Michael Reisman* (Brill, Leiden 2010) 824. In ICA, 'a dissenter will almost always be a co-arbitrator ...'—see the *Guide* (n 10), para 3-1132.

an appointing party's positions within the tribunal, thereby enhancing their future appointment prospects (see Chapter 6). Arguably, dissents violate rules on impartiality, although there is no consensus on this view. Civil law systems have long expressed hostility to dissents: they weaken a court's legitimacy by revealing the availability of more than one defensible ruling. Common law systems, which more openly acknowledge that judges make law as they resolve cases, tolerate dissents. In our view, dissents can help to legitimize third-party dispute resolution, insofar as they (a) help losers accept their fate, and (b) enable the system to correct errors. Much arbitral law is made through what is, in fact, a common law process,[148] and dissents are part of that process.

In 2015, arbitrators filed dissents in 94 per cent of all final awards decided by a majority (rather than unanimously).[149] Arbitrators may, of course, dissent for less venal purposes as well, for example, to trigger stronger scrutiny of awards, or prepare the grounds for annulment. The Court, which reviews all draft awards that contain dissents in its plenary sessions, will usually comment upon the dissent, or even demand that the tribunal address the 'strong arguments forming the basis of a dissent', when it has not done so already.[150]

The Rules strictly prohibit arbitrators from communicating with the parties throughout the drafting and scrutiny process.[151] Once approval has been obtained, and certification formalities completed, the parties will usually receive the final award 'within a matter of days'.[152] An unhappy party may seek to annul the award. Nonetheless, as the *Guide* puts it, the central purpose of the [ICC] Court's scrutiny is to stamp awards with an 'internationally recognized seal of approval, [making them] less prone to challenge or annulment'.[153] In well-developed seats of arbitration, specific courts (or specialized panels on general courts) are designated to handle such requests, and they are staffed by judges who are relatively well versed in the niceties of transnational contracting and dispute resolution. As noted, in seats that are popular with the ICC and parties, annulments are today virtually unknown.

The ICSID Convention contained a duty to give reasons from the outset;[154] and annulment committees are empowered to quash any award rendered by a tribunal that 'has failed to state the reasons on which [the award] is based'. With respect to the applicable law, the counterpart of Rule 21 (ICC) at ICSID is Rule 42(1) of the Convention:

(1) The Tribunal shall decide a dispute in accordance with such rules of law as may be agreed by the parties. In the absence of such agreement, the Tribunal shall apply the law of the Contracting State party to the dispute (including its rules on the conflict of laws) and such rules of international law as may be applicable.

---

[148] Chapters 4 and 5.
[149] The ICC reports that, of the forty-eight final awards decided by a majority vote in 2015, forty-five were accompanied by a dissenting opinion: see 2015 Statistical Report (n 4).
[150] The *Guide* (n 10), para 3-1213.   [151] ibid para 3-1219.   [152] ibid para 3-1218.
[153] ibid para 3-1182.
[154] ICSID Convention, Article 48(3) provides that the award 'shall state the reasons upon which it is based'.

In nearly all ICSID Convention cases, an investment treaty supplies the substantive law, with gaps to be filled by other applicable rules of international law, including judge-made general principles of law. National rules and practices are typically the object of the tribunal's scrutiny, not the source of the applicable law. The Secretariat is intimately involved at all stages of the arbitration, including the drafting of awards; and the Secretary-General is expressly charged with administering the certification of the final award and its distribution.

A unique feature of ICSID procedure is the availability of annulment, through the decisions of what are called 'Ad Hoc Annulment Committees' [ACs]. The procedure, governed by Article 52 of the Convention, introduces a dose of hierarchical control. Although parties activate the procedure, they otherwise have no input into how it operates. The Chairman of ICSID appoints the three-member Committees, who will then proceed under mandatory rules laid down by the Centre. ACs may annul awards on five grounds: 'failure to state the reasons'; 'manifest excess of powers'; 'that the Tribunal was not properly constituted'; 'that there was corruption on the part of a member of the Tribunal'; and 'that there has been a serious departure from a fundamental rule of procedure'.[155] While Committees are not authorized to annul an award on a tribunal's 'errors-in-law', they regularly identify and address such errors in *dicta*. Some Committees have, in effect, adopted the mantle of an appellate jurisdiction in all but name, venturing to annul awards for faulty legal reasoning, under 'the failure to state the reasons', or the 'manifest excess of powers' headings. We analyze AC decisions in detail in Chapter 4.

III. Dynamics of Institutional Change

In its ideal form, the contractual model of arbitration is predicated on party autonomy. The parties choose their law and procedures; they select the arbitrators; and the role of the house is to support the tribunals in the performance of its obligations to the parties. Largely in response to heightened adversarialism, the contractual model has steadily given way to the judicial model, wherein the house imposes its own administrative authority on parties and tribunals, through its Rules. It does so at crucial pressure points, precisely where party conflict is most likely to abort the arbitration in advance, or paralyze it once the proceedings are underway. Thus, the Rules set deadlines for the completion of the main stages in the arbitration, which apply to: the respondent's reply to the claimant's filing request; the constitution of the tribunal; the submission of the Terms of Reference—signed by the parties—to the Secretariat; the establishment of the facts; and the submission of the draft award to the Court.[156] These deadlines bind the tribunal, though the Court may extend them when it comes to particularly conflictual or complex disputes.[157] At each of these critical stages, the Secretariat supervises the tribunal's

---

[155] ICSID Convention, Article 52(1)(a)–(e).
[156] ICC Rules of Arbitration (2012), Rules 5, 12, 23, 25, 30.
[157] ICC Rules of Arbitration (2012), Rule 38.

work in fine detail; and the Rules empower the Court to take decisions necessary to keep the proceedings moving forward. When a party seeks to obstruct them, or refuses to participate altogether, the Court may intervene with binding force. To take just one example, the Court will approve the Terms of Reference for parties that withhold their consent.[158]

The judicialization of arbitral procedure has transformed the core elements of the contractual model. We do not wish to be misunderstood on this point. Party autonomy and the law of contracts remain foundational components of the judicial model. No legal system that effectively enforces contracts dispenses with the basic principles of contract law; instead, as the legal system develops, it moulds those principles to align them with its own evolving organizational imperatives and policy choices. The point fully applies to the ICC.[159] In ICC arbitration, the Terms of Reference comprise a contract involving three parties—the disputants, the tribunal, and the ICC—an agreement nested within a body of hierarchically superior, enforceable Rules. Supplementing these Rules is the *Guide*, which prescribes the standards that govern the production of the Terms, subsequent procedural orders, and the award itself. The house monitors and enforces compliance with this contract. Thus, in claiming that the contractual model is obsolete when it comes to ICC arbitration, we do not assert that contractual instruments do not matter. Rather, our claim is that how they matter is determined by the Rules of the house, by deep veins of arbitral practice that inform the Rules, and by modes of centralized supervision and control.

At ICSID, the Centre's burgeoning caseload flows from the compulsory jurisdiction established by investment treaties. The lodging of a complaint locks the respondent state into the proceedings. The ICSID Secretariat, too, is empowered to step in at the critical stages where a recalcitrant state may seek to obstruct the proceedings; and the rules authorize a tribunal to continue its work without a respondent state's participation.[160]

Taking a broader perspective, we see that the rules of the major arbitral centres do not dampen intense party conflict. Rather, they are designed to accommodate and manage adversarial legalism, in light of other goals being pursued by the house: to maintain efficiency; to enhance effectiveness; and to build the systemic autonomy of the arbitral order.

Efficiency

ICC Rules have institutionalized adversarialism, treating party conflict, procedural complexity, and recurrent delays as expected, 'normal' aspects of its docket. Given the competitive environment in which the system operates, the house nonetheless remains anxious about delays and costs. In 1935, the ICC boasted that the 'essential advantage of arbitration' was that it saved time and money compared to

---

[158] ICC Rules of Arbitration (2012), Rule 23.
[159] It also applies to the LCIA, the HKIAC, the SIAC, and the AAA-ICDR.
[160] ICSID Arbitration Rules (2006), Rule 42.

litigation, which could 'drag on for years in the ordinary Courts'.[161] Yet, as in the past,[162] the arbitration of adversarial, high value cases will often be more costly than going to a court in New York, London, or Singapore, though today the arbitral regime processes the vast bulk of such cases. The ICC's fee schedule is actually geared toward attracting complex, high stakes disputes,[163] while its capacities to administer them is unrivalled.

Since the 1930s,[164] the ICC has continuously deliberated on the efficiency of its codes and practices. Today, Rule 22(1) states that the quest for efficiency is a general obligation of the tribunal and the parties, who 'shall make every effort to conduct the arbitration in an expeditious and cost-effective manner, having regard to the complexity and value of the dispute'. The Rules lay down binding deadlines and submission requirements, in part, to enable the house to monitor compliance with Rule 22(1). 'One of the underlying aims of the revision process leading to the 2012 Rules', the *Guide* states, 'was to include ways and means of encouraging parties and arbitral tribunals to control the time and cost of arbitrations. Corporate users were particularly insistent on the importance of this aim.'[165] The 2012 Rules introduced Rule 24 which, along with Appendix 4, codified practices developed by arbitrators under the rubric of the Case Management Conference, to be 'used by the arbitral tribunal and the parties for controlling time and cost'.[166] Of course, if parties prefer an all-out, litigious brawl, if they deploy 'win at all cost' tactics in every procedural battle, tribunals are likely to lose control of costs.[167] Last, while arbitration remains the core of its dispute

---

[161] *Practical Hints* (n 23), 4. The ICC still stresses the point: 'Arbitral tribunals usually take less time than national courts to reach a final decision.' See International Chamber of Commerce, 'Frequently Asked Questions on ICC Arbitration: How much time does it take to get a final award?' <http://www.iccwbo.org/FAQs/Frequently-asked-questions-on-ICC-Arbitration/#Q16> accessed 4 January 2016.

[162] There were adversarial cases in the past as well. See, for instance, the ICC award rendered by Pieter Sanders on 6 March 1951 and published in (1951) 351 Arbitrale Rechtspraak 508. In this case, the arbitral proceedings took eight months from the date of the initiation of the proceedings to the rendering of the final award.

[163] Chapter 2.

[164] In 1955, the ICC amended its rules of arbitration in order to increase the speed of the proceedings: see (1955) 21/1 Nouvelles de la CCI 24.

[165] The *Guide* (n 10), para 3-793.

[166] ICC Rules of Arbitration (2012), Appendix IV: 'Appropriate control of time and cost is important in all cases. In cases of low complexity and low value, it is particularly important to ensure that time and costs are proportionate to what is at stake in the dispute.' See also International Chamber of Commerce, 'ICC Arbitration Commission Report on Techniques for Controlling Time and Costs in Arbitration' (2015) <http://www.iccwbo.org/Advocacy-Codes-and-Rules/Document-centre/2012/ICC-Arbitration-Commission-Report-on-Techniques-for-Controlling-Time-and-Costs-in-Arbitration/> accessed 4 January 2016.

[167] The *Guide* (n 10), para 3-794: 'In most ICC arbitrations the largest cost item is not the arbitrators' fees and expenses or the ICC administrative expenses, but rather the legal fees and other costs relating to the parties' own presentation of their cases. Lawyers' fees, expenses relating to witnesses and expert evidence and other similar expenses are generally proportionate to the length and complexity of proceedings and vary significantly depending on the manner in which a case is run. Parties sometimes insist on having multiple rounds of briefs even in relatively simple cases. Also, it is not uncommon for parties to appoint more experts than necessary or to call too many factual witnesses to testify despite the meagre contribution they are likely to make to the arbitral tribunal's fact-finding mission. Document

settlement activities, the ICC also offers parties a choice of mediation,[168] 'fast track' proceedings,[169] and settlement.[170]

The development of the CMC charts judicialization of a particularly extensive kind. In the 1980s, a group of leading arbitrators developed case management techniques for complex arbitrations, which the ICC first promoted as best-practice standards, before making them obligatory under the Rules. In the United States, a parallel evolution 'to combat undue cost and delay' in complex cases took place,[171] resulting in soft law instruments, the most important of which is the *Manual for Complex Litigation*.[172] Among other things, the *Manual* gives guidance to judges and counsel on case management. Many of these practices are now taken-for-granted, de facto rules of procedure, while others have been integrated directly into the Federal Rules of Civil Procedure.[173]

The ICSID Rules do not contain a counterpart to ICC Rule 22(1), though efficiency obligations are implied. ISA, by its nature, tends to be highly adversarial, lengthy, and expensive, not least because of the high values and state interests at stake. From the establishment of the tribunal to completion, most ICSID cases now take an average of about three-and-a-half years. The Secretariat, which closely supervises the tribunal's compliance with timetables found in the rules, reports that the house places 'a premium on addressing efficiency in case administration, while maintaining due process and a level playing field for disputing parties using ICSID facilities'.[174] Although the Convention and the Arbitration Rules are largely silent on such matters, the Secretariat today requires arbitrators: 'to establish a budget at the outset of a case outlining anticipated ... fees and expenses'; to consult with the

production, whether on paper or in electronic format, is also likely to increase costs significantly, particularly if it is conducted through a process of discovery.'

[168] On average, a successful mediation takes less than four months, costing less than 1 per cent of the disputed amount: see International Chamber of Commerce, 'Mediation and ADR statistics' <http://www.iccwbo.org/Products-and-Services/Arbitration-and-ADR/Mediation/Introduction/Mediation-and-ADR-statistics/> accessed 4 January 2016.

[169] In 1998, the ICC amended the Rules to permit '[t]he parties ... to shorten the various time limits set out in these Rules ...'. This provision is now Article 38(1) of the ICC Rules of Arbitration (2012).

[170] ICC Rules of Arbitration (2012), Article 32: the parties may request the tribunal to incorporate their settlement agreement into an award 'by consent'. In 2012, ICC arbitrators issued thirty-one consent awards (out of 491 awards issued during that year). See International Chamber of Commerce, '2012 Statistical Report' (2013) 24(1) ICC International Court of Arbitration Bulletin. See also the *Guide* (n 10), para 3-923, which encourages settlement by suggesting: 'Parties should constantly have in mind the possibility of settling their case. While an arbitral tribunal's decision may be useful or sometimes necessary, settlement is usually a better option as it can reduce time and cost and preserve commercial relationships.'

[171] Steven S Gensler, 'Judicial Case Management: Caught in the Crossfire' (2010) 60 Duke Law Journal 669.

[172] Federal Judicial Center, *Manual for Complex Litigation, Fourth* (Federal Judicial Center, Washington 2005) ['*Manual*'].

[173] For an overview of the early history of the *Manual* during the period in which the CMC was being developed at the ICC, see Andrew Simons, 'The Manual for Complex Litigation: More Rules or Mere Recommendations?' (1998) 62 St John's Law Review 493.

[174] ICSID further reports that its goal of achieving 'measurable efficiency gains' through 'technological solutions, procedural innovation, and ambitious service standards' is a continuous one. See

parties as soon as possible before and after hearings; to 'updat[e] parties on a regular basis concerning the costs expended to date'; and 'to report to the parties on the timing of outstanding decisions or awards'.[175]

Effectiveness

ICC Rules are designed to secure the effectiveness of arbitration, which we define throughout the book as the capacity of the arbitral order to attract a steady and significant caseload, and to produce final awards that are binding on the parties. Effectiveness (a variable) partly overlaps with efficiency (a variable), insofar as relative inefficiencies will make an arbitral centre less attractive to users. The Rules reflect the consolidation of the enforcement regime over the three decades following the ratification of the 1958 New York Convention.[176] The post-1990 period has been dominated by the effort to reinforce the centrality of arbitration in the context of an increasingly complex and adversarial caseload. Complex disputes—those that typically involve contending claims arising under multiple contracts connecting a multitude of parties—are common (e.g. for large construction projects). Such cases pose special challenges, which the Rules have evolved to meet.

When the ICC promulgated its 1998 Rules, 'multiparty and multicontract arbitrations were still relatively rare',[177] acknowledged only through the requirement that three-member tribunals resolve such cases.[178] The 2012 Rules codified procedures for managing such disputes, based on developments in arbitral practice and the jurisprudence of the Court under the 1998 regime. Rules 7 through 10 lay down the framework for 'joining' new parties to an existing proceeding, 'thereby accommodating complex webs of [related] claims'[179] that can be consolidated under the authority of a single tribunal. The *Guide* contains seventy-seven paragraphs of dense commentary on these changes.[180] We do not need to go into detail on these Rules, since their basic structure will be familiar by now. They fix deadlines for filings, confer decision-making discretion on tribunals, including the authority to issue procedural orders, and provide for command and control at the crucial pressure points by the Secretariat and the Court.

It is the Court, not the parties or tribunal, that ultimately decides whether a party can be joined against its will (Rule 6 [2012]). Further evidence of the decline of the contractual model, the Court has lowered its standard for joining a party. Under the 1998 Rules, the Court investigated whether the party had in fact signed the contract 'containing the relevant arbitral agreement'. Under the

---

ICSID, '2014 Annual Report' <https://icsid.worldbank.org/apps/ICSIDWEB/resources/Documents/ICSID_AR14_ENG.pdf> accessed 4 January 2015, 5.
[175] ibid 30–1.
[176] Chapter 2.   [177] The *Guide* (n 10), para 3-287.
[178] ICC Rules of Conciliation and Arbitration (1998), Article 10.
[179] The *Guide* (n 10), para 3-288.
[180] The insertion of these new Rules also meant amending Rules on filing cases (Rule 4(3)), the respondent's answers to requests for filings (Rule 5(5)), the tribunal's assessment of jurisdiction under

2012 Rules, the Court does 'not require an actual signature but simply *prima facie* evidence that the party had been or become bound by the relevant arbitration agreement'.[181] The arbitration will often proceed, even if the original claimant has settled or withdrawn. 'As arbitrations become increasingly complex', the *Guide* indicates, 'with larger numbers of parties and more tangled webs of claims, counterclaims, cross-claims and claims against additional parties, there is a greater likelihood that they will be continued despite being abandoned by the claimant'.[182]

In recent decades, ICC arbitration has become more 'court-like' in myriad other ways, a prominent instance being the house's strengthened capacity to issue 'conservatory' or 'provisional' measures ('preliminary injunctions' in the common law world). Courts typically grant such requests, to compel or restrain conduct in order to avoid harm to the other party's interests, while the dispute awaits a final decision on the merits. The ICC understood the importance of provisional measures to users early on, while recognizing that courts had distinct advantages when it came to enforcing them.[183] Under Rule 28(1) of the 2012 Rules, a party may request such orders from the tribunal, which possesses the authority to 'order any interim or conservatory measure it deems appropriate', under tests the tribunal is relatively free to develop.[184] Rule 28(2) also recognizes the 'concurrent jurisdiction'[185] of courts in the area: a party may go to a court 'in appropriate circumstances', without any deleterious effect on the arbitration agreement or the tribunal's jurisdiction. Finally, Rule 29 provides for the naming of an 'Emergency Arbitrator', who has authority to issue interim measures prior to the constitution of an arbitral tribunal, under a separate set of Rules contained in Appendix V (2012).[186] Again, explicit due process and reason-giving requirements govern these procedures; the Emergency Arbitrator is to produce a procedural timetable in consultation with the parties; and the Secretariat and the President of the Court are to supervise the process closely.

the various arbitration agreements (Rule 6(3–7)), the appointment of arbitrators (Rule 12), and advances on costs (Rule 33).

[181] The *Guide* (n 10), para 3-292.   [182] ibid para 3-279.

[183] ICC Rules of Conciliation and Arbitration (1932), Article 11: in 1932, in the context of the 'urgent cases' brought to it, the ICC gave authority to the President of the Court (before an arbitral tribunal had been constituted) or to the arbitral tribunal itself (once constituted) to appoint one or several experts to make such orders. This provision survived until 1947 before reappearing in a different form in the Arbitration Rules of 1998, which provided that the arbitral tribunal (after the file has been transmitted to it) and national tribunals (before the file has been transmitted to the arbitral tribunal and even thereafter in 'appropriate circumstances') could order interim or conservatory measures. See ICC Rules of Conciliation and Arbitration (1998), Article 23.

[184] The *Guide* (n 10), para 3-1038: 'It should also have regard to any provisions concerning interim relief in the arbitration law at the place of the arbitration. Article 17A of the 2006 version of the UNCITRAL Model Law on International Commercial Arbitration, used as the basis for many national laws, contains a list of conditions for granting interim measures.'

[185] Andrea Carlevaris and José Ricardo Feris, 'Running in the ICC Emergency Arbitrator Rules: The First Ten Cases' (2014) 25(1) ICC Court of Arbitration Bulletin 25.

[186] ICC Rules of Arbitration (2012), Article 29. Appendix V contains the 'Emergency Arbitrator Rules'.

The logics of Rules 28 and 29 are straightforward: if parties need provisional measures, then the ICC wants to meet these demands in-house, even before a tribunal has been constituted. As the *Guide* puts it:[187]

Parties may consider using the emergency arbitrator proceedings for a number of different reasons ... as an alternative to seeking relief from a competent state court. State courts may not have the necessary authority to grant interim or conservatory relief. In other instances, they can be perceived as slow, inexperienced or even biased or corrupt, leading a party to conclude that its interests may best be protected by an independent and experienced international arbitrator. Furthermore, parties may regard the emergency arbitrator proceedings as a helpful alternative where the interim relief sought concerns multiple jurisdictions and would otherwise require applications to be made in several courts in different countries.[188]

The effectiveness of interim relief may at times depend on the availability of enforcement, presumably by pro-arbitration courts. It is therefore crucial that courts in the states that constitute the major pro-arbitration, trading zones—including England, France, Singapore, and Switzerland—recognize the arbitral order's authority to issue injunctions, and will normally enforce them as a matter of routine.[189] This point made, exactly how judges and arbitrators will coordinate their joint authority to issue interim measures, and the scope of enforcement of arbitral measures by national judges, has not been fully determined.

At ICSID, the Convention stipulates that tribunals may 'recommend any provisional measures which should be taken to preserve the respective rights of either party',[190] while the Arbitration Rules outline the 'procedural framework'[191] pursuant to which such measures can be requested and granted.[192]

Autonomy

Enhancing the autonomy of the arbitral order, relative to other legal systems,[193] overlaps with effectiveness concerns. One finds overlap in certain general provisions

---

[187] The *Guide* (n 10), para 3-1052.   [188] ibid para 3-1052.
[189] For the analysis of the national law on the enforceability of interim measures orders by arbitral tribunals and emergency arbitrators, see Peter J W Sherwin and Douglas C Rennie, 'Interim Relief under International Arbitration Rules and Guidelines: A Comparative Analysis' (2010) 20 American Review of International Arbitration 317, 325–7; Raja Bose and Ian Meredith, 'Emergency Arbitration Procedures: A Comparative Analysis' (2012) 15 International Arbitration Law Review 186.
[190] ICSID Convention, Article 47.
[191] ICSID Arbitration Rules (2006), Rule 39 (Note A).
[192] ICSID Arbitration Rules (2006), Rule 39. Over time, this framework has been adjusted. ICSID Arbitration Rules (2003), Rule 39(5): The Arbitration Rules of 2003 made it clear that parties could request provisional measures before a national court prior to or during the arbitral proceedings. ICSID Arbitration Rules (2006), Rule 39(5): The Arbitration Rules of 2006 empowered the Secretary General of ICSID to solicit the parties' comments when a request for provisional measures has been made *prior to* the constitution of the arbitral tribunal as a means of gaining time for the tribunal once appointed.
[193] At ICSID, this does not come up. See *Commentary* (n 119): 'Art. 44 is the procedural counterpart to the choice of law provision of Art. 42(1). Art. 42(1) only applies to substantive questions but not to the procedure before an ICSID tribunal (see Art. 42, para. 3). Whereas Art. 42(1) contains

of ICC Rules,[194] in the decline of the importance of the seat of arbitration, and in the development of capacity to process requests for interim measures. Here we will briefly focus on a factor—the law applicable to the dispute—which, some continue to argue, fatally undermines claims to the effect that the arbitral order is a discrete legal system, meaningfully autonomous from national legal systems. Skeptics stress two facts: (a) most parties to transnational commercial contracts choose state law as the applicable law of contract; and (b) arbitrators are under a fiduciary duty 'to apply the applicable law'. In 2014, the parties selected the controlling law in 84 per cent of the new cases filed at the ICC, referring to a national law of contract in 98 per cent of cases.[195] While Chapters 4 and 5 consider these issues further, two responses to the skeptics merit repeating here. First, contractants strongly favour the law of states that are pro-arbitration, in that they emphasize party autonomy, seek to enforce the 'reasonable expectation' of the contracting parties, recognize the status of trade usages, and are hands-off when it comes to judicial review of the merits of awards.[196] Second, it is not expected that tribunals will apply national law as a domestic court would.

The *Guide* strongly discourages ICC arbitrators from attempting to don the robes of a national judge on their own initiative. A party that demands as much assumes the full burden of 'establishing the content of the relevant law', through pleadings, the provision of 'copies of the relevant code(s), statute(s), jurisprudence and/or case law', and 'the testimony of expert legal witnesses'. It is for the tribunal to 'determine the relevant content of the substantive law based on its assessment' of this evidence, and other factors of importance.[197] When counsel fails to provide sufficient evidence to make such a determination, arbitrators are 'well advised to adopt one of two approaches':

One is to ignore the point, even if it means rejecting a claim or defence. The other is to invite the parties to make submissions on those potentially relevant provisions of law.[198]

Further, the Rules embody a strong policy stance in favour of an expansive *transnational* freedom of contract and practice, and against formalistic approaches to

---

reference to the law of the State party to the dispute, Art. 44 creates a comprehensive and self-contained system that is insulated from national rules of procedure.'

[194] The ICC Rules contain strong expressions of their own autonomy. As an internal matter, ICC Rules of Arbitration (2012), Rule 41: 'In all matters not expressly provided for in the Rules, the Court and the arbitral tribunal shall act in the spirit of the Rules and shall make every effort to make sure that the award is enforceable at law.' With regard to external authority, Article 1(2) of the ICC Rules of Arbitration (2012) provides that: 'The Court is the only body authorized to administer arbitrations under the Rules, including the scrutiny and approval of awards rendered in accordance with the Rules.' The ICC Secretariat has interpreted certain provisions, including Rule 19 of the ICC Rules of Arbitration (2012), as establishing the supremacy of the ICC arbitration rules over any other procedural law that may come into play: see the *Guide* (n 10), para 3-711.

[195] International Chamber of Commerce, '2014 Statistical Report' (2015) 26(1) ICC International Court of Arbitration Bulletin.

[196] ibid. The most important laws selected, in order, were the laws of England, the United States (New York, Texas, California), Switzerland, Germany, and France.

[197] The *Guide* (n 10), para 3-768.   [198] ibid para 3-769.

the 'legal requirements and technicalities' of national contract law as interpreted by courts.

The ICC prioritizes transnational commercial practice in Rule 21(2): 'Tribunals shall take account ... of the provisions of the contract, if any, between the parties and of any relevant trade usages.' In 'some' cases, the *Guide* indicates approvingly, a 'tribunal may render its award simply by applying the terms of the contract to its factual findings, without needing to refer to the law governing the merits'.[199] In contrast, every tribunal 'must consider business practices and standards, as fixed by the parties themselves or the relevant industry sector',[200] as these constitute 'part of the essential context underlying a contract'.[201] Indeed, the *Guide* bluntly states, 'specific trade usages are in effect an implicit part of the parties' contract'.[202] Thus, the parties do not have a choice when it comes to 'relevant trade usages', which arbitrators can use to shape or even displace provisions of law selected by the parties. Today, virtually all major arbitral houses require tribunals to consider the dispute, and the applicable law, in terms of both general principles and the *Lex Mercatoria* (usually called 'rules of law' in the codes) as well the customs and usages in place in the relevant commercial or industrial sector.[203]

This evidence should weigh heavily in debates on the relative autonomy of the arbitral order, but it cannot settle them. To do so, we would need much more empirical evidence on how arbitrators make choices, when they interpret and enforce 'the applicable law'. Engaging the internal discourse of the Rules, however, does reveal a great deal about the ICC's own self-representation. Chapters 4 and 5 revisit these issues, in light of what we can observe about arbitral decision-making.[204]

IV. Conclusion

The ICC Rules of 1998 and 2012 firmly institutionalized the ICC's approach to adversarial legalism, while bolstering the house's administrative authority over disputants and tribunals. Today, the scope and density of mandatory procedures, and the intrusiveness of centralized, administrative control, surpass those in place at ICSID, which its founders significantly judicialized by design. Because the evolution of ICC procedures is a relatively pure measure of the judicialization of ICA, it provides a first order test of some of the propositions we derived from the theoretical materials presented in Chapter 1. The intensification of party conflict and adversarialism, we argued, will pressure dispute resolvers to construct procedures to maintain the legal system's effectiveness.

---

[199] ibid para 3-777.   [200] ibid para 3-778.   [201] ibid para 3-790.
[202] ibid para 3-781.
[203] The LCIA is the only major IAC not to mention trade usages, though it does refer to 'trade rules' as part of the applicable law. See Chapter 4.
[204] As noted in Chapter 2 (and discussed further in Chapters 3–6), some arbitrators interpret the phrase in Article 42(1) of the ICSID Convention—'and such rules of international law as may be applicable'—as delegating to tribunals wide-ranging authority to fill gaps in BITs, which are notoriously incomplete, with international rules, including unwritten general principles of law.

We also claimed that, as judicialization proceeded, features that distinguish the judicial from the contractual model of arbitration would appear and congeal as the foundational institutions of the system itself. These developments necessarily alter the content and scope of the arbitrator's fiduciary obligations. Under the terms of the contractual model, the arbitrator is a creature of contract owing duties only to the disputants. Under the judicial model, by contrast, a tribunal's obligations to the parties are incorporated into a matrix of duties owed to the house, that is, to the legal system constituted by the Rules. The evolution of the ICC Rules charts the decline of the contractual, and the consolidation of the judicial, model of arbitration. In one important area—policy on the appointment of arbitrators—heightened adversarialism has blocked the construction of administrative hierarchy (Chapter 4). For three-member tribunals, the parties insist on appointing their own co-arbitrators, a practice that now raises strong legitimacy concerns (Chapter 6).

Table 3.1 summarizes the core fiduciary obligations—of loyalty, accountability, and deliberative engagement[205]—of arbitrators at ICSID and the ICC, as currently codified. With one exception (the efficiency obligation in ICSID), each duty finds expression in one or more Rules of the house, and each is undergirded by supervision and sanctions for non-performance. At ICSID, centralized annulment proceedings enforce certain fiduciary obligations. Annulments can also lead to sanctions against individual arbitrators, through subsequent challenges to their competence and impartiality.[206] In the ICC, in addition to the various modes of supervision and control described above, Rule 15(2) stipulates that:

An arbitrator shall also be replaced on the Court's own initiative when it decides that the arbitrator ... is not fulfilling those functions in accordance with the Rules or within the prescribed time limits.

In addition, Rule 15(2) reinforces the ICC's authority over arbitrators in indirect ways, by making credible any well-founded threats by the parties, as well as 'warnings' of the Secretariat, to bring the arbitrator's failings to the attention of the Court.[207]

---

[205] See Chapter 1.   [206] See the case study of the 'Argentina cases' in Chapter 4.
[207] The *Guide* (n 10), paras 3-613, 3-626, 3-628.

Table 3.1 Fiduciary Duties of International Arbitrators at the ICC and ICSID

Duty	ICC	ICSID
Loyalty To the house and the Rules	– Rule 11(5): 'By accepting to serve, arbitrators undertake to carry out their responsibilities in accordance with the Rules.' – Rule 41: 'In all matters not expressly provided for in the Rules, the … arbitral tribunal shall act in the spirit of the Rules and shall make every effort to make sure that the award is enforceable at law.' – Guide 3–417: '[T]he arbitrator must put into effect and uphold the Rules and practices of the Court.'	– Art 44 Convention: 'Any arbitration proceeding shall be conducted in accordance with the provisions of this Section [on the "Powers and Function of the Tribunal"] and, except as the parties otherwise agree, in accordance with the Arbitration Rules …' – Art 52 Convention: Awards are subject to annulment on various grounds related to violations of the Rules.
To the parties: Impartiality	– Rules 11(1)/(2): 'Every arbitrator must be and remain impartial and independent of the parties involved in the arbitration. Before appointment or confirmation, a prospective arbitrator shall sign a statement of acceptance, availability, impartiality and independence.' – Guide 3–369: Rule 11(1) 'expresses a basic tenet of international arbitration … which the Court considers to be essential to the legitimacy of ICC arbitration.'	– Rule 6: 'Before or at the first session of the Tribunal, each arbitrator shall sign a declaration' of impartiality and independence. 'Any arbitrator failing to sign a declaration by the end of the first session of the Tribunal shall be deemed to have resigned.' – Art 52(1)(c) Convention: 'corruption on the part of a member of the Tribunal' is grounds for annulment.
Accountability To the parties: Efficiency	– Rule 22(1): 'The arbitral tribunal … shall make every effort to conduct the arbitration in an expeditious and cost-effective manner, having regard to the complexity and value of the dispute.' – Appendix IV: 'Appropriate control of time and cost is important in all cases.'	– No express duty. Art 60(1) Convention: Each tribunal 'shall determine the fees and expenses of its members within limits established … by the Administrative Council and after consultation with the Secretary-General.'

(*Continued*)

Table 3.1 (*Continued*)

Duty	ICC	ICSID
Choice of law	– Rule 21: The tribunal shall apply the applicable rules of law.	– Art 42(1) Convention: The tribunal shall apply the applicable law. – Art 52(1)(b) Convention: 'that the Tribunal has manifestly exceeded its powers', by failing to apply the applicable law, may be grounds for annulment.
Reason-giving	– Rule 31(2): 'The award shall state the reasons upon which it is based.' – Rule 33: Mandatory scrutiny of the award by the Court. – Guide 3–1183: The court's scrutiny 'is a corner-stone of the Rules from which [parties] cannot derogate'.	– Art 48(3) Convention: 'The award shall deal with every question submitted to the Tribunal, and shall state the reasons upon which it is based.' – Art 52(1)(e) Convention: Failure 'to state the reasons on which it is based' is grounds for annulment.
Deliberative engagement To the parties: Due process	– Rule 22(4): '[T]he arbitral tribunal shall act fairly and impartially and ensure that each party has a reasonable opportunity to present its case.' – Guide 3–814: The duty to 'act fairly and impartially and to grant each party a reasonable opportunity to make its case' is 'an overriding and fundamental principle of arbitration'.	– Art 52(1)(d) Convention: 'a serious departure from a fundamental rule of procedure' is grounds for annulment. – Rule 20(1): 'As early as possible after the constitution of a Tribunal, its President shall endeavor to ascertain the views of the parties regarding questions of procedure.'

Finally, in Chapter 1 we discussed the 'principal obligations' of arbitrators identified by Rusty Park, an influential former President of the London Court of International Arbitration.[208] Although Park aggregates and labels duties slightly differently, our approach is congruent. The first of Park's duties—'to render an accurate award'—is not expressly stated in the ICC and ICSID codes. Rather, it is implied through (a) due process requirements (related to pleadings, hearings, discovery, and evidence), (b) reason-giving and the possibility of dissenting opinion, and (c) administrative scrutiny (ICC) and annulment proceedings (ICSID). The next chapter explores the reason-giving requirement more broadly, focusing the demand for precedent-based argumentation and justification.

---

[208] See William W Park, 'The Four Musketeers of Arbitral Duty: Neither One-for-All Nor All-for-One' in Yves Derains and Laurent Lévy (eds), *Is Arbitration Only as Good as the Arbitrator? Status, Powers and Role of the Arbitrator* (ICC Publishing, Paris 2011) 25. Park is otherwise a traditionalist who regularly expresses worries that the judicialization of arbitration is going too far.

4

Precedent and Appeal

Precedent-based lawmaking enables and constrains the exercise of arbitral power, grounds discourse on the legitimacy of arbitral lawmaking and governance, and stokes demand for supervision and appeal. In the last chapter, we examined the evolution of procedural rules, a strong indicator of judicialization, that bear upon these outcomes. All major arbitral centres have codified the reason-giving requirement as a fiduciary duty of arbitrators, for example, and the ICC and SIAC Rules provide for the mandatory scrutiny of draft awards. In annulment proceedings at ICSID, parties not only routinely challenge awards for 'errors-in-law', members of ad hoc Annulment Committees (ACs) regularly succumb to the temptation to convert themselves into courts of cassation, at times annulling awards on the basis of faulty reasoning. In 2013, the AAA-ICDR created an appellate procedure that the parties may activate jointly, and the issue of appellate supervision has steadily gained salience more generally. These and other forms of hierarchical control emerged in response to heightened adversarialism, but they have also facilitated the entrenchment of precedent-based lawmaking and argumentation.

The concept of *precedent* is deeply contested by scholars, the bar, arbitrators, and officials of the major centres.[1] Everyone agrees that a notion of 'hard' precedent, conceived in terms of a *stare decisis* doctrine, is precluded, both for formal and prudential reasons. Hard precedent would require the establishment of an appellate jurisdiction with the authority to quash awards, undermining the presumption of their finality, while raising fraught issues of institutional design. A softer idea of precedent—past awards openly acknowledged as sources of persuasive authority—has broadly diffused, at least since the 1980s. In this chapter, we provide evidence that arbitrators have evolved an even more constraining notion of precedent, in the absence of a doctrine of *stare decisis* and appeal.

We define precedent as that stream of normative materials, issuing from past awards, that (a) parties plead in submissions, and (b) tribunals rely upon when they justify either their awards or their approach to decision-making. Considered in this

---

[1] For overviews on reason-giving and precedent in international arbitration, see Marta Infantino, 'International Arbitral Awards' Reasons: Surveying the State-of-the-Art in Commercial and Investment International Dispute Settlements' (2013) 5(1) Journal of International Dispute Settlement 175; Irene M Ten Cate, 'The Costs of Consistency: Precedent in Investment Treaty Arbitration' (2013) 51 Columbia Journal of Transnational Law 418 ['The Costs of Consistency']; Emmanuel Gaillard and Yas Banifatemi, *Precedent in International Arbitration* (Juris Publishing, Huntington 2008).

The Evolution of International Arbitration: Judicialization, Governance, Legitimacy. First Edition. Alec Stone Sweet and Florian Grisel. © Alec Stone Sweet and Florian Grisel 2017. Published 2017 by Oxford University Press.

way, precedent provides the components for building frameworks of argumentation and justification.[2] We observe it in practice when actors invoke doctrines, general principles, standards, tests, and interpretive techniques that are curated as case law. As an analytical matter, we distinguish between (a) 'precedent' and (b) how much any tribunal believes itself to be constrained by precedential materials, though these two phenomena may become tightly interdependent in practice. It matters what kind of authority actors are invoking when they summon precedent. As we will see, tribunals in both ICA and ISA have gradually embraced the following nascent rule: the more 'settled' is the relevant case law, the weightier is the justificatory burden placed on any tribunal that would depart from it. Such a rule, if generally adopted, would significantly harden persuasive authority, adding express presumptions and burdens to the mix.

How we understand appeal and supervision also deserves brief discussion. We define the concept of a 'system of appeal' restrictively, as any stable procedure that authorizes the annulment of a past award, depriving it of legal effect, on the basis of errors in legal reasoning. Within this category, modes of appeal can and do vary widely, on multiple dimensions.[3] At present, the AAA-ICDR is the only arbitral centre that has created such a system, in 2013, which awaits its first case. Most major centres seek to meet the demand for consistency and predictability, which has intensified with the growth in adversarial, high-stakes arbitration, through publication and supervision. Published awards should, officials expect, furnish focal points around which arbitrators will coordinate, and help to socialize new entrants. Modes of supervision can ground 'delicate' dialogues between the house and the tribunal, about the content and scope of precedent, as it does in the ICC (Chapter 3). Sophisticated parties pay attention to published awards in order to make informed decisions on the appointment of tribunals, the designation of forum, and the substance of pleadings. In ISA, states assess the evolution of arbitral jurisprudence when they consider appointments, draft new investment treaties, or contemplate exit options.

The chapter proceeds as follows. Part I focuses on how precedent emerged as a medium of judicialized, arbitral governance, not least through overcoming traditional values of arbitration that would hinder the process. Publication of awards entailed reconsidering confidentiality; requiring fully reasoned awards-in-law meant downgrading the importance of equity decision-making; and administrative supervision demanded that users tolerate a reduction in the independence of tribunals. In part II, we examine the role of precedent in ICA, in particular, how

---

[2] Barton Legum, 'The Definitions of "Precedent" in International Arbitration' in Emmanuel Gaillard and Yas Banifatemi (eds), *Precedent in International Arbitration* (Juris Publishing, Huntington 2008) ['Legum'] 7–8. A compatible version of precedent is elaborated in Alec Stone Sweet, 'Path Dependence, Precedent, and Judicial Power' in M Shapiro and A Stone Sweet (eds), *On Law, Politics, and Judicialization* (Oxford University Press, Oxford 2002) 112; Florian Grisel, 'Precedent in Investment Arbitration—The Case of Compound Interest' (2014) 2(1) PKU Transnational Law Review 216.

[3] For a comprehensive analysis of the issues, see Irene Ten Cate, 'International Arbitration and the Ends of Appellate Review' (2012) 44 NYU Journal of International Law and Politics 1109 ['Ten Cate'].

tribunals and IACs use arbitral jurisprudence to bolster their authority with respect to the parties, and the autonomy of the arbitral order in relation to state law. Part III surveys the development of precedent in ISA, followed by a detailed case study that tracks the fate of the 'necessity' defence pleaded by Argentina in a string of cases occasioned by that state's economic meltdown in the early 2000s. The so-called 'Argentina cases', more than any others, have directed attention to issues of precedent and appeal in ISA.

I. Paths to Precedent

The judicialization of international arbitration depends on the fulfilment of certain necessary conditions, including the repudiation of those orthodoxies that would hinder the emergence of notions of precedent. Arbitral centres now directly confront the key questions. First, should awards be published? If so, then the traditional commitment to confidentiality must be diluted or rescinded. Second, should arbitrators be concerned with the coherence of arbitral case law? If so, then tribunals will need to shrug off the field's association with awards-in-equity, invest heavily in reason-giving, and develop one or more conceptions of precedent. Third, to what extent should awards be supervised, and for what purposes? These questions connect reason-giving to the development of precedent and, then, to the construction of hierarchical authority.

International Commercial Arbitration

Two factors have driven the steady judicialization of ICC arbitration: the house's gradual abandonment of a strong preference for awards-in-equity, in favour of a commitment to awards-in-law; and the development of international arbitration as the dominant locus of settlement for high-stakes cases brought by parties skilled in adversarial legalism. These factors reinforced one another in ways that served: (a) to consolidate the 1958 New York Convention as an effective system for enforcing awards; (b) to organize a regulatory competition among leading states to demonstrate their pro-arbitration *bona fides*; and (c) to induce the building of organizational capacity to manage complex, adversarial cases. We examined these dynamics in Chapters 2 and 3. Here our focus is on the policy decisions taken by the ICC with regard to publication, precedent, and supervision of awards.

Publication of Awards

During the first decade of its existence, the ICC prohibited publication of awards as inimical to its project to revive the arbitral elements of the old *Lex Mercatoria*. Confidentiality would maximize the flexibility of tribunals, while reducing reputational costs to parties. 'It would be difficult to see what advantages arbitration has over ordinary legal procedure', René Arnaud, General Counsel of the ICC, insisted, 'if [the arbitrator] did not have the necessary freedom of action and ... was bound by all the formalities of procedure and a host of legal precedents'.[4] In 1929, Arnaud summarized the position of the Court of Arbitration in these blunt terms:

> In order to prevent the construction of an arbitral jurisprudence that would have the effect of creating precedent, which could hinder arbitrators in the future, it was decided to never publish the text of awards rendered in the name of the Court of Arbitration ...[5]

The prohibition complemented other core policies. ICC Rules did not require tribunals to justify awards with reasons,[6] for example, and, with rare exception, the Court's mandatory scrutiny of draft awards concentrated on the form, not the substance, of awards. Officials assumed that most awards would be based in equity, and they advised tribunals that would render awards-in-law to limit the discussion of its reasoning as a means of constraining interference by the courts.

An economic shock—the Great Depression and the attendant devaluation of the British pound sterling—compelled the ICC to reconsider its position on precedent. These deliberations opened a new developmental path that favoured judicialization. In the 1929 to 1930 period, the British pound sterling, then the pre-eminent currency of denomination for traders, fell nearly 30 per cent against the US dollar, destroying the fundamentals of countless contracts. Traders flooded the ICC with intricate disputes, the resolution of which depended partly on how to fix currency values. It quickly became clear that users would not accept resolution on a case-by-case basis, if that meant bearing the brunt of inconsistent outcomes across similar cases. Throughout 1931, the Executive Committee debated options. Some members proposed the appointment of a sole arbitrator to handle all cases related to the devaluation of the pound sterling.[7] Others advocated the creation of an appellate jurisdiction with the authority to quash awards (discussed below). In the end, the ICC chose the most modest alternative—to publish awards—thereby providing 'traders [with] guidelines for settling ... disputes of the same nature'.[8]

In a short memorandum of February 1932,[9] the ICC suggested that the potential costs of publication (that it could 'hamper the freedom of action of arbitrators in future cases' being the most important) would be outweighed by the benefits. In addition to providing a modicum of consistency, publishing awards would

---

[4] René Arnaud, 'Arbitration in the International Chamber of Commerce' (1929) 1 World Trade 116, 127.

[5] René Arnaud, 'Rapport sur l'activité de la Cour d'arbitrage' (1929) 3 L'Economie Internationale 538, 539–40. Arnaud's position reflected a prevailing view among other scholars as well—see Robert Vulliemin, *De l'arbitrage commercial particulièrement en matière internationale* (Rousseau & Cie, Paris 1931) 201–2.

[6] Until the 1930s, reasons were required in awards for enforcement purposes (e.g. the Netherlands); see Chapters 2 and 3.

[7] ICC International Court of Arbitration, 'Procès-verbal de la soixante treizième session du Comité exécutif de la Cour d'Arbitrage' (Document 4608, 30 September 1931).

[8] ICC International Court of Arbitration, 'Procès-verbal de la soixante quinzième session du Comité exécutif de la Cour d'Arbitrage' (Documents 4608 and 4690, 30 September 1931).

[9] International Chamber of Commerce, 'Publishing Arbitration Awards' (February 1932) World Trade 10.

encourage a 'free exchange of ideas' and the 'constant revision of legal concepts', while 'prevent[ing] disputes from starting at all'.[10] Confidentiality concerns, officials suggested, could be addressed through careful redaction.[11] After gathering the views of its National Committees, the ICC issued a second memorandum, informing users that it would publish redacted awards on important topics of 'general interest',[12] with 'the consent of the parties'.[13] At the same time, officials reiterated their opposition to the notion of binding precedent, announcing that published awards would be preceded by a disclaimer: 'The awards selected for publication by the Executive Committee of the Court of Arbitration cannot be considered as expressing the opinion of the ICC on the questions of principle involved, nor as constituting precedents binding the arbitrators of the ICC in future.'[14] October 1932 saw the release of 'Arbitration Awards Concerning Sterling Contracts',[15] followed by others on the same topic.[16] Awards dealing with other matters, including on the determination of the law applicable to an international contract,[17] an agent's claim to commissions,[18] the tacit acceptance of a contract,[19] and the payment of taxes on a patent,[20] appeared shortly thereafter.

After the Second World War, the ICC began in earnest to redesign arbitration as a full substitute for litigation in the courts.[21] With regard to publication, officials sought to strike a balance between two commitments: (a) the maximization of party autonomy, with freedom of contract (consent) at its core; and (b) the enhancement of arbitral authority and systemic coherence. In 1951, an ICC arbitrator took the audacious step of publishing an award without the consent of the disputing parties, albeit in redacted form.[22] Protests provoked an intense internal debate that led the Court to commission one of its members, Dr Robert Marx, to oversee the drafting

---

[10] ibid.   [11] ibid.

[12] International Chamber of Commerce, 'Publishing Arbitration Awards' (July–August 1932) World Trade 5.

[13] ibid.

[14] ibid. See also International Chamber of Commerce, 'A Recent Award Concerning Sterling Contracts' (December 1932) World Trade 11.

[15] International Chamber of Commerce, 'Arbitration Awards Concerning Sterling Contracts' (October 1932) World Trade 10.

[16] International Chamber of Commerce, 'A Recent Award Concerning Sterling Contracts' (December 1932) World Trade 11; International Chamber of Commerce, 'A Recent Decision in a Sterling Contract Dispute' (May 1933) World Trade 11.

[17] International Chamber of Commerce, 'Détermination de la loi applicable au contrat international' (March 1933) L'Economie Internationale 9.

[18] International Chamber of Commerce, 'An Agent's Claim to Commission on Business Effected Outside His Area' (June 1933) World Trade 7; International Chamber of Commerce, 'A Dispute Arising out of a Contract between a Principal and His Agent' (October 1934) World Trade 6.

[19] International Chamber of Commerce, 'Un contrat accepté tacitement peut-il être valable?' (December 1934) L'Economie Internationale 7.

[20] ICC International Court of Arbitration, 'Procès-verbal de la Quatre-Vingt-Sixième session de la Cour d'Arbitrage du 14 décembre 1932' (14 December 1932) 6.

[21] Chapter 3, Box 3.1.

[22] See ICC Award of 8 February 1951 in (1951) 365 Arbitrale Rechtspraak 511.

of a white paper on policy. The Marx Report[23] balanced in favour of transparency. If the judgments of courts operating in the international sphere were regularly published, even in sensitive cases, without withholding names, so could ICC awards. Emphasizing that the emergence of a case law would 'advantage' both counsel and arbitrators, Marx recommended that the Court be permitted to decide—'in a sovereign manner'—on publication, even in the absence of consent. Some members of the Court, including Arnaud, strongly opposed the proposal,[24] which led to further discussions on the question of how to regularize publication while respecting the principle of party consent.[25] These deliberations continue to this day, on virtually the same terms.

The present situation comprises an uneasy compromise between conflicting interests.[26] On the one hand, the modern arbitral order is founded on the ideology of party autonomy, and parties place a high value on confidentiality. It is likely that the present rule has broad support among firms: general counsel of firms will support the publication of redacted awards, but only on the basis of express consent. The 2010 *International Arbitration Survey* found that 'confidentiality is important to users of arbitration, but it is not the essential reason for recourse to arbitration'.[27] The 2015 survey found that only 33 per cent of respondents placed confidentiality among the top three reasons for choosing arbitration, placing fifth after enforceability of awards, avoiding domestic courts, flexibility, and the free selection of arbitrators.[28] Those invested in the judicialization of the arbitral order favour the development of an arbitral jurisprudence, which depends on greater transparency. Many leading arbitrators and major IACs support publication of important awards under more permissive conditions. The bar, too, has expressed its interest in the development of a more transparent case law, in that it would help counsel better serve clients. After a conflict erupts, of course, the responding party may cling to confidentiality, especially when an award goes against it. Today, when the ICC selects an award for publication, it asks the disputants concerned to express objections within a fixed time frame. Negotiations may follow, but each party ultimately

---

[23] ICC International Court of Arbitration, 'Publication des sentences de la Cour d'Arbitrage de la C.C.I.—Rapport présenté par le Dr. Robert Marx' (208th session, Document No 410/72, 26 September 1951).

[24] ICC International Court of Arbitration, 'Publication des sentences de la Cour d'arbitrage—Observations présentées par Sir Edwin S. Herbert' (210th session, Document No 410/90, 21 November 1951); ICC International Court of Arbitration, 'Publication des sentences de la Cour d'Arbitrage—Note de M. René Arnaud' (210th session, Document No 410/83, 21 November 1951).

[25] ICC International Court of Arbitration, 'Publication des sentences de la Cour d'arbitrage' (212th session, Document No 410/109, 9 January 1952).

[26] For a subtle analysis of the legal and policy interests underlying the issue of confidentiality, see Joshua Karton, 'Conflict of Interests: Seeking a Way Forward on Publication of International Arbitral Awards' (2012) 28 Arbitration International 447 ['Karton'].

[27] White & Case and Queen Mary, University of London, '2010 International Arbitration Survey: Choices in International Arbitration' <http://www.arbitration.qmul.ac.uk/docs/123290.pdf> accessed 5 April 2016, 29 ['International Arbitration Survey'].

[28] White & Case and Queen Mary, University of London, '2015 International Arbitration Survey: Improvements and Innovations in International Arbitration' <http://www.arbitration.qmul.ac.uk/research/2015/> accessed 13 June 2016, 6.

retains a veto. Most other major houses, including in Singapore (SIAC), Stockholm (SCC), Milan (Chamber of Arbitration),[29] and the US centre (AAA-ICDR) operate under a similar policy. Joshua Karton, a sophisticated commentator on these issues, favours more transparency, proposing that houses make an incremental but important change to their Rules. Under Karton's scheme, parties could object to the text of the redaction, 'but not to the fact of publication'.[30]

While the Marx Report failed to dislodge the party veto, the ICC embraced its broader approach, to promote the development of an arbitral common law through selective publication. Since 1974, the ICC has published around 700 decisions, although publication is not mentioned in the Rules.[31] In addition to five volumes of the series, *Collections of ICC Arbitral Awards*, the Court publishes new decisions on a rolling basis, in its biannual *Bulletin*, and offers an online search engine for users.[32] Among major houses, only the LCIA does not publish awards.[33]

Notions of Precedent

The development of precedent is a basic indicator of the system's judicialization. Some leading arbitrators, seemingly wedded to the dictates of the contractual model, deny that arbitrators make prospective law. Michael Mustill, a former barrister and appellate court judge in England, tells us that arbitration generates at most a 'micro *lex mercatoria*', in which 'a law is newly minted by the arbitrator on each occasion, with every contract the subject of its own individual proper law'.[34] Invoking Mustill, Kaufmann-Kohler, a leading arbitrator and professor, agrees: 'the arbitrator's sweeping freedom to apply the law that allows him or her to "mint" the rules to take account of the specificities of each case—or the case-driven propensity to transnationalise the applicable law—are in direct contradiction with the very idea of precedent'.[35] We reject the conclusion. Arbitral authority—which includes the 'sweeping freedom to interpret and apply the law'—is firmly grounded in relatively stable, precedent-based doctrines that can be empirically tracked and assessed.

It is undeniable that core features of ICA combine to hinder the development of certain forms of precedent. There exists, for example, no comprehensive body of clear, substantive rules that users can expect all arbitrators to know and consistently apply to resolve all disputes. Conceptions of precedent that depend on such a corpus of rules have never gained traction in arbitration, and we doubt that they

---

[29] Arbitration Rules of the Milan Chamber of Arbitration (2010), Article 8(1).

[30] Karton (n 26).

[31] For a full list of published awards, see International Chamber of Commerce, 'Awards' <http://www.iccdrl.com/awards_fulllist.aspx> accessed 5 April 2016.

[32] International Chamber of Commerce, 'Find Where an Award Has Been Published' <http://www.iccdrl.com/awardsfind.aspx> accessed 5 April 2016.

[33] For a comparison of confidentiality rules across major IACs, see Karton (n 26).

[34] Michael J Mustill, 'The New Lex Mercatoria: The First Twenty-Five Years' in Marteen Bos and Ian Brownlie (eds), *Liber Amicorum for the Rt. Hon. Lord Wilberforce* (Oxford University Press, Oxford 1987) 157.

[35] Gabrielle Kaufmann-Kohler, 'Arbitral Precedent: Dream, Necessity or Excuse?' (2007) 23 Arbitration International 357, 365.

exist in any effective domestic system of resolving contractual disputes. All major IACs require tribunals to embrace (a) party autonomy and freedom of contract, which generates (b) interpretive methodologies that give primacy to the intent and legitimate expectations of the parties, which they are to consider in light of (c) the applicable law, and (d) trade customs and usages relevant to the dispute.[36] The 'good' arbitrator is he or she who is skilled at fashioning a defensible award, which means taking into account each of these factors, while respecting the IAC's Rules, and any other obligations owed to parties and the house. She does so, however, on the basis of usages, general principles, and specific doctrines, that she knows other arbitrators will also curate as precedent. Major arbitral centres, for their part, codify at least some of the most important of these norms, as they emerge, on a rolling basis.[37]

These doctrines, principles, and rules comprise a foundational, common law that grounds arbitral decision-making—including the underlying bases of the tribunal's decision-making authority—enabling arbitrators to control the proceedings and fashion outcomes in light of separate streams of legal norms flowing from multiples sources. Arbitration's flexibility and sensitivity to transnational context are key components of its attraction to users. Firms and their lawyers, after all, expect a tribunal to produce better outcomes than do courts.

The essential task of the modern arbitrator—to settle disputes in light of the party's contractual choices and legitimate expectations, with due regard to the applicable law, under adversarial conditions—has shaped how precedent has emerged and evolved. The doctrines of separability and *Kompetenz-Kompetenz*, for example, serve to define key, jurisdictional features of arbitral authority vis-à-vis the parties. Both were instantiated through arbitral practice (precedent), before being codified in the codes of major arbitration centres, the *Lex Mercatoria*, and state law.[38] Tribunals generated a host of other general principles to legitimize methods of determining the reasonable expectations of the parties when interpreting contracts and filling gaps. They did so to enhance their own effectiveness, without bothering much with the question of how any specific national court would perform these same tasks. Further, some rules and general principles codify substantive arbitral law, the construction of transnational public policy being an important example (discussed below).

In short, precedent-based norms and doctrines comprise 'best-practice' standards that both enable and constrain arbitral decision-making. Some are foundational of arbitral power, settling questions of jurisdiction; others serve to secure the finality of awards in the shadow of judicial intervention; and still others are designed to help tribunals render justice to parties as agents of a transnational legal order, not merely of the parties. As important, arbitral jurisprudence regularly 'feeds back' onto the legislative activity of arbitral centres, as well as state officials. Neither Baron Mustill nor Professor Kaufmann-Kohler, both renowned, highly effective arbitrators, could do without these tools.

---

[36] Chapters 2 and 3.   [37] Chapter 3.   [38] Chapter 2.

The arbitral bar and arbitrators too have long recognized that their capacity to perform as skilled actors in the system is tied to the consolidation of an arbitral common law.[39] As early as 1982, the tribunal in ICC Case No 4131 noted that:

The decisions of … tribunals progressively create case law which should be taken into account, because it draws conclusions from economic reality and conforms to the needs of international commerce, to which rules specific to international arbitration, themselves successfully elaborated should respond.[40]

Other ICC tribunals have characterized prior published awards as 'the privileged source of law for arbitrators',[41] especially insofar as they constitute a 'consistent case law' (*jurisprudence constante*)[42] and establish 'precedents',[43] some 'remarkable and authoritative'.[44] Lawyers routinely invoke and dispute the authority of prior awards in submissions and hearings,[45] just as they would with relevant decisions of national courts, distinguishing or emphasizing similarities between prior awards and the case at hand. In such situations, arbitrators will have little choice but to do the same. Indeed, it is increasingly common for them to state whether, as one tribunal put it in 1996, they 'see any grounds for departing from the solution adopted' in an important past award.[46] Last, there is every reason to believe that parties and arbitrators would cite to more awards, if IACs published more, with less redaction.

[39] ICC Case No 3344 (1981) in Sigvard Jarvin and Yves Derains, *Collection of ICC Arbitral Awards 1974–1985* (Wolters Kluwer, New York 1994) 440: 'jurisprudence arbitrale internationale'; ICC Case No 4381 (1986) in Sigvard Jarvin, Yves Derains, and Jean-Jacques Arnaldez, *Collection of ICC Arbitral Awards 1986–1990* (Wolters Kluwer, New York 1994) 263: 'jurisprudence arbitrale'; ICC Case No 5103 (1988) in Sigvard Jarvin, Yves Derains, and Jean-Jacques Arnaldez, *Collection of ICC Arbitral Awards 1986–1990* (Wolters Kluwer, New York 1994) 361: 'jurisprudence arbitrale internationale'; ICC Case No 5030 (1992) in Jean-Jacques Arnaldez, Yves Derains, and Dominique Hascher, *Collection of ICC Arbitral Awards 1991–1995* (Wolters Kluwer, New York 1997) 475: 'jurisprudence arbitrale'; ICC Case No 6719 (1991) in Jean-Jacques Arnaldez, Yves Derains, and Dominique Hascher, *Collection of ICC Arbitral Awards 1991–1995* (Wolters Kluwer, New York 1997) 567: 'jurisprudence arbitrale internationale'; ICC Case No 14297 (2007) in Jean-Jacques Arnaldez, Yves Derains, and Dominique Hascher, *Collection of ICC Arbitral Awards 2008–2011* (Wolters Kluwer, New York 2013) 879: 'jurisprudence arbitrale CCI'.
[40] ICC Case No 4131 (1982) in Sigvard Jarvin and Yves Derains, *Collection of ICC Arbitral Awards 1974–1985* (Wolters Kluwer, New York 1994) 146.
[41] ICC Case No 5953 (1989) in Sigvard Jarvin, Yves Derains, and Jean-Jacques Arnaldez, *Collection of ICC Arbitral Awards 1986–1990* (Wolters Kluwer, New York 1994) 437.
[42] ICC Case No 10671 in Jean-Jacques Arnaldez, Yves Derains, and Dominique Hascher, *Collection of ICC Arbitral Awards 2001–2007* (Wolters Kluwer, New York 2009) 689.
[43] ICC Case No 3493 (1983) in Sigvard Jarvin and Yves Derains, *Collection of ICC Arbitral Awards 1974–1985* (Wolters Kluwer, New York 1994) 124; ICC Case No 4126 (1984) in Sigvard Jarvin and Yves Derains, *Collection of ICC Arbitral Awards 1974–1985* (Wolters Kluwer, New York 1994) 511.
[44] ICC Case No 8385 (1995) in Jean-Jacques Arnaldez, Yves Derains, and Dominique Hascher, *Collection of ICC Arbitral Awards 1991–1995* (Wolters Kluwer, New York 1997) 474.
[45] Pleadings based on arbitral precedent are documented in published awards: ICC Case No 5029 (1986) in Sigvard Jarvin, Yves Derains, and Jean-Jacques Arnaldez, *Collection of ICC Arbitral Awards 1986–1990* (Wolters Kluwer, New York 1994) 480; ICC Case No 13509 (2006) in Jean-Jacques Arnaldez, Yves Derains, and Dominique Hascher, *Collection of ICC Arbitral Awards 2001–2007* (Wolters Kluwer, New York 2009) 739; ICC Case No 14297 (2007) in Jean-Jacques Arnaldez, Yves Derains, and Dominique Hascher, *Collection of ICC Arbitral Awards 2001–2007* (Wolters Kluwer, New York 2009) 879.
[46] ICC Case No 8420 (1996) in Jean-Jacques Arnaldez, Yves Derains, and Dominique Hascher, *Collection of ICC Arbitral Awards 1996–2000* (Wolters Kluwer, New York 2009) 398, 401: Here, the

Supervision and Appeal

A system designed to produce awards-in-equity, rendered by arbitrators constituted more as mediators than judges, has no obvious need for settled doctrines,
an idea of precedent, or a mode of supervision. The ICC debated the creation
of an internal mechanism of appeal early on. In ICC Case No 207 (decided in
1930), the losing party formally requested the ICC Court of Arbitration to sit as
a 'Court of Cassation', in an effort to quash the award rendered against it.[47] The
ICC rejected the demand, on the grounds that 'the award [had] been validly rendered after review from the Executive Committee'.[48] Pressed by disgruntled users,
in 1931 the Court debated (without conclusion) a formal proposal to establish a
specialized 'Committee of Cassation' with express authority to quash awards.[49] In
the Executive Committee, Robert Marx supported the idea, arguing that the organ
would keep disgruntled parties within the system, rather than pushing them into
the domestic courts.[50] René Arnaud urged caution, proposing instead a clarifica-
tion of what was then Rule 22, in order to make it explicit that the ICC Court's
mandatory scrutiny would cover the substance of awards, not just form.[51]

By this time, the ICC Court was already reviewing the reason-giving of tribunals under the Rules, and the scrutiny process had resulted in substantial revisions
of some important awards.[52] In ICC Case No 540, a patent dispute, the Court
confronted for the first time a situation in which an arbitrator refused to revise the
substance of an award in light of the Court's comments. The meeting that ensued,
held in September 1932, revisited the question of creating an appellate court. The
published minutes of the Executive Committee of the Court are terse but revealing:

> Mr. Hansen regrets that the [Court] finds itself disarmed when facing such an award, and he
> would wish that the Rules contained a provision providing the possibility for the Committee
> itself to annul … award[s] in some cases. Mr Arnaud declares that it is normal that the form
> is often difficult to separate from the substance, but when an arbitration will have taken
> place in accordance with an arbitration agreement that gives powers to a duly-designated
> arbitrator—an arbitration agreement that is duly signed by the parties—it will be difficult
> to provide for the intervention of an organ of cassation within the ICC. Mr. Palewski thinks
> that the difficulty could be eliminated if Article 22 [of the 1932 Rules, which provided for a
> review of draft awards as to the form] were not limited to the review of form. The President

---

arbitrator refers to the award in ICC Case No 6140 with regard to two claims, accepting its authority
on one issue, while distinguishing the case on the second.
    [47] ICC International Court of Arbitration, 'Ordre du jour de la soixante-et-unième session du
Comité Exécutif de la Cour d'Arbitrage du 26 mars 1930' (61st session, 26 March 1930).
    [48] ibid.
    [49] ICC International Court of Arbitration, 'Procès-verbal de la soixante-huitième session du
Comité Exécutif de la Cour d'Arbitrage du 25 février 1931' (68th session, 25 February 1931) 5–6.
    [50] ibid 6.   [51] ibid 5.
    [52] ICC International Court of Arbitration, 'Procès-verbal de la quarante-septième session du
Comité Exécutif de la Cour d'Arbitrage du 3 octobre 1928' (47th session, 3 October 1928) 2: In ICC
Case No 264, reported in 1928, the Court called upon the arbitrator to redraft the section on compen-
sation, specify the currency in which the payment should be made, the date from which the payment
was due, and the date from which moratory interest should start running.

then observes that the Court would take the responsibility [for controlling] the substance of the award. The Committee decided to keep these observations for the next revision of the Rules concerning Article 22.[53]

The structure of this debate foreshadowed that which would take place on publication two decades later, featuring many of the same protagonists, and leading to a similar compromise.

In 1934, the ICC revised Rule 22, extending the object of the Court's scrutiny to the tribunal's reasoning:

Before completing the award, the [tribunal] shall submit the same to the Court of Arbitration, which may lay down modifications as to its form. The [Court] is not precluded from calling the attention of the [tribunal] even to points connected with the merits of the case, but with due regard to their liberty of decision.[54]

In its commentary, the ICC emphasized that the decision 'to broaden the powers of the Court' was taken in light of 'what practice had already shown to be necessary'.[55] In sum, a burst of adversarialism led the ICC to expand incrementally its existing review system rather than to invest in an altogether new form of hierarchy: an appellate court.

The revised provision, which has remained remarkably intact for more than eight decades, now appears as Rule 33 (2012). In Chapters 2 and 3, we traced the evolution of this Rule, and described the complex dialogues it organizes between the ICC Court and its tribunals. Although the Rule does not establish appellate review, the ICC's supervision of the substance of awards has become more intrusive over time.

In the 1990s, the broader arbitral community again took up the issue of appeal, generating myriad proposals.[56] It remains the case that only the ICC (since 1927) and the SIAC (since 2013), among major arbitral centres, impose mandatory pre-screening of awards before communication to the parties. In November 2013, the AAA-ICDR became the first arbitral centre to offer a mode of appeal, in its new Optional Appellate Arbitration Rules. Officials stressed that the new system was 'developed for the types of large, complex cases where the parties agree that the ability to appeal is particularly important', given the limited grounds for vacating

---

[53] ICC International Court of Arbitration, 'Procès-verbal du Comité Exécutif de la Quatre-Vingt-Quatrième session de la Cour d'Arbitrage du 28 septembre 1932' (84th session, 28 September 1932) 5–6.

[54] Article 22 of the ICC Rules of Conciliation and Arbitration (1934).

[55] International Chamber of Commerce, 'Un nouveau texte du Règlement de Conciliation et d'Arbitrage de la Chambre de Commerce Internationale' (January 1934) L'Economie Internationale 11.

[56] See 'Reconsidering a Key Tenet of International Commercial Arbitration: Is Finality of Awards What Parties Really Need? Has the Time of an International Appellate Arbitral Body Arrived?' (1999) 16 Journal of International Arbitration 57; Howard Holtzmann, 'A Task for the 21st Century: Creating a New International Court for Resolving Disputes on the Enforceability of Arbitral Awards' in Martin Hunter, Arthur Marriott, and V V Veeder (eds), *The Internationalisation of International Arbitration: The LCIA Centenary Conference* (Graham & Trotman, London 1995). For a recent reviews of the literature, see Ten Cate (n 3) and Erin E Gleason, 'International Arbitral Appeals: What Are We So Afraid of?' (2012) 7(2) Pepperdine Dispute Resolution Law Journal 269.

awards in the courts.[57] Under the Appellate Rules, no party may unilaterally activate the procedure; instead, the AAA-ICDR expects, the parties will pre-consent
to appeal in the arbitration agreement. Appellants may seek review on grounds of
(a) 'an error of law that is material and prejudicial', or (b) 'determinations of fact
that are clearly erroneous'. Three-member tribunals[58] will be selected from a pool of
former federal and state judges in the US system; and they will render final, binding awards that, in effect, replace the award under appeal.[59] The move is potentially
momentous, in that it may drive other leading centres to offer similar services, if less
American and more transnational in character.[60]

Investor-State Arbitration

By design, the founders of ICSID established an autonomous, strongly entrenched,
and relatively judicialized system of arbitration.[61] Whereas the Centre's formal
procedures have remained comparatively stable,[62] ICSID Rules concerning publication have undergone dramatic change, reflecting a policy choice in support of
precedent. Even before the explosion of ISA cases in the early 2000s, parties and
tribunals routinely invoked the authority of past awards. At the same time, a spate
of decisions featuring inconsistent reasoning[63] on the same points of law in similar
cases spurred demand for appellate supervision, which by the end of the decade had
become both noisy and impossible to ignore. Today, while virtually no one denies
the existence of arbitral precedent in treaty-based ISA, the relationship between
(a) the ICSID annulment procedure and (b) the enforcement of precedent-based
doctrine is one of the most controversial issues now and for the future.

Publication of Awards

ICSID supported publication from the beginning, if passively. Buried in the
Provisional Administrative and Financial Regulations of 1967, one finds Article 6.3
(still in force), which lays down a two-step procedure. First, the Secretary-General

---

[57] AAA President and CEO India Johnson quoted in: American Arbitration Association, 'New Optional Appellate Arbitration Rules from the AAA and ICDR Provide Further Arbitration Flexibility' <https://www.adr.org/aaa/ShowPDF?doc=ADRSTAGE2016220> accessed 5 April 2016.

[58] Upon agreement, the parties can select a sole arbitrator.

[59] Optional Appellate Arbitration Rules, Rule A-19(a) <https://www.adr.org/aaa/ShowProperty? nodeId=/UCM/ADRSTAGE2016218> accessed 5 April 2016: The appellate tribunal may '(1) adopt the underlying award as its own, or (2) substitute its own award for the underlying award (incorporat-ing those aspects of the underlying award that are not vacated or modified); or (3) request additional information and notify the parties of the tribunal's exercise of an option to extend the time to render a decision, not to exceed thirty (30) days. The appeal tribunal may not order a new arbitration hearing or send the case back to the original arbitrator(s) for corrections or further review.' The Appellate Rules are silent on a host of other issues, including standards of review and the allocation of burden of proof.

[60] International Arbitration Survey (n 27), 8: The survey reported that 23 per cent of respondents favoured the establishment of an 'appeal mechanism on the merits' for ICA, whereas 39 per cent of them favoured the same for ISA.

[61] Chapter 2.   [62] Chapter 3.   [63] See part III of this chapter.

'shall endeavour to obtain the consent of the parties to the publication' of awards. Second, once she has obtained consent, the Secretary-General will determine 'whether and in what form such publication should take place with a view to furthering the development of international law in relation to investments'.[64] In 1984, further regulation appeared in a more prominent code, the Arbitration Rules, as Rule 48(4):

The Centre shall not publish the award without the consent of the parties. The Centre may, however, [publish] excerpts of the legal rules applied by the Tribunal.

A 2006 change to Rule 48(4) placed the Centre under a positive duty to publish 'excerpts of the legal reasoning of the Tribunal', a change 'prompted by a desire to achieve greater transparency in ICSID proceedings'.[65] At the same time, no ICSID Rule has ever required parties to respect confidentiality.[66] When the issue of confidentiality arose in an early case, the tribunal refused to sanction a party that had released sensitive information to the press, since the disclosure of information to the public was not prohibited. The American Society of International Law subsequently published the decision in a prominent journal, *International Legal Materials*.[67]

Counsel immediately began to leak awards openly, in order to trumpet victories, a trend the ICSID Secretariat encouraged for more noble reasons.[68] 'When this practice first emerged', the *Commentary* recounts,[69] the 'releases' were published along with this statement, evidently drafted by the Secretariat:

We believe that the Tribunal's Decision is the product of substantial study by eminent international jurists and that its publication will not only be of interest to the international bar, but will serve generally to advance international law and order, and specifically the purposes of the [ICSID Convention].[70]

---

[64] This Rule has been updated as Regulation 22(2) of the Administration and Financial Regulations (2006), which now requires action on the part of the Secretary-General: 'If both parties to a proceeding consent to the publication of (a) reports of Conciliation Commissions; (b) arbitral awards; or (c) the minutes and other records of proceedings, the Secretary-General shall arrange for the publication thereof, in an appropriate form with a view to furthering the development of international law in relation to investments.'

[65] Christoph H Schreuer, Loretta Malintoppi, August Reinisch, and Anthony Sinclair, *The ICSID Convention: A Commentary* (2nd edn, Cambridge University Press, Cambridge 2009) Article 48, para 110 ['*ICSID Convention—A Commentary*'].

[66] ibid: Indeed, the Commentary reports that, during the drafting of the Convention, a 'party's right to [publish] was never questioned'.

[67] *Amco Asia Corporation, Pan American Development Ltd & PT Amco Indonesia* (ICSID Case No ARB/81/1), Decision of 9 December 1983, 24 ILM 365 (1985).

[68] *ICSID Convention—A Commentary* (n 65), paras 125–6: 'There are ... weighty arguments of a more general character in favour of publishing awards and other decisions. These relate not so much to the resolution of the individual dispute or to the particular parties but to the integrity and transparency of the arbitration process in general. The availability of a track record is likely to increase confidence in arbitration. Access to past decisions ought to demonstrate to potential users that the process is fair and rational. It ought to show that arbitration is not inherently slanted either in favour of the investor or the host State but that it works to their mutual advantage. This ought to induce faith in and increase use of ICSID arbitration.'

[69] *ICSID Convention—A Commentary* (n 65), para 120.

[70] The statement was attached to cases published at: 23 ILM 351 (1984); 24 ILM 365 (1985); 24 ILM 1022 (1985); 27 ILM 1281 (1988); 89 ILR 660; and 30 ILM 577 (1991).

Almost all awards rendered under the auspices of ICSID are eventually published, first on specialized websites, before diffusing more generally.[71]

Notions of Precedent

It is today clear[72] that 'a de facto doctrine of precedent'[73] is basic to arbitrating investment disputes.[74] The parties intensively plead and dispute the relevance and application of prior awards, which most arbitrators treat as a wellspring of legal reasons to justify decisions, dispositions that ICSID officials overtly encourage. As scholars and arbitrators have noted, the system has developed more or less as the common law does, if without mechanisms of coordination associated with appeal. This outcome was in no way preordained. Indeed, there were at least four good reasons to think that precedent-based argumentation and justification would not readily emerge in ISA, even in the more structured ICSID setting.

First, tribunals are typically under a formal duty to apply the substantive law laid down by a treaty, each of which comprises a discrete inter-state contract, with its own particular 'object and purpose',[75] negotiating history, and so on. It is true that most investment agreements, such as BITs and NAFTA, share certain common features, including norms that establish state liability for violations of rules on direct and indirect expropriation, the FET standard, a most favoured nation clause, and others. There is, however, no obvious reason why thousands of specific treaties should be bundled together and interpreted in the aggregate unless systemic coherence is a goal of a significant number of users, arbitrators, and officials.

Second, the interpreters of investment treaties do not sit as a permanent college, analogous to a judiciary, but rather combine in kaleidoscopic, ad hoc arrangements.

---

[71] Including the *Investment Arbitration Reporter, Investment Treaty Arbitration Law*, and *Investment Claims*. Once published, awards are discussed intensively on these websites and others, including the *Global Arbitration Review*, and are made available to standard legal search engines such as *Lexis* and *Westlaw*.

[72] As Jan Paulsson explained: 'That a special jurisprudence is developing from the leading awards in the domain of investment arbitration can only be denied by those determined to close their eyes.' See Jan Paulsson, 'International Arbitration and the Generation of Legal Norms: Treaty Arbitration and International Law' (2007) unpublished paper, widely cited and distributed and on file with the authors, 17.

[73] Domenico Di Pietro, 'The Use of Precedents in ICSID Arbitration: Regularity or Certainty?' (2007) 3 Int ALR 96. For empirical analyses of precedent in ISA, see Jeffrey P Commission, 'Precedent in Investment Treaty Arbitration: A Citation Analysis of a Developing Jurisprudence' (2007) 24 Journal of International Arbitration 129 ['Commission']; and Ole Kristian Fauchald, 'The Legal Reasoning of ICSID Tribunals—An Empirical Analysis' (2008) 19 European Journal of International Law 301 ['Fauchald'].

[74] Andrea A Bjorklund, 'The Emerging Civilization of Investment Arbitration' (2009) 113 Penn St L Rev 1269, 1273; Stephan W Schill, 'Enhancing International Investment Law's Legitimacy: Conceptual and Methodological Foundations of a New Public Law Approach' (2011) 52 Va J Int'l L 57, 82–5; Andrés Rigo Sureda, 'Precedent in Investment Treaty Arbitration' in Christina Binder et al (eds), *International Investment Law for the 21st Century: Essays in Honour of Christoph Schreuer* (Oxford University Press, Oxford 2009) 830.

[75] A tenet of interpretation imposed by Article 31(1) of the Vienna Convention on the Law of Treaties (1969) 1155 UNTS 331.

Arbitrators are of varying backgrounds, competence and reputation, and prospects for appointments to future tribunals. In three-member tribunals, they engage in strategic interactions with one another and, as a collective body, with the parties. There are several necessary conditions for precedent to emerge in such a context. Some tribunals must see it in their interest to develop the law, in ways that will serve to coordinate across treaty instruments, tribunals, and time. A rising number of counsel and arbitrators in future cases must credit legal interpretation and reasons given in past awards with at least some persuasive authority. And a substantial number of these actors must invest in a sustainable, collective process that works to permit 'the survival of good awards', while filtering out poorly reasoned ones.[76]

Third, formal law constrains the evolution of at least certain notions of precedent. While ICSID arbitrators are under an express fiduciary duty to give reasons,[77] they are not obligated to give good reasons, or to take into account the past reason-giving of their peers. Further, Article 53 of the ICSID Convention states: 'The award shall be binding on the parties.' The phrasing echoes, in part, Article 59 of the Statute of the International Court of Justice: 'The decision of the Court has no binding force except between the parties and in respect of that particular case.' These provisions are typically understood to occlude precedent conceived in *stare decisis* terms. Nonetheless, it is today widely recognized that international courts— including arbitral tribunals—can (and should) produce case law, the persuasive authority of which will depend on its longevity, coherence, and relevance to stakeholders beyond the parties.[78]

State power and international politics are a fourth potential limitation. From an agency control perspective (Chapter 1), one would predict that, the more arbitrators commit to the construction of investment treaty provisions in common, the more likely it will be that states-as-principals will react, to the extent that tribunals, through their lawmaking, displace states as the 'masters' of the regime's evolution. On the other hand, it is also true that the more tribunals owe fiduciary duties to non-state actors—the perspective of a fiduciary obligation model—the more any states-as-principals will be forced to engage other stakeholders, if states are to reform the system (see Chapters 5 and 6).

The ISA regime has surmounted these obstacles. Turning the argument on its head points toward a first-order explanation. It is precisely due to (a) the fragmentation of the sources, (b) the indeterminacy of key provisions shared by the treaties, (c) the one-shot nature of ad hoc arbitration, (d) the transient composition of tribunals, and (e) the absence of formal mechanisms of horizontal coordination between arbitrators, that the system begs for precedent. The empirical record, in fact, strongly supports a functional argument of this type. As the number of

---

[76] Commission (n 73), 156.

[77] Article 48(3) of the Convention on the Settlement of Investment Disputes between States and Nationals of Other States (1967) 575 UNTS 159 ['ICSID Convention'].

[78] See the paper published by the former President of the International Court of Justice, Gilbert Guillaume, 'The Use of Precedent by International Judges and Arbitrators' (2011) 2 Journal of International Dispute Settlement 5.

high-stakes cases flowing into the system mounted, so did the demand for precedent, which the system eventually supplied. As a result, ICSID officials,[79] tribunals, arbitrators, counsel, and scholars intensified efforts to legitimize arbitral lawmaking, using the same types of arguments long deployed to legitimize the lawmaking of courts.[80] Arbitral jurisprudence, the claim goes, serves the overlapping values of legal certainty and systemic coherence, of transparency and legitimacy, and of rule-of-law and justice. Yet, as we claimed in Chapter 1, the more judges make the law they apply, the more intractable, and the more quasi-permanent, will be the 'crisis' of legitimacy they confront. In any event, one expects that, as ISA increases in effectiveness, some state officials will contemplate reform and exit options.

While our theory of judicialization predicts such outcomes, inquiry should not stop at this level of generality. Indeed, it is obvious that more fine-grained questions beg closer examination. Noting that precedent has emerged in the regime, for example, tells us nothing about how it operates, or will evolve. In fact, the community is struggling to determine the relative dominance of differing ideas of precedent. Multiple views are in play. The first, decidedly minimalist, congrues with the contractual model. Arbitrators—scripted as faithful agents of the contracting parties—are strictly bound by state preferences. A tribunal applying treaty X has no business looking into how another tribunal has interpreted treaty Y, even when the applicable provisions are identical or similar, and even in a 'like' case. It might, however, consider how past tribunals have interpreted and applied relevant provisions of treaty X to settle similar disputes arising under treaty X.[81]

A second, much more prevalent, view holds that tribunals should consider well-reasoned, prior decisions to be sources of persuasive authority. It emerged in an explicit form in the early 2000s,[82] not least, in response to heavy reliance on past awards by parties in their submissions. By 2005, the *AES v Argentine* tribunal could articulate it as follows:

Each tribunal remains sovereign and may retain, as it is confirmed by ICSID practice, a different solution for resolving the same problem; but decisions ... dealing with the same or very similar issues may at least indicate some lines of reasoning of real interest; this Tribunal may consider them in order to compare its own position with those already adopted by its

---

[79] *ICSID Convention—A Commentary* (n 65), para 128: 'The availability of the Centre's case law should improve the predictability and quality of future decisions. It is much easier to advise parties about their chances to prevail in a potential or existing dispute on the basis of well-documented cases. The arbitration process will be more rational if the tribunals as well as the parties can build on the experience and wisdom of past decisions. While it is clear that there is no doctrine of binding precedent in ICSID arbitration, reference to earlier decisions is a useful tool in all systems of adjudication. The application of the Convention, the attendant Rules and Regulations as well as the substantive law relating to investments by a series of individually composed tribunals makes the development of a consistent case law particularly important.'

[80] This has also led to counter-arguments, the most sophisticated of which have been mounted by Ten Cate—see 'The Costs of Consistency' (n 1).

[81] A view expressed, for example, by the tribunal in *Glamis Gold Ltd v USA* (NAFTA/UNCITRAL Rules), Award of 8 June 2009, paras 3–9.

[82] Commission (n 73), 132–3: At this time, tribunals had ceased 'to disguise their outright reliance' on important 'cases' and 'precedents'.

predecessors and, if it shares the views already expressed by one or more of these tribunals on a specific point of law, it is free to adopt the same solution.[83]

Dicta of this type is today so commonplace that one can say that it comprises a basic, first-order understanding of precedent in ISA.

A third view asserts a positive arbitral duty to directly engage *la jurisprudence constante*—settled case law—when on point. Consider *Saipem Spa v Bangladesh* (2007):

> The Tribunal considers that it is not bound by previous decisions. At the same time, it is of the opinion that it must pay due consideration to earlier decisions of international tribunals. It believes that, subject to compelling contrary grounds, it has a duty to adopt solutions established in a series of consistent cases. It also believes that, subject to the specifics of a given treaty and of the circumstances of the actual case, it has a duty to seek to contribute to the harmonious development of investment law and thereby meet the legitimate expectations of the community of States and investors towards certainty of the rule of law.[84]

This conception of precedent is firmly rooted in the judicial model. Multiple forms of delegation and agency are nested within one another; and fiduciary duties to pursue doctrinal coherence are owed to the regime itself, not just to the contracting states and the disputing parties. It is also demanding notion of precedent. The Tribunal's task is to render justice in a formal sense. In the absence of 'compelling grounds', the tribunal is constrained to decide 'like' cases in 'like' fashion. These obligations flow from an unwritten, but increasingly irresistible, command to the effect that arbitrators are to maximize the stability and coherence of their jurisprudence in the name of the 'community'.

Supervision and Appeal

Given that virtually all ISA awards are published, that the parties routinely argue from the reasons given in past awards, and that tribunals have embraced the persuasive authority of their own precedents, it is no surprise that the issue of appeal has steadily moved onto the agenda. In the 2000s, a spate of inconsistent awards (see part III below) raised the political stakes for ICSID and stakeholders, generating intensive debate on the question of whether ISA needs an appellate mechanism.[85] In

---

[83] *AES Corporation v The Argentine Republic* (ICSID Case No ARB/02/17), Award of 26 April 2005, para 30.

[84] *Saipem SpA v The People's Republic of Bangladesh* (ICSID Case No ARB/05/07), Decision on Jurisdiction and Recommendations on Provisional Measures of 21 March 2007, para 67. See also *Victor Pey Casado et Fondation 'Presidente Allende' c République du Chili* (Affaire CIRDI No ARB/98/2), Sentence arbitrale du 8 mai 2008, para 119—the tribunal repeated the formula in French.

[85] See, for instance, David A Gantz, 'An Appellate Mechanism for Review of Arbitral Decisions in Investor-State Disputes: Prospects and Challenges' (2006) 39 Vanderbilt Journal of Transnational Law 39; Christian Tams, 'An Appealing Option—The Debate about an ICSID Appellate Structure' (2006) 57 Beitrage zum Transnationalen Wirtschaftsrecht 5; Claire Stockford, 'Appeal versus Annulment: Is the ICSID Annulment Process Working or Is It Now Time for an Appellate Mechanism?' in Ian A Laird and Todd J Weiler (eds), *Investment Treaty Arbitration and International Law* (Juris Publishing, New York 2012); Debra P Steger, 'Enhancing the Legitimacy of International

2004, in order 'to foster coherence and consistency in the case law', ICSID officials floated the creation of an appellate facility,[86] an agenda item it then quietly shelved as opposition emerged. Still, at least two dozen major trading nations, including the United States[87] and the European Union,[88] have at times taken positions in favour of establishing some type of appellate body for the review of ISA awards, and proposals have proliferated.[89] The collective action problems facing reform, however, are formidable, perhaps irresoluble. Revising the ICSID Convention, or creating an appellate court for the regime as a whole, would depend upon the forging of state consensus on design details; indeed, unanimity would be required. Moreover, such efforts would inevitably pose the question of formalizing substantive investment law. Would a new treaty be necessary, or would states allow an ISA appellate body to interpret the substantive law as an aggregate construction of BITs, regional arrangements, and general principles of law, as many tribunals now do? Thus, although there is incontrovertible evidence that the demand for appeal continues to rise—the 'next logical step' in the judicialization of the regime,[90] some have claimed—there is currently little prospect that a general appellate court will actually be created. We revisit this issue in Chapter 6.

At ICSID, demand for appeal has been processed through Article 52 of the Convention, which lays down an 'annulment' procedure for ICSID awards. Under Article 52 ICSID, either party 'may request annulment' within 120 days of an award being 'rendered'. Article 52 lists five headings under which claims can be brought,[91] two of which are relevant here: '(b) that the Tribunal has manifestly exceeded its powers'; and '(e) that the award fails to state the reasons on which it is based'. The parties activate the procedure, but otherwise have no control over it.

Investment Law by Establishing an Appellate Mechanism' in Armand de Mestral and Céline Lévesque (eds), *Improving International Investment Agreements* (Routledge, London 2012) ['Steger']; Ten Cate (n 3).

[86] ICSID Secretariat, 'Possible Improvements of the Framework for ICSID Arbitration' (Discussion Paper of 22 October 2004) <https://icsid.worldbank.org/apps/ICSIDWEB/resources/Documents/Possible%20Improvements%20of%20the%20Framework%20of%20ICSID%20Arbitration.pdf> accessed 5 April 2016, 14–16.

[87] As suggested in numerous model BITs and Section 2103(b)(3)(G)(iv) of the 2002 Trade Promotion Act. See Christian Tietje and Freya Baetens, 'The Impact of Investor-State-Dispute Settlement (ISDS) in the Transatlantic Trade and Investment Partnership' (Prepared for the Minister for Foreign Trade and Development Cooperation, Ministry of Foreign Affairs, The Netherlands, 24 June 2014) ['Tietje and Baetens'], 112–19.

[88] Luke Eric Peterson, 'European Commission Favors More Judicialization of ISDS in Near Term—A Multilateral Court in the Longer Term' (*International Arbitration Reporter*, 5 May 2015) <https://www.iareporter.com/articles/european-commission-favors-more-judicialization-of-isds-in-near-term-a-multilateral-court-in-the-longer-term/> accessed 26 June 2016: 'The Commission says that it is commencing preliminary work on a multilateral investment court and appellate mechanism that could be utilized by any number of governments—through an opt-in process—for resolving disputes under particular investment agreements.' See also the draft of the TTIP: European Commission, 'Transatlantic Trade and Investment Partnership' (2015) <http://trade.ec.europa.eu/doclib/html/153807.htm> accessed 5 April 2016, Article 10.

[89] For a review of the current situation, see Tietje and Baetens (n 87), 112–19. For a strong scholarly argument in favour of an appellate body, see Gus Van Harten, *Investment Treaty Arbitration and Public Law* (Oxford University Press, Oxford 2007) 160–84.

[90] Steger (n 85), 'Conclusion'.   [91] Chapter 3.

The President of the World Bank, typically in consultation with ICSID officials, appoints three 'persons' to an ad hoc Annulment Committee [AC], which proceeds under predetermined rules.[92] An annulled award may revive the original dispute: either party may request a new tribunal, upon which the process begins anew.

All participants at ICSID—the Centre's officials, tribunals and counsel, and members of ACs—fully understand the conceptual and legal distinctions between the annulment procedure and a system of appeal.[93] In 2012, in its 'Background Paper on Annulment for the Administrative Council of ICSID', the ICSID stressed that the jurisprudence of ACs had clearly established that:

(1) the grounds listed in Article 52(1) are the only grounds on which an award may be annulled; (2) annulment is an exceptional and narrowly circumscribed remedy and the role of an [AC] is limited; (3) [ACs] are not courts of appeal, annulment is not a remedy against an incorrect decision, and an [AC] cannot substitute the Tribunal's determination on the merits for its own; (4) [ACs] should exercise their discretion not to defeat the object and purpose of the remedy or erode the binding force and finality of awards; [and] (5) Article 52 should be interpreted in accordance with its object and purpose, neither narrowly nor broadly ...[94]

At a minimum, a well-functioning system of appeal corrects errors in legal reasoning committed by judges. By design,[95] Article 52 does not delegate to ACs the authority to annul awards on grounds of a tribunal's 'errors-in-law'. Rather, an AC's assigned task is to assure the procedural integrity of the award.

But participants also know that the line separating procedural and substantive review of an award is not always clear. Some blurring of boundaries may actually be desirable, to the extent that eradicating poorly reasoned awards is of value. Does a tribunal 'manifestly exceed its powers' if it manifestly applies the wrong law? Can giving the wrong reasons mean a failure 'to state the reasons' altogether? When an AC answers 'yes' to such questions, it effectively converts itself into an ad hoc appellate jurisdiction. It is significant that ACs have been doing so since the very first annulment decisions, while provoking deep controversy.[96]

---

[92] Articles 52(3) and 52(4) of the ICSID Convention.

[93] See *Patrick Mitchell v Democratic Republic of the Congo* (ICSID Case No ARB/99/7), Decision on the Application for Annulment of the Award of 1 November 2006, para 19: 'No one has the slightest doubt—all the ad hoc Committees have so stated, and all authors specializing in the ICSID arbitration system agree—that an annulment proceeding is different from an appeal procedure and that it does not entail the carrying out of a substantive review of an award.'

[94] International Centre for Settlement of Investment Disputes, 'Background Paper on Annulment for the Administrative Council of ICSID' (2012) <https://icsid.worldbank.org/apps/ICSIDWEB/resources/Documents/Background%20Report%20on%20Annulment_English.pdf> accessed 5 April 2016, para 75.

[95] ibid paras 72–3: The regime's founders unambiguously rejected appellate review of errors-in-law. As ICSID itself has emphasized, 'the drafting history demonstrates' that annulment is available only for serious violations of procedure, and 'does not provide a mechanism to appeal alleged misapplication of law or mistake in fact'.

[96] David D Caron, 'Reputation and Reality in the ICSID Annulment Process: Understanding the Distinction between Annulment and Appeal' (1992) 7 ICSID Review—Foreign Investment Law Journal 21; Christoph H Schreuer, 'Three Generations of ICSID Annulment Proceedings' in Emmanuel Gaillard and Yas Banifatemi (eds), *Annulment of ICSID Awards* (Juris Publishing, New York

We investigated the impact of the annulment procedure adapting a framework for empirical analysis developed by Aronson.[97] For each decision, an AC could proceed according to one of three approaches. Under Approach 1, the AC adopts a narrow construction of Article 52, and resists engaging in a substantive review of the legal reasoning of the tribunal. Under Approach 2, the AC engages in an 'in-depth critique' of the reasoning, but chooses not to annul the award. Under Approach 3, the tribunal annuls the award, in effect, based on the errors-in-law it contains, thereby obliterating the distinction between annulment and appeal. In addition, we examined every AC decision in order to discern whether a party pleaded faulty legal reasoning under one of the headings in Article 52, a relatively pure measure of demand for appeal in the system.

Through 2015, ICSID ad hoc Committees have rendered forty-four decisions: thirty-two rejected requests; six annulled an award in full; and six annulled in part. Strikingly, we found that in *every* annulment application leading to a final decision, applicants pleaded errors in law, often across multiple categories.[98] In thirty-three decisions, ACs adopted Approach 1,[99] although one AC took pains to agree with the reasoning of the award under review, after an intensive discussion of the international law of nationality requirements.[100] Four ACs adopted Approach 2, that is, they rejected the application while engaging in a substantive critique of the tribunal's reasoning.[101] The decision in *Togo Electricité and GDF-Suez Energie v Togo*, for example, attacks the 'confusing', 'awkward', and 'ambiguous' reasoning of the award.[102] In *Iberdrola Energía v Guatemala*, the AC rejected the tribunal's legal analysis, while refusing to annul since coherent (if wrong) reasons were, in fact,

---

2004) 17; Benjamin Aronson, 'A New Framework for ICSID Annulment Jurisprudence: Rethinking the "Three Generations"' (2012) 6 Vienna Journal on International Constitutional Law 3 ['Aronson'].

[97] Aronson (n 96). We thank Cha Moeun and Tara Zivkovic, then Yale Law School students, for their research assistance on the ACs' activity.

[98] Christoph H Schreuer, 'From ICSID Annulment to Appeal: Half Way Down the Slippery Slope' (2011) 10 Law & Prac Int'l Cts & Tribunals 211.

[99] In one of these cases, the AC annulled an award under Article 52(1)(d), as 'there has been a serious departure from a fundamental rule of procedure'. See *Fraport AG Frankfurt Airport Services Worldwide v the Republic of the Philippines* (ICSID Case No ARB/03/25), Decision of the ad hoc Committee on the Application for Annulment of Fraport AG Frankfurt Airport Services Worldwide of 23 December 2010, para 218.

[100] *Hussein Nuaman Soufraki v United Arab Emirates* (ICSID Case No ARB/02/7), Decision of the ad hoc Committee on the Application for Annulment of Mr Soufraki of 5 June 2007.

[101] *CMS Gas Transmission Company v Argentina* (ICSID Case No ARB/01/8), Decision of the ad hoc Committee on the Application for Annulment of the Argentine Republic of 25 September 2007; *Compañía de Aguas del Aconquija SA and Vivendi Universal SA (Vivendi II)* (ICSID Case No ARB/97/3), Decision on the Argentine Republic's Request for Annulment of the Award of 10 August 2010; *Iberdrola Energía, SA v Republic of Guatemala* (ICSID Case No ARB/09/5), Decision of the ad hoc Committee on the Application for Annulment of Iberdrola Energía SA of 13 January 2015; *Togo Electricité and GDF-Suez Energie Services v Republic of Togo* (ICSID Case No ARB/06/7), Decision on Annulment of Togo Electricité and GDF-Suez Energie Services of 6 September 2011.

[102] *Togo Electricité and GDF-Suez Energie Services v Republic of Togo* (ICSID Case No ARB/06/7), Decision of the ad hoc Committee on the Application for Annulment of Togo Electricité and GDF-Suez Energie Services of 6 September 2011, para 191.

given.[103] The most important AC decision in this category is *CMS Gas Transmission v Argentina*, which devoted some fifty paragraphs[104] to just one egregious 'manifest error-in-law'.[105] The *CMS* AC refused annulment on jurisdictional grounds: an AC is not, after all, a 'court of appeal' empowered 'to substitute its own view of the law … for those of the Tribunal'.[106] Nonetheless, the *CMS* AC's decision exerted enormous precedential impact on subsequent awards, as we show below (part III). Seven ACs adopted Approach 3, engaging in appellate review in all but name. Each of these invoked grounds under either Article 52(1)(b) ['that the Tribunal has manifestly exceeded its powers'] and/or Article 52(1)(e) ['that the award has failed to state the reasons on which it is based'], annulling on the basis of errors in law.[107] Thus, 27 per cent of AC decisions (n = 12) have resulted in annulment, 16 per cent on errors-in-law (n = 7).

II. Precedent and Lawmaking in International Commercial Arbitration

Major IACs publish awards to build the internal coherence, and to defend the external autonomy, of the arbitral order.[108] Neither objective could be achieved in the absence of stable and transmittable doctrine. At stake is the effectiveness of ICA. The mantra of arbitrators of cross-border commercial disputes, across many

---

[103] *Iberdrola Energía, SA v Republic of Guatemala* (ICSID Case No ARB/09/5), Decision of the ad hoc Committee on the Application for Annulment of Iberdrola Energía SA of 13 January 2015, para 131.

[104] *CMS Gas Transmission Company v Argentina* (ICSID Case No ARB/01/8), Decision of the ad hoc Committee on the Application for Annulment of the Argentine Republic of 25 September 2007, paras 101–50.

[105] ibid paras 130, 146, and 158.   [106] ibid para 135.

[107] *Klöckner I* (*Klöckner Industrie-Anlagen GmbH and others v United Republic of Cameroon and Société Camerounaise des Engrais*) (ICSID Case No ARB/81/2) Decision of the ad hoc Committee on the Application for Annulment of 3 May 1985; *Amco Asia Corporation and others v Republic of Indonesia (Amco I)* (ICSID Case No ARB/81/1), Decision of the ad hoc Committee on the Application for Annulment of 16 May 1986; *Patrick Mitchell v Democratic Republic of the Congo* (ICSID Case No ARB/99/7), Decision on the Application for Annulment of 1 November 2006; *Malaysian Historical Salvors v Malaysia* (ICSID Case No ARB/05/10), Decision of the ad hoc Committee on the Application for Annulment of 16 April 2009; *Helnan International Hotels A/S v Arab Republic of Egypt* (ICSID Case No ARB/05/19), Decision of the ad hoc Committee on the Application for Annulment of 14 June 2010; *Sempra Energy International v Argentine Republic* (ICSID Case No ARB/02/16), Decision on Annulment of 29 June 2010; *Enron Creditors Recovery Corporation (formerly Enron Corporation) and Ponderosa Assets, LP v Argentine Republic* (ICSID Case No ARB/01/3), Decision of the ad hoc Committee on the Application for Annulment of 30 July 2010.

[108] Yves Derains, a former Secretary-General of the ICC, declared in 1990 that 'the publication of this collection [of awards], since 1974, has contributed to the cohesion of the case law' of arbitral tribunals. See Sigvard Jarvin, Yves Derains, and Jean-Jacques Arnaldez, *Collection of ICC Arbitral Awards 1986–1990* (ICC Publishing, Paris 1990) 268. In 1997, Sigvard Jarvin, another former Secretary-General of the ICC, stressed that the publication of awards enables the general public 'to appreciate the evolution of arbitrators' reasoning in a continuously changing environment in the field of arbitration and substantive rules of law which, despite their diversity, have a number of common features …'. See Sigvard Jarvin, 'Preface' in Jean-Jacques Arnaldez, Yves Derains, and Dominique Hascher, *Collection of ICC Arbitral Awards 1991–1995* (ICC Publishing, Paris 1995) ix.

centuries, has been to give primacy to the intent and expectations of the contracting parties, a disposition that is now institutionalized as a fiduciary duty (Chapter 3). The obligation is rooted in a meta-principle—that of party autonomy—which is expressed in myriad ways. The regime would have failed in its mission to render final and enforceable awards if it had not developed doctrines (a) to keep parties in arbitration once a dispute has erupted, (b) to apply general principles of transnational law and trade usages, and (c) to elicit the support of courts for purposes of recognition and enforcement purposes. The arbitral order itself developed separability and *Kompetenz-Kompetenz*, dense procedures related to due process, and a long list of sub-principles that further articulate good faith, legitimate expectations, public policy, arbitral authority to tailor remedies, and so on.

Thus, the commitment to the freedom to choose arbitration entails building norms, organizational hierarchies, and capacity to dialogue with national courts within the New York Convention system. In this section, we return to the question of party autonomy and the applicable law. The parties are free to select the law that will govern their contract, whether national or transnational. Or they may leave the choice to the tribunal. As we have emphasized in previous chapters, however, even when the parties have chosen the law of state X to govern their contract, tribunals are not expected to apply that law as a court in state X would. While no one denies that tribunals are obliged to respect applicable mandatory rules, they are otherwise relatively unconstrained by state law when it comes to interpreting contracts. As transnational dispute resolvers, arbitrators are predisposed to gap-filling and fact-determination in light of transnational norms.[109] Transnational usages, general principles, and public policy not only help to express and define the scope of the parties' 'legitimate expectations', they are also important building blocks of arbitral authority. Indeed, their development has led domestic courts to adapt their own law in important ways.

Trade Usages and General Principles of Law

With regard to trade usages, those versed in the adjudication of contractual disputes in North America, Europe, and parts of Asia (Hong Kong, South Korea, and Singapore), will find themselves on familiar ground. In the United States, for example, the New York and Delaware courts have declared, again and again, that the 'cardinal rule' and 'fundamental precept' of contract interpretation is to give effect to the 'intentions' and 'the reasonable shared expectations' of the parties at the moment they contracted.[110] Faced with ambiguities and gaps in contracts and state

---

[109] Joshua Karton, 'The Arbitral Role in Contractual Interpretation' (2015) 6 Journal of International Dispute Settlement 4 ['The Arbitral Role in Contractual Interpretation'].

[110] See *Re Motors Liquidation Co* (2011) 460 BR 603 Bkrtcy SDNY: '[A] court should accord [contractual] language its plain meaning giving due consideration to "the surrounding circumstances [and] apparent purpose which the parties sought to accomplish" '; *Cordis Corp v Boston Scientific Corp* (2012) 868 F Supp 2d 342: 'The primary consideration in interpreting a contract is to "attempt to fulfill, to the extent possible, the reasonable shared expectations of the parties at the time they contracted".' This posture contrasts with that of so-called 'formalist' approaches that would seek to avoid reference to context and the 'surrounding circumstances' of the transaction.

law, judges routinely reference, or explicitly incorporate into the contract, those 'customs, practices, usages, and terminology generally understood in the particular trade or business'.[111] The assumption that the parties were familiar with such norms and practices, at the *ex ante* contractual moment, grounds the judicial interpretation of contested law and facts in an 'objective' source: the industry-specific understandings of the 'reasonably sophisticated' trader.[112] Customs and usages comprise a powerful, and ever-evolving, set of freighted norms that can overlap with, or be absorbed into, general principles. Some jurisdictions incorporate them into contracts regardless of the parties' intent. Where usages are default rules, the parties will have to take great pains to contract out of them, but, even then, they may still find themselves bound by usages through principles such as good faith, reasonableness, and legitimate expectations. Moreover, when it comes to performance, the parties will also be held to relevant conduct observed habitually by traders.[113]

The ICC and the arbitral order embraced similar presumptions long before courts did. Arbitral tribunals have a greater strategic interest in invoking trade usages and *lex mercatoria*: their vocation, after all, is to resolve transnational commercial disputes, not to enforce state law.[114] Moreover, the parties routinely choose state law that is not their own, on which counsel and arbitrators are often not expert. It is likely that incorporation serves the interests of such firms, not least, through lowering the costs of transnational contracting *ex ante*.[115]

UNCITRAL Rules, as well as the procedural rules of the ICC, the AAA-ICDR, SIAC, the Swiss Chambers, and many other IACs, treat usages as an implied term

---

[111] *RSUI Indem Co v RCG Group (USA)* (2012) 890 F Supp 2d 315: 'An ambiguity exists where the terms of an insurance contract could suggest "more than one meaning when viewed objectively by a reasonably intelligent person who has examined the context of the entire integrated agreement and who is cognizant of the customs, practices, usages and terminology as generally understood in the particular trade or business"'.

[112] *HGCD Retail Servs LLC v 44–45 Broadway Realty Co* (2006) 37 AD3d 43, 49–50, 826 NYS2d 190: '[A] contract should not be interpreted to produce a result that is absurd, commercially unreasonable or contrary to the reasonable expectations of the parties'.

[113] See US Uniform Commercial Code (1952) ['UCC'] § 1–201(3). More generally, the UCC, the relevant parts of which have been adopted more or less faithfully in all fifty states, prompts American courts to interpret contracts in light of trade usages. Indeed, usages are expected to permeate the agreement, as enforceable elements of 'the bargain of the parties'. § 1–205(2) of the UCC defines a usage as 'any practice or method of dealing having such regularity of observance in a place, vocation or trade as to justify an expectation that it will be observed with respect to the transaction in question'. For a critical overview of how American courts have used usages, see Lisa Bernstein, 'Trade Usage in the Courts: The Flawed Conceptual and Evidentiary Basis of Article 2's Incorporation Strategy' <http://chicagounbound.uchicago.edu/law_and_economics/660/> accessed 6 April 2016, Part I.

[114] Joshua Karton's empirical research shows that this disposition—which results in 'the primacy in arbitral awards to arguments based on trade usages and commercial reasonableness'—is now deeply rooted in a coherent arbitral 'culture'. See Joshua Karton, *The Culture of International Arbitration and the Evolution of Contract Law* (Oxford University Press, Oxford 2013) Chapter 4. See also 'The Arbitral Role in Contractual Interpretation' (n 109).

[115] See the argument exchange between Avery Katz, 'The Relative Costs of Incorporating Trade Usage into Domestic versus International Sales Contracts' (2004) 5 Chicago Journal of International Law 181 and Clayton Gillette, 'The Law Merchant in the Modern Age: Institutional Design and International Usages under the CISG' (2004) 5 Chicago Journal of International Law 157.

of transnational commercial contracts, and require tribunals to take them into account as part of the applicable law (Chapter 3). In 15 per cent of the ICC's new cases registered during the 2007 to 2011 period, the parties made no choice of law,[116] a situation that may lead tribunals to ground awards in the UNIDROIT Principles and other codifications of the *Lex Mercatoria*. In a typical case, the applicable law will reduce to the UNIDROIT principles, Article 1.9 of which states that 'the parties are bound by a usage that is widely known to and regularly observed in international trade by parties in the particular trade concerned except where the application of such a usage would be unreasonable'. ICC arbitrators regularly invoke usages to complement state law,[117] to fill gaps in contracts,[118] and have even disapplied provisions of national law that are incompatible with the norms and practices of transnational commerce.[119]

As it does in the world of courts, reference to custom-based norms helps arbitrators manage the 2-against-1 dynamic discussed in Chapter 1, in that they can purport to be applying 'objective', 'neutral' norms that transcend the conflict. Moreover, the application of trade usages facilitates the development of arbitral

---

[116] International Chamber of Commerce, *The Secretariat's Guide to ICC Arbitration* (ICC Publishing, Paris 2012) para 3-751, Table 31.

[117] See ICC Case No 5713 (1989) in Sigvard Jarvin, Yves Derains, and Jean-Jacques Arnaldez, *Collection of ICC Arbitral Awards 1986–1990* (Wolters Kluwer, New York 1994) 223. See also ICC Case No 6955 (1993) in Jean-Jacques Arnaldez, Yves Derains, and Dominique Hascher, *Collection of ICC Arbitral Awards 1991–1995* (Wolters Kluwer, New York 1997) 267; ICC Case No 5346 (1988) in Sigvard Jarvin, Yves Derains, and Jean-Jacques Arnaldez, *Collection of ICC Arbitral Awards 1986–1990* (Wolters Kluwer, New York 1994) 414; ICC Case No 8365 (1996) in Jean-Jacques Arnaldez, Yves Derains, and Dominique Hascher, *Collection of ICC Arbitral Awards 1996–2000* (Wolters Kluwer, New York 2009) 1078; ICC Case No 7139 (1995) in Jean-Jacques Arnaldez, Yves Derains, and Dominique Hascher, *Collection of ICC Arbitral Awards 1991–1995* (Wolters Kluwer, New York 1997) 647; ICC Case No 9333 (1998) in Jean-Jacques Arnaldez, Yves Derains, and Dominique Hascher, *Collection of ICC Arbitral Awards 1996–2000* (Wolters Kluwer, New York 2009) 575.

[118] See ICC Case No 5485 (1987) in Sigvard Jarvin, Yves Derains, and Jean-Jacques Arnaldez, *Collection of ICC Arbitral Awards 1986–1990* (Wolters Kluwer, New York 1994) 199; ICC Case No 5713 (1989) in Sigvard Jarvin, Yves Derains, and Jean-Jacques Arnaldez, *Collection of ICC Arbitral Awards 1986–1990* (Wolters Kluwer, New York 1994) 223; ICC Case No 8501 (1999) in Jean-Jacques Arnaldez, Yves Derains, and Dominique Hascher, *Collection of ICC Arbitral Awards 1996–2000* (Wolters Kluwer, New York 2009) 529; ICC Case No 2583 (1976) in Sigvard Jarvin and Yves Derains, *Collection of ICC Arbitral Awards 1974–1985* (Wolters Kluwer, New York 1994) 304; ICC Case No 7331 (1994) in Jean-Jacques Arnaldez, Yves Derains, and Dominique Hascher, *Collection of ICC Arbitral Awards 1991–1995* (Wolters Kluwer, New York 1997) 592.

[119] ICC Case No 8873 (1999) in ICC International Court of Arbitration, *ICC International Court of Arbitration Bulletin*, Vol 10(2) (ICC Publishing, Paris 1999) 78: '... les arbitres ne sont pas liés aux règles strictes d'un droit national lorsqu'il s'agit de déterminer si, et dans quelle mesure, les usages du commerce peuvent s'appliquer, éventuellement en substitution de normes dispositives de la loi applicable'. See also ICC Case Nos 2745 and 2762 (1977) in Sigvard Jarvin and Yves Derains, *Collection of ICC Arbitral Awards 1974–1985* (Wolters Kluwer, New York 1994) 326; ICC Case No 6219 (1990) in Sigvard Jarvin, Yves Derains, and Jean-Jacques Arnaldez, *Collection of ICC Arbitral Awards 1986–1990* (Wolters Kluwer, New York 1994) 428; ICC Case No 5514 (1990) in Sigvard Jarvin, Yves Derains, and Jean-Jacques Arnaldez, *Collection of ICC Arbitral Awards 1986–1990* (Wolters Kluwer, New York 1994) 459; ICC Case No 8817 (1997) in Jean-Jacques Arnaldez, Yves Derains, and Dominique Hascher, *Collection of ICC Arbitral Awards 1996–2000* (Wolters Kluwer, New York 2009) 415. Others have refused to apply usages if it would contradict the clear intention of the parties. See ICC Case No 13954 (2007) in Jean-Jacques Arnaldez, Yves Derains, and Dominique Hascher, *Collection of ICC Arbitral Awards 2008–2011* (Wolters Kluwer, New York 2013) 519, 535.

common law. Tribunals do so in a second move: they recognize a usage as embodying a general principle of law. In a widely cited 1982 case, a tribunal of three leading arbitrators, including two major theorists of the *Lex Mercatoria*, Pierre Lalive and Berthold Goldman, declared that the principles of good faith and *pacta sunt servanda* were an integral part of 'international trade usages and international law'.[120] Today, tribunals routinely rely on an arbitral jurisprudence of general principles, partly derived from trade usages, to help them deal with a wide range of issues. These include: the proper method for determining the law applicable to the merits;[121] the mitigation of damages;[122] distinctions between procedural law and substantive law;[123] the validity of the choice-of-law clause[124] and the scope of the arbitration clause;[125] challenges to separability;[126] the tribunal's competence to determine interest rates;[127] the principle of good faith in the negotiation, enforcement, and interpretation of contract;[128] *force majeure* and the hardship doctrine as regards termination of contracts;[129] the principle of 'loyalty' in transnational commerce;[130] the duty to enforce international public policy;[131] and the calculation of damages.[132]

---

[120] ICC Case No 3896 (1982) in *Journal du droit international* (1984) 58, 79.

[121] ICC Case No 4131 (1982) in Sigvard Jarvin and Yves Derains, *Collection of ICC Arbitral Awards 1974–1985* (Wolters Kluwer, New York 1994) 146.

[122] ICC Case No 3344 (1981) in Sigvard Jarvin and Yves Derains, *Collection of ICC Arbitral Awards 1974–1985* (Wolters Kluwer, New York 1994) 440.

[123] ICC Case No 4695 (1984) in Sigvard Jarvin and Yves Derains, *Collection of ICC Arbitral Awards 1974–1985* (Wolters Kluwer, New York 1994) 33.

[124] ICC Case No 5073 (1986) in Sigvard Jarvin, Yves Derains, and Jean-Jacques Arnaldez, *Collection of ICC Arbitral Awards 1986–1990* (Wolters Kluwer, New York 1994) 85.

[125] ICC Case No 5029 (1986) in Sigvard Jarvin, Yves Derains, and Jean-Jacques Arnaldez, *Collection of ICC Arbitral Awards 1986–1990* (Wolters Kluwer, New York 1994) 480; ICC Case No 5924 (1988) in Sigvard Jarvin, Yves Derains, and Jean-Jacques Arnaldez, *Collection of ICC Arbitral Awards 1986–1990* (Wolters Kluwer, New York 1994); ICC Case No 7920 (1993) in Jean-Jacques Arnaldez, Yves Derains, and Dominique Hascher, *Collection of ICC Arbitral Awards 1991–1995* (Wolters Kluwer, New York 1997) 227; ICC Case No 10671 (2001) in Jean-Jacques Arnaldez, Yves Derains, and Dominique Hascher, *Collection of ICC Arbitral Awards 2001–2007* (Wolters Kluwer, New York 2009) 689; ICC Case No 14297 (2007) in Jean-Jacques Arnaldez, Yves Derains, and Dominique Hascher, *Collection of ICC Arbitral Awards 2001–2007* (Wolters Kluwer, New York 2009) 879.

[126] ICC Case No 5485 (1987) in Sigvard Jarvin, Yves Derains, and Jean-Jacques Arnaldez, *Collection of ICC Arbitral Awards 1986–1990* (Wolters Kluwer, New York 1994) 199.

[127] ICC Case No 6219 (1990) in Sigvard Jarvin, Yves Derains, and Jean-Jacques Arnaldez, *Collection of ICC Arbitral Awards 1986–1990* (Wolters Kluwer, New York 1994) 428.

[128] ICC Case No 5953 (1989) in Sigvard Jarvin, Yves Derains, and Jean-Jacques Arnaldez, *Collection of ICC Arbitral Awards 1986–1990* (Wolters Kluwer, New York 1994) 437.

[129] ICC Case No 8486 (1996) in Jean-Jacques Arnaldez, Yves Derains, and Dominique Hascher, *Collection of ICC Arbitral Awards 1996–2000* (Wolters Kluwer, New York 2009) 321.

[130] ICC Case No 5030 (1992) in Jean-Jacques Arnaldez, Yves Derains, and Dominique Hascher, *Collection of ICC Arbitral Awards 1991–1995* (Wolters Kluwer, New York 1997) 475.

[131] ICC Case No 6719 (1991) in Jean-Jacques Arnaldez, Yves Derains, and Dominique Hascher, *Collection of ICC Arbitral Awards 1991–1995* (Wolters Kluwer, New York 1997) 567.

[132] ICC Case No 10422 (2001) in Jean-Jacques Arnaldez, Yves Derains, and Dominique Hascher, *Collection of ICC Arbitral Awards 2001–2007* (Wolters Kluwer, New York 2009) 609; ICC Case No 14359 (2007) in Jean-Jacques Arnaldez, Yves Derains, and Dominique Hascher, *Collection of ICC Arbitral Awards 2001–2007* (Wolters Kluwer, New York 2009) 931.

The synergy between usages and general principles generates expansive lawmaking dynamics that have proven irresistible; indeed, they quietly unfold in tribunal decision-making on a daily basis. In the late 1980s, Loquin and others claimed that trade usages could not be neatly distinguished from general principles, since both 'take account of the same fundamental phenomenon: the renaissance of an ancient law largely independent of national law', capable of being identified and developed by international arbitrators.[133] Emmanuel Gaillard immediately objected, arguing that national law (if chosen by the parties) strictly determines the legal status of both usages and general principles. In Gaillard's view, tribunals could take into account (or enforce) usages and general principles when expressly authorized by national law, as the French (in 1981) and Dutch (in 1987) did in revisions of their respective codes of civil procedure. On the other hand, Gaillard reasoned, it would be wrong—'illegitimate'[134]—for an arbitrator to apply usages where the national law was silent on the matter, pointing to Switzerland as the example.

One can endlessly debate the dogmatics underlying these assertions. What is undeniable is that the limitations that would be imposed on arbitrators by national law on Gaillard's account have largely dissipated, at least in the major trading zones. The norm—arbitrators 'shall take into account trade usages'—is not only enshrined in the Rules of the major IACs: it finds expression in the most important hard and soft law instruments of transnational commerce. It is directly incorporated into national law, for example, whenever states faithfully adopt the relevant provision of the UNCITRAL Model Law,[135] or accede to the 1980 Convention on Contracts for the International Sale of Goods (under which, some commentators insist, 'trade usages and the will of the parties prevail over national law with the exception of mandatory rules').[136] Consider Gaillard's counter-example. In Switzerland, the Private International Law Act (1987) governs international arbitration, but, even after being amended in 2014, the statute does *not* mention trade usages. Yet Article 33 of the Rules of the Swiss Chambers Arbitration Institution repeats word for word the formulation found in the UNCITRAL Model Law on International Arbitration (as well as the ICC Rules), although Switzerland has *not* adopted it:

In all cases, the arbitral tribunal shall decide in accordance with the terms of the contract and shall take into account the trade usages applicable to the transaction.

---

[133] Eric Loquin, 'La réalité des usages du commerce international' (1989) 2 Revue internationale de droit économique 163, cited and critiqued in Emmanuel Gaillard, 'La distinction des principes généraux du droit et des usages du commerce international' in *Etudes offertes à Pierre Bellet* (Litec, Paris 1991) ['Gaillard'] 203, 209. See also Eric Loquin, 'L'application de règles anationales dans l'arbitrage commercial international' in *L'apport de la jurisprudence arbitrale* (ICC, Paris 1986) 1, 67.

[134] Gaillard (n 133), 215.

[135] Article 28(4) of the UNCITRAL Model Law (2006): 'In all cases, the arbitral tribunal shall decide in accordance with the terms of the contract and shall take into account the trade usages applicable to the transaction.'

[136] Chalarambos Pamboukis, 'The Concept and Function of Usages in the United Nations Convention on the International Sale of Goods' (2005–2006) 25 Journal of Law and Commerce 107, 110.

Swiss courts routinely apply usages and the *Lex Mercatoria*; indeed, they will invoke the ICC's Incoterms,[137] 'even when [they] were not incorporated into the contract explicitly or implicitly ... as rules of interpretation'.[138] Switzerland acceded to the Convention on Contracts for the International Sale of Goods in 1990, thereby incorporating the primacy of trade usages as an autonomous source of applicable law. By 1990, when Gaillard wrote his piece, only eighteen states had ratified that Convention (to date, eighty-four have done so),[139] and only five states had adopted statutes based on the UNCITRAL Model Law (to date, seventy-three states have done so).[140]

Transnational Public Policy

'Transnational public policy' is a construction of arbitral jurisprudence. The process began with the so-called '*Lagergren* award' of 1963 (ICC).[141] That award, which gave primacy to (a) 'international public policy' and 'general principles' over (b) 'national rules on arbitrability', carried such prestige that tribunals routinely referred to it even before its official publication three decades later, in 1994.[142] The *Lagergren* award has since acquired the status of a stable precedent.[143] In 1986, Pierre Lalive (a well-known academic and arbitrator) published a seminal paper theorizing transnational public policy as its own domain of law.[144] Lalive conceptualized the domain as a particular set of general principles that bind tribunals and prevail over any other applicable norms, whether domestic, international, or contractual:

> The international arbitrator applies, and is limited by, an international private law [which] *can only itself be 'transnational'* that is to say, it is composed of a certain number of general principles, either common to all parties (and States) in specific domains ... some of which are even universal.[145]

---

[137] See Chapter 2.

[138] Tribunal Cantonal du Valais (2009) <http://cisgw3.law.pace.edu/cases/090128s1.html> accessed 6 April 2016. See also Leonardo Graffi, 'Remarks on Trade Usages and Business Practices in International Sales Law' (2011) 3 Belgrade Law Review 102 ['Graffi'].

[139] United Nations Commission on International Trade Law, 'Chronological table of actions: United Nations Convention on Contracts for the International Sale of Goods (Vienna, 1980)' <http://www.uncitral.org/uncitral/en/uncitral_texts/sale_goods/1980CISG_status_chronological.html> accessed 5 April 2016.

[140] United Nations Commission on International Trade Law, 'Status: UNCITRAL Model Law on International Commercial Arbitration (1985), with amendments as adopted in 2006' <http://www.uncitral.org/uncitral/en/uncitral_texts/arbitration/1985Model_arbitration_status.html> accessed 6 April 2016. (The six states are Canada, Cyprus, Nigeria, Scotland, California, and Connecticut.)

[141] ICC Case No 1110 (1963) in Jean-Jacques Arnaldez, Yves Derains, and Dominique Hascher, *Collection of ICC Arbitral Awards 1996–2000* (Wolters Kluwer, New York 2009) 1.

[142] J Gillis Wetter, 'Issues of Corruption before International Arbitral Tribunals: The Authentic Text and True Meaning of Judge Gunnar Lagergren's 1963 Award in ICC Case No. 1110' (1994) 10(3) Arbitration International 277.

[143] ICC Case No 4126 (1984) in Sigvard Jarvin and Yves Derains, *Collection of ICC Arbitral Awards 1974–1985* (Wolters Kluwer, New York 1994) 511.

[144] Pierre Lalive, 'Ordre public transnational (ou réellement international) et arbitrage international' (1986) 3 Revue de l'arbitrage 329.

[145] ibid 351 (emphasis in original).

This hierarchical feature of transnational public policy can produce constitutional effects. In ICC Case No 6320 (1992), an arbitral tribunal adjudicated a claim regarding the alleged unconstitutionality of certain provisions of the RICO statute under US law. The tribunal decided that it did not possess such authority, preferring to review the lawfulness of the same provisions under transnational public policy, comforting Lalive's construction.[146] Such decisions reveal the pluralist-constitutional model in action: transnational public policy embodies a set of higher-law norms analogous to constitutional law in the domestic sphere.

As developed by tribunals, transnational public policy includes, at the very least, the prohibition of slavery, corruption, the drug trade, terrorism, genocide, and the regulation of the trade of organs and weapons, as well as guiding principles on which the UN General Assembly or Security Council may pass important resolutions.[147] Much of this content reflects *jus cogens* norms, but it may also include other human rights and due process norms discussed with reference to the pluralist-constitutional model in Chapter 1. Acting in this quasi-constitutional mode, ICC tribunals have determined that EU competition law,[148] and the absence of a national statute of limitation,[149] for example, are compatible with transnational public policy. They have also asserted that the various transnational sub-principles of good faith,[150] the prohibition for a state to renege on an arbitration agreement on the basis of its own law,[151] and the prohibition on secret commission agreements[152] are components of it.

Although transnational public policy evolved in ICA, it has migrated into ISA, and is now a joint construction.[153] The ICSID case of *World Duty Free v Kenya* (2006) illustrates the point.[154] The dispute concerned a company incorporated on the Isle of Man and the Republic of Kenya, in connection with an agreement to construct and operate duty-free complexes at two international airports. Following the alleged expropriation of its properties by the Republic of Kenya, World Duty

---

[146] ICC Case No 6320 (1992) in ICC International Court of Arbitration, *ICC International Court of Arbitration Bulletin*, Vol 6(1) (ICC Publishing, Paris 1995) 59.

[147] Christoph Schreuer, Loretta Malintoppi, August Reinisch, and Anthony Sinclair, *The ICSID Convention: A Commentary* (2nd edn, Cambridge University Press, Cambridge 2009) 566–7.

[148] ICC Case No 8423 (1994) in (2001) XXVI Yearbook Commercial Arbitration 153, 154.

[149] ICC Case No 7263 (1994) in (1997) XXII Yearbook Commercial Arbitration 92, 102.

[150] ICC Case No 6474 (1992) in (2000) XXV Yearbook Commercial Arbitration 281: '[T]he international community has adopted the unambiguous policy of denying any recognition to and refusing to have any dealings with the territory [of the Republic of X]. The defendant contends that this must include international arbitration.'

[151] ICC Case No 10623 (2001) in (2003) 21(1) ASA Bulletin 82, 91–2.

[152] ICC Case No 6248 (1990) in (1994) XIX Yearbook Commercial Arbitration 124, 131.

[153] See *Niko Resources Ltd v Bangladesh et al* (ICSID Case Nos ARB/10/11 and ARB/10/18), Decision on Jurisdiction of 19 August 2013, para 434: 'Normally, arbitral tribunals respect and give effect to contracts concluded by the parties which agreed on the arbitration clause from which they derive their powers. However, party autonomy is not without limits. In international transactions the most important of such limits is that of international public policy. A contract in conflict with international public policy cannot be given effect by arbitrators.'

[154] *World Duty Free Company Ltd v Republic of Kenya* (ICSID Case No ARB/00/7), Award of 25 September 2006.

Free claimed restitution of the complexes, and payment of damages in the amount of US$500 million.

In the course of the proceedings, the company described in detail the conclusion of the 1989 agreement, including the payment of bribes to the then president of Kenya, Daniel Arap Moi. Kenya subsequently asked the arbitral tribunal to dismiss the proceedings on the grounds that any agreement procured through bribes was unenforceable, and that it should serve public interests more broadly.[155] The tribunal agreed, invoking transnational public policy, and only secondarily domestic public policy. The tribunal took pains to define the nature of transnational public policy, associating it with 'universal standards and accepted norms of conduct that must be applied in all fora'.[156] The award cited to the Lalive article of 1986,[157] and surveyed no less than seven ICC awards (including the *Lagergren* award). The arbitrators stressed that their reasoning was rooted in ICC arbitral practice and a particular, transnational construction of public policy.[158] Subsequent ICSID awards have adopted similar positions.[159]

Feedback Effects: National Law

One of the most important empirical issues raised by studies of judicialization concerns the extent to which the judicialization of any system of dispute resolution influences the decision-making of officials operating in other systems.[160] In previous chapters, we have emphasized the fact that officials of the major trading states have steadily adapted to the expansion of arbitration, recognizing the autonomy of the arbitral order along the way. One important, but largely unexplored, area of research concerns the impact of arbitral lawmaking on substantive state law.

Within the framework established by the New York Convention, state courts exercise a supervisory function through powers of enforcement. Article V(2)(b) of the New York Convention permits a national court to withhold the recognition and enforcement of an arbitral award that is 'contrary to [that state's] public policy'. In a classic commentary on the Convention published in 1981, van den Berg sharply distinguished the public policy principles covered by Article V(2)(b),

---

[155] ibid para 118.   [156] ibid paras 138–9.   [157] ibid para 139.
[158] ibid para 157.
[159] *EDF (Services) Ltd v Romania* (ICSID Case No ARB/05/13), Award of 8 October 2009, para 221; *Phoenix Action Ltd v Czech Republic* (ICSID Case No ARB/06/15), Award of 15 April 2009, para 113; *Millicom International Operations BV and Sentel GSM SA v Republic of Senegal* (ICSID Case No ARB/08/20), Decision on Jurisdiction of 16 July 2010, para 103; *Rumeli Telekom AS and Telsim Mobil Telekomunikasyon Hizmetleri AS v Republic of Kazakhstan* (ICSID Case No ARB/05/16), Award of 29 July 2008, paras 177 et seq; *Gustav FW Hamester GmbH & Co KG v Republic of Ghana* (ICSID Case No ARB/07/24), Award of 18 June 2010, para 123; *Fraport AG Frankfurt Airport Services Worldwide v Republic of the Philippines* (ICSID Case No ARB/03/25), Dissenting Opinion of Mr Bernardo M Cremades of 19 July 2007, para 40.
[160] Alec Stone Sweet, 'Judicialization and the Construction of Governance' (1999) 32 Comparative Political Studies 163; Alec Stone Sweet, 'The European Court of Justice and the judicialization of EU governance' (2010) 5(2) Living Reviews in European Union Governance, <http://www.livingreviews.org/lreg-2010-2>.

and the notion of 'transnational public policy', arguing that the latter do not apply to enforcement proceedings under the Convention.[161] He further asserted that the 'basis' of public policy could only be national, since it could be 'sanctioned only by a national judge'.[162] In the decade that followed, the arbitral order consolidated its own notions of 'transnational public policy', in the form of a body of pre-emptory norms that trump the application of any other applicable law.

With the consolidation of the New York Convention system, many domestic courts have recognized that 'national public policy' constrains domestic arbitration, while a separate body of principles—typically labelled either 'international' or 'transnational public policy'—constrains international arbitration. Further, the relevant domestic statutes and/or case law of the major trading nations have evolved in ways that grant wide discretion to arbitrators, insofar as they respect and enforce transnational/international public policy in their awards. Significantly, some domestic courts now process enforcement claims under Article V(2)(b) in light of international/transnational public policy: an important feedback effect. In 1992, the Court of Appeal of Milan referred explicitly to what arbitrators would call transnational public policy as the standard for assessing the enforceability of an award:

The issue ... raised by the respondent is whether the award, which is only to be reviewed formally, is consistent with public policy. [W]here this consistency is to be examined, reference must be made to the so-called international public policy, being a 'body of universal principles shared by nations of similar civilization, aiming at the protection of fundamental human rights ...'[163]

Such courts, in effect, incorporate into the notion of 'public policy', as laid down by the New York Convention, the principles of 'transnational public policy' developed by arbitrators,[164] displacing national policy requirements.[165]

---

[161] Albert Jan van den Berg, *The New York Arbitration Convention of 1958* (Kluwer Law and Taxation Publishers, Alphen aan den Rijn 1981) 361.

[162] ibid 360.

[163] *Allsop Automatic Inc v Tecnoski snc* [1992] Court of Appeal of Milan (1994) 30 Rivista di diritto internazionale private e processuale 873.

[164] Jan Paulsson, *The Idea of Arbitration* (Oxford University Press, Oxford 2013) ['Paulsson'] 209: 'Where "truly international public policy" comes into its own is in its recognition by international tribunals, which find international sources not only in national laws but also in expressions of the international community. There are thus areas where international tribunals may recognize, propagate, and consolidate universal norms ... even when they cannot find authority in a particular national law. In time, the development of this category of public policy may well influence that of national public policy.'

[165] In a 2014 enforcement case, the Supreme Court of Lithuania asserted that 'the concept of "public policy" is understood in the doctrine and practice of international arbitration [to be] international public policy, which encompasses the fundamental and universally recognized principles of law.' That Court then held that a violation of 'imperative legal norms of the Republic of Lithuania [would not be] sufficient ground to refuse the recognition of a foreign arbitral award, unless these "imperative legal norms" [coincided] with norms of transnational public policy'. See *L B v State Property Fund of the Republic of Lithuania* [2014] Supreme Court of Lithuania, Civil Case No 3K-3–363/2014 in (2014) XXXIX Yearbook Commercial Arbitration 437, 442. Gary Born, *International Commercial Arbitration* (2nd edn, Wolters Kluwer, London 2014) fn 1586: Gary Born, in his commentary of the New York Convention, cites the Luxembourg Supreme Court ('The New York Convention does not provide for any control on the manner in which the arbitrators decide on the merits, with as the only reservation, the respect of international public policy').

We observe the same trend in annulment proceedings. Unlike enforcement proceedings under the New York Convention (which can take place in the courts of any signatory state), annulment claims are reviewed only under domestic law at the seat of arbitration. In most jurisdictions, a violation of public policy constitutes a ground for annulment; and the UNCITRAL Model Law (2010) provides that: 'An arbitral award may be set aside ... only if the court finds that the award is in conflict with the public policy of this State.'[166] Again, the norm is formally a domestic one. Yet, as regulatory competition among states for arbitral business has intensified (Chapter 2), courts too have adopted transnational postures. Their reasoning is straightforward: given that arbitrators can—and should—render awards in conformity with transnational legal principles, the review undertaken by domestic judges should reflect the same standards. The result, reached by most courts in the major trading states, is that the threshold for annulling an international award on grounds of public policy is higher than it is for domestic awards. That is, judges typically defer more to international tribunals than they do to arbitrators in domestic proceedings.

The leading example is France. Paris is the most designated seat for ICC arbitration, for which the Paris Court of Appeal is the designated forum for annulment proceedings. In a decision rendered in 1960, the Supreme Court (*Cassation*), to which rulings of the Paris Court of Appeal are directly referred, construed the words 'public policy' set out in the Geneva Convention of 1927 as meaning 'international public policy',[167] and in 1961 as 'French public policy in the sense of private international law'.[168] The standard of 'international public policy' is a judicial construction, but lawmakers codified it by amending the Code of Civil Procedure of 1981,[169] as further reflected in 2011.[170] As a matter of French legal doctrine, the standard remains conceptually distinct from the 'transnational public policy' of the arbitral order.[171] Nonetheless, in a 1993 decision involving bribery, the Paris Court of Appeal refused to distinguish between the principles of international public policy (referred to in the French Code of Civil Procedure) and the transnational public policy (applied by arbitrators).[172] Other courts have followed suit. In 1994, the Federal Tribunal of Switzerland declared that the review

---

[166] Article 34(2)(b)(ii) of the UNCITRAL Model Law (2010).

[167] French Court of Cassation, Cass Civ 1ère (14 June 1960).

[168] French Court of Cassation, Cass Civ 1ère (22 November 1966): 'l'ordre public français au sens du droit international privé'. In an annulment case decided in 1976, the Court of Cassation reversed a decision of the Paris Court of Appeal (which had annulled an arbitral award for breach of 'public policy') by underscoring the more lenient standard of international public policy—see also French Court of Cassation, Cass Civ 1ère (30 June 1976), No 74-14419.

[169] See Articles 1502 and 1504(1) of the French New Code of Civil Procedure (1981).

[170] See Articles 1520 and 1525 of the French Code of Civil Procedure (2011). Article 1520(5) provides that French courts will annul an award insofar as it 'is contrary to international public policy'.

[171] Paulsson (n 164), 207–8: Jan Paulsson tellingly describes the French rule as one of 'national international' public policy, laying down 'the minimum standards appropriate in the context of cases having an international dimension'.

[172] *European Gas Turbines SA v Westman International Ltd* (30 September 1993), Paris Court of Appeal, (1994) 2 Revue de l'arbitrage 359.

of arbitral awards on the basis of national public policy would be inconsistent with the fact that arbitrators often apply substantive law other than Swiss. For that reason, the Tribunal decided that it should review arbitral awards in light of trans-national public policy.[173] Finally, in recent years, the French courts have made it even more difficult for a losing party to resist enforcement or recognition of an arbitral award, or to obtain its annulment. The claimant now must demonstrate that a tribunal's breach of international public policy was 'flagrant, effective and concrete'.[174] Some commentators have criticized the tightening of the standard, in that it would reduce the control exercised by French courts to virtually nil.[175] Today, annulments are exceedingly rare, but not unknown, events.[176]

There is also evidence of feedback beyond the New York Convention framework, as when national courts adopt doctrinal approaches to contract law developed by arbitrators. Such impact is registered, for example, when national judges, as part of pro-trade and pro-arbitration policies, apply trade usages and general principles in the context of the litigation of a transnational contractual dispute. They are required to do so, of course, when the applicable law is that of a state party to the Convention on Contracts for the International Sale of Goods, as most major trading states are. From the point of view of counsel, one of the functions of arbitration is to identify the content of trade usages and customs, as they evolve, an activity that published awards record.[177] When the same advocates find themselves before domestic courts, they are likely to invoke these decisions, as evidence of a particular usage, thereby educating those judges who might not be versed in the niceties of transnational commerce. We do not know how often such pleadings occur, or with what effects, but have every reason to believe that they are increasing.

Through this same mechanism, some national courts have adopted an arbitral tribunal's interpretation of substantive national law, displacing their own precedents. In a series of cases reported by the arbitrator and law professor François Perret, arbitral tribunals refused to abide by a decision rendered by the Italian Supreme Court (*Cassation*) on certain seller's warranties, preferring to apply Article 2496 of the Italian Civil Code (requiring a ten-year statute of limitation), rather than Article 1495 of the Italian Civil Code (mandating a one-year statute of limitation).[178] Perret notes that the arbitral tribunals were influenced by usages and customs evidenced, in part, by

[173] *F, U v W Inc* (30 December 1994), Swiss Federal Tribunal, (1995) 13(2) *ASA Bulletin* 217, 223.

[174] French Court of Cassation, Cass Civ 1ère (21 March 2000); Paris Court of Appeals (23 March 2006); French Court of Cassation, Cass Civ 1ère (4 June 2008), No 06-15320.

[175] Emmanuel Gaillard, 'La jurisprudence de la Cour de cassation en matière d'arbitrage international' (2007) 4 Revue de l'arbitrage 697, 717.

[176] In 2013, the Court of Cassation upheld the Paris Court of Appeal's annulment of an arbitral award on the ground of international public policy, rejecting claims that the Court of Appeal had not limited its inquiry to a 'flagrant, effective and concrete' character of the breach—see French Court of Cassation, Cass Civ 1ère (11 September 2013) No 11-17201.

[177] Juana Coetzee, 'The Role and Function of Trade Usage in Modern International Sales Law' (2015) 20 Uniform Law Review 243; Graffi (n 138).

[178] François Perret, 'Resolving Conflicts between Contractual Clauses and Specific Rules of the Governing Law—Strict Application of the Law or Flexible Approach' in *The Application of Substantive Law by International Arbitrators* (ICC, Paris 2014) 109.

'long-standing contractual practice inspired by the warranties and indemnity clauses of Anglo-American law'. Following these five awards, several lower courts in Rome and Milan reversed their case law, choosing to follow the tribunals' path, and disavowing the Court of Cassation.

III. Precedent and Lawmaking in Investor-State Arbitration

Arbitrators, through precedent-based reasoning and justification, have been the authors of much of the substance of international investment law since the field's take-off in the late 1990s. This section, first, provides a statistical overview of the development of precedent in ISA. We then present a detailed case study of the 'Argentina cases', focusing on how tribunals and Annulment Committees (ACs) have interpreted the 'necessity' defence provided by Article XI of the US–Argentina BIT. These awards are among the most controversial ever rendered, in that they have produced a set of inconsistent doctrinal approaches to key questions bearing on state liability in a set of high profile, 'like' cases. Nonetheless, as we show, the system succeeded in eliminating certain politically fraught interpretations of the necessity clause while leaving other issues open, with ACs operating, in effect, as appellate bodies.

Argumentation and Justification

We defined precedent (above) as those accreted materials, issuing from prior awards, that counsel and arbitrators use as building blocks to construct frameworks for argumentation and justification. Legum has defined precedent in a congruent way: (a) for counsel, 'a precedent is any decisional authority that is likely to affect the decision in the case at hand'; and (b) for arbitrators, 'a precedent is any decisional authority that is likely to justify the award to the principal audience for that award'.[179]

To help us assess the evolution of precedent, we compiled comprehensive information on citation to prior awards and judicial decisions in all final ISA awards on the merits (liability).[180] We counted every instance in which a tribunal had cited to decisions on which it positively relied, on which it expressly disagreed, and on which it engaged in order to distinguish the present from a prior case. We counted citations contained in summaries of counsels' pleadings only if the tribunal later addressed the relevant arguments in its own assessment. If the tribunal did not make it clear that a cited case informed its interpretation of the law, we did not count it. Finally, within any single award, we counted multiple citations to the same case,

---

[179] Legum (n 2).
[180] There is a paucity of empirical research on precedent in ISA despite the pioneering work of Commission and Fauchald, both publishing data ending in 2006. See Commission (n 73) and Fauchald (n 73).

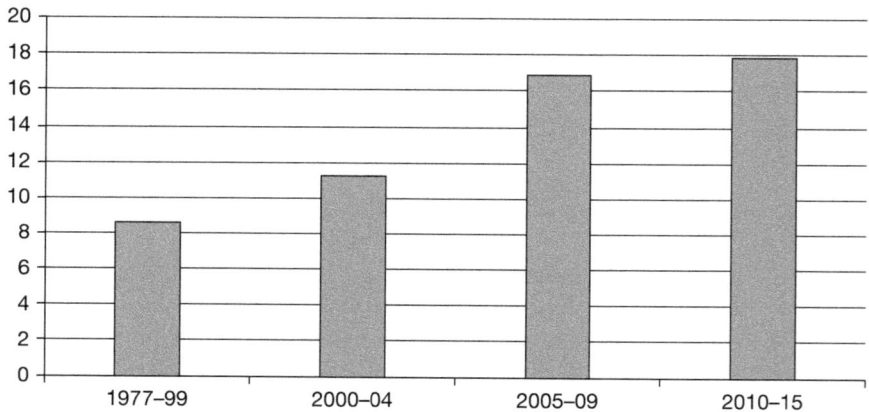

Figure 4.1 Average Number of Citations Per Award and by Period

Source: Yale Law School Data Sets on Investor-State Arbitration, compiled by Alec Stone Sweet, Sheng Li, Meng-Jia Yang, Michael Chung, Moeun Cha, and Tara Zivkovich.

on the same proposition, only once; multiple citations to the same award would be counted more than once only where a tribunal had invoked the award with regard to two or more independent propositions. Thus, the data analysed represent only those materials actually used by tribunals in the interpretation and application of the law in final awards on the merits. They are therefore a robust, relatively direct, indicator of the influence of precedent on decision-making.

Here we present descriptive statistics on citations to case law upon which tribunals explicitly relied to support their reasoning.[181] Tribunals have injected reasons into the ISA regime at a strikingly consistent rate, with the average number of citations per decision more than doubling since 2000 (Figures 4.1 and 4.2).[182] As awards have accumulated, the number of precedents in the system has grown exponentially. Indeed, 97 per cent (n = 2,108) of all citations added to the system between 1977 and 2014 have been produced since 2000, 84 per cent (n = 1,827) since 2005, and 45 per cent (n = 971) in the 2010 to 2014 period. The upshot is that, today, one can expect counsel to support every important pleading, and tribunals to defend virtually every important decision, with reference to case law.

The ISA regime has become a judicial system through reason-giving and precedent. In the pre-2000 period, tribunals tended to cite more to the International Court of Justice and other courts; thereafter, citations to their peers on ISA tribunals dominate counts (Figure 4.3). Since 2005, about 90 per cent of all awards cite to prior arbitral awards, in particular, to case law produced under the auspices of ICSID. Further, tribunals routinely site across treaty instruments. ICSID tribunals

---

[181] This part of the database was completed by Sheng Li, Meng-Jia Yang, and Alec Stone Sweet.
[182] Since 2000, ten awards have contained no counted citations, four of which have been rendered since 2004.

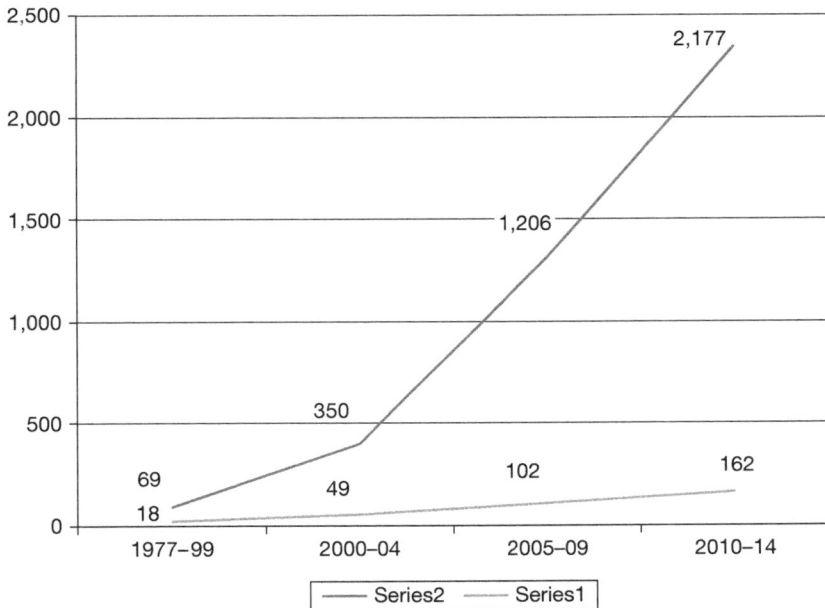

Figure 4.2 Cumulative Number of Awards and Cases Cited, by Period

Source: Yale Law School Data Sets on Investor-State Arbitration, compiled by Alec Stone Sweet, Sheng Li, Meng-Jia Yang, Michael Chung, Moeun Cha, and Tara Zivkovich.

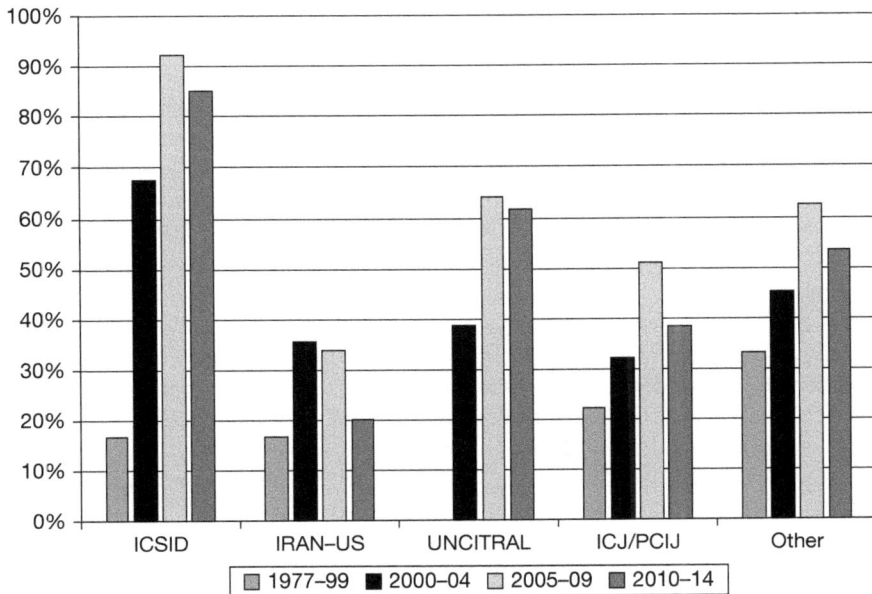

Figure 4.3 Percentage of Awards Citing to Case Law, by Source and Period

Source: Yale Law School Data Sets on Investor-State Arbitration, compiled by Alec Stone Sweet, Sheng Li, Meng-Jia Yang, Michael Chung, Moeun Cha, and Tara Zivkovich.

Table 4.1 Citation to Case Law by Legal Domain

Domain	Citations	% of All Citations Per Domain	Awards Citing to Case Law Per Domain	% of Awards Citing to Case Law Per Domain
Fair and Equitable Treatment	640	28.5%	87	51.8%
Expropriation	453	20.1%	83	49.4%
Damages	273	12.1%	55	32.7%
Protection and Security	136	6.1%	27	16.1%
Interest Assessment	91	4.1%	16	9.5%
MFN or National Treatment	89	4.0%	21	12.5%
Investment	86	3.8%	21	12.5%
Arbitrary or Discriminatory Treatment	62	2.8%	22	13.1%
Denial of Justice	60	2.7%	15	8.9%
Umbrella Clause	59	2.6%	14	8.3%
Necessity	48	2.1%	11	6.6%
Cost/Fees	44	2.0%	10	6.0%
Other	135	9.2%		
Total	2,249	100.1%		

Source: Yale Law School Data Sets on Investor-State Arbitration, compiled by Alec Stone Sweet, Sheng Li, Meng-Jia Yang, Michael Chung, Moeun Cha, and Tara Zivkovich.

freely cite to NAFTA tribunals operating under UNCITRAL rules, for example, and vice versa. The evidence strongly supports the claim that precedent-based law-making has served to consolidate the judicial model as applied to ISA.

We also compiled data at the domain level, that is, to the interpretive questions posed in specific substantive areas of treaty law. Table 4.1 reports data for all legal domains generating at least 3 per cent of total citations found in awards on the merits. In Chapter 5, we discuss in detail the construction of doctrine in the major substantive areas of investment law, including Expropriation and the Fair and Equitable Treatment standard [FET]. As we show, in many important cases, questions falling under categories such as Arbitrary or Discriminatory Treatment, Protection and Security, Denial of Justice, and an Umbrella Clause will overlap with, or be subsumed by, FET and Expropriation claims. What is clear is that legal domains have been steadily brought into closer relationship to one another as the case law has evolved, creating a system of interdependent norms.

We also examined the extent to which the arbitrators' approaches to important, recurrent questions have tended either (a) to converge around a leading case, or line of consistent precedents, or (b) to diverge, generating two or more lines of case law. We found important trends toward convergence in most areas, including in the substantive areas just listed (see Chapter 5 for further details). In other areas, a single case served to generate a high degree of consistency, where before there was no widely accepted rule, interpretation of principle, or test. The *Santa Elena v Costa Rica* award (2000), for example, initiated a powerful shift toward awarding compound interest, rather than simple interest, when calculating damages following a finding of state liability.[183] And the *Salini* test is widely used to address the problem of determining what types of assets held by the investor are protected as an 'investment'.[184]

The drive toward jurisprudential coherence is facilitated by the fact that at least one member of a relatively small group of elite arbitrators is usually present on any tribunal, and repeat arbitrators that specialize in chairing tribunals dominate the production of awards (Chapter 2). Still, there is no equivalent of the WTO Appellate Body in the regime, meaning that the process of building precedent depends on persuasion and the professional commitment of arbitrators to the value of consistency across cases, treaty instruments, and time. We therefore expect the impact of precedent on future awards to be uneven. Opposed positions on important questions remain, including, famously, on whether a breach of contractual commitments made to an investor on its own suffices to generate a breach of an 'umbrella clause',[185] triggering liability under the treaty.[186]

Our data also allow us to consider how arbitrators engage with the jurisprudence of international courts, a central preoccupation of the pluralist-constitutional model. In seventy-eight different awards—38 per cent of the total number— tribunals cite to international courts 204 times. The count understates the impact of international case law. Some of the most highly cited ISA awards have been those that invoke the authority of international courts when making major doctrinal moves. The most highly cited ISA award, *Tecmed v Mexico* (2003),[187] relied on the jurisprudence of the European Court of Human Rights [ECtHR] to introduce the proportionality principle into ISA, and to bring the doctrine of 'legitimate

---

[183] *Santa Elena v Costa Rica* (ICSID Case No ARB/96/1), Award of 17 February 2000, paras 97–105; Florian Grisel, 'L'octroi d'intérêts composés par les tribunaux arbitraux d'investissement' (2011) 3 *Journal du Droit International* 545.

[184] *Salini Costruttori SpA and Italstrade SpA v Kingdom of Morocco* (ICISD Case No ARB/05/22), Decision on Jurisdiction of 31 July 2001. We do not report data on jurisdictional decisions here unless they were cited in awards on the merits. Precedent in jurisdiction cases is also well developed, although it has a different structure. The question of determining what is or is not an 'investment' is an area of overlap, generating 6 per cent of the citations (Table 4.1).

[185] A typical example of an umbrella clause is Article X(2) of the Switzerland–Philippines BIT, which provides that: 'Each Contracting Party shall observe any obligation it has assumed with regard to specific investments in its territory by investors of the other Contracting Party.'

[186] Of thirteen awards (on the merits) invoking case law on this question, nine cite *SGS Société Générale de Surveillance SA v Islamic Republic of Pakistan* (ICSID Case No ARB/01/13), Decision on Jurisdiction of 6 August 2003, para 172 (answering in the affirmative) and ten cite *SGS Société Générale de Surveillance SA v Republic of the Philippines* (ICSID Case No ARB/02/6), Decision on Jurisdiction of 29 January 2004, para 129 (responding in the negative). Six explicitly address both awards, and most tribunals engaged the arguments they would reject in favour of the alternative.

[187] *Técnicas Medioambientales Tecmed SA v United Mexican States* (ICSID Case No ARB(AF)/00/2), Award of 29 May 2003 has been cited eighty-seven times overall and forty-eight times with respect to FET.

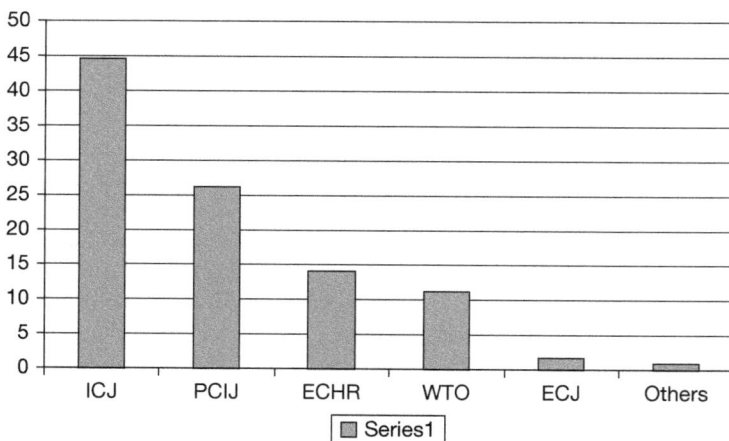

Figure 4.4 Awards Citing to International Courts: Percentage by Jurisdiction

Source: *Yale Law School Data Sets on Investor-State Arbitration*, compiled by Alec Stone Sweet, Sheng Li, Meng-Jia Yang, Michael Chung, Moeun Cha, and Tara Zivkovich.

expectations' into the FET. *Saluka v Czech Republic* (2006), a hugely influential and widely cited case[188] standing for the proposition that the 'legitimate expectations' of investors are to be balanced against the state's 'legitimate regulatory interests',[189] does not cite to international courts, but relies heavily on *Tecmed* and other ISA awards instead.[190] Thus, a tribunal may rely on the rulings of international courts to help them craft a principle that arbitrators will subsequently treat as a native fixture of foreign investment law.

Figure 4.4 compares, with respect to awards citing to international courts, the percentage of citations to five jurisdictions: the International Court of Justice (n = 91); the Permanent Court of International Justice (n = 43); the World Trade Organization (n = 23); the ECtHR (n = 29); the European Union (n = 4).[191] In most of these instances, tribunals cite to international jurisprudence to identify a principle of law for use in ISA. To take some of the most prominent examples, tribunals have cited: (a) the *Chorzow Factory* decision of the Permanent Court of International Justice in support of the principle of the full reparation of the losses suffered by the aggrieved party through financial compensation;[192] (b) the *ELSI* decision of the International Court of Justice in support of a definition of arbitrariness as an action

---

[188] *Saluka Investments BV v Czech Republic* (UNCITRAL) Partial Award of 17 March 2006. This is the eighth most cited award in the data set (n = 57), and the fourth most cited case in the domain of FET (n = 31).

[189] ibid para 306.   [190] Chapter 5.

[191] The Inter-American Court of Human Rights and the Tribunal of the Law of the Sea have each been cited once.

[192] See *Enron Corporation Pondesora Assets, LP v Argentina* (ICSID Case No ARB/01/3), Award of 22 May 2007 [hereafter '*Enron Corp*'], para 359; *Metalclad Corporation v Mexico* (ICSID Case No

that 'shocks, or at least surprises, a sense of juridical propriety';[193] (c) the separate opinion of Judge Higgins in the *Oil Platform* case (International Court of Justice) as equating the FET standard with 'legal terms of art well known in the field of overseas investment protection';[194] (d) the decision of the WTO Appellate Body in the *Korea-Beef* case with respect to the definition of 'necessity';[195] (e) the decision of the European Court of Human Rights in the *Mellacher v Austria* case with respect to the definition of expropriation;[196] and (f) the decision of the Permanent Court of International Justice in the *Oscar Chinn* case pursuant to which potential profits cannot constitute protected rights under international law.[197]

It would be a serious mistake, however, to treat ISA tribunals as passive receptors of international law. Indeed, they are actively engaging in the construction of the law. Since 1990, the ISA regime has rendered more rulings on the merits involving property rights and the necessity defence under the law of state responsibility than the courts of any other international regime outside of Europe.

We now turn to the necessity defence, and to the question of what happened when tribunals split on findings of liability in the first wave of Argentina cases.

The Argentina Cases: Arbitrating the 'Necessity' Defence

The cases generated by the Argentina crisis of 1999 to 2002 have attracted more attention than any in ICSID's history.[198] Their salience is due to sheer numbers, the high value of the compensation being claimed, and the spectacular context—an economic meltdown of cataclysmic proportions—that generated them. To add to the drama, for disputes brought under the U.S.-Argentina BIT (1991), Article XI

ARB(AF)/97/1), Award of 30 August 2000, para 122; *National Grid PLC v Argentina* (UNCITRAL), Award of 3 November 2008, para 270.

[193] See, for instance, *Técnicas Medioambientales Tecmed SA v United Mexican States* (ICSID Case No ARB(AF)/00/2), Award of 29 May 2001, para 154; *Total SA v Argentina* (ICSID Case No ARB/04/1), Decision on Liability of 27 December 2010, para 110.

[194] *Total SA v Argentina* (ICSID Case No ARB/04/1), Decision on Liability of 27 December 2010, para 108; *Unglaube v Costa Rica* (ICSID Case Nos ARB/08/1 and ARB/09/20), Award of 16 May 2012, para 247.

[195] *Continental Casualty Company v Argentina* (ICSID Case No ARB/03/9), Award of 5 September 2008, para 193.

[196] *Ronald S Lauder v Czech Republic* (UNCITRAL), Award of 3 September 2001, para 202; *Técnicas Medioambientales Tecmed SA v United Mexican States* (ICSID Case No ARB(AF)/00/2), Award of 29 May 2001, para 122.

[197] *Merrill & Ring Forestry LP v Canada* (UNCITRAL), Award of 31 March 2010, para 215; *El Paso Energy International Company v Argentina* (ICSID Case No ARB/03/15), Award of 31 October 2011, para 366.

[198] The literature on this line of cases is voluminous, having attracted more scholarly commentary than any other set of awards. Discussions in light of wider issues of comparative and international law include (in chronological order): William Burke-White and Andreas von Staden, 'Investment Protection in Extraordinary Times: The Interpretation and Application of Non-Precluded Measures Provisions in Bilateral Investment Treaties' (2007) 48 Va J Int'l L 307; William Burke-White, 'The Argentina Financial Crisis: State Liability under BITs and the Legitimacy of the ICSID System' (2008) 3 Asian J WTO & Int'l Health L & Pol'y 199; José Alvarez and Kathryn Khamsi, 'The Argentina Crisis and Foreign Investors: A Glimpse into the Heart of the International Investment Regime' in Karl Sauvant (ed), *The Yearbook on International Investment Law and Policy 2008/2009* (Oxford University Press, New York 2009) 379; Jürgen Kurtz, 'Adjudging the Exceptional at International Investment

makes available to the Contracting States a derogation clause covering acts deemed 'necessary' to meet the crisis. Argentina has systematically pleaded Article XI, and will presumably continue to do so in numerous future proceedings, testing ICSID's capacity to generate consistent outcomes absent a doctrine of *stare decisis* and appellate review. Our concern is on how the various tribunals and ACs responded to the Argentina's pleading of the necessity defense, in the awards and decisions produced to date. As we show, the annulment process generated precedential materials that destroyed certain approaches to interpreting Article XI, while leaving other questions open.

The Orrego Vicuña Approach

The cases examined here are based on the same facts, which can be briefly summarized. After overcoming military dictatorship (1973 to 1985), Argentina sought to democratize and to build an open, market-based economy. In the 1990s, it signed BITs with fifty-six countries,[199] ratified the ICSID Convention, and began privatizing state-run companies and utilities, with foreign participation. To encourage investment further, Argentina pegged its currency to the US dollar, promised that capital could move freely in and out of the country, and gave investors in some utilities rights to participate in administrative decisions that would affect revenue streams. These arrangements unraveled during the 1999 to 2002 period, when the country experienced an exploding budget deficit, a balance of payments crisis, and mounting foreign debt. In 2001, Argentina made deep budget cuts and renegotiated its debt obligations (which did not stave off default). It eventually permitted a devalued peso to float on the markets, restricted withdrawals from bank accounts, and forced conversion of dollar deposits into pesos—so-called *pesification*. It would probably be impossible to unravel the precise causal relationships that connected (a) the onset and deepening of the economic crisis, (b) mounting political instability, and (c) the increasingly desperate steps taken by the Argentine state to stave off collapse of its currency and banking system. Each of these processes fed into the other two, leading the situation to spiral out of control at a breathtaking pace. These questions of fact and causation were among the most difficult arbitrators faced.

What is undeniable is that Argentina's response to the crisis destroyed the regulatory environment upon which foreign investors had relied *ex ante*. Dozens turned to arbitration at ICSID claiming, among other things, that Argentina violated the FET requirement, not least, by reneging on explicit promises. Article 2(a) of the

---

Law: Security, Public Order and Financial Crisis' (2008) 59 International and Comparative Law Quarterly 325; José Alvarez and Tegan Brink, 'Revisiting the Necessity Defense: Continental Casualty v. Argentina' (2012) 9 Transnat'l Disp Mgmt 319 [hereafter 'Alvarez and Brink']; Giorgio Sacerdoti, 'The Application of BITs in Times of Economic Crisis: Limits to their Coverage, Necessity, and the Relevance of WTO Law' in G Sacerdoti (ed), *General Interests of Host States in International Investment Law* (Cambridge University Press, Cambridge 2014) 3.

[199] Investment Policy Hub, 'International Investment Agreements Navigator' <http://investment-policyhub.unctad.org/IIA> accessed 6 April 2016.

US–Argentina BIT states: 'Investment shall at all times be accorded fair and equitable treatment ...', but the FET is otherwise left unqualified.[200] There is virtually no disagreement that Argentina's responses to the crisis, but for Article XI BIT, would constitute a violation of FET standards in the cases brought. Article XI of the US–Argentina BIT stipulates that:

This Treaty shall not preclude the application by either party of measures necessary for the maintenance of public order, the fulfillment of its obligations with respect to the maintenance or restoration of international peace or security, or the protection of its own essential security interests.[201]

Article XI thus provides a 'carve-out' exemption from BIT obligations for state acts designed to achieve certain, specified state purposes, while presenting an obvious, first-order interpretive problem. Assuming that a derogation claim is not self-judging, how should a tribunal evaluate a measure's 'necessity'?

To date, ICSID tribunals have issued six final awards on such claims: *CMS* (May 2005); *LG&E* (October 2006); *Enron* (May 2007); *Sempra* (September 2007); *Continental Casualty* (September 2008); and *El Paso* (October 2011).[202] Each tribunal found that Argentina had violated the FET standard, and, cumulatively, they ordered Argentina to pay nearly $650 million plus interest in damages, on original requests totaling about $2 billion. In addition, ACs have rendered final decisions on five of these awards (the parties in *Sempra* withdrew from the annulment process). Each of these Committees discussed at length the tribunals' various approaches to Argentina's necessity defence, adding to the corpus of reasons available for use by future parties and tribunals. These ten rulings provide strong support for the judicial model: we can directly observe the evolution and enforcement of precedent as it emerges and congeals.

They also raise intriguing questions about the system's porousness, and capacity to adapt, to jurisprudential developments taking place in other international regimes. To anyone familiar with how WTO, EU, and ECtHR judges have interpreted derogation clauses, Article XI seems a prime candidate for the application of the proportionality framework, at least on its face.[203] Further, no language in the US–Argentina BIT would preclude the development of such an approach, including the deployment of a less restrictive means [LRM] test, a narrow tailoring requirement in American parlance. Under a proportionality-based approach, arbitrators

---

[200] Article II of the Treaty Concerning the Reciprocal Encouragement and Protection of Investment (US–Argentina) (14 November 1991) S Treaty Doc No 103-02 [hereafter 'US–Argentina BIT'].

[201] ibid Article XI.

[202] In chronological order: *CMS Transmission Co v Arg Republic* (ICSID Case No ARB/01/8), Award of 12 May 2005 [hereafter '*CMS Transmission*'], para 332; *LG&E Energy Corp v Arg Republic* (ICSID Case No Arb/02/1), Decision on Liability of 3 October 2006 [hereafter '*LG&E Energy Corp*'], para 202; *Enron Corp, Ponderosa Assets, LP v Arg Republic* (ICSID Case No Arb/01/3), Award of 22 May 2007, para 322; *Sempra Energy Int'l v Arg Republic* (ICSID Case No Arb/02/16), Award of 28 September 2007 [hereafter '*Sempra Energy*'], para 364; *Cont'l Cas Co v Arg Republic*, (ICSID Case No ARB/03/9), Award of 5 September 2008 [hereafter '*Cont'l Cas Co*'], para 58; *El Paso Energy Int'l Company v Arg Republic* (ICSID Case No ARB/03/15), Award of 31 October 2011 [hereafter *El Paso*].

[203] Alec Stone Sweet and Jud Mathews, 'Proportionality Balancing and Global Constitutionalism' (2008) 47 Columbia Journal of Transnational Law 72 [hereafter 'Stone Sweet and Mathews'].

would first decide if the crisis was severe enough to fall under one of the headings that make the necessity defence available. As a matter of comparative law (especially in the French and Spanish traditions), the notion of 'public order' is a broad concept, encompassing core public policy concerns that state officials, including national judges, are under a duty to protect. Yet even if the parties to the BIT meant 'the maintenance of public order' to apply only to threats to public security, it arguably covers the Argentina crisis. December 2001 saw rioting in the streets, a run on the banks, hyperinflation, and political turmoil. Five presidents were appointed in a ten-day period beginning on 20 December 2001, in the shadow of credible threats of preparation for a military coup. By the end of 2002, one-quarter of all urban workers were unemployed, and a majority of the population lived under the official poverty line. Argentina could also claim that the situation posed a threat to its 'essential security interests'.

If a tribunal did find that at least one of these headings covered the crisis, it would then probe the means-ends nexus which is at the heart of proportionality. In a first phase of analysis, the tribunal ensures that the measure was, in fact, taken to ameliorate the crisis.[204] If so, the arbitrators would turn to a necessity test, which involves LRM testing—did the measure harm investors more than was necessary to meet the crisis? Necessity analysis may include, or be followed by, an overall balancing of interests. If Argentina fails any of these tests, the defence would be rejected.

In the first four awards rendered, each on privatized gas concessions, no ICSID tribunal embraced proportionality. The *CMS, Enron,* and *Sempra* tribunals found that Argentina had breached its obligations, while rejecting Argentina's necessity claim. These tribunals were all chaired by Francisco Orrego Vicuña, a Chilean professor of public international law, who took a similar approach to Article XI in each case. Thus, subsequent awards cut and pasted holdings from prior ones, in particular, that of *CMS.*

What we are calling the 'Orrego Vicuña approach' looks to customary international law [CIL] for interpretive guidance to the necessity defence, which led the *CMS, Enron,* and *Sempra* tribunals to deny that Article XI was an autonomous source of law. Under this approach, the CIL defence of necessity subsumes Article XI. It is widely agreed that Article 25 of the Draft Articles on the Responsibility of States for Internationally Wrongful Acts (2001), produced by the International Law Commission (ILC), best expresses the CIL of necessity.[205] Article 25 ILC reads:

1. Necessity may not be invoked by a State as a ground for precluding the wrongfulness of an act not in conformity with an international obligation of that State unless the act: (a) is the only way for the State to safeguard an essential interest against a grave and

---

[204] The state would lose, therefore, if the measures were taken for an improper purpose (e.g. to punish an investor), or if means bore scant relationship to the purported ends. For a fuller discussion of proportionality analysis, see Chapter 6.
[205] In all of the rulings discussed here, all parties and arbitrators agreed that Article 25 ILC was authoritative. For an overview of the necessity defence in customary international law, see Robert D Sloane, 'On the Use and Abuse of Necessity in the Law of State Responsibility' (2012) 106 American Journal of International Law 447.

imminent peril; and (b) does not seriously impair an essential interest of the State or States towards which the obligation exists, or of the international community as a whole.
2. In any case, necessity may not be invoked by a State as a ground for precluding wrongfulness if: (a) the international obligation in question excludes the possibility of invoking necessity; or (b) the State has contributed to the situation of necessity.[206]

Article XI BIT and Article 25 ILC are differently formulated. Article 25 is more restrictive: necessity may be invoked to excuse an act that violates international law when it is the 'only way' a state can 'safeguard an essential interest', in the context of a 'grave and imminent peril'. Article XI BIT expressly permits state measures under headings that cover a broader range of contexts, thereby precluding a finding of violation of the treaty in the first place. Whereas Article 25 ILC appears to favour an 'only way' test for necessity, Article XI BIT looks tailor-made for an LRM test, at least to anyone versed in proportionality.

Grounding the analysis in Article 25 ILC, the *CMS, Enron*, and *Sempra* tribunals rejected Argentina's necessity defence on three grounds. First, as the *Enron* and *Sempra* awards stated in identical terms, the economic crisis did not implicate an 'essential interest of the State', since it did not threaten the 'very existence of the State and its independence'.[207] The *CMS* tribunal emphasized that 'the Argentine crisis ... did not result in total economic and social collapse', while indicating that it would take into account the state's travails in the damages phase.[208] Second, the *CMS* Tribunal interpreted the 'only means' requirement under Article 25 to be fatal to the necessity plea, if *any means other than those chosen* had been available to Argentina. Since the record showed that experts and others disagreed on what mix of measures Argentina could have taken, the means chosen could not qualify as the 'only means'. Third, the *CMS* Tribunal held that Argentina's efforts to mitigate the crisis had actually contributed to it.

Meanwhile, the *LG&E* tribunal, which weighed in after the *CMS*, but before the termination of the *Enron* and *Sempra*, proceedings, also found breaches of the FET standard, but it accepted the necessity defence under both Article XI BIT and Article 25 ILC, separately. The Tribunal excused Argentina of liability, but only for measures taken during a specific period of 'crisis' (December 2001 to April 2003). The approach conflicts with that of Orrego Vicuña. In *CMS*, the Tribunal had stated that 'the plea of state of necessity may preclude the wrongfulness of an act, but it does not exclude the duty to compensate the owner of the right ... sacrificed',[209] a holding later echoed in the *Enron* and *Sempra* awards.[210] The level of damages assessed by the *LG&E* Tribunal ($57.4 million on claims of $268 million) was far below the compensation ordered by the Orrego Vicuña tribunals in *CMS* ($133 million on claims of $261.1 million), *Enron* ($106 million on claims

---

[206] Article 25 of the Draft Articles on Responsibility of States for Internationally Wrongful Acts (2001) 53 UN GAOR Supp (No 10), UN Doc A/56/10.
[207] *Enron Corp* (n 192), para 306; *Sempra Energy* (n 202), para 348.
[208] *CMS Transmission* (n 202), paras 354–6.   [209] ibid para 388.
[210] *Enron Corp* (n 192), para 345; *Sempra Energy* (n 202), para 394.

ranging between $388 and $543 million), and *Sempra* ($128 million on claims of $209.4 million). Finally, the Tribunal invoked proportionality, but only to indicate that Argentina had not violated the principle;[211] the award otherwise shows no indication that arbitrators engaged in serious proportionality analysis [PA].

The Impact of the Annulment Procedure

We turn now to the decisions of the ACs in *CMS, Sempra,* and *Enron,* which eviscerated the Orrego Vicuña approach.[212] As discussed above, although ACs are not empowered to annul awards on grounds of 'errors-in-law', they routinely address such errors in *dicta*, and some have annulled awards for faulty reasoning under other available headings, in particular, 'failure to state the reasons' and 'manifest excess of powers'. Although the AC chose not to annul the *CMS* award, it devoted a long section of its decision to a pointed criticism of the Orrego Vicuña approach. Less modestly, the ACs in *Enron* and *Sempra* annulled the tribunals' awards, on the basis of deficient analysis of Article XI BIT, citing as authority the *AC-CMS* ruling.

ICSID officials, it would appear, sought to hard-wire the doctrinal authority of the AC in *CMS* in advance, appointing two members of the International Court of Justice, including the then-President of that Court, Gilbert Guillaume, and James Crawford who, as the ILC's Special Rapporteur on State Responsibility, oversaw the drafting of Article 25 ILC. In its decision, the *AC-CMS* stressed that it did not have the authority to act as an appellate court; in particular, it could not quash an award on the basis of errors in law, no matter how serious. The Committee then painstakingly detailed the 'manifest' errors of interpretation committed by the *CMS* tribunal, the most important being the conflation of Article XI BIT and Article 25 ILC. In the AC's estimation, the *CMS* tribunal should have analysed pleadings under the two norms separately, given their different functions. CIL makes available the necessity defence for a breach of international law, once such a breach has been admitted or found. In contrast, the plea under Article XI (BIT), if accepted, precludes the finding of a treaty violation in the first place. In blunt *dicta*, the Committee then went on to state:

---

[211] *LG&E Energy Corp* (n 202), para 195: '… the State has the right to adopt measures having a social or general welfare purpose. In such a case, the measure must be accepted without any imposition of liability, except in cases where the State's action is obviously disproportionate to the need being addressed.'

[212] *CMS Transmission Co v Arg Republic* (ICSID Case No ARB/01/8), Decision of the ad hoc Committee on the Application for Annulment of 25 September 2007 [hereafter '*CMS Transmission*, Annulment Proceedings']; *Sempra Energy Int'l v Arg Republic* (ICSID Case No Arb/02/16), Decision on the Argentine Republic's Request for Annulment of the Award of 29 June 2010 [hereafter '*Sempra Energy*, Annulment Proceedings']; *Enron Corp, Ponderosa Assets, LP v Arg Republic* (ICSID Case No Arb/01/3), Decision on the Application for Annulment of the Argentine Republic of 30 July 2010 [hereafter '*Enron Corp*, Annulment Proceeding']; *Continental Cas Co v Arg Republic* (ICSID Case No ARB/03/9), Decision on the Application for Partial Annulment of Continental Casualty Company and the Application for Partial Annulment of the Argentine Republic of 16 September 2011 [hereafter '*Cont'l Cas Co*, Annulment Proceedings']; *El Paso Energy Int'l Company v Arg Republic* (ICSID Case No ARB/03/15), Decision on the Application for Annulment of the Argentine Republic of 22 September 2014 [hereafter '*El Paso*, Annulment Proceedings'].

[The] errors made by the Tribunal could have had a decisive impact on the operative part of the Award ... In fact, it did not examine whether the conditions laid down by Article XI were fulfilled and whether, as a consequence, the measures taken by Argentina were capable of constituting, even *prima facie*, a breach of the BIT. If the Committee was acting as a court of appeal, it would have to reconsider the Award on this ground.[213]

These and other findings immediately impacted the work of tribunals and ACs, already underway.

A second AC annulled the *Sempra* award on like terms, citing extensively to the *AC-CMS* decision. Echoing the latter's views, the *Sempra-AC* noted that while 'it may be appropriate to look to customary law as a guide to the interpretation of terms used in the BIT', '[i]t does not follow ... that [Article 25 ILC] establishes a "peremptory definition of necessity and the conditions for its operation"'.[214] The Committee then went on to hold that the Tribunal's failure to separately analyse and apply Article XI BIT constituted a 'total' failure to apply the law, and thus a 'manifest excess of powers' warranting annulment.[215] Under this view, the Tribunal should have determined, first, whether Article XI BIT (the 'primary' law governing the issue) covered the measures under review; only if Article XI did not apply should the Tribunal have moved to consider if breaches of the BIT were excused under CIL (the secondary law governing the issue). In contrast, the Tribunal had proceeded as if Article 25 ILC simply 'trumped' Article XI BIT.[216]

The *AC-Enron* took a different tack, directing attention to the Tribunal's deployment of an 'only means' test. Among other problems, the AC found that the Tribunal had failed to give reasons for how it interpreted the 'only way' clause of Article 25 ILC. The AC opined that necessity analysis under Article 25 could just as well accommodate an LRM test, or an assessment of the effectiveness of the state measure under review in light of its harm to investors, both of which are congruent with the proportionality principle.[217] The *Enron* Tribunal had (apparently) relied solely on the expertise of one economist to justify its rejection of Argentina's defence—it failed an 'only way' test—without considering the matter further. The *AC-Enron* refused to indicate whether it agreed with the Tribunal's conflation of Article XI BIT and the CIL defence. It saw no point in doing so, in part, because it had found that the Tribunal's rejection of the necessity defence under both Article XI and Article 25 ILC were thoroughly 'tainted by annullable error'.[218]

In sum, the annulment committees destroyed the Orrego Vicuña approach, expressing strong disagreement with each of its core components.[219]

---

[213] *CMS Transmission*, Annulment Proceedings (n 212), para 135.
[214] *Sempra Energy*, Annulment Proceedings (n 212), para 197.   [215] ibid paras 213–14.
[216] ibid paras 214–19.
[217] *Enron Corp*, Annulment Proceedings (n 212), paras 369–71.   [218] ibid para 405.
[219] Investors have brought new proceedings in both the *Sempra* and *Enron* cases, and the *LG&E Energy* annulment application was withdrawn by the parties.

Necessity and Proportionality

In the fifth award, *Continental Casualty v Argentina*[220]—chaired by a former member of the WTO-Appellate Body, Giorgio Sacerdoti—the Tribunal gave proportionality pride of place, just as another Tribunal (also chaired by Sacerdoti) would do for purposes of FET analysis in *Total v Argentina* (see Chapter 5). Continental Casualty, a provider of employment compensation insurance in Argentina, maintained a portfolio of low-risk capital investments in Argentine financial institutions. Much of the value of this portfolio was lost with *pesification* and the rescheduling of payments on various debt instruments held by the company. The company asked for $114 million in compensation. Citing to the *AC-CMS* decision, Sacerdoti focused on Argentina's necessity plea under Article XI BIT, relegating CIL to virtual irrelevance. He then confronted the crucial issue left open by the *AC-CMS*: what methodology should arbitrators use when they assess an Article XI BIT defence?

In response, Sacerdoti adapted the WTO-AB's approach to adjudicating 'necessity' in the derogation clauses found in Article XX of the GATT 1947. He justified the move as follows:

Since the text of Art. XI derives from the parallel model clause of the U.S. Friendship, Commerce, and Navigation treaties, and these treaties in turn reflect the formulation of Art. XX of GATT 1947, the Tribunal finds it more appropriate to refer to the GATT and WTO case law which has extensively dealt with the concept and requirements of necessity in the context of economic measures derogating to the obligations contained in GATT, rather than to refer to the requirement of necessity under customary international law.[221]

The award also notes that the investor had pleaded the case law of the WTO AB on Article XX GATT in the hearings.[222]

The Tribunal found that the economic crisis fell within the coverage of Article XI, under both the 'maintenance of public order' and 'essential security interests' headings. It then recognized, citing to the case law of the ECtHR, that the state possessed, *ex ante*, 'a significant margin of appreciation' in the determination of how to meet the crisis, thus setting the stage for necessity analysis. Sacerdoti then meticulously laid out the approach developed by the WTO-AB, extensively quoting from the leading cases.[223] The necessity of a measure would, accordingly, be determined through 'a process of weighing and balancing of factors', including the relative importance of interests furthered by the challenged measures, the contribution of the measure to the realization of the ends pursued, and the restrictive impact of the measure on international exchange. The Tribunal then assessed the state measures under review with regard to a list of alternatives that, the claimant had argued, were just as effective and reasonably available, but which would have done less harm to the investor. With one minor exception (worth a scant $2.8 million), the Tribunal

---

[220] *Cont'l Cas Co* (n 202).   [221] ibid para 192.   [222] ibid.
[223] ibid paras 193–4 (citing to the decisions of the WTO Appellate Body in the *Korea-Beef* and *EC-Tyres* cases).

rejected these arguments, finding that Article XI BIT indeed covered Argentina's measures.[224]

The award survived annulment. The *AC-Continental Casualty* stressed its agreement with the reasoning of the *AC-CMS* and *AC-Sempra* on the distinction between Article XI BIT and the CIL defence of necessity.[225] With regard to the Tribunal's use of proportionality, the *AC-Continental Casualty* rejected the company's claims to the effect that the Tribunal had 'erred in its analysis' of WTO jurisprudence. 'The Tribunal was clearly not purporting to apply that body of law', the AC held, 'but merely took it into account as relevant to determining the correct interpretation and application of Article XI of the BIT'.[226]

The most recent award is *El Paso*, also involving an international energy company that invested heavily in the oil and natural gas sector. Much of the investment was lost by the time it sold its holdings, in the midst of a crisis in full bloom. The Tribunal, relying heavily on Sacerdoti's *Continental Casualty* award and the ruling of the *AC-CMS*, focused on Article XI BIT, treating Article 25 ILC as 'secondary law' (to be applied 'only' once Article XI is found not to apply).[227] Contrary to the *LG&E* and *Continental Casualty* tribunals, however, the *El Paso* Tribunal rejected Argentina's necessity defence, on a finding that the state's measures under review had 'contributed to the crisis to a substantial extent, so that Article XI cannot come to its rescue'.[228] Expressing a dissenting opinion within the award itself, Brigitte Stern (one of the most active repeat arbitrators, typically appointed by states) declared that she would have taken the position of *Continental Casualty* on the necessity of Argentina's measures.[229] In Stern's view, the complexity of the situation made it all but impossible for any tribunal to unravel the precise causes of the crisis so as to impute them to acts by Argentina. At annulment, Argentina raised these and other arguments, which the AC rejected: the tribunal alone possessed the competence to determine the facts[230] bearing on the necessity plea.[231]

Assessment

In the Argentina case, annulment proceedings operated as a mechanism for generating precedent. While each successive tribunal engaged with existing awards on the books, the *AC-CMS* functioned as a focal point for ongoing coordination among

---

[224] The Tribunal found a breach of the FET standard on only one claim. Its acceptance of Argentina's plea of necessity under Article XI of the BIT meant rejecting the others.

[225] *Cont'l Cas Co*, Annulment Proceedings (n 212), paras 127–8.   [226] ibid para 133.

[227] *El Paso Energy Int'l Co v Arg Republic* (ICSID Case No ARB/03/15), Award of 31 October 2011, paras 552–5. The Tribunal also agreed that 'the protection offered by the BIT to the Claimant's investment is suspended to the extent that Article XI is applicable'. See ibid para 649.

[228] ibid para 665; see also ibid para 624 (finding that necessity cannot be invoked if the party has substantially contributed to it).

[229] ibid paras 666–70.

[230] Under the *Kompetenz-Kompetenz* principles and ICSID Rule 34(1).

[231] *El Paso*, Annulment Proceedings (n 212), paras 168, 193–203.

tribunals and ACs. The process steadily reduced the range of defensible decisions available to tribunals.

The arbitral process has firmly settled the following legal questions, a remarkable result given the small number of awards. First, Article XI BIT is the primary law; where it applies, the customary law of necessity, as expressed by Article 25 ILC, is largely 'superfluous'.[232] Second, Article XI can cover measures that are necessary to respond to an economic crisis of the kind experienced by Argentina in the 1999 to 2002 period. Third, the successful invocation of the necessity defence renders 'inapplicable' the BIT's 'protections', thereby precluding compensation.[233] Fourth, it is not appropriate to apply an 'only means' test to assess the necessity of Argentine measures under Article XI BIT. Indeed, arbitrating the necessity defence has produced viable alternatives to the 'only means' test, namely, the LRM tests suggested by the *AC-Enron* (in the context of Article 25 ILC), and by Sacerdoti (in the context of the US–Argentina BIT) in *Continental Casualty*.

Not everyone agrees. José Alvarez and his collaborators have taken diametrically opposed positions on each of these four issues. In a first paper,[234] Alvarez and Khamsi argued that the *CMS, Enron*, and *Sempra* Tribunals got it right in virtually all important respects, and that the AC in *CMS* got it wrong. In a follow-up paper devoted to criticising *Continental Casualty*, Alvarez and Brinks aggressively advocate the basics of *CMS*, supported mainly by analysis of the historical origins of Article XI BIT (but exclusively from the US point of view). They sum up their view as follows: 'Article XI was essentially an attempt to preserve existing customary defenses and not to derogate from them.'[235]

In the face of progressive arbitral lawmaking, an appeal to the original intent of US treaty-makers is perhaps the only lawyerly way to defend the Orrego Vicuña approach that remains. But it is also a rear-guard effort designed to revive propositions that have been defeated through networked decision-making. It is a blunt fact that none of the five ACs that have weighed in thus far provides any support for the view put forth by Alvarez and Khamsi and Alvarez and Brinks. Recall that the *AC-CMS* characterized the conflation of Article XI BIT and Article 25 ILC as 'a manifest error in law'.[236] The *AC-Sempra* put it this way: 'It is apparent ... that Article 25 does not offer a guide to *interpretation* of the terms used in Article XI. The most that can be said is that certain words or expressions are the same or similar.'[237] Moreover, faulty necessity analysis—of exactly the same kind as that endorsed by Alvarez and his co-authors—led to annulment of the *Enron* and *Sempra* awards. Even if one were to accept their arguments as defensible, in theory, the present state

[232] *Cont'l Cas Co* (n 202), para 162; *El Paso Energy* (n 202), para 552 (quoting *Continental Casualty*).
[233] *Cont'l Cas Co* (n 202), para 164.
[234] José E Alvarez and Katheryn Khamsi, 'The Argentina Crisis and Foreign Investors: A Glimpse into the Heart of the International Investment Regime' in Karl Sauvant (ed), *The Yearbook on International Investment Law and Policy 2008/2009* (Oxford University Press, New York 2009) 379, 441.
[235] Alvarez and Brink (n 198), 334, n 9 (discussing alleged methodological problems with the decision, and advocating for alternative rules of interpretation).
[236] *CMS Transmission*, Annulment Proceedings (n 212), para 146.
[237] *Sempra Energy*, Annulment Proceedings (n 212), para 199 (emphasis in the original).

of the jurisprudence on Article XI BIT renders them, at best, academic. In any event, we assign more weight to the positions taken by the President of the ICJ, a second Justice of the ICJ, and the ILC's *Special Rapporteur on State Responsibility* (the composition of the *CMS* Annulment Committee) than to Alvarez. Arbitrators with responsibilities to make the authoritative choices in law have done so as well.

It has since come to light that Orrego Vicuña was dismissed in 2013 from an ICSID tribunal for lacking impartiality with regard to his views on the necessity defence, namely, that an 'essential security' clause of the kind found in Article XI BIT 'should be interpreted so as to conform to the "state of necessity" test under CIL'.[238] The disqualification[239] was decided by the Vice-President of the International Court of Justice, Peter Tomka. In the words of a commentator with access to the full decision, Tomka stressed that:

Prof. Orrego Vicuña has stuck to this view through three arbitral awards, but also in an academic [paper] defending this view in the aftermath of the partial or total annulment of the … arbitral awards in question … Indeed, Judge Tomka laid particular weight upon Prof. Orrego Vicuña's 2011 [contribution to a *Festschrift* in honor of Michael Reisman],[240] where he discloses that he has reviewed the reasoning of the various ICSID ACs, but hewed to the same view as earlier.[241]

Prior to the decisions of the ACs in *CMS, Enron,* and *Sempra*, Professor Orrego Vicuña had served as president of more ICSID tribunals than any other arbitrator. After these decisions, he has been exclusively nominated for appointment by investors. In this line of case, the regime evolved and enforced a relatively hard version of precedent.

We now turn to *Continental Casualty*. Alvarez argues that Sacerdoti did not give an adequate justification for importing a proportionality-based approach into ISA, and Alvarez and Brinks go so far as to accuse Sacerdoti of indolence: 'the Tribunal simply reached for an off-the-shelf model presumably because it was familiar—at least to the President of that tribunal'.[242] Sacerdoti, recall, after noting parallels between Article XI BIT and Article XX GATT, had considered it more appropriate

---

[238] Luke Eric Peterson, 'Francisco Orrego Vicuna is Disqualified from Sitting in India BIT Arbitration Due to Appearance of Having Fixed View as to Meaning of "Essential Security" Standard' (*IA Reporter*, 9 October 2013) <https://www.iareporter.com/articles/francisco-orrego-vicuna-is-disqualified-from-sitting-in-india-bit-arbitration-due-to-appearance-of-having-fixed-view-as-to-meaning-of-essential-security-standard/> accessed 6 April 2016 ['Peterson']. The disqualification decision was rendered on 30 September 2013 in the UNCITRAL arbitration *CC/Devas (Mauritius) Ltd et al v India* (UNCITRAL) Decision of 30 September 2013.

[239] Francisco Orrego Vicuña was nominated by the investor-claimant. Two more challenges were filed against Orrego Vicuña in separate cases, one unsuccessfully (*Repsol SA and Repsol Butano SA v Argentine Republic* (ICSID Case No ARB/12/38)) and the other successfully (*Burlington Resources Inc v Republic of Ecuador* (ICSID Case No ARB/08/5)). See also Peterson (n 238).

[240] Francisco Orrego Vicuña, 'Softening Necessity' in M Arsanjani et al (eds), *Looking to the Future: Essays on International Law in Honor of W. Michael Reisman* (Martinus Nijhoff, The Hague 2011).

[241] Peterson (n 238): Judge Tomka's comments apply fully to Alvarez et al's defence of these same views.

[242] Alvarez and Brink (n 198), 356.

to look to established doctrine in international economic law, than to shoehorn Article XI BIT into CIL.

The Tribunal could have taken another route. By the time the award in *Continental Casualty* was rendered, most of the world's most powerful national and international courts had recognized it as an unwritten general principle of law.[243] Indeed, PA had become the unrivalled, best-practice procedure for adjudicating derogation clauses found in constitutions and many treaties. Judges have, in effect, read into derogation clauses an LRM test, and other types of balancing, in order to help them assess the 'necessity' of state measures. The adoption of proportionality by courts in the European Union, the ECtHR, and the WTO took place without explicit justification.[244] The *Continental Casualty* award is actually a rare exception. Sacerdoti could have simply declared proportionality to be a general principle of international economic law, citing to the WTO-AB and other courts. General principles, of course, are a recognized source of international law[245] that ICSID arbitrators, arguably, are obliged to apply.[246] In any event, it remains an open question whether an LRM test, or proportionality more generally, will become the doctrinal standard for necessity analysis in future awards, the *El Paso* Tribunal having eschewed it. We take up the development of proportionality analysis, with regard to the FET in particular, in Chapters 5 and 6.

IV. Conclusion

There are three necessary conditions for the development of arbitral governance (Chapter 1). First, the system must attract a steady caseload, without which arbitrators would be unable to accrete authority over the system's institutional development. Second, once activated, tribunals must resolve these disputes, on the basis of defensible reasons. In doing so, they will produce the raw materials that future users may fashion into usable doctrine. Third, a minimally robust conception of precedent must develop for a doctrinal 'system' to emerge at all. Combined, these factors

---

[243] Stone Sweet and Mathews (n 203).

[244] For a more extensive discussion of these points, see Alec Stone Sweet and Giacinto della Cananea, 'Proportionality, General Principles of Law, and Investor-State Arbitration' (2014) 46/3 NYU Journal of International Law and Politics 911.

[245] Article 38 of the Statute of the International Court of Justice (1945) TS 993 recognizes general principles as a source of international law.

[246] Under Article 31(3)(c) of the Vienna Convention on the Law of Treaties (1969) 1155 UNTS 331, judges are to take into account the 'relevant rules of international law applicable in the relations between the parties' when they interpret treaties; and under Article 42(1) of the ICSID Convention: 'The Tribunal shall decide a dispute in accordance with such rules of law as may be agreed by the parties. In the absence of such agreement, the Tribunal shall apply the law of the Contracting State party to the dispute (including its rules on the conflict of laws) and such rules of international law as may be applicable.' Arguably, as is our position, proportionality is a 'relevant' and 'applicable' rule.

will lead an increasing number of tribunals to treat past awards as a wellspring of reasons for justifying decisions. These conditions have largely been fulfilled, in both ICA and ISA. The result has been a steady institutionalization of the judicial model, and the emergence of practices that undergird the pluralist-constitutional model of arbitration.

In ICA, the development of precedent is a direct indicator of judicialization. As early as the 1930s, the ICC began to rethink house policies that disfavoured precedent. By the 1950s, it had abandoned them altogether, through enhanced reason-giving requirements, dispositions favouring publication of important awards, and the strengthening of mandatory supervision of draft awards (Chapter 3). The ICC did so in order to secure its authority over the arbitral process, and to strengthen its autonomy vis-à-vis states within the evolving pluralist legal system established by the New York Convention.

As we argued in Chapter 3, the values of party autonomy and freedom of contract do not disappear when we shift from the contractual to the judicial model. Instead, as judicialization has proceeded, the arbitral order has reconstructed the meaning of party autonomy in light of its own priorities. The parties' choice of law, for example, is subject to the evolution of trade usages and general principles, including the doctrine of legitimate expectations, which are components of the *Lex Mercatoria* that arbitrators help to construct. These precedent-based norms not only fill gaps in incomplete contracts; they will, at times, authoritatively displace other choices contractants have made, including with respect to applicable state law. Nevertheless, the fact that the most important awards remain secret has stunted the growth of precedent, and ICA's capacity to govern in a coherent and effective manner (Chapters 5 and 6).

Judicialization generates hierarchies (Chapters 2 and 3). In ICA, we can distinguish between two forms of hierarchy, which overlap in important ways. The first is organizational: tribunals develop authority over the parties; IACs develop authority over tribunals; and the arbitral order asserts its own authority, as a legal system, with respect to state law. The second is normative: the arbitral order develops doctrine that asserts its own primacy. The community expects arbitral constructions, including general principles and transnational public policy, to prevail in any conflict with norms issuing from, say, national systems. In the next chapter, we examine in more detail the question of how ICA tribunals have dealt with mandatory law and the public interest.

In ISA, because most awards are available, the analyst can track and assess the development of precedent and its influence. The evidence shows that the regime has evolved into a tightly networked judicial system, through precedent-based practices. Repeat players with an interest in doctrinal coherence have sustained what is, in effect, a common law process of lawmaking, in the absence of a formal mechanism of coordination and appeal. Doctrine not only networks arbitrators, it networks treaties. As a result, states routinely find themselves subject to constructions that did not emanate from treaties to which they consented, but from treaty provisions the tribunals have interpreted in the aggregate. The record also supports the claims of proponents of the pluralist-constitutional model. The Argentina cases, for example, have placed the proportionality principle, which tribunals invoked through engagement with the case law of the ECtHR and WTO courts, at the top of the agenda. The next chapter continues examination of precedent-based lawmaking, focusing on the question of how, and the extent to which, tribunals balance and, therefore, govern.

5

Balancing and the Public Interest

Chapter 4 charted the evolution of precedent, a necessary condition for the emergence of judicialized governance. This chapter focuses on balancing, in the context of pleadings that oppose property rights and public interest, a mode of decision-making directly implicated in governance.[1] Part I provides a brief summary of the basics of our approach. Part II shows that, in the context of commercial disputes, tribunals and the major arbitration centres have moved aggressively to assert their own competence to apply mandatory state law, in complicity with the courts of the most important trading states. Today, tribunals routinely take into account and balance public interests, even in sensitive policy areas once thought to be inarbitrable. In part III, we examine how tribunals, in resolving investment disputes, have managed similar problems, in particular, through the dynamic construction of the 'fair and equitable treatment' standard [FET]. Today, the FET is also the doctrinal site of recurrent skirmishes in an intensifying war of authority between arbitrators and states, which raises Principal–Agent dynamics that we assess in light of a new generation of treaty-making.

I. Orientations

As previous chapters have made clear, we base our approach to arbitral governance on considerations that need only brief restatement here.

First, we do not make a sharp theoretical distinction between public and private law and process.[2] In domestic legal contexts, (a) the emergence of the regulatory, welfare, and administrative states before the Second World War, (b) the development of the 'horizontal effect' of constitutional rights thereafter, and (c) the impact of privatization and globalization since the 1980s have combined to blur the boundaries separating the 'private' from the 'public'. In state courts, public interests permeate the adjudication of private law disputes in multifarious ways.[3] At the international level, the effectiveness of transnational legal systems depends critically on the making and enforcement of norms that directly govern relations between

---

[1] See Chapter 1.   [2] See Chapter 6 for further discussion.
[3] Michel Rosenfeld, Alain Supiot, Peter Goodrich, and Judith Resnik, 'Symposium: The Boundaries of Public Law' (2013) 11 International Journal of Constitutional Law 125.

The Evolution of International Arbitration: Judicialization, Governance, Legitimacy. First Edition. Alec Stone Sweet and Florian Grisel. © Alec Stone Sweet and Florian Grisel 2017. Published 2017 by Oxford University Press.

private actors.[4] For their part, legal philosophers, such as Hans Kelsen, have found the distinction 'useless' for 'a general systematization of law'.[5] As discussed in earlier chapters and the next section of this one, ICA too has evolved in ways that deny the distinction. For now, it is enough to stress that the nature of the dispute and the applicable law are likely to determine how arbitrators take public-regarding decisions, not whether it is a contract or an investment treaty that provides the source of jurisdiction. We would expect, for example, to find more public-regarding arbitral decision-making in (a) a commercial dispute in which mandatory state law is material or controlling than in (b) an investment dispute in which a host state has allegedly reneged on specific, quasi-contractual, commitments made to an investor, but to no other entity.

The second point follows from the first. As arbitration came to replace litigation for high-stakes, adversarial disputes, that is, as it became an effective substitute for domestic courts, tribunals found themselves in the same kinds of balancing situations as their peers on the bench. Domestic judges routinely consider the extent to which public policy considerations impinge upon freedom of contract; and, under the New York Convention, they may refuse to enforce the arbitral awards of those tribunals that fail to do the same. In complex transnational disputes, pleadings routinely involve the interpretation of specific statutory requirements. In such cases, the tribunal will have no choice but to take into account public policy concerns which, often enough, will require balancing. As a strategic matter, balancing also enables dispute resolvers to split differences between the parties, and to fashion awards that will harm the loser as little as possible. In ISA, where states-as-respondents directly plead the public interest in their defence, adopting a balancing posture is a straightforward means of countering charges of investor bias.

Third, arbitral governance is delegated governance. In ICA, states have increasingly conferred upon arbitrators broad powers to interpret and apply domestic law, even in sensitive areas of public policy. As we argue below, these duties have congealed as a distinct set of fiduciary obligations to take into account the public interest. In ISA, as we will show, tribunals developed a precedent-based balancing framework that integrates public interest concerns. In contrast to ICA, some states are actively using their treaty-making powers to provide more guidance to arbitrators when it comes to important state interests.

II. International Commercial Arbitration and Mandatory Domestic Law

In ICA, tribunals bring public interests to bear on the parties whenever they (a) resolve a case in light of applicable, mandatory state law, and (b) apply public

---

[4] See 'Symposium: Public and Private Law in the Global Adjudication System' (2008) 18(2) Duke Journal of International and Comparative Law 253–549.

[5] Hans Kelsen, *General Theory of Law and State* (Anders Wedberg tr, Harvard University Press, Cambridge 1961), quoted in Michel Rosenfeld, 'Rethinking the Boundaries between Public Law and Private Law for the Twenty First Century' (2013) 11 International Journal of Constitutional Law 125.

policy, whether domestic or transnational (Chapter 4). In the vast majority of disputes, the parties themselves made the law of state X the applicable law; further, the law of state Y may also be applicable, for example, in light of a connection with the place of performance. 'No law is foreign law in international arbitration', goes the maxim.[6] The extent to which arbitrators take into account public interests in their awards is an empirical question that no analyst can study satisfactorily, given the fact that the regime publishes so few awards, and virtually none in full. Extant scholarship is largely anecdotal and normative, strongly biased in favour of celebrating the regime's triumphs. As in previous chapters, we adopt a second-best strategy. We track the development of the effectiveness of the arbitral system,[7] focusing on changes in the policies and rules of IACs, in the case law of domestic courts, and in representative, published awards. With the consolidation of the New York Convention system, the interests of the IACs, arbitrators, the bar, and states have gradually aligned in ways that enhance the role of arbitration in transnational governance.

Arbitral Autonomy and State Delegation

It is commonplace to conceptualize ICA as a purely private process, whose legitimacy is rooted in party autonomy. Through freedom of contract, private parties have built their own sphere of private justice, reducing the practical relevance of state interests as expressed in law. In the early days of the ICC, theorists had already begun to argue that parties could contract around domestic legal constraints, with the sole exception of public policy.[8] Today, this view is a core ideological component of the arbitral regime. Lévy and Robert-Tissot express it in terms that are congruent with what we have called the contractual model:

Arbitrators are not 'without law,' [for] they are not 'without contract' and … must therefore insure that the interpretation of the applicable law corresponds to the expectations of the parties. [A]rbitrators prioritize contractual rather than legal analysis, deciding strictly with reference to the specific dispute at hand. [They] are not bound by precedent, whether arbitral or judicial (except with respect to 'rules of public policy that are truly international' …) because their mission is founded on the parties' agreement. The approach of judges is similar, but to a lesser degree, due to their duty to preserve legal security in general, and to their attachment to a specific legal order.[9]

Although we accept much of this characterization, we would highlight important features of arbitral law and practice that Lévy and Robert-Tissot leave out. First, the effectiveness of tribunals in highly adversarial disputes depends heavily

---

[6] Chapters 3 and 4 discuss sources and mixes of applicable law.
[7] The notion of *effectiveness* is defined in the book's previous chapters.
[8] See Robert Vulliemin, *De l'arbitrage commercial particulièrement en matière internationale* (Rousseau & Cie, Brussels 1931) 17: 'Rien n'empêche par conséquent les parties de permettre à l'arbitre toute dérogation à la loi que le respect de l'ordre public n'interdirait pas.'
[9] Laurent Lévy and Fabrice Robert-Tissot, 'L'interprétation arbitrale' (2013) 4 Revue de l'arbitrage 861, 877.

on an accreted jurisprudence of general principles that undergirds arbitral authority (Chapters 2 and 4). Second, ICC Rules, at least, place tribunals under the direct supervision of house officials, including with respect to their reasoning in law (Chapter 3). Third, and most important for present purposes, most parties that arbitrate in major IACs have chosen state law as the governing law in their contract, a choice that requires tribunals to engage that law, though not necessarily as judges would do in a similar case (Chapters 3 and 4).

The ICC would not have succeeded in its mission—to construct a private, transnational dispute resolution to replace domestic courts—without arbitration becoming more hierarchical, coordinative—that is, more 'court-like'. In the vast majority of high-value cases, the parties have chosen state law; and where a dispute implicates mandatory law, at least one of the parties is likely to devote enormous resources to arguing about how the Tribunal ought to apply that law. The ICC addresses this situation in its *Guide to ICC Arbitration* (2012) as follows:

3–771 … An arbitral tribunal must apply all relevant and applicable provisions of the rules of law that the parties have chosen or the arbitral tribunal has determined to be applicable to the merits of the dispute. In addition, it may occasionally be required to apply laws that are mandatory in a different jurisdiction.

3–772 … Laws characterized as mandatory are intended to implement fundamental public policy in the legal system to which they belong. This means that the parties cannot avoid or derogate from those laws in the context of that legal system.[10]

Further, ICC Rules encourage tribunals to oppose settlement between the parties that would lead to an 'agreement [that] is contrary to mandatory law or public policy'.[11] And the Rules provide for heightened review of awards by the ICC Court where a mandatory law of the seat is involved.[12]

From the very beginning, ICC tribunals have reviewed contractual rights in light of public interests expressed in statutory provisions. In 1927, for example, a tribunal interpreted and applied the English Income Tax Act of 1918, in a dispute concerning tax on the royalties owed under a licensing agreement.[13] In 1951, an ICC tribunal conferred on itself the capacity to review the conformity of a sales contract with certain French exchange regulations, which one of the parties had pleaded as mandatory law. In the ensuing annulment proceeding, the Paris Court of Appeal confirmed the award, agreeing that the contract did not offend public policy or otherwise violate French law.[14] Once the New York Convention entered into force, tribunals evolved their own version of public policy, and asserted an autonomous

---

[10] Jason Fry, Simon Greenberg, and Francesca Mazza, *The Secretariat's Guide to ICC Arbitration* (ICC, Paris 2012) ['the *Guide*']. The *Guide* then describes examples from recent cases, including a delicate dispute involving Sharia law. See ibid paras 3-773–3-776.

[11] ibid para 3-1172.

[12] ibid para 3-1182: '[W]hen performing its scrutiny function the Court will consider, to the extent practicable, the requirements of mandatory law at the place of the arbitration.'

[13] See International Chamber of Commerce, 'Income Tax Deductions on British Patent Royalties' (January 1933) World Trade 14.

[14] International Chamber of Commerce, 'Sanctity of Contracts—Paris Court of Appeal Confirms an ICC Arbitral Award' (September–October 1953) World Trade 5.

capacity to review state law in light of (transnational) public policy, where needed (Chapter 4).

How state officials would respond to these moves has been, across many decades now, the crucial question. Would states resist arbitral assertions of authority, or would they use their recognition and enforcement powers under the New York Convention to circumscribe them? We can align the positions taken by states on a continuum, stretching from maximally restrictive to maximally permissive, with most states on points between these poles. On the restrictive end, state officials treat any dispute that depends for their resolution on the application of mandatory law as inarbitrable, and treat all mandatory law as covered by the 'public policy' exception of the New York Convention. This position was, in fact, the dominant one in 1958, even in the major trading states. At the permissive pole, state officials expressly delegate the enforcement of mandatory law to arbitrators; they reduce the scope of the inarbitrability exception to nil; and they presumptively accept arbitral control of international/transnational public policy as a legitimate substitute for judicial control of national public policy.

It is an indisputable fact that, since 1958, the major trading states have steadily moved to strongly permissive positions. In a process accelerating in the 1980s, these states have delegated massive authority to arbitrators when it comes to enforcing mandatory law. The result has been transformative. A brief review of the French and American situations will suffice to make the point.

During the 1789 Revolution, intense political hostility to judicial authority turned officials toward arbitration.[15] The revolutionaries gave arbitrators jurisdiction over public claims, including those brought by individuals against French municipalities in land distribution disputes arising under the Great Terror.[16] The Napoleonic codes reversed this course. Having tamed the courts, legislators favoured a narrower view of the arbitral function. The Code of Civil Procedure, first adopted in 1806, prohibited the use of arbitration to resolve disputes that involved 'public policy, the State, the public domain, [and] municipalities'.[17] The *travaux préparatoires* for the Code justified this restriction as follows:

Only purely private interests can be subject to a contract: no one can insert any provision that would touch upon public policy ... These issues are too [important] for the decision to be abandoned to arbitrators, who, no matter how instructed and wise they may be, never offer to society the same guarantee, the same independence as judges instituted by law, and invested by the Chief of State of his authority.[18]

---

[15] Article 1, Statute of 16/24 August 1790.

[16] For further discussion, see Florian Grisel, 'Public Arbitration under French Law: Tradition and Transition' in Stephan Schill (ed), forthcoming.

[17] Articles 86 and 1004, Code of Civil Procedure (1806).

[18] Jean-Guillaume Locré, *Esprit du Code de procédure civile, ou Conférence du Code de procédure avec les discussions du Conseil, les observations du Tribunat, les exposés des motifs, les discours des orateurs du Tribunat* (P Didot l'Aîné, Paris 1816) Vol 4, 359–60. See also one of the first commentaries of the Code of Civil Procedure: Boitard (published by Gustave de Linage), *Leçons sur le code de procédure civile* (4th edn, Gustave Thorel, Paris 1847) Vol 2, 447–54.

After 1972, the Civil Code formulated the prohibition as follows: 'No one may enter into an arbitration agreement pertaining to ... disputes involving public entities and organizations, and more generally in any field that touches upon public policy.'[19]

In the 1960s, shortly after the entry into force of the New York Convention, French courts began to produce divergent readings of the restriction. In 1961, the Orleans Court of Appeal held that 'submission to arbitration is void whenever the settlement of the arbitration presupposes the interpretation and application of a public policy rule'.[20] In 1965, the Paris Court of Appeal drew a line between disputes touching upon public policy (arbitrable) and disputes involving breaches of public policy (inarbitrable).[21] The case law of the Paris Court of Appeal is of fundamental importance, since that Court is the designated forum for the annulment of arbitral awards rendered in France, and that Paris is the most popular seat for ICC arbitration.[22] In 1960, the French Supreme Court (*Cour de Cassation*) had already declared that, for international awards, judges were to apply 'international public policy', a standard that gives more leeway to international arbitrators compared to their domestic counterparts.[23] Legislators finally codified this jurisprudence in 1981, and the courts have continued to loosen the constraints placed upon arbitrators by national public policy ever since.[24]

The seminal *Ganz* case of 1991 dealt directly with a tribunal's public policy analysis. In its ruling in that case, the Paris Court of Appeals declared that arbitrators possessed the 'power to apply the principles and rules belonging to international public policy and sanction their possible breach, subject to judicial control at the annulment stage'.[25] In the subsequent *Labinal* case (1993), that court held that arbitrators had the power to enforce breaches of public policy in the context of EU competition law.[26] More generally, as commentators put it, French courts had delegated these powers subject to *ex post* judicial review of 'compliance with the fundamental requirements of [international] public policy'[27] at the annulment or enforcement stage. At least since these rulings, instances of French courts annulling awards on international public policy grounds are very unusual (see also Chapter 4).

---

[19] Article 2060(1), Civil Code (2015).

[20] *Société Jean Tardits & Cie v Korn og Foderstof Kompagniet* (Orléans Court of Appeal) (1962) 1 *Journal du Droit International* 140, 149.

[21] *Société J Meulemans v Robert* (Paris Court of Appeal) (1965) 1 *Journal du Droit International* 113, 116: '[A]lthough it is forbidden to enter into arbitration agreements concerning disputes implicating public policy, that rule does not mean that any dispute arising from an agreement or operation governed in some respects by a mandatory regulation, cannot be submitted to arbitration on those grounds.'

[22] In 2014, Paris was the most popular seat in ICC arbitrations. See International Chamber of Commerce, '2014 ICC Dispute Resolution Statistics' (2015) 1 ICC Dispute Resolution Bulletin.

[23] Cass Civ 1ère (14 June 1960).   [24] See Chapter 4.

[25] *Société Ganz et al v Société Nationale des Chemins de Fer Tunisiens* (Paris Court of Appeal, 29 March 1991).

[26] *Société Labinal v Société Mors* (Paris Court of Appeal, 19 May 1993).

[27] John Savage and Emmanuel Gaillard, *Fouchard Gaillard Goldman on International Commercial Arbitration* (Kluwer Law International, Alphen aan den Rijn 1999) para 566.

With respect to delegation and supervision, the situation today resembles that of the US courts, under the so-called 'second look' doctrine.

In the United States, the first federal statutes did not expressly establish public policy grounded rules of arbitrability. The Federal Arbitration Act (1925) provided for the validity of arbitration agreements, 'save upon such grounds as exist at law or in equity for the revocation of any contract'.[28] In *Wilko v Swan* (1953), however, the Supreme Court held that arbitration was not suitable for the adjudication of claims arising from the Securities Act, a view it would later extend to anti-trust law, the Racketeer Influenced and Corrupt Organizations Act, bankruptcy, the Carriage of Goods by Sea Act, and others.[29] By 1974, the Court could state as settled policy that the arbitrator 'has authority to resolve only questions of contractual rights', but has 'no general authority to invoke public laws that conflict with the bargain between the parties'.[30]

For transnational arbitration,[31] the turning point is the Court's 1985 ruling in the *Mitsubishi* case.[32] At issue was whether the courts could compel arbitration of a dispute involving US anti-trust law, a challenge to the presumption of inarbitrability under the *Wilko* line of cases. The dispute attracted the attention of the ICC, which filed an *amicus* brief arguing that its arbitrators were 'no less qualified than federal judges' to hear anti-trust and other statutory claims,[33] given that its tribunals were composed of highly competent judges, scholars, and practising lawyers.[34] In its decision, the Court comforted the ICC's position:

[T]he international arbitral tribunal owes no prior allegiance to the legal norms of particular states; hence, it has no direct obligation to vindicate their statutory dictates. The tribunal, however, is bound to effectuate the intention of the parties. When the parties have agreed that the arbitral body is to decide a defined set of claims which includes, as in these cases,

---

[28] Section 2, Federal Arbitration Act (enacted 12 February 1925).

[29] Gary Born, *International Commercial Arbitration* (2nd edn, Kluwer Law International, Alphen aan den Rijn 2014) 964–5.

[30] *Harrell Alexander Sr v Gardner-Denver Co* (US S Ct, 1974) 415 US 36, 56–7.

[31] For domestic arbitration, a similar move took place a few years later (but see *Scherk v Alberto-Culver Co* (1974) 417 US 506). *Rodriguez de Quijas v Shearson/Am Express, Inc* (1989) 490 US 477: This case was followed quickly by a series of cases, which reversed the *Wilko* line of case law. See Judith Resnik, 'Diffusing Disputes: The Public in the Private of Arbitration, the Private in Courts, and the Erasure of Rights' (2014–15) 124 Yale Law Journal 2680 ['Resnik'], cases cited in footnotes 281–96. See also Resnik, ibid, for an analysis of the effects of these changes on litigation and rights protection.

[32] On the *Mitsubishi* case, see Jean Robert, 'Une date dans l'extension de l'arbitrage international: l'arrêt Mitsubishi c/ Soler' (1986) 2 Revue de l'arbitrage 173; Hans Smit, 'Mitsubishi: It Is Not What It Seems to Be' (1987) 4(3) Journal of International Arbitration 7; Jacques Werner, 'A Swiss Comment on Mitsubishi' (1986) 3(4) Journal of International Arbitration 82 ['Werner'].

[33] At least one practitioner has criticized the ICC for undermining the contractual model. See Werner, ibid: 'Here is a major arbitral institution … which, inexplicably, comes to forget the very basics of arbitration which it preached for so many years, namely that arbitration and arbitrators do exist only by the clear agreement of the parties to that effect, and within the limits set by such agreement.' The ICC General Counsel, Mr Sigvard Jarvin, responded to the effect that the ICC's position reflected dominant arbitral practice. See Sigvard Jarvin, 'Mitsubishi—ICC comment' (1987) 4(1) Journal of International Arbitration 87.

[34] *Amicus* brief filed by the ICC in the case of *Mitsubishi Motors Corporation v Soler Chrysler Plymouth* (17 December 1984), 15–17.

those arising from the application of American antitrust law, the tribunal therefore should be bound to decide that dispute in accord with the national law giving rise to the claim.[35]

In wide-ranging *dicta*, the Court then expressly delegated the authority to enforce mandatory state law to the arbitral order:

By agreeing to arbitrate a statutory claim, a party does not forego the substantive rights afforded by statute; it only submits to their resolution in an arbitral, rather than a judicial, forum. It trades the procedures and opportunity for review of the courtroom for the simplicity, informality, and expedition of arbitration.

… As international trade has expanded in recent decades, so too has the use of international arbitration to resolve disputes arising in the course of that trade. The controversies that international arbitral institutions are called upon to resolve have increased in diversity as well as complexity. Yet the potential of these tribunals for efficient disposition of these legal disagreements has not yet been [fully] tested. If they are to take their place in the international legal order, national courts will need to 'shake off the old judicial hostility to arbitration' … To this extent, it will be necessary for national courts to subordinate domestic notions of arbitrability to the international policy favoring commercial arbitration.[36]

The Court then insisted that it would retain the power of the 'second look', to review the application of public policy by arbitrators at the enforcement stage in order 'to ensure that the legitimate interest in the enforcement' of such policy 'has been addressed'.[37]

In *Mitsubishi*, the Court treats arbitration as an autonomous system of dispute resolution; and it recognizes the system's functionality for traders, as well as its underlying autonomy and legitimacy. Considered in light of delegation theory, the Court scripts tribunals as agents of the US legal order, to the extent that a dispute calls upon them to enforce mandatory law. From the perspective of the New York Convention, the decision provides formal recognition, by a major court, of the pluralist nature of a regime. Cooperation between state courts and the arbitral order, in mutual recognition of one another's legitimate authority, is required for transnational governance to be effective. As in France, the 'second-look' in the United States has had little bite. Since 1970, it appears that US courts have only twice refused to enforce foreign arbitral awards, and then, only in part.[38]

Enforcing Mandatory Law

Arbitrators are under a fiduciary duty to enforce the parties' choice of law, as the 'applicable law'. Nonetheless, tribunals are under no obligation to enforce

---

[35] *Mitsubishi Motors v Soler Chrysler-Plymouth* (1985) 473 US 614, 636–7.   [36] ibid.
[37] ibid 614, 638.
[38] Reported in David Stewart, 'National Enforcement of Arbitral Awards under Treaties and Conventions' in Richard B Lillich and Charles N Brower (eds), *International Arbitration in the 21st Century: Towards 'Judicialization' and Conformity?* (Transnational, Irvington 1992) 191–2. We are not aware of any refusal on the part of American courts to enforce awards based on public policy considerations after *Mitsubishi*.

applicable state law as domestic judges of that law do, even in cases involving mandatory law or public policy (Chapters 3 and 4). Indeed, the ICC not only advises arbitrators not to attempt to do so,[39] it warns counsel that they should not expect a tribunal to be expert in applicable state law.[40] The more a dispute involves the interpretation of mandatory rules, the more autonomy the Tribunal is likely to have with respect to the parties, and their agreement. As the International Law Association's Committee on International Commercial Arbitration puts it:

Mandatory rules expressing public policy norms may warrant special consideration by arbitrators. When such laws [are] implicated in a dispute, arbitrators should, with respect to such issues, generally have more freedom to probe, to set the agenda, and to drive the development of the legal analysis than is typically the case when no such issues are present.[41]

Arbitrators themselves insist that even 'when an arbitrator disregards a mandatory rule of the applicable law, his decision does not yet amount to a violation of public policy',[42] a position now endorsed by the courts in most trading states as a component of pro-trade, pro-arbitration policies.

A tribunal's primary duty is to render an award that, in fact, applies the applicable law. Most complex, important disputes involve a kaleidoscope of sources of law and usages that the Tribunal must take into account. Taking an aggregate perspective allows us to observe certain patterns of activity. Not surprisingly, those domains of state law that impinge most directly on transnational commerce activate arbitrators the most. All leading arbitrators, for example, have extensive experience resolving disputes involving intellectual property, anti-trust, and bankruptcy, domains of law that states once considered inarbitrable.

Intellectual Property

Between 1990 and 1995, about 12 per cent of all new cases filed at the ICC contained a 'significant intellectual property aspect'.[43] In many of these cases, arbitrability issues prompted jurisdictional challenges, not least because most states did not recognize the arbitrability of IP disputes.[44] The most important states have

---

[39] The *Guide* (n 10), paras 3-768 and 3-769.

[40] Jacob Grierson and Annet van Hooft, *Arbitrating under the 2012 ICC Rules* (Kluwer Law International, Alphen aan den Rijn 2012) 169. 'Unlike a judge in a national court, an arbitrator in an ICC arbitration should not be presumed to know the law, and will therefore need to be provided source material for any legal principles that he or she is requested to apply, unless the arbitral tribunal expressly states otherwise.'

[41] International Law Association, *Ascertaining the Contents of the Applicable Law in International Commercial Arbitration* (2008) 21.

[42] François Perret, 'Resolving Conflicts between Contractual Clauses and Specific Rules of the Governing Law—Strict Application of the Law or Flexible Approach' in *The Application of Substantive Law by International Arbitrators* (ICC, Paris 2014) 109.

[43] ICC Commission on International Arbitration, 'Final Report on Intellectual Property Disputes and Arbitration' (1998) 9(1) ICC International Court of Arbitration Bulletin 37, 40.

[44] ibid 41–5.

reversed this position,[45] in one of two ways. Some, including Switzerland and the United States, give *erga omnes* effect to relevant arbitral awards that are recorded in the Register of Patents; others, such as France, give arbitral awards only *inter partes* effect.[46]

The number of IP disputes submitted to arbitration has expanded,[47] or remained 'significant',[48] for good reasons. IP rights are territorial, and thus disputes may lead to multiple judicial proceedings in various countries, rather than bundled into one arbitral proceeding.[49] IP disputes often involve trade secrets, leading parties to seek the cover of confidentiality. And their resolution often requires technical expertise that domestic courts may lack.[50] Parties usually submit these disputes to the major centres, such as the AAA/ICDR or the ICC, where the parties can access technical support in complex cases.[51] In March 2016, the Hong Kong International Arbitration Centre [HKIAC] established 'a new panel of arbitrators' to settle IP disputes, a move that followed the revisions of Hong Kong law explicitly withdrawing public policy objections from the enforcement of IP awards in that territory's courts. Some cases go to the World International Property Organization (based in Geneva and Singapore), which has administered about 400 mediation, arbitration, and expert determination cases, the bulk of which were filed in recent years.[52] In addition, the literature on IP arbitration has grown significantly in recent years, testifying to the increasing importance of the subject.[53]

Most IP proceedings take place pursuant to a licensing agreement containing an arbitration clause.[54] A typical case arises when one party asserts that the agreement permits it to distribute or manufacture products, a claim denied by the other party, who holds the IP rights. The Tribunal will then assess these entitlements, often enough, through balancing the parties' rights against broader public interests. An ICC award issued in 1989 is an example. In ICC Case 6036, a company X, the claimant, owned exclusive patent rights for a polyethylene bottle used in the packaging of soft drinks, the validity of which ran until 1985. X granted a licence

---

[45] Jacques de Werra, 'Arbitrating International Intellectual Property Disputes: Time to Think Beyond the Issue of (Non) Arbitrability' (2012) 3 IBLJ 299, 311 ['de Werra'].

[46] See François Dessemontet, 'Party Autonomy and the Law Applicable to the Arbitrability of IP Rights and Licensing Transactions' (2013) 5 IBLJ 421, 424.

[47] de Werra (n 45), 311; Patrick Nutzi, 'Intellectual Property Arbitration' (1997) 19(4) EIPR 192 ['Nutzi'].

[48] Trevor Cook and Alejandro I Garcia, *International Intellectual Property Arbitration* (Kluwer Law International, Alphen aan den Rijn 2010) 49 ['Cook and Garcia'].

[49] Alessandro L Celli and Nicola Benz, 'Arbitration and Intellectual Property' (2002) 3(3) EBOR 593, 596.

[50] Nutzi (n 47), 193.

[51] Murray Lee Eiland, 'The Institutional Role in Arbitrating Patent Disputes' (2009) 9(2) PDRLJ 283, 321.

[52] World Intellectual Property Organization, 'WIPO Caseload Summary' <http://www.wipo.int/amc/en/center/caseload.html> accessed 10 March 2016. WIPO has also heard more than 30,000 cases in domain name disputes.

[53] Cook and Garcia (n 48); William Grantham, 'The Arbitrability of International Intellectual Property Disputes' (1996) 14(1) Berkeley Journal of International Law 173; Thomas D Halket (ed), *Arbitration of International Intellectual Property Disputes* (Juris Publishing, New York 2012).

[54] Kamen Troller, 'Intellectual Property Disputes in Arbitration' (2006) 72(4) Arbitration 322, 323.

for the exploitation of the patent to company Y, which assigned the licence to its subsidiary, the defendant in the case. In the meantime, the Italian Government, using an administrative Ordinance and a decree, extended the life of patents, while entitling licensees to obtain a five-year extension on licences, free of charge. After company Y took advantage of the new rules, company X initiated proceedings, claiming that company Y owed fees to it for the extension. The Tribunal firmly asserted jurisdiction:

> The Arbitral Tribunal cannot accept Defendant's contention that the dispute should not be arbitrable because 'the issue on the breach of the agreement coincides with the determination of the right of Defendant under ... the Ordinance, a subject which in the opinion of Defendant is not arbitrable.' ... Defendant's conclusion that the dispute is not arbitrable has no other basis than its own view that the [subsequent] Decree has confirmed its right to discontinue the payment of royalties, while it is precisely that view that Claimant challenges in front of the Arbitral Tribunal. As rightly stressed by Claimant, the question at stake is 'whether, in the context of the Decree, Defendant has a continuing obligation under the contract to pay over to Claimant royalties collected from its customers.' This question calls for interpretation of the contract, in light of all relevant elements of law and fact, including the [administrative acts in question], and the Arbitral Tribunal is empowered by the arbitration clause of the Agreement to make such an interpretation.[55]

While we do not have access to the complete award, the arbitral tribunal positioned itself to be the primary decision-maker, finding that it had jurisdiction 'to decide whether Defendant is entitled to discontinue the payment of the contractual royalties ...'.[56]

Competition Law

Tribunals regularly enforce competition law[57] in proceedings involving licensing agreements, distribution contracts, and non-compete clauses that, one party alleges, span over a period that is too long, or whose territorial scope is too broad. ICC arbitrators began interpreting and applying mandatory domestic law in this area long before courts began to delegate this authority in the 1980s and 1990s.[58] In two cases decided in 1966, for example, ICC tribunals rejected claims that contractual agreements breached, respectively, US anti-trust law[59] and the competition rules of the Treaty of Rome.[60] Both tribunals asserted authority to enforce

---

[55] Final Award in ICC Case No 6036 (1989) in (1994) 5(1) ICC International Court of Arbitration Bulletin 67.

[56] ibid.

[57] Gordon Blanke and Philip Landolt, *EU and US Antitrust Arbitration: A Handbook for Practitioners* (Kluwer Law International, Alphen aan den Rijn 2011) 2063, Annex 3: In the 1964 to 2007 period, the ICC reported that it processed at least fifty-seven anti-trust cases. The actual number is unknown.

[58] For instance, the question of whether arbitrators should apply US anti-trust law was raised long before the 1980s. See Robert Pitofsky, 'Arbitration and Antitrust Enforcement' (1969) 44 New York University Law Review 1072.

[59] Unpublished ICC award (1966).

[60] ICC Case No 1397 (1966) in (1974) 2 *Journal du droit international* 878.

competition law, the second tribunal invoking a clear 'duty' to enforce European competition rules.[61] As the proportionality principle evolved within the European Union, at least some arbitrators embraced proportionality. In ICC Case No 12127 (2003), the question of whether a territorial limitation to patent rights set out in a licence agreement complied with French and European competition law had emerged as central; in response, the Tribunal moved to assess whether the restriction was 'disproportionate in respect of its finality and did not excessively restrict the operation of the licensee'.[62]

Today, tribunals routinely enforce competition law, and may do so even without prompting by the parties. The ICC's *Guide* refers to a case, decided in 2004, in which an arbitral tribunal enforced EU competition law on its own initiative:

[T]he parties were in a dispute over two agreements relating to the exchange of glass production technology and its use in Europe and elsewhere. The agreements restricted the parties' use of each other's technology in other regions of the world, raising competition issues. In particular, the respondent claimed that the first contract was null and void under European competition law, which the arbitral tribunal regarded as mandatory within Europe. However, the respondent did not formally plead for relief in relation to the alleged nullity. German law applied to the first contract. As European law is an integral part of German law, the relevant EU competition law was clearly applicable. The arbitral tribunal ultimately found that the contract complied with that law and, despite the fact that the matter had not been pleaded by the respondent, also addressed the issue of mandatory laws in relation to the second contract.[63]

The literature on competition law in ICA, too, has exploded in the past two decades.[64] Much of the scholarship emphasizes problems of coordination between the arbitral order and competition authorities.[65] The fragmented nature of European governance is a prime instance. Until 2003, the EU Commission had exclusive

---

[61] ibid 880: '[N]o arbitration agreement could substitute a private judge for a public judge to resolve a dispute concerning public policy *in se* and per se ... However, if in the context of a private law dispute a party claims as a defense that the contract on which the other party relies is void on the grounds of public policy and in particular for a breach of Article 85 of the Treaty of Rome, the arbitrator has a duty to examine whether the disputed contract satisfies the substantive and legal conditions leading to the application of the said article.'

[62] ICC Case No 12127 (2003) in (2008) Yearbook Commercial Arbitration 82.

[63] The *Guide* (n 10), para 3-776.

[64] See, on a non-exhaustive basis, Walid Abdelgawad, *Arbitrage et droit de la concurrence— Contribution à l'étude des rapports entre ordre spontané et ordre organisé* (LGDJ, Paris 2001); Luca Radicati di Brozolo, 'Antitrust: A Paradigm of the Relations between Mandatory Rules and Arbitration—A Fresh Look at the "Second Look" ' (2004) 7(1) International Arbitration Law Review 23; Philip Landolt, *Modernised EC Competition Law in International Arbitration* (Kluwer Law International, Alphen aan den Rijn 2006); Gordon Blanke (ed), *European Business Law Special Edition—Arbitrating Competition Law Issues* (Kluwer Law International, Alphen aan den Rijn 2008) Vol 19(11); Georgios I Zekos, 'Antitrust/Competition Arbitration in EU versus EU Law' (2008) 25(1) Journal of International Arbitration 1; Gordon Blanke and Philip Landolt (eds), *EU and US Antitrust Arbitration: A Handbook for Practitioners* (Kluwer Law International, Alphen aan den Rijn 2011); Charles N Brower, 'Arbitration and Antitrust: Navigating the Contours of Mandatory Law' (2011) 59(5) Buffalo Law Review 1127.

[65] Renato Nazzini, 'International Arbitration and Public Enforcement of Competition Law' (2004) 25(3) European Competition Law Review 153.

authority to grant competition law exemptions under the EU Treaty,[66] which raised obvious difficulties when a disputing party requested an exemption from a tribunal.[67] Since 2003, arbitrators directly process such claims on their own.[68] These developments inevitably raise a further architectural issue: is a tribunal a 'court' for the purposes of enforcing EU law and, thus, under a duty to request and obtain preliminary rulings from the European Court of Justice [ECJ] when interpretation of that law is at issue?[69] Or should tribunals permit a disputing party to request a judge of the seat of the arbitration to refer the question to the ECJ?[70]

While these issues remain unsettled, the ICC has established a 'Task Force for Arbitrating Competition Law Issues' to deal with them. The Task Force has highlighted the need to strike a balance between public interests (values contained in competition law) and the private character in ICA, in dialogue with the EU Commission as *amicus*:

In assessing the appropriateness and desirability of the Commission's involvement as *amicus curiae* in arbitral … proceedings [involving EC competition law], it has to be borne in mind that by their very nature, EC competition law proceedings as such ultimately seek to protect the EC interest and are therefore pursued in defence of the public interest more generally … Such considerations have to be balanced against the strictly private and confidential nature of the underlying arbitral proceedings.[71]

Similarly, despite initial skepticism, the EU Commission relies increasingly on the arbitral order to enforce EU competition law,[72] particularly in the area of merger control.[73] In 1992, the EU Commission delayed the initiation of an anti-trust investigation 'pending the outcome of the arbitration proceedings':

… the Commission has established a policy of reinforcing the role which national courts play in the enforcement of the EEC Treaty's competition rules. It would seem that cases of arbitral proceedings dealt with by standing institutions … where arbitrators base their findings on the law can be treated in an analogous manner to national judges.

---

[66] Consolidated version of the Treaty on the Functioning of the European Union 2008/C 115/01, Article 101(3).

[67] Maurits Dolmans and Jacob Grierson, 'Arbitration and the Modernization of EC Antitrust Law: New Opportunities and New Responsibilities' (2003) 14(2) ICC International Court of Arbitration Bulletin 37 ['Dolmans and Grierson'], 41–2.

[68] ibid 49.

[69] *Nordsee Deutsche Hochseefisherei BmbH v Reederei Mond Hochseefischerei Nordstern AG & Co KG and Reederei Friedrich Busse Hochseefischerei Nordstern AG & Co, KG* (23 March 1982) [1982] ECR 1095: The Court held that an arbitral tribunal is not a 'court or tribunal of a Member State' that can raise preliminary questions to the ECJ.

[70] Gordon Blanke and Renato Nazzini, 'Arbitration and ADR of Global Antitrust Disputes: Taking Stock' (2008) Global Competition Litigation Review 133, 136.

[71] 'ICC Draft Best Practice Note on the European Commission Acting as Amicus Curiae in International Arbitration Proceedings' in Gordon Blanke (ed), *European Business Law Special Edition—Arbitrating Competition Law Issues* (Kluwer Law International, Alphen aan den Rijn 2008) 198.

[72] Hamid G Gharavi, 'EC Competition Law and the Proper Scope of Arbitration' (1997) 63(1) Arbitration 59.

[73] Gordon Blanke, 'The Transformation of International Arbitration and the Emergence of the Supranational: Lessons from EC Merger Control' (2005) 8(6) International Arbitration Law Review 211.

... Arbitration is anchored in numerous legal national orders and the award delivered can be enforced under national law ... In the present case [where an arbitration clause required the rendering of an award within 6 months], a decentralized application will provide a particularly quick and efficient way of bringing to an end any possible infringement and providing legal certainty.[74]

Again, public officials, in this case of the European Union, have delegated to arbitrators competences they had already claimed to possess.

Bankruptcy

Conflicts between contract and mandatory law also arise with regularity once a party declares or contemplates bankruptcy. These conflicts typically revolve around the issue of whether arbitrators should ignore, or defer to, bankruptcy proceedings underway under domestic law. In most jurisdictions, a debtor initiates proceedings before a special court, in order to restructure debts, or to distribute remaining assets to creditors. In response, a creditor may look to arbitration in order to obtain a title against the debtor, or to circumvent the bankruptcy proceedings entirely.

As Kirgis stresses, cross-border problems of insolvency have given rise to competition between national courts and arbitral tribunals,[75] which have progressively been resolved in favour of 'coordination'.[76] In 2009, the ICC Secretary-General mentioned the 'numerous cases [brought to the ICC over the years] in which one or more of the parties were subject to bankruptcy proceedings'.[77] This is an undeniably messy area of law and practice, not least, since domestic laws differ as to the effect of insolvency on the validity of arbitration agreements.[78] Further, even when the domestic law is clear, conflict of law rules may dictate divergent outcomes.[79]

For present purposes, what is important is that tribunals now routinely confront, as the Tribunal in ICC Case No 16369 (2011) put it, 'a conflict between the private nature of arbitration and the collective insolvency procedures provided for under domestic laws, which are driven by public-policy considerations'.[80] The conflict is unavoidably one of 'competing policy objectives',[81] in which a state-driven process

---

[74] Dolmans and Grierson (n 67), 38.

[75] Paul F Kirgis, 'Arbitration, Bankruptcy, and Public Policy: A Contractarian Analysis' (2009) 17(2) American Bankruptcy Institute Law Review 503.

[76] Philippe Fouchard, 'Arbitrage et faillite' (1998) 3 Revue de l'arbitrage 471.

[77] Jason Fry, 'Introductory Note' (2009) 20(1) ICC International Court of Arbitration Bulletin 3.

[78] Famously, in the *Elektrim* case, an LCIA tribunal (seated in London) and an ICC tribunal (seated in Geneva) arrived at opposed conclusions to the same question. While the LCIA tribunal asserted its jurisdiction under the *lex arbitri* (English law), the ICC Tribunal dismissed its jurisdiction on the basis of Article 142 of the Polish Law on Bankruptcy and Reorganisation (which invalidates arbitration agreements in case of bankruptcy proceedings). See Doug Jones, 'Insolvency and Arbitration: An Arbitral Tribunal's Perspective' (2012) 78(2) Arbitration 123, 125.

[79] Gabrielle Nater-Bass and Olivier Mosimann, 'Effects of Foreign Bankruptcy on International Arbitration' (2011) Austrian Yearbook on International Arbitration 163.

[80] ICC Case No 16369 (2011) in (2014) XXXIX Yearbook Commercial Arbitration 169, paras 52–4. See also Emmanuel Jolivet, 'Quelques exemples de traitement du droit des procédures collectives dans l'arbitrage' (2006) 3 Cahiers de l'Arbitrage—Gazette du Palais 16.

[81] Doug Jones, 'Insolvency and Arbitration: An Arbitral Tribunal's Perspective' (2012) 78(2) Arbitration 123.

giving 'total control of the debtor's affairs [to] the bankruptcy court'[82] comes into tension with the arbitral commitment to preserve the parties' choice of arbitration. Not surprisingly, tribunals have not shied from asserting their own autonomy. In ICC Case No 10507 (2009), for example, the Tribunal considered that the parties' arbitral agreement must prevail over the asserted primacy of bankruptcy courts:

> [R]eference may be made to the principle of *pacta sunt servanda* in favour of maintaining the validity of the arbitration agreement beyond the declaration of bankruptcy of one of the parties. In an international relationship, as in the present matter, the parties very often agree on arbitration as the dispute settlement procedure in order to avoid that disputes have to be decided by the courts in the country of one of the two parties. By opting for arbitration, the parties [have] express[ed] their willingness to submit any dispute to a neutral panel, of which one member is normally designated by each party. There are no sufficiently strong reasons [that] could justify [a decision that would frustrate] a foreign contractual partner in his reasonable expectations to see his case decided by such panel, and thus be compelled to submit the dispute to the Bankruptcy Court of the State in which the opposing party has its place of business.[83]

How state courts will respond to such decisions remains an open question, but we expect to see more adaptation than state resistance and retrenchment.

An Assessment

Most of the major trading states, as well as the European Union,[84] have adopted pro-arbitration policies; indeed, states are engaged in fierce regulatory competition with one another to attract arbitral business (Chapter 2). In judicial decisions like *Mitsubishi*, courts play catch-up, delegating to cover what arbitrators are already doing. Judges retain the authority to review awards that may infringe upon public policy, while arbitrators proclaim their own competence to enforce mandatory state law, and to create transnational/international public policy on an ongoing basis (Chapter 4). These positions starkly reveal the pluralist nature of the New York Convention regime.

How well do national courts actually supervise what arbitrators are doing when they enforce mandatory law and public policy? The answer is clear: poorly. The reasons, too, are clear (Chapters 2 and 4). First, in the major trading zones, domestic law of contract enshrines party autonomy, including the freedom to choose arbitration. Second, states that make up these zones have limited *ex post* review of awards on the merits to virtually nil. Third, the clear, dominant strategy of transnational

---

[82] Jay Lawrence Westbrook, 'The Coming Encounter: International Arbitration and Bankruptcy' (1983) 67 Minnesota Law Review 595, 598.

[83] ICC Case No 10507, cited in Dominique Vidal, 'Arbitration and Insolvency Proceedings: Comments on ICC Awards and Other Recent Decisions' (2009) 20(1) ICC International Court of Arbitration Bulletin, para 63.

[84] The Court of Justice of the European Communities, in the *Eco Swiss v Benetton* case, implicitly delegated to arbitrators the authority to rule on violations of EC competition law, subject to the review exercised by domestic courts.

business is (a) to select the law of pro-arbitration states as the 'applicable law', and (b) to seat the arbitration in jurisdictions that take a hands-off approach to the merit review of awards. These choices secure the autonomy of the arbitrator. Fourth, the New York Convention is a decentralized enforcement regime: while one jurisdiction may block an award, another may enforce it.

How well do arbitrators take into account the public interest, through balancing or other means? The answer: no one knows. Just as in state courts, most commercial cases will turn on the contract and the facts, not on the application of mandatory law or the enforcement of public policy. Nonetheless, nearly all ICA awards in which tribunals do interpret and apply mandatory law, or take into account the public interest in other ways, are unavailable. Present policies on publication of awards give primacy to confidentiality interest (Chapter 4), which makes it impossible for scholars, judges, other state officials, NGOs, the media, and the broader public to evaluate arbitral decision-making. In our view (see Chapter 6), these policies are no longer justifiable.

III. Balancing and the Public Interest in Investor-State Arbitration

In ISA, tribunals routinely review official acts that states seek to defend in light of sovereign prerogatives and the duty to act in the name of the public interest. In this section, we address four overlapping questions. First, what types of state measures do tribunals review? Second, how do tribunals arbitrate claims in which states plead the general interest? Arbitrators could adopt a relatively ad hoc approach (the contractual model); they could seek to construct a common approach, as a relatively cohesive college (the judicial model); they could also view such cases as opportunities to dialogue with domestic courts, or to help build common frameworks for enforcing international economic law (the pluralist-constitutional model). Third, do tribunals balance investors' entitlements against the state's regulatory prerogatives? We are interested not only in who wins and loses, but in the extent to which they take into consideration a state's 'right to regulate'. Fourth, have states used their treaty-making authority to constrain arbitrators going forward? As we show, arbitrators have been the authors of much of the substance of international investment law since the field's take-off in the late 1990s. In the past decade, states-as-principals and primary lawmakers have rematerialized.

Review of State Measures: An Overview

In a first step toward addressing these questions, we gathered information on the types of measures attacked by investors as violations of a host state's treaty obligations, as recorded in the cases contained in our data set on final awards on the merits. We were able to obtain such information on 139 awards, the largest number of such decisions yet analysed. We paid particular attention to the distinction between general measures—a state act that regulates activity, or applies to all persons active, in a particular policy domain[85]—and individual acts that apply to a specific invest-ment. When tribunals engage in the review of general measures, states will rou-tinely plead public interests. The distinction will blur insofar as the Tribunal finds it impossible to review an individual measure without examining a general measure to which it is connected. In all cases, we analysed the pleadings of the parties, focusing on claims brought under the expropriation and FET headings. We then examined each tribunal's decision, paying particular attention to how arbitrators dealt with situations in which the state pleaded its regulatory prerogatives or a public interest.

The Review of 'General' Measures

Investors claimed that at least one general measure was a source of an investment treaty violation in forty awards (29 per cent). Some of these rulings concern the same set of measures. The 'Argentina cases', disputes based on the effects of a set of emergency measures adopted to meet that state's economic crisis of 1999 to 2002, comprise the largest such cluster, generating fourteen awards. In each of these cases, claimants attacked pesification and bank controls, among other measures, prevail-ing in twelve.[86] In three NAFTA awards—*ADM, Cargill,* and *Corn Products*—a Mexican tax on corn sweeteners used in soda drinks, a measure designed as a trade counter-measure, favouring Mexican sugar producers, produced three violations.[87] The third cluster, of three awards, involves Ecuador's Law 42 (2006) and a further implementing regulation. In 2006, Ecuador adopted a statute imposing a 50 per cent windfall profits tax on foreign oil companies which, eighteen months later, it raised to 99 per cent. Tribunals found state liability in all three cases, Law 42 and the amending decree being the direct source of two such violations. Tribunals found general measures to be the source of a violation in seven other, discrete cases; and they rejected such claims in the remaining sixteen. Table 5.1 summarizes this data.

The Argentina cases are the most politically and legally significant group of awards that review general measures of host states, in that they gave a series of tri-bunals the opportunity to take a position on similar pleadings.[88] Tribunals dealt with public interest arguments, including the necessity defence, in diverse ways, but none failed to take into account these interests at the liability or damages stage (see also Chapter 4). In the Mexican cases, arbitrators engaged the rulings of a WTO panel and the Appellate Body (which had found that the same law violated WTO

---

[85] Statutes are presumptively general measures, while some administrative decisions would also meet the criteria, e.g., a revision of the tax code through ministerial decree.

[86] See Chapter 4.

[87] *Archer Daniels Midland Company and Tate & Lyle Ingredients Americas, Inc v The United Mexican States* (ICSID Case No ARB(AF)/04/5), Award of 21 November 2007; *Cargill, Incorporated v United Mexican States* (ICSID Case No ARB(AF)/05/2), Award of 19 September 2009; *Corn Products International, Inc v United Mexican States* (ICSID Case No ARB(AF)/04/1), Award of 18 August 2009.

[88] For an overview of the cases from the perspective of public interests, see Giorgio Sacerdoti, 'General Interests of Host States in the Application of the Fair and Equitable Treatment Standard' in Giorgio Sacerdoti (ed), *General Interests of Host States in International Investment Law* (Cambridge University Press, Cambridge 2014) 3–25.

Table 5.1 Review of State Measures: Pleadings and Outcomes

	Claims	Violations	No Violation
General Measures	40	22	18
Argentina Cases	14	12	2
Non-Argentina Cases	26	10	16
Individual Measures*	109	58	51
Total	139	80	69

* This count excludes the 14 Argentina awards, and those 12 awards in which a tribunal found a violation of a general measure. The number of awards that contain either (i) a claim concerning at least one general measure, or (ii) one targeting at least one individual measure (n = 149), is higher than the total number of awards (n = 139), because tribunals may have rejected a pleading against a general measure, while accepting a claim targeting an individual measure. We do not count cases in which the investor claims a breach of a contract only.

Source: *Yale Law School Data Sets on Investor-State Arbitration*, compiled by Alec Stone Sweet, Sheng Li, Meng-Jia Yang, Michael Chung, Moeun Cha, and Tara Zivkovich.

rules).[89] All three tribunals found that Mexico had intentionally adopted the law to harm foreign interests based on facts left virtually unchallenged by Mexico. In the disputes raised under Ecuador's Law No 42, two tribunals—in *Occidental* (2012) and *Perenco* (2014)—found that these measures violated FET standards. While arbitrators acknowledged that 'there cannot be any doubt that a sovereign State has the undisputable sovereign authority to enact laws in order to raise revenue for the public welfare', such a 'right' is also subject to 'rule of law'.[90] Both tribunals also found, and Ecuador did not dispute,[91] that officials had taken these measures in order to coerce oil companies to renegotiate their participation contracts with the state. As the *Perenco* Tribunal put it: 'Law 42 at 99% unilaterally converted the Participation Contracts into *de facto* service contracts while the State developed a new model of such contracts which it demanded the contractor to sign.'[92] In the third case (*Burlington*), the Tribunal rejected the tax claim, but found a violation for the physical seizure of the investor's oil field (which we coded as an individual measure).

The number of non-Argentina cases in which a pleading against a general measure is registered is twenty-six, most of which (n = 18) involve discriminatory taxes, subsidies, or export controls. In most of these case (n = 15), claimants target changes in taxation. The remaining cases concern a variety of specific statutes or regulations

[89] For an analysis of the law and politics of the WTO disputes and their settlement, see Magda Kornis, 'U.S. Corn Sweeteners and Mexican Sugar: Agreement at Last!' (2008) 1 Journal of International Commerce and Economics 51.
[90] *Occidental Petroleum Corporation and Occidental Exploration and Production Company v The Republic of Ecuador* (ICSID Case No ARB/06/11), Award of 5 October 2012, para 529.
[91] *Perenco Ecuador Ltd v The Republic of Ecuador and Empresa Estatal Petróleos del Ecuador (Petroecuador)* (ICSID Case No ARB/08/6), Decision on the Remaining Issues of Jurisdiction and on Liability of 12 September 2014, para 409.
[92] ibid para 409.

allegedly tailored to harass the investor, or to unravel specific commitments the host state had made to induce the investment in the first place. Of the non-Argentina cases in this group (n = 26), sixteen (62 per cent) rejected investors' claims. As discussed below, many tribunals, first, expressly recognized a state's 'police power' prerogatives under customary international law [CIL], also called the 'regulatory power exception',[93] or the state's 'right to regulate',[94] and then, in effect, defer to the state's discretion to change the law in light of changing circumstances.[95]

The Review of 'Individual' Measures

In more than 70 per cent of the awards in our data set (n = 99), investors do not attack general measures. In virtually all of these cases, investors alleged that state officials took specific decisions or legal actions designed to harass them,[96] to interfere with their operations,[97] or to alter unilaterally investor–state contracts or agreements.[98] Claimants typically allege that these acts violate standards of due process, failing requirements of transparency, notice, the right to be consulted and heard, and reason-giving, often in breach of that state's own public law requirements when it comes to domestic governance.[99] Arbitrators developed the FET, in part, to cover

---

[93] *Saluka Investments BV v The Czech Republic* (UNCITRAL), Award of 17 March 2006 ['*Saluka v Czech Republic*'], para 471.

[94] *Total SA v The Argentine Republic* (ICSID Case No ARB/04/01), Award of 8 December 2010 ['*Total v Argentina*'], para 123; *El Paso Energy International Company v The Argentine Republic* (ICSID Case No ARB/03/15), Award of 31 October 2011 ['*El Paso v Argentina*'], paras 72–6.

[95] In *Chemtura Corporation v Government of Canada* (UNCITRAL), Award of 2 August 2010, the claimant challenged measures that would phase out use of a certain pesticide it produced, a tribunal composed of three elite arbitrators (Gabrielle Kaufmann-Kohler, Charles Brower, and James Crawford) deferred to the scientific expertise of Canadian regulators and noted Canada's 'margin of appreciation': paras 123, 134–8. It then engaged in comparative analysis of the environmental regulation in other states, and of relevant international instruments, in the style of the WTO and ECtHR courts (at para 135). See Alec Stone Sweet and Thomas Brunell, 'Trustee Courts and the Judicialization of International Regimes: The Politics of Majoritarian Activism in the ECHR, the EU, and the WTO' (2013) 1 Journal of Law and Courts 61.

[96] Recent awards in which violations were found for harassment include: *Joseph Charles Lemire v Ukraine* (ICSID Case No ARB/06/18), Award of 28 March 2011; *Gemplus SA, SLP SA, Gemplus Industrial SA de CV v The United Mexican States* (ICSID Case No ARB(AF)/04/3), Award of 16 June 2010; *Mr Franck Charles Arif v Republic of Moldova* (ICSID Case No ARB/11/23), Award of 8 April 2013.

[97] Recent awards in which violations were found for interference include: *Alpha Projektholding GmbH v Ukraine* (ICSID Case No ARB/07/16), Award of 8 November 2010); *Hulley Enterprises Ltd (Cyprus) v The Russian Federation* (UNCITRAL, PCA Case No AA 226), Award of 18 July 2014; *Mobil Corporation, Venezuela Holdings, BV, Mobil Cerro Negro Holding, Ltd, Mobil Venezolana de Petróleos Holdings, Inc, Mobil Cerro Negro, Ltd, and Mobil Venezolana de Petróleos, Inc v Bolivarian Republic of Venezuela* (ICSID Case No ARB/07/27), Award of 9 October 2014.

[98] Recent awards in which violations were found with regard to contractual obligations undertaken include: *AES Summit Generation Ltd and AES-Tisza Erömü Kft v The Republic of Hungary* (ICSID Case No ARB/07/22), Award of 23 September 2010; *Railroad Development Corporation v Republic of Guatemala* (ICSID Case No ARB/07/23), Award of 29 June 2012; *Gold Reserve Inc v Bolivarian Republic of Venezuela* (ICSID Case No ARB(AF)/09/1), Award of 2 September 2014.

[99] Recent awards finding violations for failures to provide due process, as provided for by domestic law, include *The Rompetrol Group NV v Romania* (ICSID Case No ARB/06/3), Award of 6 May 2013; *Hassan Awdi, Enterprise Business Consultants, Inc and Alfa El Corporation v Romania* (ICSID Case

these latter pleadings. As Table 5.1 reports, claimants prevailed in their pleadings against an individual measure about 53 per cent of the time (n = 58).

An Assessment

To what extent have tribunals failed to take seriously the public interest when pleaded by the state? Have they, in effect, placed a thumb on the scales in favour of investors? We accept that even the most informed observers may disagree on the proper response to these questions. Indeed, they have given rise to a great deal of controversy. Our approach was to address them empirically, as systematically as possible, considering every case in the data set in light of these issues.

Three of our findings deserve emphasis. First, we found no influential award that we would classify as an obvious failure on the part of the Tribunal (a) to deliberate the scope of the state's sovereign prerogatives, or (b) to consider carefully the public interest. In virtually all cases in which tribunals reviewed general measures and found against states (n = 22), they gave defensible reasons, including for how they had balanced. Most tribunals stressed that they were not sitting in judgment of statutes or other general measures, but, rather, considering the application of these measures to the investor in context, hence the importance of the FET and principles related to due process (below). The Argentina awards in this set of cases (n = 12) involved general measures upon which the investor had relied, and which the host state had explicitly promised would be maintained. Observers will differ in how they assess the quality of the reasons given by tribunals when they review state measures and balance, but we found no glaring examples of negligence. In the vast majority of awards, tribunals made good faith efforts to take seriously the state's 'right to regulate' (see below). Second, we found no evidence for the view that FET doctrine biases tribunals against states in any structural sense. As we report in the next section, the success rate for arbitrating FET claims (and claims targeting individual measures, more generally), hovers around 50 per cent. This figure is akin to what one finds in the free movement of goods domain in the European Union,[100] and it conforms to certain well-known theories of adjudication, including Priest-Klein, which predicts a 'tendency toward 50% plaintiff victories among litigated cases', under conditions of uncertainty.[101] In balancing situations, it is the factual context, not the law per se, that varies across cases, which is a strong condition of uncertainty. Third, we found no evidence for the view that arbitrating the FET has led to regulatory freeze or paralysis, and we know of no empirical scholarship demonstrating the contrary.

No ARB/10/13), Award of 2 March 2015; *William Ralph Clayton, William Richard Clayton, Douglas Clayton, Daniel Clayton and Bilcon of Delaware Inc v Government of Canada* (UNCITRAL, PCA Case No 2009-04), Award of 17 March 2015.

[100] Alec Stone Sweet, *The Judicial Construction of Europe* (Oxford University Press, Oxford 2004) Chapter 3.

[101] George Priest and Benjamin Klein, 'The Selection of Disputes for Litigation' (1984) 13 Journal of Legal Studies 1.

Readers should consider these findings in light of the evolution of the FET standard, to which we now turn.

Constructing the Fair and Equitable Treatment Standard

The evolution of the FET is a stunning example of expansive arbitral lawmaking. ICSID tribunals have developed the FET as a type of 'master norm', an overarching, quasi-'constitutional' principle.[102] The result is that, today, it is settled case law that the FET is comprised of a wealth of relatively elastic sub-principles, including: good faith;[103] due process, the reason-giving requirement, and access to justice;[104] regulatory consistency and transparency; reasonableness, non-arbitrariness, and non-discrimination; and the proportionality principle. A succession of tribunals gradually assembled these norms under a covering principle, the 'legitimate expectations' of the investor [LE]. The move enables the assessment of virtually every aspect of the relationship between the investor and the host state in what is, today, a relatively stable doctrinal structure.[105]

Inserting the FET into investment treaties reduced states' contracting costs *ex ante*, while delegating massive interpretive authority to arbitrators *ex post*. Tribunals embraced the FET for its flexibility, enabling them to tailor their rulings to the facts under the rubric of principles. Today, a jurisprudence of general principles comprises the core of the law and politics of ISA, including debates about if and how to curtail arbitral lawmaking power.

The FET is a paradigmatic example of an open-ended, incomplete norm, combining expansive functional logics, indeterminacy, and breadth.[106] Different formulations of the standard could lead arbitrators to wide variance in outcomes. Consider the following examples, taken from agreements that entered into force in the 1990s, which we reproduce in their entirety:

- NAFTA (entered into force, 1995): 'Each Party shall accord to investments of investors of another Party treatment in accordance with international law, including fair and equitable treatment and full protection and security.'

---

[102] Roland Kräger, *Fair and Equitable Treatment in International Investment Law* (Cambridge University Press, Cambridge 2011) ['Kräger'] 308–16: see for a discussion on the view that the FET comprises a 'master norm', as well as a mechanism of 'constitutionalisation'.

[103] According to some tribunals, the principles bundled under the FET are derivable from good faith. See *Tecmed v Mexico* (ICSID Case No ARB(AF)/00/2), Award of 29 May 2003 ['*Tecmed v Mexico*'], paras 153–5.

[104] For an analysis of developments in these areas, see Giacinto della Cananea, *Due Process of Law Beyond the State: Requirements of Administrative Procedure* (Oxford University Press, Oxford 2016) Chapters 3 and 4.

[105] Kenneth J Vandevelde, 'A Unified Theory of Fair and Equitable Treatment' (2010) 43 NYU Journal of International Law and Politics 43 ['Vandevelde']; Rudolph Dolzer, 'Fair and Equitable Treatment: Today's Contours' (2013) 12 Santa Clara Journal of International Law 7.

[106] In the important awards interpreting the FET, the tribunals themselves acknowledge the challenges posed by the FET's incompleteness, e.g., *Saluka v Czech Republic* (n 93), paras 263–5.

- US–Argentina BIT (entered into force, 1994): 'Investment shall at all times be accorded fair and equitable treatment, shall enjoy full protection and security and shall in no case be accorded treatment less than that required by international law.'
- The France–Mexico BIT (entered into force, 1998): 'Each Contracting Party shall extend and ensure fair and equitable treatment in accordance with the principles of International Law to investments made by investors of the other Contracting Party in its territory or in its maritime area, and ensure that the exercise of the right thus recognized shall not be hindered by law or in practice.'
- *The European Energy Charter* (entered into force, 1998): 'Each Contracting Party shall, in accordance with the provisions of this Treaty, encourage and create stable, equitable, favourable and transparent conditions for Investors of other Contracting Parties to make Investments in its Area. Such conditions shall include a commitment to accord at all times to Investments of Investors of other Contracting Parties fair and equitable treatment.'

The NAFTA provision—Article 1105—is included under the heading, 'Minimum Standard of Treatment' thereby invoking the CIL standard owed to aliens, which pre-dates the emergence of the FET. The FET found in the US–Argentina BIT closes with reference to international law, as a floor below which treatment may not fall, whereas the France–Mexico BIT version connects the FET to 'the principles' of international law, expressly conferring a justiciable 'right' on the investor. The Energy Charter announces the FET without mentioning international law at all, which is the case of most BITs.

Two general points deserve emphasis up-front. First, in the great wave of investment agreements signed in the 1990s, states provided virtually no guidance on how the FET was to be interpreted, leaving it to arbitral process. Drafters mostly cut and pasted from a basic template. Second, an FET provision qualified by international law will not necessarily restrict lawmaking; indeed, reference to international law might just as well provoke it. There is no consensus, after all, on the content and scope of the minimal standard of treatment owed to aliens, or on the degree to which other relevant CIL standards might subsume the minimal standard. In deciding whether and how to apply a CIL norm, judges assess the consistency of state practice in light of *opinio juris*, which typically leads them to survey relevant decisions by other courts and officials, as well as doctrinal commentary. CIL evolves over time through state practices (including their treaty-making activities), judicial decisions, and legal scholarship. It would be defensible for an arbitrator to find that the FET has evolved through (a) practice, as evidenced by the explosion of investment treaties that contain it, and (b) arbitral interpretation and enforcement. If so, one could find evidence of emergent CIL norms in the arbitral interpretation of investment treaties.

Where an FET provision references international law without mentioning CIL, arbitrators could appeal to the 'general principles of law' to justify a major lawmaking move. General principles are unwritten, judge-made legal norms on which courts have long relied upon to build their own legal systems, ostensibly to 'fill' important 'gaps'.[107] Moreover, general principles comprise an autonomous source of international law,[108] fully applicable in arbitrations under the ICSID Convention.[109] Tribunals may also mould the FET into a placeholder for a general principle. Looking forward, some tribunals have constructed the FET as an autonomous principle, at times in synergy with an evolving CIL. In doing so, they assert their own primacy over the law's evolution, which we find neither surprising nor controversial.[110] In any event, all of these bodies of norms—the FET, CIL, and general principles—are incomplete. States can respond to lawmaking they do not like by stating as much, appointing arbitrators presumed to be allies, drafting and publishing new model BITs, renegotiating existing treaties, and considering exit strategies.

BIT Arbitration: Legitimate Expectations and the Right to Regulate

The FET has evolved in relation to three other important substantive protections in BITs. First, all investment treaties prohibit expropriations that fail to meet certain legal standards,[111] the most common of which are non-discrimination, due process, the showing of an important public purpose, and the payment of prompt, adequate, and effective compensation. Second, virtually all BITs prohibit so-called 'indirect' expropriation, that is, measures taken to have an 'equivalent effect' to expropriation. These might include regulatory takings, 'creeping' incursions on property rights, failure to regulate, and other state omissions—interferences that, in effect, would 'substantially deprive' the investment of its value. Third, most but not all BITs contain a so-called 'umbrella clause', which covers breaches of specific promises to an investor, most obviously, of contractual commitments entered into

---

[107] Alec Stone Sweet and Giacinto Della Cananea, 'Proportionality, General Principles of Law, and Investor-State Arbitration: A Response to Jose Alvarez' (2013–14) 46 NYU Journal of International Law and Politics 911.

[108] Statute of the International Court of Justice TS 993, Article 38.

[109] Convention on the Settlement of Investment Disputes between States and Nationals of Other States (1967) 575 UNTS 159, Article 42. See also Chapter 2.

[110] Organisation for Economic Co-operation and Development [OECD], 'Intergovernmental Agreements Relating to Investment in Developing Countries' (27 May 1984) Doc No 84/14: In 1984, well before the emergence of FET jurisprudence, the OECD published a study of the post-Second World War origins of the FET, along with an analysis of state responses to survey questions regarding the standard's source and status. The report summarized these views in the following terms: 'According to all Member countries which commented on this point, the FET introduced a substantive legal standard referring to general principles of international law even if this is not explicitly stated and is a general clause which can be used for all aspects of the treatment of investments, in the absence of more specific guarantees. In addition it provides general guidance for the interpretation of the agreement and the resolution of difficulties which may arise.' The origins and evolution of the FET is traced again in a 2004 update of the 1984 report—see OECD, 'Fair and Equitable Treatment Standard in International Investment Law' (2004/03) OECD Working Papers on International Investment <http://dx.doi.org/10.1787/675702255435> accessed 10 May 2016.

[111] If an expropriation meets these standards, then it is lawful under the treaty. Typically, the investor will then be compensated for the value of the investment at the date of the taking. If the expropriation violates the treaty, the state may be liable for lost profits as well.

by a state entity.[112] Umbrella clauses can shift to ISA disputes that, in ICA, would be treated as contractual. Arbitrators have developed the FET in ways that can supplement the purpose of these norms, or even supplant them altogether, which has recast the law and politics of ISA in important ways.

As a strategic matter, a state inclined to expropriate or encroach on an investment in other ways will have an interest in disguising its intentions, which the indirect expropriation heading means to smoke out and capture. In this cat and mouse game, a state may turn to ever more subtle forms of encroachment. We can expect a tribunal to rely on expropriation norms in a clear and egregious case, but these provisions are blunt and stigmatizing instruments. Like the FET, they are also products of incomplete treaty-making. In BITs adopted prior to 2005[113] (to date, no final award on liability under a BIT adopted after 2003 has yet appeared), states did not provide interpretive guidelines, or criteria, for arbitrating indirect expropriation claims. Simplifying a complicated and somewhat disjointed jurisprudence, arbitrators have mixed and matched several different approaches, all of which express a certain anxiety toward aggressive enforcement.[114] First, there is broad consensus on the 'substantial deprivation' doctrine: the 'effects' of state acts on the investment must be comparable to the effects of an express expropriation. Second, in the 2002 to 2007 period, a series of influential awards held that the regulatory power exception[115] effectively insulated general state measures from censure if they met standards of due process and non-discrimination, and were taken for some *bona fide* public purpose.[116] Third, a set of significant awards rendered more recently blends these two approaches in ways that favour adoption of a balancing posture.[117]

---

[112] A standard formulation reads: 'Each Contracting Party shall observe any obligation it may have entered into with regard to the treatment of investments of nationals of the other Contracting Party.' Claims made pursuant to an umbrella clause have concerned licensing agreements, contract-based concessions for the provision of public services, and tax exemptions and other inducements. Arbitral case law on umbrella clauses is notoriously inconsistent. See Jarrod Wong, 'Umbrella Clases in Bi-Lateral Investment Treaties: Of Breaches of Contract, Treaty Violations, and the Divide between Developing and Developed Countries in Foreign Investment Disputes' (2006) 14 George Mason Law Review 135.

[113] For an important early assessment of indirect expropriation law, see W Michael Reisman and Robert D Sloane, 'Indirect Expropriation and Its Valuation in the BIT Generation' (2004) 74 British Year Book of International Law 115.

[114] Prabhash Ranjan and Pushkar Anand, 'Determination of Indirect Expropriation and Doctrine of Police Power in International Investment Law: A Critical Appraisal' in Leila Choukroune (ed), *Judging the State in International Trade and Investment Law* (Springer 2016) (forthcoming).

[115] *Saluka v Czech Republic* (n 93), para 252: '[I]t is now established in international law that States are not liable to pay compensation to a foreign investor when, in the normal exercise of their regulatory powers, they adopt in a nondiscriminatory manner *bona fide* regulations that are aimed at the general welfare.'

[116] ibid; *Marvin Roy Feldman Karpa v United Mexican States* (ICSID Case No ARB(AF)/99/1), Award of 16 December 2002; *Methanex Corporation v United States of America* (UNCITRAL), Award of 3 August 2005.

[117] *Total v Argentina* (n 94); *El Paso v Argentina* (n 94).

Table 5.2 Cases, Claims, and Violations Found in Investor–State Arbitration: Expropriation, Umbrella Clauses, and Fair and Equitable Treatment

	Total		ICSID*		NAFTA		Other**	
Cases	141		83		22		36	
Claims	341		212		39		90	
Direct Expropriation	57		35		2		20	
Indirect Expropriation	117		70		18		29	
Umbrella Clause	44		35		NA		9	
FET	123		72		19		32	
Violations Found		Success Rate		Success Rate		Success Rate		Success Rate
Cases	90	64%	55	66%	9	41%	26	72%
Claims	113	33%	78	37%	6	15%	29	32%
Direct Expropriation	11	19%	8	23%	0	0%	3	15%
Indirect Expropriation	29	25%	19	27%	1	1%	9	31%
Umbrella Clause	9	20%	8	23%	NA	NA	1	11%
FET	64	52%	43	60%	5	25%	16	50%

* We include both ICSID Convention and ICSID Additional Facility cases here, excluding NAFTA from the latter category.
** We include UNCITRAL arbitrations here, except NAFTA cases arbitrated under UNCITRAL Rules.
Source: *Yale Law School Data Sets on Investor-State Arbitration*, compiled by Alec Stone Sweet, Sheng Li, Meng-Jia Yang, Michael Chung, Moeun Cha, and Tara Zivkovich.

As developed by arbitrators, the FET has proved more flexible, enabling arbitrators to assess every important fact bearing on the dispute, as they accumulate episodically, and then to fashion decisions and remedies that are appropriate to the overall situation. Over the past fifteen years, claimants have routinely pleaded both indirect expropriation and FET on what are essentially the same facts. The FET may also partly overlap with an umbrella clause, each furnishing materials for evaluating claims in the other domain. In the absence of an umbrella clause, tribunals may deploy the FET to fill the gap. Indeed, tribunals now rely heavily on the covering principle of LE to manage situations wherein an investor has relied on express guarantees given by the state to induce the investment in the first place.

Table 5.2 reports data on pleadings and findings of violation across these domains in all final, publicly available awards on the merits. In 141 ICSID, NAFTA, and non-NAFTA UNCITRAL cases, investors brought 341 separate claims under expropriation, indirect expropriation, umbrella clauses, and the FET. In 103 cases, investors pleaded both indirect expropriation and FET. Of these, tribunals found a violation of both in sixteen cases (16 per cent); a violation of indirect expropriation but not of the FET in eight cases (8 per cent); and a violation of the FET but not of indirect expropriation in forty-one cases (40 per cent). Although states neither intended nor foresaw this outcome, tribunals have gradually settled on a clear preference for using the FET rather than indirect expropriation as the basis for findings of liability.[118] In cases in which investors plead both provisions, tribunals usually assess each claim in turn, generating a great deal of redundant assessment of identical materials. Tellingly, some recent tribunals go directly to FET analysis and, having found a violation, forego assessment of the indirect expropriation claims altogether.[119] FET claims also have a higher success rate (52 per cent) compared to indirect expropriation claims (25 per cent); indeed, the number of FET violations exceeds those found under the other three headings put together.

In the domain of the FET, ICSID tribunals have overcome the various obstacles to building stable doctrinal frameworks (Chapter 4). Indeed, a powerful feedback loop—a key mechanism of judicialization—has been forged.[120] A steady stream of FET claims has led tribunals to develop an increasingly dense and articulated arbitral jurisprudence, which, in turn, has structured new rounds of pleadings. As Schill puts it, 'arbitral jurisprudence' in this domain is itself a 'source of expectations' for investors and states.[121]

Beginning in 2006, some arbitrators began to take great pains to survey the development of the FET. They carefully traced its evolution from a handful of very important BIT and NAFTA awards,[122] as well as from general principles recognized by domestic and international courts, in a clear effort to standardize the domain's logics and content going forward.[123] Within five years, a series of prominent awards were on the books. Written by renowned jurists and former judges of major international courts, they featured sophisticated commentary on the LE as a general principle of law, and laborious LE-FET analysis. Four notable

---

[118] In an influential dissent, Thomas Wälde expressed the view openly: 'the legitimate expectation principle ... provides a more supple way of providing a remedy appropriate to the particular situation as compared to the more drastic determination and remedy inherent in concept of regulatory expropriation. It is probably partly for these reasons that "legitimate expectation" has become for tribunals a preferred way of providing protection to claimants in situations where the tests for a "regulatory taking" appear too difficult, complex and too easily assailable ...'. See *International Thunderbird Gaming Corporation v Mexico* (NAFTA/UNCITRAL), Award of 26 January 2006, Separate Opinion Thomas Wälde ['Wälde'], para 37. See also Katia Yannaca-Small, *Fair and Equitable Treatment Standard, in Arbitration under International Investment Agreement* (Oxford University Press, Oxford 2010) 385, 399: 'obligations entailed in the expropriation clause and those of fair and equitable treatment do not necessarily differ in quality but just in intensity'.

[119] *Ioan Micula and others v Romania* (ICSID Case No ARB/05/20), Award of 11 December 2013.

[120] As discussed in Chapter 6, the proposed *Trans-Pacific Partnership* agreement places the principle of legitimate expectations not within FET provisions—phrased as 'distinct, reasonable, investor-backed expectations'—but within indirect expropriation. These appear only in Annex 9-B—Expropriation; and Article 9.7.1, footnote 36, which concerns Expropriation and Compensation.

[121] Stephan W Schill, 'Fair and Equitable Treatment, the Rule of Law, and Comparative Public Law' in Stephan W Schill (ed), *International Investment Law and Comparative Public Law* (Oxford University Press, Oxford 2010) 156–7.

[122] *SD Myers Inc v Canada* (UNCITRAL/NAFTA) 40 ILM 1408, First Partial Award of 13 November 2000; *Pope and Talbot v Canada* (UNCITRAL/NAFTA), Award on the Merits of Phase 2 of 10 April 2001; *Mondev International Ltd v United States* (ICSID Case No ARB(AF)/99/2), Award of 11 October 2002 ['*Mondev v USA*']; *Técnicas Medioambientales Tecmed, SA v Mexico* (ICSID Case No ARB(AF)/00/2) 43 ILM, Award of 29 May 2003 (2004).

[123] Wälde (n 118); *Saluka v Czech Republic* (n 93); *Total v Argentina* (n 94); *El Paso v Argentina* (n 94).

examples[124]—*Saluka* (2006), the dissent in *Thunderbird* (2006),[125] *Total* (2010), and *El Paso* (2011)—share common traits. Each is the product of a self-conscious effort to rationalize LE-FET doctrine in the face of inconsistencies,[126] through elucidating the source, content, and scope of application of the legitimate expectations doctrine, and its relationship to other substantive protections found in BITs. Further, each contains intensive engagement with past awards, approving, distinguishing, or rejecting existing lines of case law.[127] Read together, one finds consensus on the basic materials that subsequent tribunals can easily assemble into a general framework for FET analysis. This same period saw a stream of scholarly articles designed to synthesize the case law, including Thomas Vandevelde's treatise-like reconstruction, portentously entitled, 'A Unified Theory of Fair and Equitable Treatment'.[128]

From the point of view of arbitral governance, the most important outcome of this process concerns the development of a coherent balancing framework within the FET.[129] Under this framework, the Tribunal balances (a) the investor's 'legitimate' (or 'basic') 'expectations', which are generated, for example, when the investor relies on specific commitments proffered by the host state, against (b) the state's sovereign prerogatives to regulate in the public interest. An investor's LE may include an entitlement to some minimal level of stability in the regulatory environment, and more if expressly promised by the state to induce the investment in the first place. But entitlements associated with the FET and LE are not absolute. As tribunals from *Saluka* forward have made clear, investors cannot legitimately expect regulatory arrangements to be frozen in place. In effect, the state possesses a 'right to regulate', which the *Saluka* Tribunal referred to as the state's 'legitimate regulatory interests'[130] to pursue important public purposes, even if changes to arrangements would harm the investor. When used for the purposes of balancing, tribunals regularly treat the doctrine as subsuming other FET-derived norms, such as due process, non-discrimination, and transparency. Balancing permits arbitrators to consider a wider range of elements than would be plausible under the standards developed for

---

[124] Wälde (n 118), paras 9–58; *Saluka v Czech Republic* (n 94), paras 282–309; *Total v Argentina* (n 95), paras 105–34; *El Paso v Argentina* (n 94), paras 328–79.

[125] Though *Thunderbird* is a NAFTA case, Wälde, in his separate opinion, focuses on the FET as a common principle at the heart of investment law, irrespective of the treaty instrument or source.

[126] The *El Paso* Tribunal worried, for instance, that 'ICSID case-law has developed in a way that generates some confusion and overlap between these different standards of protection found in most BITs'. See *El Paso v Argentina* (n 94), para 226. The Tribunal then goes on to lay out its views on the distinction between (a) FET and (b) other substantive protections more generally, including indirect expropriation (paras 226–31), before applying these views to the facts (paras 380–519).

[127] In a recent paper, Michele Potestà claims, inexplicably, that tribunals have given 'little justification' for the principle, preferring simply to follow precedent. In fact, Potestà covers exactly the same ground as these four opinions, citing them. We note this fact not to criticize Potestà, but rather to highlight the great efforts the authors of these awards made to provide the field with exactly what Potestà asserts is absent. See Michele Potestà, 'Legitimate Expectations in Investment Law: Understanding the Roots and the Limits of a Controversial Concept' (2013) 28 ICSID Review—Foreign Investment Law Journal 88.

[128] Vandevelde (n 105); Kräger (n 102).

[129] The process has not been a linear one, and not all leading arbitrators have invested in it.

[130] *Saluka v Czech Republic* (n 93), para 306.

expropriation or indirect expropriation. And, to repeat, it enables tribunals to assess virtually all relevant facts and arguments under one flexible standard.

It is crucial to stress that tribunals, in the absence of any express state consent, purposefully read into the FET both the doctrine of 'legitimate expectations' and the state's 'right to regulate'. Arbitrators did not camouflage their lawmaking. Instead, they adopted the posture of a judge whose task it is to identify and apply general principles of law. Where tribunals have interpreted the LE-FET in light of CIL, they typically arrive at the same conclusions as tribunals that engage more explicitly in a jurisprudence of general principles.[131] This common disposition networks treaties and tribunals, while creating a dynamic through which the FET and CIL evolve synergistically.

The 2003 award in *Tecmed v Mexico* first announced the LE doctrine, in the context of Article 4(1) of the Spain–Mexico BIT stipulating that states shall 'guarantee' the FET to investors 'according to International Law'. The *Tecmed* award is the most cited in the history of ISA, notably for the proposition that LE constitutes a '*bona fide* principle recognized in international law',[132] derivable from an even broader principle, that of 'good faith':

> The Arbitral Tribunal considers that [Art. 4(1)], in light of the good faith principle established by international law, requires the Contracting Parties to provide to international investments treatment that does not affect the basic expectations that were taken into account by the foreign investment to make the investment. The foreign investor expects the host State to act in a consistent manner, free from ambiguity and totally transparently ... so that it may know beforehand any and all rules and regulations that will govern its investments, as well as the goals of the relevant policies and administrative practices or directives, to be able to plan its investment and comply with such regulations.[133]

This passage immediately attracted the attention of the arbitral community. It also generated strong criticism from those who worried that the construction would produce a pro-investor bias, insofar is it would hold states to a standard of 'perfect regulation in a perfect world'.[134] The paragraph actually closes on a softer line, stressing that the LE-FET captures clearly 'arbitrary' 'state action' that 'shocks ... a sense of judicial propriety',[135] not all measures that fail to meet the ideal just expressed.

The *Tecmed* Tribunal only impliedly recognized a state's 'right to regulate' in the domain concerned—that of environmental protection.

---

[131] *El Paso v Argentina* (n 94), para 335: As the *El Paso* Tribunal affirmed, seeking to determine if the FET-as-principle constrains states more than the FET within CIL would be a 'somewhat futile' exercise since 'the scope and content of the minimum standard of international law is as little defined as the BITs' FET standard. The issue is not one of comparing two undefined or weakly defined standards; it is to ascertain the content and define the BIT standard of fair and equitable treatment.'

[132] *Tecmed v Mexico* (n 103), para 153.   [133] ibid para 154.

[134] Zachary Douglas, 'Nothing If Not Critical for Investment Treaty Arbitration: Occidental, Eureko, and Methanex' (2006) 27 Arbitration International 27, 28.

[135] *Tecmed v Mexico* (n 103), para 154.

Upon making its investment, the fair expectations of the Claimant were that the Mexican laws applicable to such investment, as well as the supervision, control, prevention and punitive powers granted to the authorities in charge of managing such a system, would be used for the purpose of assuring compliance with environmental protection, human health and ecological balance goals underlying such laws.[136]

The Tribunal found that the Mexican Federal Government had abused its regulatory prerogatives, closing down the investor's waste disposal operations through a series of unilateral decisions targeting the investor, using various forms of coercion along the way. Federal officials did so in response to intensifying local opposition to the landfill site, after elections at the municipal and state levels. The tribunals also found, unanimously, that the company had not 'endangered public health economic balance or the environment'.[137] In fact, the company had proposed the development of an alternative site, bearing the costs of its own relocation, the permit for which the authorities refused.

Explicit recognition of a 'right to regulate', conceived as a necessary corollary to LE, emerged in Thomas Wälde's dissent in *Thunderbird v Mexico* (2006), a NAFTA case. Wälde considers the development of LE—as a general principle of international law tied to the good faith principle[138]—in light of the case law of the European Union, the ECtHR, the WTO Appellate Body, and national administrative law courts, in addition to the relevant scholarship of comparative public law. For present purposes, two aspects of the dissent are important. First, the opinion emphasizes that LE analysis inevitably drives the arbitrator into a balancing posture, wherein the Tribunal takes into account both the 'needs for flexible public policy and the legitimate reliance on particular investment-backed expectations'.[139] Second, Wälde defends an approach to the FET that highlights, rather than disguises, the role of judges in progressively constructing the law as a set of 'objective', 'authoritative', and 'universal' principles of 'modern national and international economic law'.[140] Tribunals are not only under an obligation to apply such general principles; their jurisprudence on general principles ought to knit together the various sources of international law into a coherent whole:

While individual arbitral awards by themselves do not as yet constitute ... binding precedent, a consistent line of reasoning developing a principle and a particular interpretation of specific treaty obligations should be respected; if an authoritative jurisprudence evolves, it will acquire the character of customary international law and must be respected. A deviation from well and firmly established jurisprudence requires an extensively reasoned justification. This approach will help to avoid the wide divergences that characterise some investment arbitral awards ... But it is also mandated by the reference to applicable rules of international Law (Art. 1131 NAFTA) and thereby Art. 38 of the Statute of the ICJ: An increasingly continuous, uncontested and consistent modern arbitral jurisprudence is part of the authoritative source of international law embodied in 'judicial decisions' [ICJ Statute, Art. 38 (1)(d)] and will develop, with an even greater legally binding effect, into 'international custom' [ICJ

---

136 ibid para 157. 137 ibid para 162. 138 Wälde (n 118), para 25.
139 ibid para 30. 140 ibid.

Statute, Art. 38 (1)(b)], in particular as an arbitral jurisprudence defines in a contemporary treaty and factual context the 'general principles of law' [ICJ Statute, Art. 38 (1)(d)].[141]

Wälde's preferred approach not only takes for granted the dictates of the judicial model, it forcefully invokes duties associated with the pluralist-constitutional model.

In this case, the *Thunderbird* corporation, faced with a Mexican statute that prohibited gambling in the context of 'luck-related' games, had asked the relevant regulatory authority if it would permit a skill-oriented game, 'where chance and wagering or betting is not involved'. Officials replied that they would permit games based on skill, but not on luck. This response, the corporation would later claim, created an LE. In fact, Thunderbird ran slot machines. By the company's own admission, the 'skill' needed to win entailed aligning 'different symbols on the [machines'] screen' through a player's act of 'pushing buttons'.[142] The Tribunal found for Mexico, holding that the investor's own conduct helped to create a situation in which authorities shut down its operations. As Valenti has stressed,[143] tribunals in previous LE-FET cases, including in *Tecmed*, had examined the investor's conduct as a factor in its overall decision. In *Thunderbird*, the investor's disingenuous representations, among other actions, proved to be fatal to its claim.[144] At the same time, the *Thunderbird* Tribunal accepted at face value the government's public interest arguments.

Two months later, the Tribunal in *Saluka v Czech Republic*, citing to *Tecmed* as well as to subsequent BIT and NAFTA awards,[145] asserted that LE was the 'dominant element' of the FET.[146] Yet it pointedly denied that investors possessed a presumptive entitlement to regulatory 'stability'[147] which, if 'taken too literally ... would impose upon host States' obligations [that] would be inappropriate and unrealistic'.[148] Instead, arbitrators should balance:

No investor may reasonably expect that the circumstances prevailing at the time the investment is made remain totally unchanged. In order to determine whether frustration of the foreign investor's expectations was justified and reasonable, the host State's legitimate right subsequently to regulate domestic matters in the public interest must be taken into consideration as well ... The determination of a breach of [the FET] therefore requires a

---

[141] ibid para 16.

[142] *International Thunderbird Gaming Corporation v Mexico* (NAFTA/UNCITRAL), Award of 26 January 2006, para 50.

[143] Mara Valenti, 'The Protection of Interests of Host States in the Application of the Fair and Equitable Treatment Standard' in Giorgio Sacerdoti (ed), *General Interests of Host States in International Investment Law* (Cambridge University Press, Cambridge 2014) 48–50.

[144] Wälde (n 118), paras 94–5: Wälde sides with the investor. State officials had formally given the investor a response to a formal question from which, they knew, the investor would draw 'comfort' and confidence.

[145] *Saluka v Czech Republic* (n 93), paras 302–3.

[146] ibid para 302. See also ibid paras 307–8.

[147] Including *Occidental Exploration and Production Company v The Republic of Ecuador* (LCIA Case No UN3467), Award of 1 July 2004: 'The *stability* of the legal and business framework is thus an essential element of fair and equitable treatment' (emphasis in the original). See also *Saluka v Czech Republic* (n 93), para 183.

[148] *Saluka v Czech Republic* (n 93), para 304.

weighing of the Claimant's legitimate and reasonable expectations on the one hand and the Respondent's legitimate regulatory interests on the other ... having due regard [for] all relevant circumstances.[149]

Saluka concerned the recent privatization of an important Czech bank (IPB) that had experienced severe debt problems when the global financial crisis hit in 1998. As the crisis progressed, the government intervened ever more intrusively into IPB's affairs, eventually placing the bank under forced administration (after dispatching armed police to remove managers). Not only were other large Czech banks in comparable situations spared this treatment, but:

the Forced Administrator was not left with his usual discretion to find the most appropriate solution for IPB's future based on an objective and unbiased assessment of all relevant factors. Instead, he was instructed by the Government to implement immediately the transfer of IPB's business to CSOB and he was even provided a financial incentive to follow exclusively the Government's instruction.

After examining a long list of related claims under the rubric of LE-FET, the Tribunal found that Czech authorities had engaged in discriminatory treatment, while breaching due process and transparency norms.[150] It also rejected several claims, including an alleged 'failure' on the part of the state 'to ensure a predictable and transparent framework for Saluka's investment'.[151]

In 2010 to 2011, two awards—*Total v Argentina* and *El Paso v Argentina*—consolidated what is now the standard approach to LE, and thus to the FET writ large. Presiding arbitrators, who were perfectly at home with such a balancing construct, produced the awards. Giorgio Sacerdoti, a former WTO Appellate Body judge, drafted the *Total* award; and Lucius Caflisch, a former justice on the European Court of Human Rights [ECtHR], drafted *El Paso*. Both tribunals invoked *Saluka*,[152] noting the importance of an investors' LE,[153] while firmly rejecting any view to the effect that the FET guarantees 'the stability of the *legal* and *business framework*'.[154] As the *El Paso* Tribunal put it: 'Economic and legal life is by nature evolutionary',[155] and in any event:

[I]t is inconceivable that any State would accept that, because it has entered into BITs, it [could] no longer modify pieces of legislation which might have a negative impact on foreign investors, in order to deal with modified economic conditions and must guarantee

---

[149] ibid paras 305–6, 309.

[150] The Tribunal declared that it was not 'second-guessing' the 'Government's privatization policies', which it characterized as 'perfectly legitimate'. Nonetheless, '[o]nce it had decided to bind itself by the Treaty to accord "fair and equitable treatment" to investors of the other Contracting Party, [the Czech Republic] was bound to implement its policies, including its privatisation strategies, in a way that did not lead to unjustified differential treatment unlawful under the Treaty'.

[151] ibid paras 498–502.

[152] ibid para 302: 'The standard of "FET" is ... closely tied to the notion of legitimate expectations which is the dominant element of that standard.'

[153] *El Paso v Argentina* (n 94), para 348: 'There is an overwhelming trend to consider the touchstone of FET to be found in the legitimate and reasonable expectations of the Parties, which derive from the obligation of good faith.'

[154] ibid para 352 (emphasis in the original).   [155] ibid.

absolute legal stability. In the Tribunal's understanding, [the] FET cannot be designed to ensure the immutability of the legal order, the economic world and the social universe, and [to] play the role assumed by stabilisation clauses specifically granted to foreign investors with whom the State has signed investment agreements.[156]

The *Total* Tribunal began an extensive doctrinal construction of the LE by addressing states directly:[157]

On the one hand, stability, predictability and consistency of legislation and regulation are important for investors in order to plan their investments, especially if their business plans extend over a number of years. Competent authorities of States entering into BITs in order to promote foreign investment in their economy should be aware of the importance for the investors that a legal environment favourable to the carrying out of their business activities be maintained. On the other hand, signatories of such treaties do not thereby relinquish their regulatory powers nor limit their responsibility to amend their legislation in order to adapt it to change and the emerging needs and requests of their people in the normal exercise of their prerogatives and duties. Such limitations upon a government should not lightly be read into a treaty which does not spell them out clearly nor should they be presumed.[158]

Having positioned themselves as balancing tribunals, the crucial questions concerned what and how to balance.

Both the *El Paso* and the *Total* Tribunals emphasized the importance of context— the general political and economic circumstances surrounding the investment—to the various ways in which LE and the right to regulate reciprocally limit one another. The investor can never expect 'economic stability',[159] and the FET is not a general stabilization clause.[160] Nonetheless, the LE-FET protects investors in at least two, often overlapping, situations. First, a state triggers liability by re-regulating, or applying existing regulations, in ways that breach core FET norms (due process, non-discrimination, and so on), which are captured, in balancing, by the principle of proportionality. Second, liability ensues when a state reneges on a 'specific commitment directly made

---

[156] ibid paras 367–8.

[157] *Total v Argentina* (n 94), para 124: This award also puts investors on alert, stating that BITs '"are not insurance policies against bad business judgments" and that the investor has its own duty to investigate the host State's applicable law'.

[158] ibid paras 114–15. See also *Continental Casualty v Argentina* (ICSID Case No ARB/03/9), Award of 5 September 2008 ['*Continental Casualty v Argentina*']: The Tribunal opined that 'it would be unconscionable for a country to promise not to change its legislation as time and needs change, or even more to tie its hands by such a kind of stipulation in case a crisis of any type or origin arose. Such an implication as to stability in the BIT's Preamble would be contrary to an effective interpretation of the Treaty; reliance on such an implication by a foreign investor would be misplaced and, indeed, unreasonable'. Both the *Total* and the *Continental Casualty* Tribunals were presided by the same arbitrator, Giorgio Sacerdoti.

[159] *El Paso v Argentina* (n 94), para 366.

[160] *Total v Argentina* (n 94), para 120: 'A general stabilization requirement would go beyond what the investor can legitimately expect.' See also ibid para 117; *El Paso v Argentina* (n 94), para 368: 'In the Tribunal's understanding, FET cannot be designed to ensure the immutability of the legal order, the economic world and the social universe and play the role assumed by stabilisation clauses specifically granted to foreign investors with whom the State has signed investment agreements.' See also *Parkerings-Compagniet AS v Republic of Lithuania* (ICSID Case No ARB/05/8), Award of 11 September 2007, para 332.

to the investor, on which the latter has relied'.[161] Such commitments 'limit the right of the host State to adapt the legal framework to changing circumstances',[162] at least without paying compensation. In either case, the next step is to balance. The *Total* Tribunal, borrowing an approach to balancing from WTO jurisprudence, put it this way:

The circumstances and reasons (importance and urgency of the public need pursued) for carrying out a change impacting negatively on a foreign investor's operations on the one hand, and the seriousness of the prejudice caused on the other hand, compared in the light of a standard of reasonableness and proportionality are relevant. The determination of a breach of the standard requires, therefore, 'a weighing of the Claimant's reasonable and legitimate expectations on the one hand and the Respondent's legitimate' [citing to *Saluka*]. Thus an evaluation of the fairness of the conduct of the host country towards an investor cannot be made in isolation, considering only their bilateral relations. The context of the evolution of the host economy, the reasonableness of the normative changes challenged and their appropriateness in the light of a criterion of proportionality also have to be taken into account.[163]

As the *El Paso* Tribunal put it, the FET is 'a standard entailing reasonableness and proportionality' and 'a means to guarantee justice to foreign investors'.[164]

Total and *El Paso* concerned Argentina's response to its economic meltdown of the early 2000s, which generated a series of findings of violations of the FET, notably in the energy sector (see Chapter 4). The *Total* Tribunal dismissed most of the oil company's claims, holding that the measures did not violate the principles of non-discrimination and proportionality. In the Tribunal's view, the enormity of the crisis justified, even required, the taking of onerous state measures, even though they could not but harm investors. The *Total* Tribunal found a breach of the LE-FET only with regard to the government's abandonment of certain agreed-upon procedures to adjust tariffs on a regular basis with the participation of the investor. For its part, the *El Paso* Tribunal stressed that the measures under examination, considered individually in light of the public interests pursued, would not violate the energy company's LE. It nonetheless held that 'the cumulative effect of the measures was a total alteration of the entire legal [framework] for foreign investments', thus comprising a type of 'creeping violation of the FET'.[165]

Although there remain important disagreements concerning the content and scope of the LE-FET, it is indisputable that the arbitral process has largely determined its basic parameters, as the dominant argumentation and justification framework in this domain of law.[166]

---

[161] *El Paso v Argentina* (n 94), para 375. See also *Continental Casualty v Argentina* (n 158), para 261: 'Representations made by the host State are enforceable and justify the investor's reliance only when they are specifically addressed to a particular investor.' See also *Total v Argentina* (n 94), paras 119, 309.

[162] *Total v Argentina* (n 94), paras 119, 309.   [163] ibid para 123.

[164] *El Paso v Argentina* (n 94), para 373.   [165] ibid paras 517–18.

[166] This claim should be evaluated in light of counter-evidence. Sacerdoti, for example, was not able to achieve consensus within the *Total* Tribunal on the interpretation of the FET. The claimant-appointed member of the Tribunal, Henri Alvarez, filed a separate opinion, citing to *Tecmed*, asserting that Argentina had failed to meet an obligation to maintain the stability of the legal framework promised. The

NAFTA: The Struggle for Authority

In BIT arbitration, tribunals disaggregate the LE into component principles that they will then balance, selectively, against the state's right to regulate. The most important awards characterize the FET as an autonomous provision of BITs linked to a cluster of related general principles. In BITs that tie the FET to CIL, the most influential tribunals have held that the customary standard—nominally a 'minimum standard of treatment' owed to foreigners—contains virtually the same list of general principles covered by the doctrine of LE (e.g. *El Paso*). As a number of tribunals have pointed out,[167] methodological differences between these two approaches are more superficial than real.[168] Tribunals typically consider the ubiquity of FET provisions in investment treaties as evidence that CIL has evolved in light of state practice; and they assess state practice in synergy with the arbitral case law on the FET, the latter being a repository of general principles. In BIT arbitration, tribunals interpreting the FET in terms of CIL routinely invoke the jurisprudence of general principles, and tribunals that begin in the realm of general principles typically consult the case law rooted in CIL analysis.

In NAFTA arbitration, these dynamics have generated an ongoing war of authority between states and arbitrators. Chapter 11 of NAFTA (establishing the ISA of the regime) announces the FET in Article 1105:

Minimum Standard of Treatment
1. Each Party shall accord to investments of investors of another Party treatment in accordance with international law, including fair and equitable treatment and full protection and security.

state-appointed arbitrator, Luis Herrara Marco, asserted that the doctrine of LE did not guarantee stability and should cover only the most 'abusive' and 'manifestly unfair' state acts—reported by Luke Eric Peterson, 'Co-Arbitrators in Total v. Argentina case take Widely-Divergent Views of Argentina's Fair and Equitable Treatment Obligation under Investment Treaty' (*Investment Arbitration Reporter*, 30 March 2011) <https://www.iareporter.com/articles/co-arbitrators-in-total-v-argentina-case-take-widely-divergent-views-of-argentinas-fair-and-equitable-treatment-obligation-under-investment-treaty/> accessed 10 May 2016. It is important to stress that this debate has taken place within the LE-FET construct, defending propositions on the margins of the LE and the right to regulate respectively. In *Suez, Sociedad General de Aguas de Barcelona, SA and Vivendi Universal, SA v Argentine Republic*, ICSID Case No ARB/03/19, Separate Opinion of Arbitrator Pedro Nikken of 30 July 2010, paras 3–27, decided before *Total v Argentina* (n 94) and *El Paso v Argentina* (n 94), the state-appointed arbitrator, Pedro Nikken, dissented, arguing that the doctrine of LE was purely a construction of arbitral case law and lacked legitimacy, given the absence of explicit state consent. Separate Opinion, ibid paras 31 and 33: Nikken, nonetheless, cites approvingly *Saluka v Czech Republic* (n 93) and Sacerdoti's *Continental Casualty v Argentina* (n 158) award (in which Sacerdoti took a similar stance to that of *Total v Argentina* (n 94); see Chapter 4) for the proposition that states presumptively possess what we are calling a 'right to regulate'.

[167] *Azurix Corp v The Argentine Republic* (ICSID Case No ARB/01/12), Award of 14 July 2006 ['*Azurix*'], para 361: The relevant standard 'has evolved and the Tribunal considers that its content is *substantially similar* whether the terms are interpreted in their ordinary meaning, as required by the Vienna Convention, or in accordance with customary international law' (emphasis in the original).

[168] *El Paso v Argentina* (n 94), para 335: The *El Paso* Tribunal, addressing the question as to whether the FET imposes a higher standard when conceived (a) as a general principle or an autonomous provision of investment treaties or (b) in terms of CIL, stated that it 'consider[ed] this discussion to be somewhat futile, as the scope and content of the minimum standard of international law is as little

In 2001, the state parties (Canada, Mexico, and the United States) jointly issued an interpretive statement to the effect that CIL—as the contracting parties interpret that law, not arbitrators—is the exclusive source of norms governing treatment owed to investors by host states under the NAFTA. They did so to stunt the development of the LE doctrine.

State parties acted in response to three NAFTA awards rendered in 2000 and 2001, that is, prior to *Tecmed* in the BIT context.[169] These awards strongly support the proposition that NAFTA tribunals, on their own, would have developed an approach closely resembling that which BIT tribunals evolved thereafter. In one of these cases, the *Pope and Talbot v Canada* arbitration,[170] the investor argued that the FET should be established under 'all the sources of international law found in Article 38 of Statute of the ICJ', which would include general principles, CIL, and judicial opinions (as a subsidiary source). Canada, joined by the United States as a third party, insisted that the customary standard effectively subsumed the FET. In Canada's view, CIL covered only 'egregious misconduct' of the state, resulting in a 'shocking denial of fairness'. The position implied that the standard had not evolved since the inter-war years, as expressed by the so-called *Neer* test (1926). To violate that test, the state's treatment of an alien must 'amount to an outrage, to bad faith, to wilful neglect of duty, or to an insufficiency of governmental action so far short of international standards that every reasonable and impartial man would readily recognize its insufficiency'.[171]

The *Pope and Talbot* tribunal rejected Canada's argument, as seconded by the United States, intervening as a third party. It held, instead, that the 'fairness' elements in Article 1105 were 'additive to the requirements of CIL', and that the network of existing treaties was their source.[172] 'There are', insisted the Tribunal, 'very strong reasons for interpreting the language of Article 1105 consistently with the language in the BITs',[173] and thus for the rejection of older standards such as those embodied in the *Neer* test.[174] In its interim award on liability of April 2001,

defined as the BITs' FET standard, and as the true question is to decide what substantive protection is granted to foreign investors through the FET'.

[169] The awards are *Metalclad Corporation v United Mexican States* (ICSID Case No ARB(AF)/97/1/NAFTA), Award of 30 August 2000; *SD Myers Inc v Canada* (UNCITRAL/NAFTA), First Partial Award of 13 November 2000; *Pope & Talbot v Canada* (UNCITRAL/NAFTA), Award on the Merits of Phase 2 of 10 April 2001 ['*Pope and Talbot v Canada*'].

[170] *Pope and Talbot v Canada* (n 169), paras 107–15.

[171] *LFH and Pauline Neer (United States v Mexico)* (1926) 4 RIAA 60: The case concerned the killing of an American citizen (Paul Neer) in Mexico.

[172] *Pope & Talbot Inc v Canada (UNCITRAL/NAFTA)*, Award of 31 May 2002 ['*Pope & Talbot Inc v Canada*, 31 May 2002'], paras 57–60: 'Canada considers that the principles of customary international law were frozen in amber at the time of the *Neer* decision. It was on this basis that it urged the Tribunal to award damages only if its conduct was found to be an "egregious" act or failure to meet internationally required standards.'

[173] *Pope and Talbot v Canada* (n 169), para 115.

[174] ibid para 118: '[T]he Tribunal interprets Article 1105 to require that covered investors and investments receive the benefits of the fairness elements ... without any threshold limitation that the conduct complained of be [sic] "egregious", "outrageous" or "shocking", or otherwise extraordinary. For this reason, the Tribunal will test Canadian implementation of the SLA against the fairness elements without applying that kind of threshold.'

the *Pope and Talbot* Tribunal then went on to dismiss four of the investor's claims, while accepting two of them (violations of the principles of non-discriminatory treatment, and due process and transparency). It then scheduled further hearings between the parties on damages.

Acting in the guise of the NAFTA Free Trade Commission [FTC],[175] state parties to NAFTA issued the following *Note of Interpretation*:

1. Article 1105 prescribes the CIL minimum standard of treatment of aliens as the minimum standard of treatment to be afforded to investments ...
2. The concepts of 'FET' and 'full protection and security' do not require treatment in addition to ... that which is required by the CIL minimum standard of treatment of aliens.
3. A determination that there has been a breach of ... a separate international agreement, does not establish that there has been a breach of Article 1105.[176]

State parties presumed their own capacity to control outcomes. Article 2000 NAFTA, after all, confers on the FTC authority 'to supervise the implementation' of the treaty, 'oversee its further elaboration', and to 'resolve disputes that may arise regarding its interpretation or application'. Under Article 1131 NAFTA, 'an interpretation by the Commission of a provision of this Agreement shall be binding' on tribunals.

In response, the *Pope and Talbot* Tribunal obtained disclosure by Canada of the *travaux préparatoires* of NAFTA, to help it determine whether the FTC had sought to 'amend', rather than merely 'interpret', Article 1105. In yet another interim award (of May 2002), the arbitrators held that the FTC had sought to revise the treaty, but through the wrong procedure:

[The documents] show that no reference was ever made to CIL, and, of course, one must accept that the negotiators of NAFTA, as sophisticated representatives of their governments, would have known that, as is made clear in Article 38 of the Statute of the ICJ, international law is a broader concept than CIL, which is only one of its components ... Canada has argued to this Tribunal that CIL is limited to what was required by the cases of the *Neer* era of the 1920s, whereas international law in its entirety would bring into play a large variety of subsequent developments. For these reasons, were the Tribunal required to make a determination whether the Commission's action is an interpretation or an amendment, it would choose the latter.[177]

The Tribunal asserted, nonetheless, that its interpretation of the 'fairness' duties owed by States under Article 1105 was compatible with the FTC's *Note*, at least as the arbitrators interpreted it. 'Canada's views', it suggested, 'were perhaps shaped by its erroneous belief that only some 70 bilateral investment treaties [had] been negotiated; however, the true number, now acknowledged by Canada, is in excess of 1800. Therefore, applying the ordinary rules for determining the content of

---

[175] Pursuant to Article 2001 NAFTA.

[176] NAFTA Free Trade Commission, 'FTC Notes of Interpretation of Certain Chapter 11 Provisions' 1 (31 July 2001) <http://www.sice.oas.org/tpd/nafta/Commission/CH11understanding_e.asp> accessed 10 May 2016.

[177] *Pope & Talbot Inc v Canada*, 31 May 2002 (n 172), paras 46–7.

custom in international law, one must conclude that the practice of states is now represented by those treaties.'[178]

We now know that state parties to NAFTA failed to constrain doctrinal developments. To be sure, since the FTC issued its *Note*, every NAFTA tribunal has engaged in the analysis of CIL in order to determine the scope of the FET. One tribunal adopted a restrictive approach, holding that the *Neer* test remained relevant, once adapted to new circumstances.[179] The rest have held that the 'minimum standard of treatment' has evolved a good deal beyond *Neer*, in favour of investors.[180]

In *Mondev v the US*, a case decided immediately after *Pope and Talbot*, proceedings focused heavily on the FTC *Note*. The investor, 'profess[ing] to be "somewhat bewildered"', complained[181] that:

state parties saw fit 'to change the meaning of a NAFTA provision in the middle of the case in which that provision plays a major part,' and questioned whether it could do so in good faith ... In the view of the Claimant, the [*Note*] added to the text of Article 1105 ... the word, 'customary', while treating the terms 'fair and equitable treatment' and 'full protection and security' as surplusage.[182]

Canada claimed that the *Neer* standard remained the controlling law. The Tribunal, which included Ninian Steven (former justice of the High Court of Australia), James Crawford (then an influential member of the International Law Commission, and now a justice on the International Court of Justice [ICJ]), and Stephen Schwebel

---

[178] ibid para 62.

[179] *Cargill v Mexico* (ICSID Case No ARB(AF)/05/2, NAFTA), Award of 18 September 2009, para 284: 'The Tribunal observes a trend in previous NAFTA awards, not so much to make the holding of the *Neer* arbitration more exacting, but rather to adapt the principle underlying the holding of the *Neer* arbitration to the more complicated and varied economic positions held by foreign nationals today. Key to this adaptation is that, even as more situations are addressed, the required severity of the conduct as held in *Neer* is maintained.'

[180] *Glamis Gold, Ltd v The United States of America* (UNCITRAL), Award of 8 June 2009, para 627: The *Glamis Gold* Tribunal appears to have taken a hybrid position. That tribunal found that the 'claimant has not met its burden of proving that something other than the fundamentals of the *Neer* standard apply'. However, it also held that: '[s]uch a breach may be exhibited by a "gross denial of justice or manifest arbitrariness falling below acceptable international standards", or the creation by the State of objective expectations *in order to induce* investment and the subsequent repudiation of those expectations' (emphasis in original). The LE principles, of course, cover the latter situation, which would render the *Neer* standard obsolete. The Tribunal addressed this tension as follows: 'although the standard for finding a breach of the CIL minimum standard of treatment therefore remains as stringent as it was under *Neer*; it is entirely possible that, as an international community, we may be shocked by State actions now that did not offend us previously'. See ibid para 27. See also ibid: In any event, the tribunal engaged in LE analysis (paras 812–30), explicitly using the language of 'legitimate expectations' (para 813) and 'reasonable expectations' (para 812).

[181] Parts of the arbitral community also criticized the *Note* as a thinly disguised attack on arbitral independence, given that the *Note* has appeared before the conclusion of the *Pope & Talbot v Canada* proceedings. See Gabrielle Kaufmann-Kohler, 'Interpretive Powers of the Free Trade Commission and the Rule of Law' in Emmanuel Gaillard and Frédéric Bachand (eds), *Fifteen Years of NAFTA Chapter 11 Arbitration* (Juris Publishing, New York 2011) 175.

[182] *Mondev v USA* (n 122), para 102.

(former justice of the ICJ), disagreed unanimously, in terms that have been widely cited by subsequent tribunals:

[Since *Neer* was decided,] both the substantive and procedural rights of the individual ... have undergone considerable development. In the light of these developments, it is unconvincing to confine the meaning of 'FET' and 'full protection and security' of foreign investments to what those terms ... might have meant in the 1920s ... To the modern eye, what is unfair or inequitable need not equate with the outrageous or the egregious. In particular, a State may treat foreign investment unfairly and inequitably without necessarily acting in bad faith. [Moreover,] the vast number of bilateral and regional investment treaties ... almost uniformly provide for [the FET], and largely provide for full security and protection ... Investment treaties run between North and South, and East and West, and between States in these spheres *inter se*. On a remarkably widespread basis, States have repeatedly obliged themselves to accord foreign investment such treatment. In the Tribunal's view, such a body of concordant practice will necessarily have influenced the content of rules governing the treatment of foreign investment in current international law. It would be surprising if this practice and the vast number of provisions it reflects were to be interpreted as meaning no more than the *Neer* Tribunal (in a very different context) meant ...[183]

The *Mondev* Tribunal then engaged in full-fledged FET analysis, only to dismiss the investor's claims.

Most NAFTA tribunals have followed the path cleared by *Pope and Talbot* and *Mondev*. They have held, or strongly implied, that CIL protects investors beyond the minimum standard expressed in *Neer*, citing to one another, drawing evidence from BITs, and even invoking FET jurisprudence beyond NAFTA.[184] Pushing further, the Tribunal in *Waste Management v Mexico* (2004) engaged in LE analysis in all but name:

In applying [the FET] it is relevant that the treatment is in breach of representations made by the host State which were reasonably relied on by the claimant.[185]

The *Waste Management* Tribunal, too, dismissed all of the investor's claims. Along with *Tecmed* and *Saluka*, the NAFTA awards in *Mondev* and *Waste Management* are among the five most cited cases in the FET domain, and tribunals in non-NAFTA proceedings regularly cite to the latter.

A case decided in 2010, *Merrill & Ring v Canada*, brought the LE issue to a head. The investor, referencing *Saluka*, argued that the Tribunal should interpret Article 1105 in light of all sources of international law, not just CIL.[186] In its

---

[183] ibid paras 116–17.

[184] *ADF Group Inc v United States* (ICSID Case No ARB(AF)/00/1, NAFTA), Award of 9 January 2003; *Waste Management v Mexico* (ICSID Case No ARB(AF)/00/3, NAFTA), Award of 30 April 2004, 43 ILM 967; *Merrill & Ring Forestry LP v Canada* (UNCITRAL/NAFTA), Award of 31 March 2010; *William Ralph Clayton, William Richard Clayton, Douglas Clayton, Daniel Clayton and Bilcon of Delaware Inc v Government of Canada* (UNCITRAL, PCA Case No 2009-04), Award on Jurisdiction and Liability of 17 March 2015.

[185] *Waste Management Inc v United Mexican States* (ICSID Case No ARB(AF)/00/3), Award of 30 April 2004, para 98.

[186] *Merrill & Ring Forestry LP v The Government of Canada* (ICSID Administered Case, UNCITRAL) of 31 March 2010, para 160.

view, given the absence of a substantive difference between the FET standard as expressed in (a) stand-alone BIT provisions and (b) CIL,[187] the NAFTA version must also contain the principle of LE.[188] Canada reiterated the terms of the FTC *Note*, which it insisted would exclude good faith and legitimate expectations altogether.[189] On this point, the arbitrators sided with the investor,[190] agreeing that the BIT and CIL standard had converged:

[G]eneral principles of law ... have a role to play in this discussion. Even if the Tribunal were to accept Canada's argument to the effect that good faith, the prohibition of arbitrariness, discrimination and other questions raised in this case are not stand-alone obligations under Article 1105(1) ... and might not be a part of customary law either, these concepts are to a large extent the expression of general principles of law and hence also a part of international law.[191]

While the tribunal acknowledged the 'binding' nature of the FTC *Note*, it declared, *Pope and Talbot* style, that CIL could not be considered 'frozen in amber' or incapable of evolution.[192] In the Tribunal's assessment, the CIL standard was 'now broader than that defined [by] *Neer* and its progeny', providing 'for the FET of ... investors within the confines of reasonableness'.[193] Turning to the dispute, the *Merrill and Ring* Tribunal found no violation of the FET.

The most recent and, arguably, most controversial, NAFTA award is *Bilcon v Canada* (2015). The *Bilcon* Tribunal, citing at length to *Merrill and Ring* with regard to CIL,[194] and to *Waste Management* with regard to LE,[195] stated bluntly that:

[T]he international minimum standard exists and has evolved in the direction of increased investor protection precisely because sovereign states—the same ones constrained by the standard—have chosen to accept it. States have concluded that the standard protects their own nationals in other countries and encourages the inflow of visitors and investment.

The Tribunal then went on to apply a version of LE-FET analysis, finding that an environmental assessment undertaken by a provincial government had violated a Canadian federal statute, on which the investor had relied. In *Bilcon*, for the first time in a NAFTA proceeding, LE analysis had real bite.

Assessment

The evolution of FET doctrine provides an important illustration of judicialization theory in action. Tribunals have self-consciously treated innovative awards as focal points for horizontal coordination with one another, across treaty instruments and time. The result has been the steady construction of FET doctrine that provides a stable framewok for argumentation and justification. Tribunals that have resisted these dynamics, as they have gathered force, have been marginalized, their awards

---

[187] ibid para 161. [188] ibid para 167. [189] ibid paras 168–70.
[190] ibid paras 184–6. [191] ibid para 187. [192] ibid para 192.
[193] ibid para 213. [194] ibid para 435.
[195] ibid paras 442–4: The Tribunal relied on *Waste Management* for the proposition that the FET covers 'reasonably relied-on representations by a host state, and a recognition that injustice in either procedures or outcomes can constitute a breach'.

ignored in subsequent proceedings. The case study provides direct and overwhelming evidence for the applicability of the judicial model. The judicialization of ISA has rendered the contractual model obsolete, at least as an empirical matter.

Judicialization begets triadic governance. Through their own lawmaking, arbitrators have taken on a duty to balance the LE of investors against a host state's regulatory prerogatives. Consider this outcome in light of the balancing postures adopted by the most powerful international courts, when they enforce international economic law. The WTO-AB, the Court of Justice of the European Union, and the European Court of Human Rights all adjudicate derogation clauses, carve-outs that permit states to pursue important public policy purposes notwithstanding treaty obligations.[196] When states plead these provisions in defence, the regimes' courts carefully review the reasons that states give to justify the proposed derogation. The judges do so in light of the principle of proportionality, a relatively intrusive standard of review that has replaced (or strengthened) 'reasonableness' tests and other standards across the world.[197] Each of these courts has eschewed the development of express deference doctrines. Instead, under the banner of effectiveness, each embraced a version of the proportionality framework to ensure that states do not use derogation clauses to subvert treaty objectives.[198]

It is remarkable that the most influential ISA tribunals reached a comparable position, through a jurisprudence of general principles. Arbitrators did so, on their own, without express treaty authorization. Proportionality entered into ISA through *Tecmed*, citing to the case law of the ECtHR with regard to indirect expropriation; *Saluka* insisted that tribunals should balance LE against the right to regulate; and a host of tribunals have since balanced with reference to the proportionality principle. The Tribunals in *Continental Casualty v Argentina* and *Total v Argentina* (both presided by Sacerdoti) embraced approaches developed in the WTO. We discuss the advantages and potential costs of using proportionality at length in Chapter 6.

State Responses to Arbitral Lawmaking

In treaty-based ISA, states are Principals who have conferred juridical authority on arbitrators—their Agents. States delegate authority both directly and indirectly (Chapter 1). They delegate directly through treaties. The regime for ISA rests on

---

[196] Prominent derogation clauses include: (a) for the WTO, Article XX of the General Agreement on Tariffs and Trade (1947) 55 UNTS 194 and Article XIV of the General Agreement on Trade in Services (1994) 1869 UNTS 183; for the European Union, Articles 30 and 36 of the Treaty Establishing the European Community (Consolidated Version), Rome Treaty (1957), now Articles 33 and 36 of the Treaty on the Functioning of the European Union 2008/C 115/01, and Articles 8–11 of the European Convention for the Protection of Human Rights and Fundamental Freedoms (1953) ETS 5. With regard to the latter, the European Court of Human Rights read into the right to property (Protocol No 1) an implied derogation clause, which it then adjudicates in light of the proportionality principle.

[197] Alec Stone Sweet and Jud Mathews, 'Proportionality Balancing and Global Constitutionalism' (2008) 47 Columbia Journal of Transnational Law 73.

[198] Alec Stone Sweet and Thomas Brunell, 'Trustee Courts and the Judicialization of International Regimes: The Politics of Majoritarian Activism in the ECHR, the EU, and the WTO' (2013) 1 Journal of Law and Courts 61.

BITs, regional and sectoral investment treaties, and two multilateral agreements (the ICSID and New York Conventions). To the extent that investment treaties embody incomplete contracts, states have indirectly delegated lawmaking powers. Such powers inhere in arbitral authority, given that tribunals are under a duty to resolve disputes according to the terms of these treaties. As we have shown, arbitrators have constructed the FET, an incomplete provision par excellence, as a site of progressive lawmaking. This lawmaking has transformed the underlying law and politics of the regime.

State officials, arbitrators, and scholars are now intensively debating the extent to which the present regime is experiencing backlash from states (see Chapters 1, 2, and 6). One standard argument holds that traditional capital-exporting (i.e. advanced industrial) states will seek to curtail arbitral power insofar as they become recipients of FDI emanating from traditional capital-importing states, thereby exposing their own regulatory arrangements to review. A second argument suggests that to the extent that states in the developing world learn, or come to believe, that the current regime is biased against them, the more they will pursue treaties that are tailored to insulate them from liability, while reasserting state autonomy and regulatory prerogatives. To the extent that these hypotheses hold, states of both types would find it in their interest to design new treaties that would effectively insulate regulatory arrangements from arbitral review. We accept the premises of these propositions.

From the standpoint of delegation theory, the crucial empirical question concerns how states, as Principals, have responded to the lawmaking of their Agents. States have the power to destroy the system, reform it, or exit. They may select an exit option, and denounce BITs and the ICSID Convention, as a small handful of states have done.[199] They may draft and sign new treaties that leave indirect expropriation and the FET out altogether; or they may design such provisions to limit arbitral discretion, or to guide the tribunals' decision-making in other ways. In Chapter 6, we examine some of the choices states have made from perspectives given by current legitimacy debates. Here, we focus on the empirical side, in particular, on the extent to which states have deployed their treaty-making powers in response to the arbitral lawmaking charted in this chapter.

To address this issue, we compiled data[200] on every BIT signed between 2002 and the end of 2015, for which the text is available in English: n = 398.[201] Figure 5.1 charts the cumulative number of (a) new BITs signed during this period and (b) new

---

[199] Ecuador terminated nine BITs in 2008; Venezuela terminated one BIT in 2009; and, since 2014, Indonesia has terminated fourteen BITs. Bolivia (2007), Ecuador (2009), and Venezuela (2012) denounced the ICSID Convention. See Gabrielle Kaufmann-Kohler and Michele Potestà, 'Can the Mauritius Convention Serve as a Model for the Reform of Investor-State Arbitration in Connection with the Introduction of a Permanent Investment Tribunal or an Appeal Mechanism? Analysis and Roadmap', Geneva Center for International Dispute Settlement (paper commissioned by UNCITRAL), 3 June 2016, p 10.

[200] In this area, we are indebted to the efforts of a research assistant, Michael Chung (Yale JD, 2017), who holds the primary claim to this part of the data set.

[201] The UNCTAD database makes available a further 137 BITs which are not available in English. UNCTAD Division on Investment and Enterprise, 'Investment Policy Hub' <http://investmentpolicyhub.unctad.org> accessed 10 May 2016.

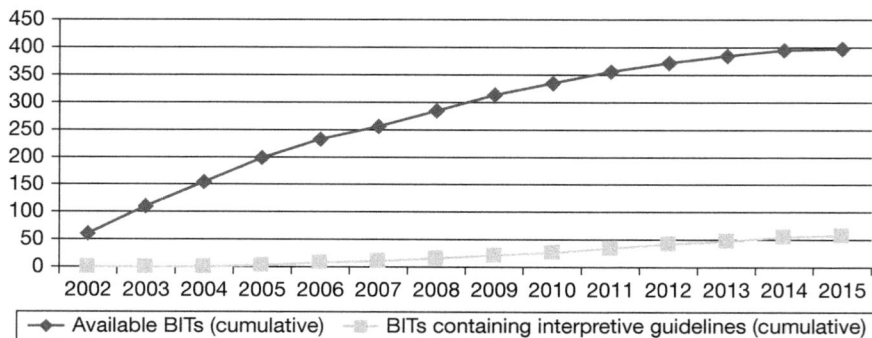

Figure 5.1 Cumulative Number of New BITs and New BITs Containing Interpretive Guidelines for Indirect Expropriation and the FET, 2002–2015

Source: 'Data Set of New BITs Signed since 2002', *Yale Law School Data Sets on Investor-State Arbitration*, compiled by Michael Chung.

BITs that contain substantive criteria for interpreting either indirect expropriation (n = 46) or the FET (n = 40). One finding deserves emphasis up-front. Of the final awards on the merits contained in our data set (n = 141), only four involved the arbitration of any treaty signed after 1999, the latest involving a BIT signed in 2003. Thus, no one will be able to assess the direct impact of new treaties on final awards until new rulings, interpreting a new generation of treaties, appear.

Analysis of the data provides no support for the view that the regime has generated 'backlash' in any systemic sense. On the contrary: (a) states continue to negotiate and sign investment treaties; (b) the mix of treaty protections on offer has remained remarkably stable; and (c) what states have mostly done is to consolidate the system in line with how arbitrators have, in fact, developed it in their awards on liability. We do not mean to downplay the importance of states as treaty-makers. New treaties can consolidate the main lines of arbitral case law, once jurisprudence has congealed. When states, in effect, codify certain arbitral approaches to liability, they presumptively reduce the parameters of choice available to future tribunals. States also possess the capacity to destroy influential lines of case law, or to block future developments. To date, however, they have not done so in any significant way. We are aware of only one other completed empirical study of these same issues, and it shares our main conclusions.[202]

Indirect Expropriation

Only 2 of the 398 new treaties in our data set leave out expropriation provisions.[203] Within the expropriation domain, a small subset of new treaties (n = 46; 12 per

---

[202] Tomer Broude, Yoram Z Haftel, and Alexander Thompson, 'Who Cares About Regulatory Space in BITs? A Comparative International Approach,' in A Roberts, P-H Verdier, M Versteeg, and P Stephan (eds), *Comparative International Law* (Oxford University Press, Oxford forthcoming).
[203] BLEU–Qatar BIT (2007) and BLEU–Montenegro BIT (2010).

cent) include substantive criteria for determining indirect expropriation. All forty-six of these BITs codify the main approach to indirect expropriation, as developed in arbitral case law, including the recognition of 'creeping expropriation'. The standard formula reads:

It is understood that indirect expropriation results from a measure or series of measures of a Contacting Party having an equivalent effect to direct expropriation without formal transfer of title or outright seizure.

With regard to methodology, the most common set of guidelines, variations of which are included in 33 new BITs, comforts both (i) the basic arbitral approach to indirect expropriation, which had taken shape by 2003 at the latest, and (ii) the formulation announced in the U.S. Model BIT of 2004.[204] Article 7 of the Colombia-Turkey BIT of 2014, for example, builds on the phraseology of the U.S. 2004 Model BIT, stipulating that review requires 'fact-based inquiry' focusing on:

[T]he scope of the [measures]; [their] economic impact; the level of interference on the reasonable ... expectations concerning the investment; [their] character in accordance with the legitimate public objectives searched.

In such way that [their] effect ... is equivalent to the expropriation of the whole investment, a significant part of it, or prevents its use or the reasonable expected economic benefit from it. The sole fact of ... measures having adverse effects on the economic value of an investment does not imply that an indirect expropriation has occurred.

The same treaty, joined with minor variation by the other forty-five BITs in the subset, goes on to state that:

It is understood that non-discriminatory measures of a Contracting Party that are designed and applied for public purposes or social interest or with objectives such as public health, safety and environment protection, do not constitute indirect expropriation.

The carve-out gives expression to the dominant thrust of the leading arbitral awards in this domain, as discussed above. The vast majority of tribunals, after all, have rejected most expropriation claims that target general measures in precisely these terms.

A second carve-out related to public interests provides the clearest example of treaty-making seeking to hinder the development of an approach to liability found in an arbitral award: *Santa Elena v Costa Rica* (2000).[205] The dispute involved the taking of a property that was home to a rich mix of flora and fauna situated near a national park. The investor had purchased the property with the aim of developing a tourist resort, which Costa Rica expressly expropriated in order to preserve it, while incorporating it into the park. Costa Rica agreed that it owed compensation. The Tribunal's task therefore reduced to determining the amount to be paid, a question on which the parties disagreed. Along the way, the Tribunal stated that:

[T]he purpose of protecting the environment for which the Property was taken does not alter the legal character of the taking for which adequate compensation must be paid. The

---

[204] On-line at: https://ustr.gov/sites/default/files/U.S.%20model%20BIT.pdf.
[205] *Compañia del Desarrollo de Santa Elena SA v Republic of Costa Rica* (ICSID Case No ARB/96/1), Award of 17 February 2000.

international source of the obligation to protect the environment makes no difference. Expropriatory environmental measures—no matter how laudable and beneficial to society as a whole—are, in this respect, similar to any other expropriatory measures that a state may take in order to implement its policies: where property is expropriated, even for environmental purposes, whether domestic or international, the state's obligation to pay compensation remains.[206]

Of the new BITs signed since 2002, forty-two (10.5 per cent) declare that general measures taken for purposes of 'health, safety and environmental protection' do not, in and of themselves, constitute expropriation. It is doubtful that the public health, safety, and environment protection carve-out would apply to an expropriation decree, and Costa Rica did not even plead the matter.

In any event, these provisions largely conform to the positions taken by the most cited awards on exactly this issue. In 2006, the *Saluka* Tribunal, in one of the most cited ISA awards, had held that:

In the opinion of the Tribunal, the principle that a State does not commit an expropriation and is thus not liable to pay compensation to a dispossessed alien investor when it adopts general regulations that are 'commonly accepted as within the police power of States' forms part of customary international law today. There is ample case law in support of this proposition. As the tribunal in *Methanex Corp. v. USA* said recently in its final award, '[i]t is a principle of CIL that, where economic injury results from a *bona fide* regulation within the police powers of a State, compensation is not required.'[207]

With the exception of certain awards issuing from the Argentina crisis, no important award dating after *Saluka* announces the contrary.

In any event, only five of the forty-two new BITs containing the 'health, safety, and environmental protection' carve-out pre-date *Saluka*, and four of those involve India.[208] A formulation common to the China–India (2006) and Canada–Peru (2006) BITs stipulates that:

Except in rare circumstances, such as when a measure or series of measures is so severe in the light of its purpose that it cannot be reasonably viewed as having been adopted and applied in good faith, non-discriminatory measures of a Party that are designed and applied to protect legitimate public welfare objectives, such as health, safety and the environment, do not constitute indirect expropriation.[209]

The provision fits comfortably with the dominant arbitral approach to the same issue. We doubt that many arbitrators would consider it a reining-in of their powers.[210]

---

[206] ibid paras 71–2.   [207] *Saluka v Czech Republic* (n 93), para 262.
[208] India–Trinidad and Tobago BIT (2007); India–Jordan BIT (2006); China–India BIT (2006); and India–Saudi Arabia BIT (2006).
[209] Canada–Peru BIT (2006): Annex B.13.1.c. Compare to China–India BIT (2006): Article 6(2)(c).
[210] *El Paso v Argentina* (n 94), paras 240–1: As the *El Paso* Tribunal put it: A 'general regulation', such as a statute or regulation that applies to all within a domain of activity, 'is a lawful act rather than an expropriation if it is non-discriminatory, made for a public purpose and taken in conformity with due process'. However, when the state enacts 'unreasonable, *i.e.* arbitrary, discriminatory, disproportionate

The FET

In the FET domain, critics and proponents agree that arbitral lawmaking has expanded the scope of pleadings and made review more intrusive. In response, states could excise the provision (leaving the customary international law standard in place), or limit its scope, prohibiting coverage of an investors' LE, for example. Of the 398 BITs in our data set, only 7 (1.8 per cent) do not contain the FET.[211] Two of these mandate the 'minimal standard of treatment', respectively, of international law[212] or CIL.[213] Thus, five BITs, negotiated among only six states, contain no provision related to the treatment of an investor by the host state; and only one of these dates from after 2005.[214]

Of the new BITs that contain the FET or a standard of treatment owed investors (n = 393), states negotiated interpretive guidelines in forty. Within this subset of new BITs (barely 10 per cent), the most important development is the diffusion of the terms of the FTC Note, primarily through new BITs signed by Canada (n = 17), Mexico (n = 9), Japan (n = 5), China (n = 5), and the United States (n = 2). Fully thirty-four of the forty treaties in this category (85 per cent) contain both guidelines, stating:

(1) 'The concepts of "FET" and "full protection and security" do not require treatment in addition to ... that which is required by the CIL minimum standard of treatment of aliens'; and

(2) 'A determination that there has been a breach of ... a separate international agreement, does not establish that there has been a breach of [the FET].'

Of these forty BITs, one contains the first guideline only;[215] four include only the second guideline;[216] and only one leaves both out.[217] Perhaps the migration of the FTC guidelines from NAFTA into BITs will eventually change the basics of FET doctrine, but we are skeptical. Given that the NAFTA FTC failed to constrain NAFTA tribunals, there is little reason to think that tribunals arbitrating these same provisions in BITs will be more inclined to depart from the established case law.

No new BIT, including those signed by NAFTA parties, removed the LE of investors from consideration under the FET. This outcome counts against backlash

---

or otherwise unfair' measures, they may be 'considered as amounting to indirect expropriation if they result in a neutralisation of the foreign investor's property rights'.

[211] Five BITs whose formulations depart slightly from the standard FET provision are included in the FET count: two (Dominican Republic–Italy BIT (2006) and Italy–Yemen BIT (2004)) announce a 'just and fair treatment' standard; two (Albania–Moldova BIT (2004) and Botswana–Ghana BIT (2003)) call for 'equitable treatment'; and one (Italy–Nicaragua BIT (2004)) provides for 'fair treatment'.

[212] Azerbaijan–Estonia BIT (2010).　　　[213] Guatemala–Trinidad and Tobago BIT (2013).

[214] Morocco–Serbia BIT (2013); Turkey–UAE BIT (2005); Libya–Malta BIT (2003); Malta–Turkey BIT (2003); Italy–Malta BIT (2002).

[215] Morocco–Vietnam BIT (2012).

[216] China–Uzbekistan BIT (2011); Belarus–Mexico BIT (2008); Colombia–India BIT (2009); China–Japan–South Korea BIT (2012).

[217] Australia–Mexico BIT (2005).

claims, dispositively in our view. Meanwhile, some of the forty new BITs that added substantive criteria actually codify elements of FET case law. Some BITs now stipulate that the treatment owed to investors covers explicit promises made to them by host states.[218] Article 5 of the trilateral agreement between China, Japan, and South Korea (2012), for example, announces the FET and then immediately states that:

Each Contracting Party shall observe any written commitments in the form of an agreement or contract it may have entered into with regard to investments of investors of another Contracting Party.[219]

Further, a long list of states—including Belgium and Luxembourg, Canada, Colombia, India, Japan, Mexico, and the United States—took pains to establish, within the rubric of the FET, the prohibition of denial of justice, and obligations of due process, transparency, notice, and comment.[220] In sum, we observe states working to consolidate the FET as a framework for the development of general principles, while doing virtually nothing to dismantle it.

General Exceptions

States may also generate derogation clauses, in the form of non-precluded measures provisions. An exception might apply only to selected provisions.[221] A derogation clause might also apply generally, to most or all of a treaty, as does Article XX GATT (1947), or Article XIV of the GATS (1994). The most prevalent general exception clause is found, with only slight variation, in every new BIT to which Canada is a party (n = 17). The Canadian formulation is also the widest in scope. Modelled on WTO clauses, it creates a carve-out for measures that are 'necessary to protect human, animal or plant life or health', as well as 'for the conservation of living or non-living exhaustible natural resources'. It adapts the 'chapeau' of Article XX GATT to investment, specifying that the derogation is only available for measures that are not 'applied in a manner that constitutes arbitrary or unjustifiable discrimination between investments or between investors', or constitute 'a disguised restriction on international trade or investment'. It stipulates that the BIT does not 'prevent a Contracting Party from adopting or maintaining reasonable measures for prudential reasons' in the banking and finance sector. And it does the same for

---

[218] Japan–Laos BIT (2012); Colombia–Japan (2011).

[219] Article 5(2), China–Japan–South Korea BIT (2012).

[220] BLEU–Colombia BIT (2009); India–Mexico BIT (2007); Rwanda–USA BIT (2008); Canada–Jordan BIT (2009); China–Japan–South Korea BIT (2012).

[221] We discussed clauses that apply to emergency situations and essential security interests in Chapter 4. For the domain of expropriation, see the discussion above. With regard to the FET, we found only two treaties that contained substantive carve-outs. Article 2(4) of the Morocco–Vietnam BIT (2012) prohibits the application of the FET for 'measures that have to be taken by either Contacting Party for reasons of public security, order or public health or protection of environment provided that such measures are not applied in a manner which would constitute a means of arbitrary or unjustified discrimination'. Under the Australia–Mexico BIT (2005), investors may attack taxation measures under the expropriation (but not the FET) heading.

measures 'necessary to protect … essential security interests', and to 'fulfill obligations' when it comes to international security arrangements.[222]

In our view, Canada's boilerplate exception clauses would push tribunals into exactly the kind of proportionality-based posture that some of the most influential tribunals have already adopted (e.g. in *Total*). The same point applies to the other BITs that contain GATT-style derogation provisions, including those of Jordan–Singapore (2004), Colombia–India (2009), Colombia–Japan (2012), Colombia–Turkey (2014), and Japan–Peru (2008). We discuss non-precluded measures provisions, and the appropriateness of proportionality balancing, at length in Chapter 6.

IV. Conclusion

The judicialization of arbitration has meant that tribunals govern, more or less as courts do, when they resolve contractual disputes, and when they determine liability for compensation under investment treaties. In ICA, tribunals apply and make law, including in sensitive domains of state law and policy. Judges and legislators in most of the major trading states have expressly delegated broad authority to arbitrators to enforce mandatory state law, withdrawing objections to arbitrability, and narrowing the public policy grounds for challenging awards in the courts to insignificance. State delegation underwrites the effectiveness of the arbitral order, while raising pressing issues of accountability. In our view, state courts are no longer in a position to supervise effectively how tribunals balance when they take into account the public interest. Because arbitral centres publish so few awards, how ICA tribunals actually govern, to what effect, remains a mystery. In ISA, the task of balancing investors' entitlements in relation to the host state's right to regulate now occupies the very core of the arbitral mission. States have broadly acquiesced to arbitral lawmaking when it comes to indirect expropriation and the FET. Indeed, in negotiating a new generation of treaties, they have done more to consolidate major strands of arbitral case law than they have to block the extension of that jurisprudence by future tribunals.

In the next chapter, we consider proposals for wider structural reforms in light of our findings in Chapters 2 through 5.

---

[222] Expressing a particular Canadian sensitivity, BIT protections also do not apply to measures regulating the 'cultural industry' and the media.

6

Legitimacy and Reform

The arbitral order has developed features of hierarchy that enable it to assert power over the disputing parties, and to defend its own autonomy with respect to other legal systems. While the regime interacts intensively with the domestic law and courts, these processes have strengthened the status of arbitral law-making, rather than subordinating it to state priorities. Indeed, arbitrators themselves have made much of the law that grounds the exercise of their own authority.

The regime's judicialization has also meant that legitimacy debates that have long swirled around courts, and their lawmaking, now beset arbitration. The literature on the legitimacy of judicial lawmaking, as a mode of governance, is both vast and contentious. There are no commonly accepted definitions, bodies of theory, or empirical measures of legitimacy when it comes to judge-made law. Instead, judicial lawmaking chronically produces anxiety, which is expressed in a variety of well-rehearsed legitimacy discourses. Organized by different normative precepts and analytical criteria, these discourses are typically incommensurate.

In this chapter, we approach legitimacy issues from multiple perspectives. Part I considers a functional notion of legitimacy that follows from the terms of our theory (Chapter 1) and findings (Chapters 2 to 5). The explosive success of arbitration took place only because an increasing number of companies, law firms, legal scholars, and state legislatures and courts chose to invest in it. In part II, we address debates that are directly relevant to the book. It is a blunt fact that, today, there is far more critical and reform-minded discussion than existed even a decade ago. We treat the growing intensity of structural criticism as important data to be assessed. Part III expresses our own normative views on proposals for institutional reform, from the perspective of judicialized arbitral governance. We argue that the institutional evolution of the field has generated its own peculiar legitimacy dilemmas that are best resolved through further judicialization. We advocate, in particular, routine publication of important awards, the development of mechanisms of appellate supervision, and an enhanced interface between tribunals and courts, both domestic and international. We also strongly favour the deployment of a more structured proportionality analysis when it comes to balancing property rights (of contractants and investors) and the public interest.

The Evolution of International Arbitration: Judicialization, Governance, Legitimacy. First Edition. Alec Stone Sweet and Florian Grisel. © Alec Stone Sweet and Florian Grisel 2017. Published 2017 by Oxford University Press.

I. Functional Dynamics

The theory that guided our research focuses empirical attention on (a) the sources of social demand for new institutions and (b) the extent to which these demands are supplied by actors who accrue competences to do so, through (c) specific dynamics of pressure and feedback, including those issuing from legitimacy concerns. Virtually all social science theorizing about institutions—rules, principles, procedures (that is, law)—is permeated by functionalist logics. For the economist as much as the sociologist, the capacity of a rule system to reproduce itself over time, given recurrent crises and changing circumstances, is among the most important measures of that system's legitimacy. From this standpoint, the arbitral order is presumptively legitimate because the scope and significance of its authority has expanded, as powerful actors have invested in its development. Put differently, the actors that have the capacity to destroy the system—especially state officials in the major trading and capital-exporting states—have either acquiesced to the authority claims of the arbitral order, or actively supported those claims.

Judicialization

In Chapter 1, we proposed a theory of how arbitration would evolve as a legal system. Deductive and abstract, the theory does not purport to explain everything of importance, or to predict outcomes of discrete episodes. Instead, it focuses attention on a small number of specific mechanisms that are basic to institutional change and the accretion of judicialized authority. Under certain conditions, these mechanisms will combine to produce a causal system that connects three processes: (a) the delegation of disputes to arbitrators for settlement; (b) arbitral decision-making; and (c) the development of hierarchy such that the decision-making of tribunals would produce prospective lawmaking effects. We also claimed that outcomes predicted by the theory could be evaluated with respect to three 'models of arbitration' derived, in part, from delegation theory—the Principal–Agent [P–A] framework developed by social scientists. The judicialization of arbitration entails the steady obsolescence of the 'contractual model' and the emergence of the 'judicial model'. As the coherence of the regime developed, the arbitral order will gain capacity to defend its autonomy as a legal system in its own right, within an evolving pluralist-constitutional model, and to participate in the construction of international law. And, with any shift away from the contractual model, tribunals will owe a thicker set of fiduciary duties to a growing number of stakeholders.

The broad claim is that judicialization can be empirically tracked with reference to these models. Had the contractual model remained viable, then relatively little judicialization would have taken place. But that is not what one finds. Chapters 2 to 5 demonstrate that the core elements of the contractual model have either been abandoned altogether, or remoulded in ways that fit and undergird the judicial model. Today, tribunals owe primary fiduciary duties not only to the parties, but to arbitral centres and the wider regime. These obligations, codified in the procedural rules of the major international arbitration centres [IACs], ground the effectiveness of the system. They confer authority on tribunals to manage recalcitrant parties, and of IAC officials to manage wayward tribunals (Chapters 2 and 3). Tribunals are required to give reasons for their decisions. Counsel and arbitrators, for their part, have long treated reasons as building blocks of precedent-based argumentation and justification (Chapters 4 and 5). Today, parties, tribunals, and IACs presume that settled lines of case law—*la jurisprudence constante*—will not be ignored, at least not without good reason. The more the judicial model has been institutionalized, the more inconsistent decisions are treated as signatures of (treatable) pathology.

The upshot is that the arbitrators are now major actors in transnational governance. The regulation of transnational economic activity involves a kaleidoscope of public and private organizations exercising authority for quite different purposes, not all of which are compatible. But transnational regulation, as a domain of governance, is not without structure,[1] arbitration being a prime example. Commercial and investment disputes are resolved, and awards enforced, with regard to an increasingly articulated, treaty-based interface, a legal 'field'[2] that organizes dialogue between the arbitral order, domestic legal systems, and public international law (Chapters 1 and 2). The system is pluralistic, in that its viability depends upon mutual recognition, by otherwise autonomous regimes, of the authority of others that occupy the field. When one observes the outcomes produced within this field, through the lenses of the pluralist model, certain 'constitutional' elements come into view. The New York and ICSID Conventions, after all, require national judges to recognize the authority of arbitrators, while strongly implying that arbitrators take seriously the priorities of states as regards important public interests. One crucial frontier question is whether a fiduciary obligation, binding on arbitrators, to take into account the public interest will be codified, and by whom.

Delegation

Delegation theory, too, rests on functional logics that absorb some deeply held normative commitments. Express authorization does not resolve all legitimacy dilemmas, but it does narrow and focus debate. Consider a written constitution, containing a judicially enforceable charter of rights, enacted through popular referendum. Mainstream contemporary constitutional ideology has it that the sovereign People have delegated to a court (or to the judiciary) the responsibility to supervise the rights-regarding decisions of all other public officials. These arrangements fulfil the basic principles of formal legitimacy. Further, the drafters delegate inherent lawmaking powers to judges, to the extent that the rights provisions they write are substantively incomplete. Despite authorization, (seemingly irresolvable) debates

---

[1] Nico Krisch, *Beyond Constitutionalism: The Pluralist Structure of Postnational Law* (Oxford University Press, Oxford 2010); Alec Stone Sweet, 'The Structure of Constitutional Pluralism' (2013) 11(2) International Journal of Constitutional Law 491.

[2] Neil Fligstein and Doug McAdam, *A Theory of Fields* (Oxford University Press, Oxford 2012).

on the democratic legitimacy of judicial review rage on. It would seem that the more robustly judges perform their duties, the more their political legitimacy will be contested.

The arbitral order benefits from, and actively harnesses, the functional logics of delegation-as-authorization. In the commercial law of the most important legal systems in the world, the contract—a placeholder for the sanctity of party autonomy—is a privileged source of legitimation of the judge. Those who contract need enforcement; those who write incomplete contracts need an interpreter; those who interpret the law help to make it. These truisms apply to courts, and they apply to the arbitral tribunals that replace courts. It is a matter of great importance that the main source of the legitimacy of ICA is the contract, specifically, the arbitration agreement. National legislatures and courts in the major trading zones, too, have expressly delegated to the arbitral order, under the banner of party autonomy (Chapters 2, 4, and 5). Again, formal authorization—in this case, by contracting parties and state officials—does not preclude or settle legitimacy debates. But the stronger the normative commitment to transnational freedom of contract by IACs, users, scholars, and state officials, the more ineffectual critiques of ICA's political legitimacy are likely to be when it comes to reform.

The major source of legitimation in international law is the treaty, a contract between two or more states. Investment treaties establish arbitral authority and, to the extent that they are incomplete contracts, they confer inherent lawmaking powers on tribunals. As Chapters 4 and 5 have documented, arbitrators have been the authors of much of the substance of international investment law in the domains of the fair and equitable treatment standard [FET] and indirect expropriation, the two most important causes of action. When states, as Principals, have responded, they have mostly acted to codify the main tenets of arbitral case law; efforts to block the development of the jurisprudence have floundered (Chapter 5). It may be that recently produced model BITs, new draft treaties, and a wave of signed BITs that include WTO-style 'general exceptions' will combine to alter the development of ISA, a topic discussed further below. At this point, it suffices to restate the point just made with respect to contracts. States, as treaty-makers, have fully authorized arbitral lawmaking; ISA meets the basic criteria of formal legitimacy; but legitimacy debates have not been extinguished.

Structures of Norms and Authority

To reproduce itself—to remain viable—a legal system must either meet the functional needs of users, or endure attempts to build more effective arrangements. Mechanisms of institutional change are therefore of critical importance (Chapter 1). The evolution of ICA is an extraordinary example of a private, transnational community that has built an adaptive legal system from the ground up. The International Chamber of Commerce [ICC], the dominant organizational actor in the field for nearly a century, continuously consults users, legislates soft law as well as obligatory rules, recruits and socializes arbitrators into the system, supervises awards, and directly engages national officials, including judges, at crucial points in the interface between the arbitral order and state law (Chapter 3). ICA is characterized by flexibility: multiple major IACs compete with the ICC for market share, which gives firms a variety of procedural arrangements from which to choose. And, because most awards are not published, arbitrators may feel freer to tailor awards to users' priorities. At least on the surface, treaty-based ISA is far more rigid: treaties are difficult to change, and the majority of awards will be published. Strong entrenchment and enhanced transparency has meant that tribunals, not states, have been the major substantive lawmakers in the domain of foreign investment (Chapters 4 and 5). Tribunals also initiated some important procedural innovations with implications for legitimacy debates, including the move to accept *amici* briefs from third parties, to which states acceded (Chapter 3).

As the arbitral order evolved its own systemic properties and institutional logics, its relationship with state law and national courts became more structured. Indeed, as we have stressed throughout the book, the formal legitimacy of ICA, as a legal regime, rests in part on institutional isomorphism, with respect to law and courts at the domestic level. Isomorphic processes produce convergence in norms and forms across organizational boundaries, facilitating the emergence and institutionalization of new 'fields' (Chapter 1). Although domestic legal systems and the arbitral order are formally separate realms, isomorphic dynamics have made the evolution of each system partly dependent on that of the other. The law of contract of the most important trading states has absorbed the basics of the new *Lex Mercatoria* when it comes to transnational contract law, for example. The ICC has always given a privileged place to party autonomy, and to trade usages when interpreting the parties' expectations as contractants. State officials have steadily adapted to the transnational community's approach to these and many other issues, not least through adopting model laws and conventions on contracts, arbitration, and recognition and enforcement of awards (Chapters 2, 3, and 4). For their part, arbitrators have developed case law that overlaps that of states, transnational/international public policy being a prime example (Chapter 4). Tribunals, when enforcing mandatory state law, do so in dialogues with state officials, taking cues from domestic approaches to similar legal questions (Chapter 5). This isomorphism has favoured the ongoing delegation, by state officials, of authority to the arbitral order. Without institutional convergence, and the ongoing negotiation of cooperative terms of engagement, serious conflicts of authority would be chronically produced, to arbitration's detriment.

What is indisputable is that a field of governance for transnational commerce, covering at least the major trading zones, has been institutionalized in law. The structure of authority within ICA is pluralist, and functionally divided, most obviously, in that arbitrators produce awards—typically interpreting and applying state law along the way—which courts enforce. These pluralist features are rooted in the New York Convention, which furnishes an indispensable, formal interface between the arbitral and domestic legal systems. Since 1958, the New York Convention has never been revised. At the same time, the terms of engagement between courts and tribunals, and between the officials of IACs and states, have evolved to favour further convergence.

In treaty-based ISA, we found evidence, as others have,[3] that tribunals are engaged in increasingly structured interactions with other international legal systems. As the international investment regime has gained in coherence, not least through the consolidation of arbitral case law, so has its capacity to engage across jurisdictional boundaries. It is today a blunt fact that tribunals in ISA produce more legal rulings applying general international law (general principles of law, the MFN principle, state responsibility and state police powers, and so on) than does the International Court of Justice [ICJ] or the World Trade Organization [WTO] courts, for example. ICSID has 214 pending disputes in arbitration (as of July 2016),[4] and other IACs, including the ICC and SIAC, are actively positioning themselves to become bigger players in ISA. The density of the caseload, and the growing sophistication of the case law, means that the law made by tribunals is increasingly likely to impact the development of international economic law. It remains to be seen whether a stable field—in which the various legal regimes make and enforce international economic law in mutually regarding ways—will develop and how.

In sum, this matrix—of contracts, treaties, and convergent institutions and expectations—embeds international arbitration in a resilient legal field that is presumptively legitimate in a strong sociological sense. These points made, functional logics do not exhaust legitimacy concerns, and often obscure significant ones. Academic lawyers, in particular, have long engaged in more searching inquiry into the normative principles that underwrite systemic legitimacy, raising issues to which we now turn.

II. Whither Hierarchy?

The institutionalization of the judicial model is registered in the construction of hierarchies: those non-derogable rules of IACs that subject the disputing parties to the authority of tribunals (Chapter 2), and tribunals to the authority of IACs (Chapter 3). These rules are, today, reinforced in a pluralist, transnational regime. In ICA, domestic judges routinely enforce arbitral agreements, closing access to the courts;[5] and tribunals and IACs strive to make judicial enforcement of their awards automatic. Hierarchy in arbitration serves the goal of effectiveness

---

[3] Jürgen Kurtz, *The WTO and International Investment Law: Converging Systems* (Cambridge University Press, Cambridge 2016) ['Kurtz']. See also the contributors to Giorgio Sacerdoti (ed), *General Interests of Host States in International Investment Law* (Cambridge University Press, Cambridge 2014); Pierre-Marie Dupuy, Francesco Francioni, and Ernst-Ulrich Petersmann (eds), *Human Rights in International Investment Law and Arbitration* (Oxford University Press, Oxford 2009).

[4] This figure includes cases in annulment proceedings. See 'ICSID Pending Cases with Details' <https://icsid.worldbank.org/apps/ICSIDWEB/cases/pages/pendingcases.aspx?status=p> accessed 7 July 2016.

[5] They recognize, for example, the doctrine of the separability of the arbitration agreement and that of the *Kompetenz-Kompetenz* of tribunals—see Chapters 2 and 4.

(Chapters 2 and 3). With the growth of a highly adversarial caseload, many of arbitration's consensual elements were abandoned, or fell into desuetude (Chapter 3). From this standpoint, coercive authority structures are justified, not least for those who contract and dispute, to the extent that they are necessary conditions of effectiveness. It is a striking fact that judicialization produced hierarchy precisely at the most important pressure points in proceedings, where collective action problems are most acute, and parties may seek to defect, and where judges may intervene on their own authority.

The construction of hierarchy has, nonetheless, proceeded unevenly. Some arbitral institutions have remained stubbornly resistant to judicialization, the most obvious of which are rules governing (a) the appointment of tribunals, (b) access to internal appellate review, and, for ICA, (c) the publication of awards. It is therefore a matter of great importance that resistance to more 'court-like' arbitration is coming under assault, in the name of the system's legitimacy, by power-holders *within* the system. With judicialization, the types of arrangements that count as necessary to the effectiveness of the regime going forward have expanded, to include criteria of legitimacy once thought to be antithetical to the very idea of arbitration.

Resistance: Appointment, Confidentiality, Appeal

As we have emphasized throughout the book, the arbitral order did not develop by design, or in a linear fashion. Rather, the structural properties that now organize the field evolved piecemeal, at different rates, in response to different stimuli, for varied purposes. While judicialization has transformed arbitration in important ways, it has also been blocked in others. Until recently, virtually all scholarly commentary from within the field has been supportive, even celebratory of the regime's triumphs. Elite arbitrators-turned-publicists have long laboured to explain and rationalize the evolving system, and to counter legitimacy critiques, as part of broader market-building agenda. They also urge appropriate reforms, if periodically and on the margins, either to satisfy users' demands, or in response to external challenges. What is new and important is that, in the past decade, powerful insiders have begun to question more openly principles of arbitration long considered to be foundational. These principles, remnants of concepts traditionally invoked to distinguish arbitration from adjudication, are challenged as sources of, rather than solutions to, ascendant legitimacy problems.

Consider one of the most resilient features of arbitration: the rules governing the constitution of the tribunal. In Chapter 3, we presented a simple strategic model of appointments under adversarial conditions that explains party-dominated appointments when it comes to three-member tribunals, and that of the house in proceedings to be conducted by a sole arbitrator. Most high stakes disputes will be settled by three-member tribunals, in which each party names a 'co-arbitrator' who then jointly selects a 'presiding arbitrator'. The procedures resolve some basic coordination problems, while comprising an important start-up mechanism: through an act of express delegation, the parties legitimize the tribunal. In both ISA and ICA, they are also attacked as failing basic criteria of legitimacy, the most important of which are derived from the principle of impartiality that grounds notions of judicial independence. In ICA, what is being challenged is primordial, namely, the claim that a valid arbitral agreement is virtually all that is required to secure the legitimacy of all that follows.

The view that party-driven appointments would undermine the impartiality of arbitrators is as old as the ICC. But so is the view, fully consistent with the dictates of the contractual model, that party autonomy covers the constitution of the tribunal. If the dispute is a purely private, contractual affair, then there is no social benefit to be gained from constraining party autonomy in order to secure impartiality. In 1935, the ICC, struggling to centralize appointments in its own offices, warned users that 'it happens more often than not that the arbitrators chosen by the parties merely act as [party] advocates'.[6] But, when adversarialism exploded during that same decade, users insisted on retaining control. Today, as a distinguished arbitrator puts it, the constitution of the tribunal is guided by 'the unique principle of international arbitration that a party is entitled to appoint, as one of the three decision-makers, a person of its own choosing …'.[7]

For its part, the ICC relented, but not without pronouncing what is now a fiduciary duty of impartiality, today expressed as ICC Rule 11(1):[8]

Every arbitrator must be and remain impartial and independent of the parties involved in the arbitration.

Nonetheless, powerful incentives drive co-arbitrators to ensure that the pleadings of their respective appointing party are fully considered. Worse are those situations, of which experienced arbitrators routinely complain, wherein parties continuously feed co-arbitrators positions that they are expected to advocate within the tribunal, at each stage of the proceedings.[9] In contrast to other areas of procedure, heightened adversarialism has not led to the loss of party control. Instead, savvy counsel now take great pains to vet candidates for appointment, in background checks and interviews (Chapter 3). Some go so far as to elicit a pre-commitment to espouse the appointing party's pleadings going forward.[10]

---

[6] International Chamber of Commerce, *International Commercial Arbitration—Practical Hints* (ICC Publishing, Paris 1935) 4.

[7] Charles N Brower, 'The Ethics of Arbitration: Perspectives from a Practicing International Arbitrator' (2010) 5(1) Berkeley J Int'l Publicist 4.

[8] ICC Arbitration Rules (2012): This duty appeared relatively late in the history of international arbitration. For instance, it is only in 1975 that party-appointed arbitrators were required to 'be independent of the party nominating' them—see Article 2(4), ICC Rules of Conciliation and Arbitration (1975). The duty to 'act fairly and impartially' only appeared in 1998—see Article 15(2), ICC Rules of Conciliation and Arbitration (1998).

[9] See Serge Lazareff, 'L'arbitre singe ou comment assassiner l'arbitrage' in *Global Reflections on International Law, Commerce and Dispute Resolution: Liber Amicorum in honour of Robert Briner* (ICC Publishing, Paris 2005) 477.

[10] Gerald Aksen, 'The Tribunal's Appointment' in Lawrence W Newman and Richard D Hill (eds), *The Leading Arbitrators' Guide to International Arbitration* (Juris, New York 2014) 337.

This tension also finds expression in the growing practice of issuing dissenting opinions. Dissents were originally discouraged, as a threat to the collegiality of tribunals and the authority of awards. Indeed, the first dissent to an ICC award was removed by the ICC Court.[11] Today, the major IACs permit dissenting opinions, which are no longer rare (Chapter 3). It may well be that the purpose of such dissents is to highlight weaknesses in the award, in anticipation of annulment proceedings, a not ignoble objective in the context of the judicial and pluralist models. But, critics lament, many dissenting opinions are written primarily with an eye toward securing future appointments. Dissents, after all, are almost always written by co-arbitrators appointed by the losing party, in both ICA[12] and ISA,[13] and available dissents typically restate the positions of the appointing party.

Discomfort with this situation has now burst into the open. Most important, Jan Paulsson (a leading practitioner, arbitrator, publicist, Vice-President of the ICC Court, Board Member of the AAA-ICDR, former President of the LCIA, among many other important positions) has sternly called for the abandonment of unilateral party appointments. For Paulsson, 'the notion that the mere proclamation of an ethical rule achieves a legitimizing effect is obviously a mirage', given the fact that 'whatever the qualities of the nominee, the appointing party is focused on winning, not on ensuring the ideal of impartiality'. In his view, 'the practice of unilateral nominations' is itself 'antagonistic to the idea of arbitration'—a rhetorical reversal of the classic view.

The best way [forward] is clearly to abandon the practice of unilateral appointments. This would involve a significant change in prevailing conduct and rules. References are occasionally made to 'the fundamental right' to name one's arbitrator. But there is no such right. Moreover, if it existed, it would certainly not be fundamental. The original concept that legitimates arbitration is that of an arbitrator in whom both parties have confidence. Why would any party have confidence in an arbitrator selected by its unloved opponent?[14]

Paulsson's proposals include the creation of an elite college of arbitrators from which the parties (acting jointly), IAC officials, or some other neutral body would appoint.

While some elite arbitrators side with Paulsson,[15] other luminaries, including Brower, deny that there is any problem at all, while starkly rejecting reform

---

[11] ICC Case No 850 (unpublished). See also Florian Grisel, Emmanuel Jolivet, and Eduardo Silva Romero, 'Aux origines de l'arbitrage commercial contemporain: l'émergence de l'arbitrage CCI (1920–1958)' (2016) 2 Revue de l'arbitrage 1, 30–1.

[12] Alan Redfern, 'Dissenting Opinions in International Commercial Arbitration: The Good, the Bad and the Ugly' (2004) 20 Arbitration International 223.

[13] Albert Jan van den Berg, 'Dissenting Opinions by Party-Appointed Arbitrations in Investment Arbitration' in Mahnoush H Arsanjani, Jacob Katz Cogan, Robert D Sloane, and Siegfried Wiessner (eds), *Looking to the Future: Essays on International Law in Honor of W. Michael Reisman* (Martinus Nijhoff, Leiden 2010) 821. According to van den Berg's data, nearly all dissenting opinions were issued by the arbitrator appointed by the losing party—see ibid 824.

[14] Jan Paulsson, *The Idea of Arbitration* (Oxford University Press, Oxford 2014) Chapter 5: 'Ethical Challenges'.

[15] John Fellas, 'Book Review: The Idea of Arbitration (Clarendon Law Series) by Jan Paulsson' (2014) 30 Arbitration International 589.

proposals: 'any proposal that would alter any of the fundamental elements of international arbitration constitutes an unacceptable assault on the very institution of international arbitration'.[16] The first of these fundamental elements is, according to Brower et al, 'the disputing parties' freedom to play a direct role in the design of their arbitration, particularly including the right freely to select, individually and collectively, the members of the tribunal'.[17]

Barring a cataclysmic event, any scheme to create a stable college of private judges within ICA faces major hurdles. Given the decentralized, competitive environment in which the major IACs find themselves, the risk involved in moving first, without the prior consent of users, is a strong deterrent. There exist no grounds for thinking that users will support giving up their authority over appointments. A more likely first step would be for a major IAC to give each party a veto over the other's choice—that is, the constitution of the tribunal would proceed under a consensus rule—thus reversing the default position. When parties deadlock, ICC officials choose (see Chapter 3). A list of IAC-preferred candidates, vetted for their commitment to impartiality, might well create a focal point for coordination, which could also favour the development of a *de facto* college.

In the meantime, the major IACs have strengthened procedures for challenging arbitrators for lack of impartiality and independence. The move is undergirded by the promulgation of an important statement of soft law that purports to express 'best current international practice':[18] the International Bar Association's *Guidelines on Conflicts of Interest in International Arbitration* (2004, revised in 2014). In 2006, the London Court of International Arbitration began to publicize the decisions of its Court on challenges to arbitrators;[19] and, in 2015, the ICC moved to communicate the decisions of its Court on arbitrator challenges and replacement proceedings, if only to the disputing parties.[20] In a 'Note' released in February 2016, the

[16] Charles N Brower, Michael Pulos, and Charles B Rosenberg, 'So Is There Anything Really Wrong with International Arbitration As We Know It?' in Arthur W Rovine (ed), *Contemporary Issues in International Arbitration and Mediation—The Fordham Papers (2012)* (Martinus Nijhoff, Leiden 2013) 3 ['Brower et al']. See also Charles N Brower and Charles B Rosenberg, 'The Death of the Two-Headed Nightingale: Why the Paulsson-van den Berg Presumption that Party-Appointed Arbitrators Are Untrustworthy Is Wrongheaded' (2013) 25 Arbitration International 7.

[17] Brower et al (n 16). See also V V Veeder, 'The Historical Keystone to International Arbitration: The Party-Appointed Arbitration—From Miami to Geneva' in David D Caron, Stephan W Schill, Abby Cohen Smutny, and Epaminontas E Triantafilou (eds), *Practicing Virtue: Inside International Arbitration* (Oxford University Press, Oxford 2016) 148: 'The right of each party to appoint an arbitrator makes the arbitration the *parties'* arbitrator, deciding *their* dispute with *their* tribunal. The preference by users for arbitration over litigation has many explanations, but one manifest reason is the sense of ownership by a party over the arbitral process because it has participated in the formation of the tribunal as to which all parties have consented' (emphasis in the original).

[18] International Bar Association, 'IBA "Guidelines on Conflicts of Interest in International Arbitration"' <http://www.ibanet.org/ENews_Archive/IBA_July_2008_ENews_ArbitrationMultipleLang.aspx> accessed 16 June 2016 ['IBA Guidelines'], 2.

[19] Thomas W Walsh and Ruth Teitelbaum, 'The LCIA Court Decisions on Challenges to Arbitrators: An Introduction' (2011) 27 Arbitration International 283.

[20] The President of the ICC Court stated that: 'Providing reasons as to Court decisions will further enhance the transparency and clarity of the ICC arbitration process.' See International Chamber of Commerce, 'ICC Court to communicate reasons as a new service to users' (8 October 2015)

ICC announced that transparency would henceforth be an objective to be pursued in defence of arbitration's legitimacy:

> The Court endeavours to make the arbitration process more transparent in ways that do not compromise expectations of confidentiality that may be important to parties. Transparency provides greater confidence in the arbitration process, and helps protect arbitration against inaccurate or ill-informed criticism.[21]

The ICC will now publish information on such cases registered after 1 January 2016, including the arbitrators' names, nationality, the method of their appointment, and whether the proceedings are ongoing or closed,[22] aligning it with practice at ICSID.

In ICA, confidentiality continues to trump transparency when it comes to publication of awards. All majors IACs pledge to guarantee, subject to waiver by the parties, confidentiality (Chapter 4), and it remains the mainstream view that ICA cannot do without it.[23] In the most recent White & Case/Queen Mary University survey of users (2015), 33 per cent of respondents ranked 'confidentiality' as 'one of the three most valuable characteristics of international arbitration', fifth on the list after 'enforceability of awards', 'avoiding' national legal systems, 'flexibility', and party 'selection of arbitrators'.[24]

In ISA, confidentiality has steadily ceded ground to transparency, so much so that the former is virtually no longer defended (Chapter 4). All new ISA awards will eventually be published, we can now expect, even without a party's consent. Oral pleadings no longer take place behind closed doors, indeed, some are even televised. Legitimacy concerns have driven these changes. The more a proceeding involves the public interest and performance of public officials,[25] the greater the perceived need for transparency. In ICA, remnants of the traditional view, to the effect that arbitration is a purely private affair, still remain, and these legacies hamper the development of arbitral governance. Today, ICA tribunals frequently arbitrate important public interests in policy areas once considered 'inarbitrable' in

---

<http://www.iccwbo.org/News/Articles/2015/ICC-Court-to-communicate-reasons-as-a-new-service-to-users/> accessed 16 June 2016.

[21] International Court of Arbitration, 'ICC Note to Parties and Arbitral Tribunals on the Conduct of the Arbitration under the ICC Rules of Arbitration' (22 February 2016) <https://international-arbitration-attorney.com/wp-content/uploads/not-to-partices-on-conduct-of-ICC-arbitration.pdf> accessed 16 June 2016, para 27.

[22] ibid para 28.

[23] Lazareff bluntly characterizes the 'postulate that confidentiality is not part and parcel of commercial arbitration' as an 'absurdity': 'it is inconceivable that such a procedure, whether domestic or international, should take place in the public eye'. See Serge Lazareff, 'Confidentiality and Arbitration: Theoretical and Philosophical Reflections' in International Chamber of Commerce, *Confidentiality in Arbitration: Commentaries on Rules, Statutes, Case Law and Practice* (ICC Publishing, Paris 2009) 81.

[24] White & Case and Queen Mary, University of London, '2015 International Arbitration Survey: Improvements and Innovations in International Arbitration' (2015) <http://www.arbitration.qmul.ac.uk/research/2015/> accessed 16 June 2016, 6.

[25] Most ISA proceedings involve pleadings to the effect that a public official has taken decisions that do not meet procedural or substantive standards found in domestic law.

all major court systems, while these same courts have renounced robust review of awards (Chapter 5).[26] Further, states are often parties to ICA proceedings; in 2015, the ICC reported that 13 per cent of new filings involved a state or state entity.[27] In our view, present policies privileging confidentiality are intensely vulnerable on legitimacy grounds (Part III below). To the degree that IACs participate in transnational governance, rather than merely providing discreet triadic dispute resolution services, they should be held to the transparency requirements of courts.

Scholars are now actively debating the 'confidentiality-transparency problem',[28] and the major IACs are re-evaluating their policies on publishing awards[29] (Chapter 4). While the ICC has been issuing redacted awards since the 1930s, some of the other major IACs have only just begun to do so. The AAA-ICDR began publishing awards in its *Bulletin* in 2012,[30] joined by the SIAC that same year.[31] Others continue to resist. The SCC makes available only a handful of awards per year, while the Hong Kong Centre[32] releases none at all. The LCIA indicates, in its rules, that it will only publish awards upon the written consent of the parties,[33] but the provision is contradicted by the LCIA's own 'Notes for Parties' stating that the Centre 'does not publish Awards, or parts of Awards, even in redacted form'.[34]

As with party-dominated appointments, it is unlikely that an IAC would risk moving first to abolish the veto on publication, although the ICC, the SIAC, and the Milan Arbitration Chamber are on record as wanting to publish more awards, even without express consent. At the same time, present policies not only hinder the development of precedent and other aspects of judicialized governance, they undermine the arbitral order's own claims to operate in the public interest.

With regard to appeal (Chapter 4), the fundamental tension between two values, (a) the finality of awards and (b) legal certainty, has not been resolved. In both ICA and ISA, we find a growing demand for appellate mechanisms that has not been met, partly for fear of reproducing the adversarial, delay-ridden

---

[26] See also Florian Grisel, *L'arbitrage international ou le droit contre l'ordre juridique* (LGDJ, Paris 2011) ['Grisel'], para 379.

[27] International Chamber of Commerce, '2015 ICC Dispute Resolution Statistics' (2016) 26(1) ICC International Court of Arbitration Bulletin 9.

[28] For an overview of the debate, see Joshua Karton, 'Conflict of Interests: Seeking a Way Forward on Publication of International Arbitral Awards' (2012) 28(3) Arbitration International 447; Catherine A Rogers, 'Transparency in International Commercial Arbitration' (2006) 54 U Kan L Rev 1301 ['Rogers'].

[29] For a survey of the publication policies of the major IACs, see New York City Bar, 'Report by the Committee on International Commercial Disputes: Publication of International Arbitration Awards and Decisions' (February 2014) <http://www2.nycbar.org/pdf/report/uploads/20072645-PublicationofInternationalArbitrationAwardsandDecisions.pdf> accessed 16 June 2016 ['Publication of International Arbitration Awards and Decisions'].

[30] The AAA-ICDR changed its rules to permit publication under certain conditions only in 2010.

[31] In 2013, the SIAC amended its rules to allow it to 'publish any award with the names of the parties and other identifying information redacted': see Article 28.10, SIAC Arbitration Rules (2013).

[32] The HKIAC states that, although publication is possible, it has never received a request to do so by the parties: see 'Publication of International Arbitration Awards and Decisions' (n 29), 9.

[33] Article 30, LCIA Arbitration Rules (2014).

[34] London Court of International Arbitration, 'LCIA Notes for Parties' (4 April 2016) <http://www.lcia.org//adr-services/lcia-notes-for-parties.aspx> accessed 16 June 2016.

pathologies of courts.[35] ICSID initiated internal assessments of the annulment system,[36] and the establishment of an appellate body.[37] The SIAC[38] has established a system of internal control similar to the ICC's, empowering its 'Registrar' to review 'draft awards' prior to their certification as final (Chapter 3). And the AAA-ICDR is the first to initiate a formal appeal process (Chapter 4), through its Optional Appellate Arbitration Rules of 2013,[39] while taking pains to express its strong attachment to the finality of awards. In the meantime, a determined minority of arbitrators and scholars propose the creation of an 'international court' for reviewing arbitral awards, which would have jurisdiction over annulment, enforcement, and recognition of awards, specifically in ICA.[40] And in ISA (discussed below), some major states are now seriously contemplating the creation of an appellate court, and Gabrielle Kaufmann-Kohler and Michele Potestà have recently produced a white paper for UNCITRAL proposing what appears to be a productive way forward.[41]

Models

As arbitration's importance has grown, so has scholarship that grounds normative reflection in a comparative-institutional analysis of judicial authority (see Chapter 1). The most important critical research in this vein focuses on ISA, following a seminal paper of 2006, written by Gus Van Harten and Martin Loughlin, in which the authors argue that ISA comprises a form of 'global administrative law'.[42] Van Harten and Loughlin stress similarities of function between public law courts and ISA tribunals, while highlighting important differences between ISA and ICA:

---

[35] Florian Grisel, 'Control of Awards and Re-Centralisation of International Commercial Arbitration' (2006) 25 Civil Justice Quarterly 166, 171 et seq.

[36] International Centre for Settlement of Investment Disputes, 'Background Paper on Annulment for the Administrative Council of ICSID' (10 August 2012) <https://icsid.worldbank.org/apps/ICSIDWEB/resources/Documents/Background%20Report%20on%20Annulment_English.pdf> accessed 16 June 2016.

[37] International Centre for Settlement of Investment Disputes, 'Possible Improvements of the Framework for ICSID Arbitration' (22 October 2004) <https://icsid.worldbank.org/apps/ICSIDWEB/resources/Documents/Possible%20Improvements%20of%20the%20Framework%20of%20ICSID%20Arbitration.pdf> accessed 16 June 2016.

[38] Rule 28.2, SIAC Arbitration Rules (2013).

[39] AAA-ICDR Optional Appellate Arbitration Rules (2013).

[40] Stephen M Schwebel, 'The Creation and Operation of an International Court of Arbitral Awards' in Martin Hunter, Arthur Marriott, and V V Veeder (eds), *The Internationalisation of International Arbitration* (Graham & Trotman and Martinus Nijhoff, London 1995) 115; Howard M Holtzmann, 'A Task for the 21st Century: Creating a New International Court for Resolving Disputes on the Enforceability of Arbitral Awards' in Hunter et al (eds), *The Internationalisation of International Arbitration*, 109.

[41] Gabrielle Kaufmann-Kohler and Michele Potestà, 'Can the Mauritius Convention Serve as a Model for the Reform of Investor-State Arbitration in Connection with the Introduction of a Permanent Investment Tribunal or an Appeal Mechanism? Analysis and Roadmap', Geneva Center for International Dispute Settlement (paper commissioned by UNCITRAL), 3 June 2016 ['Kaufmann-Kohler and Potestà'].

[42] Gus Van Harten and Martin Loughlin, 'Investment Treaty Arbitration as a Species of Global Administrative Law' (2006) 17 European Journal of International Law 121.

Commercial arbitration originates in an agreement between private parties to arbitrate disputes between themselves in a particular manner, and its authority derives from the autonomy of individuals to order their private affairs as they wish. Investment arbitration, by contrast, originates in the authority of the state to use [it] to resolve disputes arising from the exercise of public authority. Investment arbitration is constituted by a sovereign act, as opposed to a private act, of the state and this ... makes investment arbitration more closely analogous to domestic juridical review of the regulatory conduct of the state.

Because the judicial review of public acts is inevitably implicated in governance, the political legitimacy of such arrangements should not be presumed but, rather, closely scrutinized.

When one actually does so, they argue, ISA is found lacking. Party-dominated appointment procedures in ISA are relatively more problematic, 'since it is not uncommon for a prominent figure in investment arbitration simultaneously to be sitting as an arbitrator in one case, representing an investor or state in another, and generally advising other clients on investment law'.[43] Further, when one considers ISA as a mode of administrative review and regulatory control, one notices that the regime has not developed stable standards of review, or appropriate doctrines of deference to public interests, as one expects well-functioning judiciaries to do. In 2006, when their article was published, the process of developing such standards was in its infancy, and remains incomplete today (Chapter 5). In the past decade, Van Harten[44]—who advocates formal judicialization, including the creation of an appellate jurisdiction[45]—and a growing group of scholars have taken up these issues in earnest.[46]

We clearly embrace the ISA-as-governance formulation and, for reasons stated, believe that ICA should be subjected to the same searching questions. The fact remains, however, that ISA blends some relatively weak 'public law' functions with strong 'private law' remedies. Tribunals are charged with reviewing the treaty-conformity of state acts but, unlike a national administrative or constitutional court, they do not possess the power to invalidate such acts judged to be unlawful. Put differently, they exercise no sovereign authority *within* the legal order of the respondent state. Instead, tribunals award compensation where liability is found. The remedy—damages to successful claimants, rather than invalidation or

---

[43] ibid 148.

[44] Gus Van Harten, *Sovereign Choices and Sovereign Constraints: Judicial Restraint in Investment Treaty Arbitration* (Oxford University Press, Oxford 2013).

[45] Gus Van Harten, *Investment Treaty Arbitration and Public Law* (Oxford University Press, Oxford 2007) ['Van Harten']; Gus Van Harten, 'A Case for an International Investment Court' (2008) Working Paper No 22/08, Society of International Economic Law Inaugural Conference (Geneva) <http://papers.ssrn.com/sol3/papers.cfm?abstract_id=1153424> accessed 16 June 2016.

[46] William Burke-White and Andreas von Staden, 'The Need for Public Law Standards of Review in Investor-State Arbitrations' in Stephan W Schill (ed), *International Investment Law and Comparative Public Law* (Oxford University Press, Oxford 2010) 689; Stephan W Schill, 'Deference in Investment Treaty Arbitration: Reconceptualizing the Standard of Review' (2012) 3(3) Journal of International Dispute Settlement 577; Caroline Henckels, 'Balancing Investment Protection and the Public Interest: The Role of the Standard of Review and the Importance of Deference in Investor-State Arbitration' (2013) 4(1) Journal of International Dispute Settlement 197.

performance orders—gives to ISA a 'private law' complexion, akin to ICA in this respect.

As Anthea Roberts has argued, the choice of analogy by arbitrators and scholars can powerfully frame legal and normative arguments, often driving them to a conclusion.[47] If the analyst's point of departure is the available remedy, rather than the nature of the act under review, a different set of analogies, with different normative implications, emerges. ISA instantiates a system of liability assessment for breach whose basic function is to override the 'hold-up' problem when it comes to foreign investment. States sign treaties to signal their commitment to investor protections; and they confer authority on arbitrators as a means of securing the credibility of those commitments (Chapter 2). It is the basic function of tribunals to assess liability and the level of compensation when states breach their obligations. States may well choose to breach promises made to investors,[48] including for sound public policy reasons. Under this view, the review of state acts is essential to the task of determining how much it will cost the state to breach the property rights of an investor, for any purpose the state may deem important. The view analogizes in the direction of an efficient breach model,[49] in which a duty to compensate comprises an escape hatch with respect to performance. Liability found, the judge's role is to determine the appropriate compensation to the successful claimant, not to order performance on the part of the state. Because investors are the vulnerable parties when it comes to non-performance on the part of states, arbitral deference to the state is not presumptively warranted. Rather, tribunals should determine liability and damages on a case-by-case basis, through a process that will include an assessment of the importance of legitimate public interests, which is precisely what most tribunals do most of the time (see Chapter 5).

It bears emphasis that comparative-institutional analysis presumes that appropriate analogies are to be found in the judicial world—where debates about standards of review, deference, and efficient breach are commonplace—rendering traditional models of arbitration obsolete and irrelevant.

States as Critics

International arbitration is partly a creature of state delegation. Urged on by powerful private actors, the major trading states ratified the 1958 New York Convention (largely a project of the arbitral community) and withdrew objections to tribunals' asserted authority to interpret and apply mandatory law. The extraordinary development of the New York Convention regime, as a quasi-constitutional interface between domestic courts and arbitrators, has been driven by competition among

---

[47] Anthea Roberts, 'Clash of Paradigms: Actors and Analogies Shaping the Investment Treaty System' (2012) 106 American Journal of International Law 1.

[48] Many tribunals have found that so-called 'umbrella clauses' and the FET cover specific promises made to investors by host states—see Chapter 5.

[49] Krzysztof Pelc and Johannes Urpelainen, 'When Do International Economic Agreements Allow Countries to Pay to Breach?' (2015) 10(2) Review of International Organizations 231.

these same states for arbitral business. Although there remain pockets of resistance, once disparate 'islands of transnational governance' have become a global archipelago (Chapter 2). In ICA, broad acquiescence on the part of states to arbitral authority has created important gaps in accountability, which we address in the next section. Most important, the absence of transparency in ICA renders it vulnerable to challenges to its political legitimacy. It is no longer acceptable, if ever it was, to conceptualize ICA as a purely private dispute resolution regime.

In ISA, states are both Principals (as treaty-makers) and respondents in proceedings. Tribunals become Agents of the same states over which they exercise authority, once a third-party beneficiary of an investment treaty—the investor—brings suit. From the standpoint of delegation theory, the peculiarity of the situation is explained by the nature of the commitment problem to be resolved. At the same time, the analyst expects states to monitor the performance of their Agents and, when dissatisfied, to seek to change how tribunals take decisions. Nonetheless, the *banc* of repeat arbitrators possesses distinct advantages over states in any specific proceeding. Respondent states are subjects of pre-existing treaty rules; states are locked in to arbitration; and their actions are the object of control with respect to arbitral case law whose evolutionary dynamics have proved difficult to constrain.

States can seek to reassert control over development of the regime by altering the determinants of the latter's decision-making. The book reports findings on new investment treaties negotiated and signed since 2002. In one area of relative discontent—the application of the most favoured nation rule to dispute resolution procedures—states have largely succeeded in predicating compulsory jurisdiction on explicit state consent (Chapter 2). In other areas that have generated controversy, including interpretation of indirect expropriation and the fair and equitable treatment standard [FET], states have adapted to the main lines of arbitral case law, legitimizing that lawmaking (Chapter 5). This finding is important since, as the data show, most of the action takes place in these two domains.

States reveal their preferences, and weigh-in on the acceptability of current arrangements, through publishing model BITs and floating drafts of new treaties. We examined these texts in light of the P–A issues raised in the book. Two trends merit emphasis (as well as deeper consideration than we can give to them here).

First, when states have considered departures from the standard template for BITs,[50] the more radical proposals have been removed or diluted. The scaling back of reform ambitions has taken place during the drafting process itself, and after the release of a 'draft model BIT' for public comment. In the United States, the business community's worries about reducing investment protections, including with regard to the FET, prevailed over those who sought to strengthen regulatory

---

[50] Brazil, which has signed but not ratified any BITs, has recently negotiated two new BITs, with Mozambique and Angola. The treaties, whose 'ratification prospects … remain dim', do not provide for the FET or indirect expropriation, and arbitration can be initiated only by states (not an investor). See Clovis Trevino, 'A Closer Look at Brazil's Two New Bilateral Investment Treaties' (*Investment Arbitration Reporter*, 10 April 2015) <http://www.iareporter.com/articles/a-closer-look-at-brazils-two-new-bilateral-investment-treaties/> accessed 16 June 2016.

prerogatives.[51] In the end, the 2012 US Model BIT made only marginal adjustments to the 2004 Model it replaced. In 2008, the Norwegian Government issued a draft model that contained several revisionist features, including a requirement that investors exhaust local remedies before filing for arbitration. The Government dropped the provision in the 2015 version, after Norwegian business leaders and investors mounted protests.

The Indian Government has produced the most innovative model, which it submitted for comment in April 2015. The March draft: required exhaustion of local remedies; insulated from arbitral review 'any legal issue' that had been 'finally settled by any judicial authority of the Host State'; and prohibited a tribunal from reviewing a host state's determination that a state act under review was taken in the public interest, and thus deserving substantial deference. It left out the FET, preferring a 'treatment of investment' provision prohibiting 'fundamental breaches of due process' and 'manifestly abusive treatment, such as coercion, duress and harassment', presumably to block application of the case law on the 'legitimate expectations' of investors to disputes involving India (Chapter 5). Most intriguing, the March 2015 model contained a long list of investors' 'duties' (anti-corruption, disclosure, and compliance with environmental and consumer protection law, human rights, and labour regulations, and so on), headings under which a host state could counter-sue the investor. After opposition by Indian business groups, and the publication of a critical commentary by its own Law Commission (composed of judges and representative of the bar),[52] the draft was revised. In its final Model BIT, revealed in December 2015, the Indian Government maintained its stance on the 'treatment of investment', and limited the exhaustion of remedies requirement to a period of five years, but excised completely the other initiatives just mentioned.[53]

The second important trend concerns derogation clauses, the addition of which reflects states' concern for defending their regulatory prerogatives. The insertion of a 'general exceptions' provision, typically modelled on Article XX GATT (1947) or Article XIV GATS (1994), and the creation of carve-outs for 'essential security interests', taxation, and other sensitive areas, has clearly gained momentum. Canada initiated the practice, which then spread to a small handful of other states, as evidenced in BITs signed since 2002 (see Chapter 5). Virtually all of the new Model BITs and draft treaties we examined contain such general exceptions and

---

[51] Luke Eric Peterson, 'Analysis: United States Unveils "New" Model Bilateral Investment Treaty that Retains Protective Core, and Makes a Few Tweaks on Periphery' (*Investment Arbitration Reporter*, 22 April 2012) <http://www.iareporter.com/articles/analysis-united-states-unveils-new-model-bilateral-investment-treaty-that-retains-protective-core-and-makes-a-few-tweaks-on-periphery/> accessed 17 June 2016.

[52] Government of India, Law Commission of India, 'Report No. 260: Analysis of the 2015 Draft Model Indian Bilateral Investment Treaty' (August 2015) <http://lawcommissionofindia.nic.in/reports/Report260.pdf> accessed 16 June 2016.

[53] Government of India, Law Commission of India, 'Model Text for the Indian Bilateral Investment Treaty' <https://mygov.in/sites/default/files/master_image/Model%20Text%20for%20the%20Indian%20Bilateral%20Investment%20Treaty.pdf> accessed 16 June 2016 ['Model Indian BIT'].

carve-outs, as well as statements to the effect that 'it is inappropriate to encourage investment by weakening or reducing the protections afforded in domestic labor [or environmental] laws'.[54] To the extent that these preferences are consolidated in new treaties, they will favour further doctrinal integration of the trade and investment regimes,[55] as well as a more structured development of the proportionality principle (see below).

We do not consider these developments to be straightforward indicators of 'backlash', as others might. On the contrary, experienced arbitrators are likely to welcome these moves, insofar as they (a) comfort approaches to the 'right to regulate' developed by the most influential tribunals themselves (Chapters 4 and 5), and (b) leave tribunals less exposed as primary lawmakers. Significantly, new models and drafts also explicitly assert the host state's 'right to regulate', including the Draft Model BITs of Norway and India, the draft Comprehensive Economic and Trade Agreement between Canada and the European Union [CETA], and the Trans-Pacific Partnership [TPP],[56] signed in February 2016 by twelve Pacific Rim states, including Australia, Canada, Japan, the United States, and Singapore.

Why have states not pursued a more radical reform agenda? In response, we would highlight three main factors. First, the generic problems of contracting and coordination are acute in international economic law. States have found it difficult to write more complete contracts when it comes to the most highly arbitrated domains of investment law: the provisions on indirect expropriation and the FET illustrate the point. The provisions of most new BITs, revised models, and draft treaties in these areas have consolidated, not repudiated, approaches that had already been mapped in major strains of arbitral jurisprudence. When it comes to broader issues of regime design, the decision-rule governing treaty-revision—consensus—favours inertia. Second, even when states have contemplated proposals to expressly restrict treaty protections for foreign investment, domestic investors and the national bar have pushed back. India has become a major capital exporter, and Indian investors want the same protections that their counterparts from other countries enjoy. Third, it has proven difficult, even for the most skeptical and disgruntled states (and scholars), to demonstrate that the regime is biased in favour of investors in a systemic sense,[57] or against developing states.[58] While more than

---

[54] Article 13(2), US Model Bit (2012). Such statements are also found in dozens of BITs signed since 2002.

[55] Kurtz (n 3).

[56] Office of the United States Trade Representative, 'Trans-Pacific Partnership' <https://ustr.gov/trade-agreements/free-trade-agreements/trans-pacific-partnership/tpp-full-text> accessed 16 June 2016.

[57] Susan D Franck, 'The ICSID Effect? Considering Potential Variations in Arbitration Awards' (2011) 51(4) Virginia Journal of International Law 825. To our knowledge, the only relatively systematic empirical study that purports to have found pro-investor bias concerns decisions on jurisdiction; Gus Van Harten, 'Arbitrator Behaviour in Asymmetrical Adjudication: An Empirical Study of Investment Treaty Arbitration' (2012) 50 Osgoode Hall Law Journal 211.

[58] Susan D Franck, 'Conflating Politics and Development? Examining Investment Treaty Arbitration Outcomes' (2014) 55(1) Virginia Journal of International Law 13.

25 per cent of all filings are settled,[59] states prevail in most cases at the merits stage, their winning percentage topping 56 per cent.[60] Further, dominant lines of arbitral doctrine fully recognize their regulatory prerogatives.[61] These points add up to a rather banal conclusion: most states, even those that are reform-minded, find the basics of the present regime to be in their interest. Scholars who have examined these same issues, in the light of relatively systematic data collection and analysis, have reached the same conclusions.[62]

We do not want to be misunderstood. Structural reform is in the reach of states. Indeed, if even a handful of powerful states converged on preferences to remake the regime in some fundamental way, they would very likely succeed. They would need only to contract the new arrangements with one another, abandon old agreements, and then insist that their partners in BITs and regional treaties do likewise or be excluded from what would be, in effect, a new regime.

While the most powerful states continue to extend the scope of treaty-based ISA, the potential for structural change has recently opened up in the related areas of appointment and appeal. A potential game-changer comes in the form of the draft of the Canada–EU CETA, which the parties released, 'for information purposes', in February 2016. The text proposes extensive judicialization, in the form of a permanent body of arbitrators and an appellate court, pushed by the European Commission and Germany.[63] (They thus embrace reform ideas advocated by Van Harten and others.) The parties envision the creation of a 'multilateral investment tribunal and appellate mechanisms', which would feature a 'Tribunal' to be composed of 'at least 15 individuals' possessing 'expertise' in international trade law. According to an 'Ethics' provision, persons named to this roster would be required to 'refrain from acting as counsel or as party-appointed expert or witness in any pending or new investment dispute under this or any other international

---

[59] International Bar Association, 'Investor-State Dispute Settlement: The Importance of an Informed, Fact-Based Debate' (23 April 2015) <http://www.ibanet.org/Article/Detail.aspx?ArticleUid=1dff6284-e074-40ea-bf0c-f19949340b2f> accessed 16 June 2016.

[60] Statistics reported in Chapter 2.

[61] Chapter 5. In *Charanne and Construction Investments v Spain* (SCC), Award of 21 January 2016, the first award to deal with the abolition of tax and tariff incentives for solar energy under the European Energy Charter, the Tribunal rejected the investors' indirect expropriation and FET claims. The *Charanne* Tribunal stressed that, in a 'highly regulated sector such as energy', investors must exercise due diligence when it comes to the risk of regulatory change. In the absence of a contractually based stabilization clause, the Tribunal held, investors could not reasonably expect 'that an existing regulatory framework will remain unchanged'. At least twenty such cases are now pending against Spain, along with proceedings brought against Germany, Italy, and other European countries that have pursued similar policies. The award is discussed in Luke Eric Peterson and Zoe Williams, 'Spain Prevails on Merits in First of Many Energy Charter Treaty Claims in the Solar Sector' (*Investment Arbitration Reporter*, 25 January 2016) <https://www.iareporter.com/articles/breaking-spain-prevails-on-merits-in-first-of-many-energy-charter-treaty-claims-in-the-solar-sector/> accessed 25 June 2016.

[62] Chapter 5; Tomer Broude, Yoram Z Haftel, and Alexander Thompson, 'Who Cares about Regulatory Space in BITs? A Comparative International Approach' in A Roberts, P-H Verdier, M Versteeg, and P Stephan (eds), *Comparative International Law* (Oxford University Press, forthcoming). Among other findings, the authors show that states have chosen to reduce, not widen, their own 'regulatory space'.

[63] The 2004 and 2012 Model BITs of the United States contain a similar provision.

agreement', and to 'comply' with the IBA Guidelines (noted above).[64] With regard to appointments, the parties, aided by the Chair of the CETA Joint Committee (an administrative official who represents state parties), would select members of arbitral 'Panels'. Where parties fail to agree, the Chair of the Joint Committee would organize appointment through the drawing of lots, from three lists of members of the Tribunal provided, respectively, by each party and the Chair herself.[65]

The draft treaty also foresees the creation of an Appellate Tribunal, to be appointed by the Joint Committee. According to draft Article 8.28(1), disputants would be able to 'appeal an award ... within 90 days after its issuance'. Appeals would be processed by a three-member 'division', drawn at random from members of the Appellate Tribunal. Appellate Divisions would be authorized to 'uphold, modify or reverse a Tribunal's award' on grounds of 'errors in the application or interpretation of applicable law', 'manifest errors in the appreciation of the facts, including the appreciation of relevant domestic law', and under the grounds of annulment set out in Article 52(1) of the ICSID Convention.[66] In draft Article 8.29, the CETA parties declare their commitment to pursuing, along 'with other trading partners', the creation of 'a multilateral investment tribunal and appellate mechanism for the resolution of investment disputes'.

The draft CETA, which already has been the subject of sharp criticism by both proponents and opponents of reform,[67] is now being widely discussed by officials, arbitrators, and scholars. Kaufmann-Kohler and Michele Potestà, in their 2016 white paper for UNCITRAL, propose a relatively detailed blueprint for building an appellate regime, on the basis of the usual reasons (to build a coherent jurisprudence, to reduce instances of legal error, and so on; see Chapter 4). Their plan entails the creation of an appellate tribunal by multilateral convention, on which states would confer jurisdiction through an opt-in for parties to existing investment treaties, and through express provision in new treaties. They are fully aware of the risks involved:

First, if appeals were possible, they would soon become the rule, as states and investors who have lost a case could not afford *not* to file an appeal, be it only for reasons of internal accountability. Second, as 'ICSID experience with ad hoc annulment committees show, even corrective mechanisms intended to be severely restricted (indeed allowing no appeal even on points of law) have a tendency to duplicate the arbitral process itself in terms of duration, cost, complexity ...'[68] This could prove especially detrimental for States and investors with limited resources.[69]

---

[64] IBA Guidelines (n 18), Article 29(8).   [65] IBA Guidelines (n 18), Article 29(7).

[66] The annulment system at ICSID is discussed in Chapter 4.

[67] Douglas Thomson, 'Canada Agrees to EU Proposals on ISDS' (*Global Arbitration Review*, 3 March 2016) <http://globalarbitrationreview.com/news/article/34787/canada-agrees-eu-proposals-isds/> accessed 16 June 2016; Alison Ross, 'Schwebel criticises EU Act of "appeasement"' (*Global Arbitration Review*, 24 May 2016) <http://globalarbitrationreview.com/news/article/35352/schwebel-criticises-eu-act-appeasement/> accessed 16 June 2016.

[68] Quoting Jan Paulsson, 'Avoiding Unintended Consequences' in Karl P Sauvant and Michael Chiswick-Patterson (eds), *Appeals Mechanism in International Investment Disputes* (Oxford University Press, New York 2008) 241, 260 (emphasis in the original).

[69] Kaufmann-Kohler and Potestà (n 41), 32.

The authors focus on appeal, and do not advocate important changes in the rules governing proceedings at the 'lower' level at which the dispute is settled in the first instance. Because the proposal seeks to minimize adjustment costs, largely eliminating the need for states to renegotiate agreements, and for arbitrators to alter their approach to the law, the proposal may have a chance of succeeding. We strongly support it.

III. Arbitral Governance and Reform

We advocate a series of reforms that would enhance the legitimacy of arbitral governance which, we assume, will continue to widen in scope and deepen in importance.

Transparency and Accountability

ICA suffers an accountability deficit that undercuts its claims to legitimacy as a transnational legal system. In our view, the present situation is unacceptable.

On the one hand, the regime has largely secured its own autonomy and effectiveness, the most compelling indicator of which is the routine recognition and enforcement of its award on the part of national judges of the major trading states in the world, without review on the merits. On the other hand, the vast majority of awards remain confidential. We thus have no means of assessing how arbitrators are doing their jobs, even when they are interpreting and applying mandatory state law (Chapter 5), and developing transnational/international public policy (Chapter 4). Tribunals hold hearings behind closed doors; they almost never allow submission of *amicus* briefs; and their awards are kept secret. The forces favouring inertia are powerful, but not always honourable.[70]

Insofar as arbitration replaces courts in the regulation of transnational business, it should be subject to principles of public accountability, which entails meeting basic transparency requirements. These requirements should apply when the dispute (a) involves the distribution of an important public good, (b) is likely to have a substantive impact on third parties, or (c) involves 'public policy'—domestic or transnational/international. At the very least, enhanced transparency would cover disputes involving important consumer and environmental regulation, the arms trade, energy concessions, bribery and corruption, competition, and bankruptcy, as well as those involving the fundamental rights of third parties, whether expressed in international or domestic charters of rights. These conditions are more likely to be fulfilled when the parties to the dispute are public entities, but some disputes involving private firms will meet them as well.[71]

---

[70] As Hans Smit, a renowned arbitrator, once affirmed, 'arbitration can't be credible unless there is a certain measure of transparency, yet [c]onfidentiality exists because [corporate] executives don't want the public to know what stupid mistakes they make'—cited in Michael Goldhaber, 'The Court that Came in from the Cold' (*The American Lawyer*, May 2001).

[71] Grisel (n 26), para 379. See also Florian Grisel and Jorge E Vinuales, '*L'amicus curiae* dans l'arbitrage d'investissement' (2007) 23 ICSID Review—Foreign Investment Law Journal 380, 430–1.

In every proceeding in which these conditions are met, IACs should require the publication of the award, or a synopsis of the terms of settlement, redacted in appropriate ways to protect sensitive business information and trade secrets. Moreover, tribunals should possess the authority to open part or all of the proceedings to the public, where public interests are compelling, and to entertain *amicus* briefs from third parties. As we noted above, however, none of the leading institutions has an incentive to take the first step, for fear of offending users.

Publication would serve the value of legal certainty, promoting the building of a more coherent, precedent-based jurisprudence. It would ground the deference granted to awards by courts in legally defensible practices.[72] The ICC and other IACs already engage in more intrusive supervision of tribunals when the proceedings raise significant public policy concerns. Publishing the resulting awards ought to confirm our trust in how they perform these important tasks, given that the ICC has long claimed that it performs as well or better than courts when it enforces mandatory law and public policy. To the extent that such a rule would backfire, driving parties into the courts, the advantages of arbitration, beyond secrecy, will be exposed as an exaggeration.

If arbitration does not embrace enhanced transparency, then the domestic courts in pro-arbitration states should review important awards more robustly. In 2012, responding to the rise and 'judicialization'[73] of arbitration in Asia, the new Chief Justice of the Singapore Supreme Court strongly criticized the practice of unilateral party appointments and the absence of 'visibility and public accountability' of its decisions and lawmaking.[74] In 2016, the Chief Justice of England and Wales attacked the confidentiality of ICA proceedings as an unjustified affront to the principles of 'open justice', a 'hallmark of democratic society'.[75] The New York City Bar Association, a strong supporter of international arbitration, recently reviewed the publication policies of the leading IACs, in order to 'stimulate the ongoing debates within the international arbitration community about the pros and cons of publication and the different ways in which it can be done'.[76] It nonetheless found that, as of 2014, no IAC 'reported any active consideration of changing policies or practices on publication of awards'.[77]

Our view is predicated on the rejection of any sharp distinction between ICA and ISA, when it comes to transnational governance (Chapter 5). ICA does not always involve more 'private' than 'public' law and interests, even relative to ISA.

---

[72] It would also lower the cost of entry to new users and arbitrators, helping to socialize them into the system.

[73] Sundaresh Menon, 'International Arbitration: The Coming of a New Age for Asia (and Elsewhere)' in Albert Jan van den Berg (ed), *International Arbitration: The Coming of a New Age? (ICCA Congress Series No 17)* (Wolters Kluwer, Alphen aan den Rijn 2013).

[74] ibid para 48.

[75] Lord Chief Justice of England and Wales Thomas of Cwmgiedd, 'Developing commercial law through the courts: rebalancing the relationship between the courts and arbitration' (9 March 2016), The Bailii Lecture 2016 <https://aberdeenunilaw.files.wordpress.com/2016/05/lcj-speech-bailli-lecture-201603091.pdf> accessed 16 June 2016, paras 38–9.

[76] Publication of International Arbitration Awards and Decisions (n 29), 1.   [77] ibid 11.

In the types of ICA disputes that would meet the criteria just listed, the public interest is directly implicated, whereas, in some ISA disputes, it is clearly not. ISA, however, meets minimal standards of transparency. In 2006, states amended the ICSID Rules to permit tribunals to entertain third-party *amicus* briefs, and to broadcast hearings, innovations that tribunals had previously evolved on their own (Chapter 3).[78] New investment treaties and models routinely provide for the same, and the UNCITRAL Rules on Transparency in Treaty-Based Investor-State Arbitration, which requires publication of pleadings and awards, went into effect on 1 April 2014.[79]

The rapid institutionalization of rules enhancing transparency and accountability in ISA may well exert an influence on the situation in ICA. As Rogers put it as early as 2006:

Investor-state arbitration may create pressure or at least inspiration for greater transparency. Even if the two systems are distinct in many ways, the membrane between the two systems is rather permeable. Many of the lawyers and arbitrators who staff investment arbitration established themselves in international commercial arbitration and continue to shuttle back and forth between the systems. Precedents and procedures from the investment context also migrate into the international commercial arbitration. Given the vigor of pressures for increased transparency in investment arbitration, it seems doubtful that they will stop at the blurred boundary between the two systems.[80]

Today, even executives of IACs champion transparency,[81] and now openly challenge the presumption of confidentiality,[82] though concrete proposals for reform are lacking. One promising avenue might be for UNCITRAL to consider adapting some of its 'Rules on Transparency' for ISA, to ICA.[83]

Arbitral Lawmaking and General Principles

When judges develop general principles of law, they become architects of their own legal systems, acting as primary lawmakers. Consider how scholars and judges

---

[78] Aurélia Antonietti, 'The 2006 Amendments to the ICSID Rules and Regulations and the Additional Facility Rules' (2006) 21 ICSID Review—Foreign Investment Law Journal 427.

[79] United Nations Commission on International Trade Law, 'UNCITRAL Rules on Transparency in Treaty-based Investor-State Arbitration' (2014) <http://www.uncitral.org/uncitral/en/uncitral_texts/arbitration/2014Transparency.html> accessed 16 June 2016.

[80] Rogers (n 28), 1334–5.

[81] See the remarks of the newly appointed President of the ICC International Court of Arbitration: Alexis Mourre, 'ICC Court to communicate reasons as a new service to users' (8 October 2015) <http://www.iccwbo.org/News/Articles/2015/ICC-Court-to-communicate-reasons-as-a-new-service-to-users> accessed 16 June 2016.

[82] Stefano Azzali (then Secretary-General of the Milan Chamber of Arbitration and Secretary Treasurer of the International Federation of Commercial Arbitration Institutions), 'Confidentiality vs. Transparency in Commercial Arbitration: A False Contradiction to Overcome' (28 December 2012), NYU Transnational Notes <http://blogs.law.nyu.edu/transnational/2012/12/confidentiality-vs-transparency-in-commercial-arbitration-a-false/> accessed 17 June 2016.

[83] Robert Argen, 'Ending Blind Spot Justice: Broadening the Transparency Trend in International Arbitration' (2014) 40(1) Brooklyn Journal of International Law 207.

describe their various functions. General principles, it is claimed, lay 'down the essential elements of the legal order',[84] express the 'fundamental legal concepts and essential values of any legal system',[85] and legitimate 'all or any of the more specific [legal] rules in question'.[86] It is no exaggeration to state that much of the basic normative infrastructure of domestic and international law has been constituted by judge-made general principles. Arbitral tribunals, too, have made a great deal of constitutive law under the cover of a jurisprudence of principles, not least, to enhance their own authority and autonomy (Chapters 3 to 5). Since they cannot do without them, tribunals ought to develop general principles of law more transparently, and deploy them more consistently. When it comes to assessing the importance of public interests in the resolving of dyadic disputes, they can do no better than to develop a more structured version of proportionality analysis [PA].

General Principles

The 'general principles of law'[87] comprise an authoritative and autonomous source of legal norms that international judges are under a duty to apply when relevant to a dispute at bar. At the same time, there is no codified statement of their content, and no authoritative, prescribed method for identifying them.[88] In domestic public law, the most important principles materialized in national judicial decisions as self-evident propositions, beginning in the late nineteenth century in Europe. Ever since, judges have only very rarely provided explicit justification for the appearance of a new principle. They have tended to rely on incremental doctrinal consolidation to do the work of legitimation, or on a citation to an elliptical judgment of another court. Once institutionalized in subsequent case law and scholarly commentary, judges will apply the principle as if it were an inherent component of the rule of law itself. In most important cases, judges rely on principles to compensate for the absence of basic texts, such as a charter of rights. The leading example is that of the French Supreme Administrative Court, the *Conseil d'État*, whose methods of discovery and consolidation broadly diffused across Europe, and then globally.

---

[84] Armin von Bogdandy, 'Doctrine of Principles' (2003) 10 NYU Sch of Law Jean Monnet Ctr, Working Paper No 9/03 <http://www.jeanmonnetprogram.org/archive/papers/03/030901-01.pdf> accessed 16 June 2016.

[85] Meinhard Hilf and Goetz Goettsche, 'The Relation of Economic and Non-Economic Principles in International Law' in Stefan Griller (ed), *International Economic Governance and Non-Economic Concerns: New Challenges for the International Legal Order* (Springer, New York 2003).

[86] Neil MacCormick, *Legal Reasoning and Legal Theory* (Oxford University Press, Oxford 1978) 152.

[87] Article 38(1)(c), Statute of the International Court of Justice 33 UNTS 993: 'The Court, whose function is to decide in accordance with international law such disputes as are submitted to it, shall apply ... the general principles of law recognized by civilized nations.' We understand 'by civilized nations' to mean 'in legal systems based on the rule of law'.

[88] Unlike 'judicial decisions' and the 'writings of learned publicists' (Article 38(1)(d), Statute of the International Court of Justice), the general principles are not defined as 'subsidiary sources' of law under Article 38. Instead, they are an autonomous source of legal norms whose legitimacy as positive international law is not in question. At the same time, Article 38(1)(c) is itself incomplete, in that it does not indicate how general principles, left unenumerated, are to be identified, let alone applied.

While the jurisprudence of general principles reveals strong features of judicial empowerment, much of the law actually made is defensive in nature (see Chapter 1). Due process norms are designed to assure disputants of the fairness of proceedings. Others serve to constrain the judge's lawmaking, or at least the process through which the judge decides. The proportionality principle, for example, with its distinctive series of tests, requires judges to evaluate arguments, and to justify their decisions, in particular ways. Courts can deploy principles to promote coherence in systems threatened by fragmentation, and to ground adjustments of the law in the face of external shocks and changing circumstances. At this point in the evolution of international law and courts—notoriously fragmented,[89] incomplete,[90] and (seemingly) beset by quasi-permanent crises of legitimacy, international judges and arbitrators need general principles more than their peers on established national courts.

Throughout this book, we have emphasized the gap-filling functions of general principles, as tools for managing dilemmas of incomplete commitment and contracting, but not to disguise arbitral lawmaking. The effectiveness of arbitration rests on a jurisprudence of general principles, the production of which is a robust indicator of judicialization, and of the applicability of the judicial and pluralist-constitutional models. In ICA, this jurisprudence comprises a foundational common law, anchoring claims of authority (from the standpoint of a tribunal's relationship to parties, Chapters 2 and 3) and of autonomy (from the perspective of the arbitral order's relationship to state law, Chapters 4 and 5). Much of this law is procedural in nature, though reason-giving requirements undergird substantive lawmaking in obvious ways. Further, 'transnational/international public policy' is arbitrator-made law, which important state courts have recognized as legitimate. In ISA, tribunals can and ought to develop general principles to fill gaps.[91] States have expressly empowered arbitrators to enforce investor entitlements that are announced, typically, in provisions that are open-textured. The most obvious example is the FET, a protection that is common to virtually all investment treaties. Relatively quickly, arbitrators constructed the FET as a repository for a long list of general principles (also found in virtually all well-functioning domestic systems) that they use to assess the acts of host states (Chapter 5).

In the arbitral world, tribunals control the enumeration and application of principles. Nonetheless, the law they make, it is asserted, already exists to the extent

---

[89] International Law Commission, 'Fragmentation of International Law: Difficulties Arising from the Diversification and Expansion of International Law' (13 April 2006, UNGA Doc A/CN.4/L.682) <http://legal.un.org/ilc/documentation/english/a_cn4_l682.pdf> accessed 16 June 2016.
[90] In virtually all important treaty-based judicial systems, including those of the European Union, the GATT-WTO, and the ECtHR, states did not legislate a code of procedures, for example, and they left crucial provisions, such as derogation clauses, incomplete. See Alec Stone Sweet and Thomas Brunell, 'Trustee Courts and the Judicialization of International Regimes: The Politics of Majoritarian Activism in the ECHR, the EU, and the WTO' (2013) 1(1) Journal of Law and Courts 61 ['Stone Sweet and Brunell'].
[91] Emmanuel Gaillard and Yas Banifatemi, 'The Meaning of "and" in Article 42(1), Second Sentence, of the Washington Convention: The Role of International Law in the ICSID Choice of Law Process' (2003) 18(2) ICSID Review—Foreign Investment Law Journal 375.

that judges elsewhere have embraced the same principle. Those who worry about the legitimacy of judicial lawmaking will find no comfort in a jurisprudence that justifies newly minted law with reference to past episodes of judicial lawmaking. Still, general principles do not simply enable lawmaking; they constrain it in ways that help arbitrators meet the 'crisis of legitimacy' that besets all third-party dispute resolvers (Chapter 1). Due process and reason-based justification are today codified fiduciary duties of arbitrators (Chapter 3), owed to users, IACs, and state parties under the New York and ICSID Conventions.

The time has come for the arbitral community to be more forthcoming about the sources and purposes of the principles they use. Over the past century, general principles have accreted enough legitimacy to permit arbitrators to be more open (compared to their pioneering judicial counterparts) about why they need general principles, and to be clearer about how they derive them.[92] In ICA, due to publication policies, we have virtually no reliable means of assessing the concrete impact of their deployment in any important domain of the law. In ISA, by contrast, tribunals are increasingly anxious to explicate the doctrinal foundations of the general principles they deploy, in light of the relevant practices of courts at both the national and international levels.[93] All arbitral tribunals, in both ICA and ISA, should be accountable to all stakeholders for how they govern through general principles.

Proportionality

Over the past sixty years, PA has become a centerpiece of the jurisprudence of the world's most powerful national and international courts.[94] Today, it is the unrivalled, best-practice standard for adjudicating constitutional rights that are 'qualified' by limitation clauses that permit the state to burden the exercise of rights for important public purposes. Most rights found in modern constitutions (post-Second World War) are qualified, that is, very few rights are expressed in 'absolute' terms. At the international level, the proportionality principle has been adapted for use by the courts of the European Union, the European Convention on Human Rights [ECHR], and the WTO, in particular, to adjudicate treaty provisions that

---

[92] Stephan W Schill, 'International Investment Law and Comparative Public Law: An Introduction' in Stephan W Schill (ed), *International Investment Law and Comparative Public Law* (Oxford University Press, Oxford 2010) 27–33.

[93] See the awards cited in Chapter 5, including: *International Thunderbird Gaming Corporation v Mexico* (NAFTA/UNCITRAL), Award of 26 January 2006, Separate Opinion of Thomas Wälde, paras 9–58; *Saluka Investments BV v The Czech Republic* (UNCITRAL), Award of 17 March 2006, paras 282–309; *Total SA v The Argentine Republic* (ICSID Case No ARB/04/01), Award of 8 December 2010, paras 105–34; *El Paso Energy International Company v The Argentine Republic* (ICSID Case No ARB/03/15), Award of 31 October 2011, paras 328–79.

[94] See Alec Stone Sweet and Jud Mathews, 'Proportionality Balancing and Global Constitutionalism' (2008) 47 Columbia Journal of Transnational Law 68 ['Stone Sweet and Mathews'] (tracing the migration of proportionality from Germany to Canada, Israel, New Zealand, South Africa, and across Europe and to the European Union, the ECtHR, and the WTO); Aharon Barak, *Proportionality: Constitutional Rights and Their Limitations* (Cambridge University Press, Cambridge 2012) (discussing the diffusion of proportionality from Germany to Canada, Ireland, the United Kingdom, New Zealand, and to national legal systems in Asia and Latin America, as well as to international regimes).

permit states to claim derogations from their treaty obligations in the pursuit of important policy interests.[95]

The proportionality principle is operationalized through a sequence of tests.[96] A state measure that fails any one of these tests is outweighed by a right or entitlement held by the claimant. In the first, 'legitimacy', stage, the judge ensures that the act under review was taken in pursuance of a proper governmental purpose. In the next, the 'suitability' stage, the government must demonstrate that the relationship between (a) the means chosen and (b) the ends pursued is rational and appropriate.[97] Governments rarely lose in the first two stages. The third step—'necessity'—includes what Americans call a 'narrow tailoring' requirement, and has far more bite. At its core is a less restrictive means [LRM] test, through which the judge ensures that the measure under review does not curtail the right being pleaded more than is necessary for the government to achieve its declared purposes. In practice, judges do not invalidate a measure simply because they can imagine one less restrictive alternative to the law under review. Instead, the claimant typically bears the burden of presenting to the court one or more less harmful alternatives that were 'reasonably' available. The third step—balancing *stricto sensu*—is also known as 'proportionality in the narrow sense'. In the paradigmatic balancing situation, judges consider the marginal social benefits of the act (already found to have been narrowly tailored) in relation to the marginal costs incurred to the rights claimant, in light of the facts. They do so in order to ensure that a relatively trivial addition to the public weal does not, say, extinguish a right in an important domain of liberty (disproportionately). Judges who rely heavily on this stage (notably, members of the German Federal Constitutional Court and the Israeli Supreme Court) also emphasize that balancing allows them to 'complete' the analysis, in order to check that no factor of significance to either side has been overlooked in previous stages.[98]

We advocate the development of PA within ISA, and ICA where appropriate or all but required,[99] for a number of overlapping reasons. First, it would be clearly inappropriate (and probably fatal to the regime) for tribunals to treat investors' protections as placeholders for, or functional equivalents of, absolute rights. As

---

[95] Stone Sweet and Brunell (n 90).

[96] Not all courts use this four-stage version of PA, combining two stages (steps one and two, for example, or steps three and four) into one—see Stone Sweet and Mathews (n 94).

[97] This mode of scrutiny is broadly akin to what Americans call 'rational basis' review, though, under PA, the appraisal of government motives and choice of means is more searching. See Jud Mathews and Alec Stone Sweet, 'All Things in Proportion? American Rights Doctrine and the Problem of Balancing' (2011) 60 Emory LJ 102–6 ['Mathews and Stone Sweet'].

[98] Dieter Grimm, 'Proportionality in Canadian and German Constitutional Jurisprudence' (2007) 57 U Toronto L.J. 393–5; Mathews and Stone Sweet (n 97), 106–8.

[99] It is appropriate when the mandatory law of a state requires proportionality analysis (see Chapter 5 with regard to European anti-trust law). Under German law, the judge is under a duty to ensure that his decision takes proper account of the constitutional rights in play (e.g. freedom of expression), in accordance with the proportionality principle—see Mattias Kumm, 'Who Is Afraid of the Total Constitution? Constitutional Rights as Principles and the Constitutionalization of Private Law' (2006) 7 German Law Journal 341. In the European Union, many labour and social rights are directly effective—that is they can be pleaded by one private party against another at bar—see Alec Stone Sweet, *The Judicial Construction of Europe* (Oxford University Press, Oxford 2004) Chapter 4.

charted in Chapter 5, the most influential tribunals have adopted a balancing posture, which has driven some of them to deploy PA. In the domains of the FET and indirect expropriation—the two most important sources of pleadings and findings of liability in ISA—the strong trend is for tribunals to balance (a) an investor's entitlements under an investment treaty against (b) the host state's 'right to regulate', the latter being a competing principle[100] also conceived in limited, not absolute, terms. Second, PA furnishes a ready-made balancing structure, the effectiveness and legitimacy of which have been firmly established by the world's most prestigious courts. Standardizing its use would render the arbitral process more doctrinally consistent and transparent. A comprehensive framework of legal argumentation, it organizes how lawyers make claims and counterclaims, and how judges justify their rulings.

Third, PA enhances the flexibility of judges, all but requiring them to tailor rulings to the fact-specific contexts of disputes. It is important to emphasize that in balancing situation it is not the law, but the factual context, that varies across cases. Because PA does not tell the judge how to weigh the various interests and values at play in any case, it does not dictate correct legal answers to legal questions. Balancing 'interests'—or 'values'—that are incommensurate is a famously indeterminate mode of decision-making, to which PA provides procedural determinacy. Even in similar cases, different tribunals could well come to opposed conclusions about the proportionality (lawfulness) of a state act under review. If they are using PA, however, we would know exactly why— on what legal grounds and assessment of facts—they came to their respective conclusions.[101]

In ISA, states have not only countenanced balancing, they increasingly favour it. As noted, states now draft and sign treaties that contain WTO-style general exceptions that are likely to push tribunals toward the PA-based modes of analyses developed by the WTO Appellate Body. It is worth recalling that some tribunals have already embraced the Appellate Body's approach to proportionality, even in the absence of a general exceptions clause; they did so, in effect, by reading one into treaties in the guise of a host state's 'right to regulate' (Chapter 5). In this mode, the judge evaluates whether the means adopted by a state to pursue a legitimate public policy aim is 'necessary' to achieve that end.[102] Even states that have declared their ambition to constrain arbitral discretion have not renounced necessity analysis. The original draft of India's Model BIT, for example, prohibited arbitrators from examining whether a state act was taken for a legitimate purpose, in a lawful manner,

---

[100] A host state's 'right to regulate' can be understood as a general principle or derived from the traditional police power doctrines of customary international law: see Prabhash Ranjan and Pushkar Anand, 'Determination of Indirect Expropriation and Doctrine of Police Power in International Investment Law: A Critical Appraisal' (unpublished draft) <http://papers.ssrn.com/sol3/papers.cfm?abstract_id=2728839> accessed 16 June 2016.

[101] See Chapters 4 and 5 for an analysis of relevant awards.

[102] Not all tribunals deployed an LRM test, but their decisions would have been more convincing had they done so. In the European Union and the ECtHR, where one finds clauses that permit derogations from treaty obligations on the basis of 'necessity', judges use PA to adjudicate such claims.

which would have foreclosed PA altogether. The consultation process excised that provision. The published Indian Model BIT contains a general exceptions provision in Article 32(1), mimicking Article XIV of the GATS (1994):

Nothing in this Treaty shall be construed to prevent the adoption or enforcement by a Party of measures of general applicability applied on a nondiscriminatory basis that are necessary to:

(i)   protect public morals or maintaining public order;
(ii)   protect human, animal or plant life or health;
(iii) ensure compliance with law and regulations that are not inconsistent with the provisions of this Agreement;
(iv)   protect and conserve the environment, including all living and nonliving natural resources;
(v)   protect national treasures or monuments of artistic, cultural, historic or archaeological value.

A footnote to this provision echoes WTO case law, stating that: 'In considering whether a measure is "necessary", the Tribunal shall take into account whether there was no less restrictive alternative measure reasonably available to a Party.'[103]

Scholarly discussion of the development of the proportionality principle within ISA has taken off.[104] The most important work, a recent book by Caroline Henckels,[105] comprehensively traces the evolution of PA and alternatives in the existing case law, against the backdrop of the principle's institutionalization in the case law of the WTO, the European Court of Human Rights [ECtHR], and the European Union. Henckels argues that tribunals have much to gain from fully embracing PA, but that its benefits can be fully realized only through consistent application of its sequence of tests. We fully agree on this point. Henckels also elaborates a normative framework for considering the linked questions of deference and standard of review, to which PA provides at least partial answers.

---

[103] Model Indian BIT (n 53): Article 32: General Exceptions, fn 6.
[104] Jasper Krommendijk and John Morijn, ' "Proportional" by What Measure(s)? Balancing Investor Interests and Human Rights by Way of Applying the Proportionality Principle in Investor-State Arbitration' in Pierre-Marie Dupuy, Ernst-Ulrich Petersmann, and Francesco Francioni (eds), *Human Rights in International Investment Law and Arbitration* (Oxford University Press, Oxford 2009); Alec Stone Sweet, 'Investor-State Arbitration: Proportionality's New Frontier' (2010) 4(1) Law and Ethics of Human Rights 47; Caroline Henckels, 'Indirect Expropriation and the Right to Regulate: Revisiting Proportionality Analysis and the Standard of Review in Investor-State Arbitration' (2012) 15(1) Journal of International Economic Law 223; Benedict Kingsbury and Stephan W Schill, 'Investor-State Arbitration As Governance: Fair and Equitable Treatment, Proportionality and the Emerging Global Administrative Law' (2012) 8 Transnational Dispute Management <https://www.transnational-dispute-management.com/article.asp?key=1700> accessed 16 June 2016 ['Kingsbury and Schill']; Alec Stone Sweet and Giacinto della Cananea, 'Proportionality, General Principles of Law, and Investor-State Arbitration' (2014) 46 NYU Journal of International Law and Politics 911.
[105] Caroline Henckels, *Proportionality and Deference in Investor-State Arbitration: Balancing Investment Protection and Regulatory Autonomy* (Cambridge University Press, Cambridge 2015) ['Henckels'].

Deference

States delegated extensive lawmaking powers to arbitrators, both directly and indirectly, and arbitral lawmaking has determined much of the regime's evolution. The greater ISA community has struggled to find an appropriate balance between discretion, delegated to arbitrators for the protection of foreign investment, and the deference owed to states. A major strain of critical scholarship maintains that tribunals should give far more deference to states than they have, a stance predicated on concerns about pro-investor bias in the system. The 'public law' nature of treaty-based ISA, it is asserted, supports this position, while pointing the analyst to the world of public law courts for analogical guidance. Proponents of greater deference also worry that arbitrators may be comparatively ill-equipped to engage in the judicial review of public acts, compared to judges on well-functioning, domestic administrative and constitutional law courts.[106] Arbitrators are outsiders to the system in which they intervene, the argument goes. Predisposed to viewing a dispute narrowly, in terms of their own mandate to enforce investment treaties, they will miss a dispute's wider public dimensions. They will typically lack the expertise required to make competent policy judgments in the context of complex and foreign regulatory environments. More broadly, robust, pro-investor bias threatens to constrict national policy space,[107] and to foreclose reforms in times of economic crisis,[108] when they are most needed. Tribunals, therefore, should explicitly develop deferential standards of review that reflect these risks.[109]

However well founded these worries might be, the extant empirical research provides no support for the claim that awards on liability in ISA are biased in favour of investors. No study has shown that awards have reduced the policy space of host states, or deterred regulatory reforms. Further, tribunals have taken pains to recognize the regulatory prerogatives of states, either as an expression of the doctrines of 'police powers' in customary international law, or as a general principle of law. They then use the right to regulate as a doctrinal frame for showing deference, and for evolving standards of review, however inchoate such standards remain in the aggregate (Chapter 5). The most important lines of case law in this vein do, in fact, lay out a defensible theory of deference, albeit within a balancing posture that some may nonetheless consider objectionable. With regard to general measures, the vast majority of tribunals begin with a presumption of deference that can be rebutted by

---

[106] For a strong defence of these arguments, see Van Harten (n 45).

[107] Stephan W Schill, 'Deference in Investment Treaty Arbitration: Re-Conceptualizing the Standard of Review' (2012) 3(3) Journal of International Dispute Settlement 578 ['Schill']: 'One central concern—among others—is that arbitral tribunals use the vague standards of investment protection to intrude into the regulatory space of host states and become the ultimate controller of central public policy decisions as they limit domestic courts and domestic regulators in exercising jurisdiction.'

[108] William Burke-White and Andreas von Staden, 'Private Litigation in a Public Law Sphere: The Standard of Review in Investor-State Arbitrations' (2010) 35 Yale Journal of International Law 283; Jürgen Kurtz, 'Adjudging the Exceptional at International Investment Law: Security, Public Order and Financial Crisis' (2010) 59 International and Comparative Law Quarterly 325.

[109] Schill (n 107), 577–607.

showing that a state has manifestly abused its right to regulate, against the backdrop of treaty obligations to which the state has freely entered.[110]

In our view, it would be inappropriate for tribunals to adopt formal deference doctrines, except insofar as the latter is required by express treaty provisions. Formal deference doctrines include those that classify an issue as per se non-justiciable (e.g. a categorical 'political question doctrine'), or that place a burden on the claimant that is so high as to make review of state acts, in practice, all but impossible (e.g. under the so-called 'Wednesbury unreasonableness' test). In our view, PA ought to furnish the basic standard of review, at least under the indirect expropriation and FET headings. The objects of such pleadings should not be limited in advance. PA provides ample room for the expression of de facto deference to the states' right to regulate.[111] How tribunals do so should depend on facts of the case, not on the basis of a priori categorical reasoning. We sketch the basics of the position here.

In the realm of treaty-based ISA, arbitrators are judges bound by the Vienna Convention on the Law of Treaties (1969). The Vienna Convention provides no support for formal deference doctrines. Instead, judges are bound by Article 31(1), the 'general rule of interpretation':

A treaty shall be interpreted in good faith in accordance with the ordinary meaning to be given to the terms of the treaty in their context and in the light of its object and purpose.

Where treaties are silent on the question, arbitrators possess inherent powers to determine the standard of review, in light of the purpose of the treaty—that is, the effective protection of foreign investment. Moreover, where treaties do not make derogation clauses self-judging, but rather justiciable under a necessity clause or doctrine, there is little of a formal nature to limit the tribunals' discretion. In our view, tribunals ought to maximize effectiveness, of investment treaties and the regime as a whole; but this goal can *not* be achieved without appropriate deference to states' regulatory prerogatives.

PA provides a well-tested framework for doing so. To be sure, PA embodies an intrusive standard of review, in which states bear the burden to justify, in light of legitimate public interests, acts that burden a right or entitlement. Judges and arbitrators can and do invoke a state's 'margin of appreciation'—a corollary of the right to regulate—thereby building 'deference' into the framework. But PA itself determines the size of a state's 'margin of appreciation', in the context of a specific dispute.

Judges and arbitrators can express deference at each stage of PA. Arbitrators could use the first stage—that of 'proper purpose'—to capture state acts expressly designed to punish, or coerce, an investor. A finding that the act under review also violates domestic law, as determined by the host state's own courts, would strengthen such a decision. Notwithstanding such instances, the prong would serve

---

[110] Giorgio Sacerdoti, 'The Application of BITs in Time of Economic Crisis: Limits to Their Coverage, Necessity and the Relevance of WTO Law' in Giorgio Sacerdoti (ed), *General Interests of Host States in International Investment Law* (Cambridge University Press, Cambridge 2014) 3.

[111] Kingsbury and Schill (n 104), 22.

as a placeholder for a tribunal's expression of consideration and respect. The same is true of the 'suitability' phase which, in the context of the review of general measures, commonly reduces to a weak version of a rationality test. 'It is clear that the law under review is an appropriate instrument for pursuing an important objective in the public interest', the tribunal can declare, without undermining its authority to determine liability on more searching grounds in the next stage of the analysis. If tribunals in ISA follow their counterparts on, say, the courts of the European Union and the WTO, necessity analysis will do most of the work. Why should it ever be acceptable for a host state to infringe on an investor's entitlements *more than is necessary to achieve the state's regulatory objectives*? It is indisputable that LRM testing pushes judges into a policymaking mode, in that it requires them to consider, counterfactually, the efficacy of alternative measures. Yet, even here, international judges have held that states have a right to determine the 'desired level of protection with respect to the objective pursued', and that the complainant bears the burden of identifying the 'alternatives to the measure at issue that the responding Member could have taken'.[112] Some tribunals in ISA have followed.[113] Finally, the role of balancing in the strict sense is to ensure that a measure has not destroyed the viability of the investment in the name of securing a relatively trivial measure of a social good.

Balancing in the strict sense has been attacked for permitting judges to either protect a right too little or too much. Judges may 'balance a right away', or they might be tempted to substitute their own policy judgment for that of public officials.[114] For this latter reason, and for reasons of relative institutional competence and political legitimacy, Henckels[115] now argues that tribunals in ISA should conclude PA at the necessity stage. Judges should never move to balancing in the narrow sense. On this point, we disagree with Henckels. We see no compelling justification for arbitrators to refuse to take into consideration the marginal costs and benefits of the interests at play in an investment dispute. In 2012, Henckels agreed:

[R]esidual review of strict proportionality should be retained ... Not proceeding to this analytical stage in order to avoid explicit balancing may result in a measure being adjudged lawful even if its impact is especially severe relative to the importance of the measure and

---

[112] World Trade Organization, Report of the Appellate Body (AB-2007-4), 'Brazil—Measures Affecting Imports of Retreaded Tyres', 156: 'It rests upon the complaining Member to identify possible alternatives to the measure at issue that the responding Member could have taken. [I]n order to qualify as an alternative, a measure proposed by the complaining Member must be not only less trade restrictive than the measure at issue, but should also "preserve for the responding Member its right to achieve its desired level of protection with respect to the objective pursued." If the complaining Member has put forward a possible alternative measure, the responding Member may seek to show that the proposed measure does not allow it to achieve the level of protection it has chosen and, therefore, is not a genuine alternative.'

[113] Henckels (n 105), 169–70.   [114] Stone Sweet and Mathews (n 94), 77.

[115] Henckels (n 105), 168: 'The proportionality *stricto sensu* stage by its very nature can only operate to reduce the regulatory autonomy of states compared to the application of a necessity test, as it can result in a tribunal ruling unlawful the only way that the government has available to achieve its aim. It is strongly arguable, therefore, that least-restrictive means analysis should be the limit of review in investor-state arbitration.'

its objective—or where the measure and its objective could not reasonably be regarded as significant and important vis-à-vis its expropriatory effect. In such cases, tribunals would retain the power to employ strict proportionality analysis to declare expropriatory the only reasonable way of achieving what has already been judged to be a legitimate aim.

At the very least, tribunals ought to be able to assess state liability under an investment treaty in circumstances in which (a) the state has implemented a law in ways that extinguish an investment, and (b) implementation only achieves a very low level of social benefit.

We would also emphasize two additional points. First, in the world of domestic public law adjudication, the balancing judge possesses a formal veto, and reasons given in support of the veto will constrain future episodes of policymaking. Again, the available remedy ought to weigh heavily on the normative argument. In ISA, a finding of liability under the treaty (a matter of international not national law) will lead to an award of damages, but not to the invalidation or quashing of the measure under review. The logics of efficient breach are relevant to debates about deference. Second, if the balancing stage is closed off altogether, we would expect the relevant arguments, and the balancing, to flow into the proper purpose and necessity prongs.[116] The 'hydraulic' dynamics of shifting burdens within balancing frameworks found elsewhere would likely manifest themselves with full force in the domains that matter the most in ISA: the FET and indirect expropriation.[117] Such an outcome would undermine transparency, as well as the tribunal's capacity to express deference precisely where it is due.

Transnational Legal Pluralism

Pluralism is a defining property of international arbitration. In any given proceeding, tribunals typically take into account diverse sets of norms issuing from different authorities: national lawmakers, treaty-makers, the codifiers of the *Lex Mercatoria*, contracting parties, and IACs. The situation is one of 'source pluralism'. Comprised of independent IACs in competition with one another for business and influence, the arbitral regime is also pluralistic in a jurisdictional sense. At the international level, the New York Convention formally organizes a regime in which functions are divided: arbitrators render awards that domestic courts enforce. Pluralism means that the authority of arbitral awards—their legitimacy as enforceable legal acts—is produced through the coordination of two or more discrete systems of law. The judicialization of arbitration has altered how the

[116] International courts, including the CJEU, the ECtHR, and the WTO, often carry out the balancing exercise at the necessity stage, collapsing the second and third steps.
[117] For 'hydraulic' accounts of the effects of doctrinal change, see Ernest Young, 'Executive Preemption' (2008) 102 NWUL Rev 880: 'There is a hydraulic quality to federalism doctrine: weakening one set of constraints on national power tends to create pressure to tighten others if the overall objective of meaningful balance is to be maintained.' See also David Han, 'The Mechanics of First Amendment Audience Analysis' (2014) 55 Wm & Mary L Rev 1647, 1705–10, 1716: '[L]egal doctrine is often hydraulic in nature; whenever the rigidity in one doctrinal area exerts pressure on courts' decisionmaking, that pressure often seeks release in other areas of the doctrine'.

New York Convention regime works, not least through the isomorphic dynamics discussed above.

A frontier issue, which we do not purport to settle in the book, is the extent to which these pluralist regimes are developing 'constitutional' properties (Chapter 1). We recognize that the usage of the word 'constitutional' to describe any legal system beyond the state is highly charged, symbolically and politically.[118] We primarily use the term in a descriptive sense, in order to focus attention on the structural properties of the New York Convention as a legal regime. In our view, any stable legal framework that organizes how discreet legal systems coordinate with one another in ways that produce legal effects is 'constitutional' in a basic sense. The norms that undergird federal systems, allowing the federal and state 'levels' to interact productively with one another, are an obvious example; and it is worth noting that the first federal constitutions were typically considered to be compacts between sovereign states. To take a more contemporary analogue, since the 1980s, scholars and the Court of Justice of the European Union [CJEU] have asserted that the European Union underwent a profound process of 'constitutionalization' with the acceptance, by the national courts, of the basics of the CJEU's doctrines of direct effect, supremacy, and other principles.[119] At stake was whether EU legal norms would be enforced directly by national courts, upon request by a private party.[120] The New York Convention requires national courts to acknowledge the autonomy of the arbitral order, and to enforce its awards, subject to the inarbitrability and public policy exceptions.

Looking forward, further judicialization in the form of existing proposals to establish new forms of hierarchy within the arbitral regime would fundamentally alter how arbitrators and domestic judges engage one another under the New York Convention, in a constitutional pluralist direction. What would happen if the ICC moved to publish all important awards in which the tribunal applied mandatory law and enforced public policy, which state courts actually reviewed as proposed above? How would domestic judges react to the creation of a centralized appellate jurisdiction for ICA or ISA? Others have considered establishing a preliminary reference system,[121] in which tribunals could request an interpretation of the applicable law from a court, when that law is unsettled on sensitive areas of public interest and policy. We could go on, but the answers to such hypotheticals appear clear. Assuming good faith on both sides, the dialogues between judges and arbitrators

---

[118] See Neil Walker, 'Taking Constitutionalism beyond the State' (2008) 56 Political Studies 519.

[119] For an overview of this literature, see Alec Stone Sweet, 'The European Court of Justice and the Judicialization of EU Governance' (2010) 5 Living Reviews in European Union Governance <http://europeangovernance.livingreviews.org/Articles/lreg-2010-2/> accessed 25 June 2016.

[120] The regime remains pluralist, however. Among other indicators, the CJEU asserts that EU law is directly applicable by national judges, and reserves for itself the final determination of the lawfulness of any EU act; in contrast, national constitutional courts typically assert the right to review the legality of EU law with reference to national charters of rights. Alec Stone Sweet, 'A Cosmopolitan Legal Order: Constitutional Pluralism and Rights Adjudication in Europe' (2012) 1 Journal of Global Constitutionalism 53, 60–2.

[121] Grisel (n 26), paras 431 et seq.

would become more structured, intensifying pressure to produce a coordinated jurisprudence on important questions implicating public interests. The potential for inter-judicial conflict, too, would be significantly increased. A supreme arbitral jurisdiction would not only be charged with defending the arbitral mission, but its own *bona fides* as a court, within a system of courts.

IV. Conclusion

We have argued that a judicialization process, which has steadily gathered force since the mid-1960s, has transformed international arbitration. Three factors have combined to sustain this process. First, the explosion in trade generated high-stakes disputes that, in turn, drove parties into highly adversarial postures. Second, the major IACs and a cadre of elite arbitrators decided that the future of the system hinged on its capacity to replace domestic courts. Since the early 1950s, they have worked steadily to build the institutional infrastructure that would allow them to succeed. Although all major IACs, including ICSID, continue to make provision for mediation and equity decisions, they now compete with one another to provide what is, in effect, private adjudication of transnational disputes. Third, states (treaty-makers), and the national courts of the major trading zones (enforcement mechanisms), have not only accommodated the expansion of adversarial arbitration, they have heavily invested in it (albeit with some lingering doubts), extending its reach and effectiveness. Today, what goes on in proceedings is hardly 'arbitration' at all, in the traditional sense of that term. The judicialization process has also fundamentally altered the political environment in which arbitration is embedded, spawning legitimacy dilemmas that press for more, not less, judicialization. The elements of the traditional model that remain in place—confidentiality (in ICA), party-dominated appointment procedures, and the absence of appeal—are under sustained attack, on legitimacy not efficiency grounds.

International arbitration has largely become a form of litigation, a substitute for courts. And the legitimacy crises that affect judicial governance, and the most effective of courts, are never settled.

Index

Milton Keynes UK
Ingram Content Group UK Ltd.
UKHW051644310823
427734UK00024BA/462

9 780198 739739